The Egyptians

The Peoples of Africa

General Editor: Parker Shipton

This series is about the African peoples from their origins to the present day. Drawing on archaeological, historical and anthropological evidence, each volume looks at a particular group's culture, society and history.

Approaches will vary according to the subject and the nature of the evidence. Volumes concerned mainly with culturally discrete peoples will be complemented by accounts which focus primarily on the historical period, on African nations and contemporary peoples. The overall aim of the series is to offer a comprehensive and up-to-date picture of the African peoples, in books which are at once scholarly and accessible.

Published

The Shona and their Neighbours*
David Beach

The Berbers*
Michael Brett and Elizabeth Fentress

The Egyptians*
Barbara Watterson

In preparation

The Masai, the Dinka and the East African Pastoralists
Peter Robertshaw and Neil Sobania

The Ethiopians*
Richard Pankhurst

Island of Gold: The Peoples of the Middle Niger*
R. J. McIntosh and S. J. McIntosh

The Swahili
Mark Horton and John Middleton

The Nubians
W. Godlewski and S. Jacobielski

The Black Peoples of Southern Africa
Timothy Maggs and W. Guest

The Kenyans
John Middleton

*Indicates title commissioned under the general editorship of Dr David Phillipson of Gonville and Caius College, Cambridge

The Egyptians

Barbara Watterson

BLACKWELL
Publishers

First published 1997

2 4 6 8 10 9 7 5 3 1

Blackwell Publishers Ltd
108 Cowley Road
Oxford OX4 1JF
UK

Blackwell Publishers Inc.
238 Main Street
Cambridge, Massachusetts 02142
USA

British Library Cataloguing in Publication Data
A CIP catalogue record for this book is available from the British Library.

Library of Congress Cataloging-in-Publication Data
Watterson, Barbara.
    The Egyptians / Barbara Watterson.
        p.   cm. – (The Peoples of Africa)
    Includes bibliographical references and index.
    ISBN 0-631-18272-1
    1. Egypt–History. I. Title. II. Series.
IN PROCESS
962–dc20   96-19205
                                             CIP

Typeset in 11 on 12¹/₂pt Sabon
by Best-set Typesetter Ltd., Hong Kong
Printed in Great Britain by Hartnolls Limited, Bodmin, Cornwall

This book is printed on acid-free paper.

For Juan, Juana and Paul

Contents

Plates

Maps

Series Editor's Preface

The Peoples of Africa series has been designed to provide reliable and up-to-date accounts of what is known about the development and antecedents of the diverse populations in that continent, and about their relations with others near or far. It is hoped that the series will enjoy a wide readership in many parts of the world, including Africa itself.

This series has counterparts relating to other continents, and it may be appropriate to discuss here aspects specific to a series dealing with Africa. Africa is a continent of contrasts – not only in its physical environments and in the life-styles and economies of its peoples, but also in the extent to which writing has influenced its development and recorded its past. Parts of Egypt have one of the longest histories of literacy in the world; on the other hand, some interior regions – notably in south-central Africa – remained wholly unrecorded in writing up to a hundred years ago. The historical significance of this contrast has been both varied and far-reaching.

The books in this series variously combine perspectives of archaeology, anthropology and history. It will be obvious that someone studying the past of a non-literate people will adopt techniques very different from those that are at the disposal of historians who can base their work on written sources. The relevance of archaeology is by no means restricted to non-literate contexts, but it is clearly a pre-eminent means of illustrating even the comparatively recent past in those parts of Africa where writing was not employed. It may be less obvious to those not familiar with Africa that non-literate peoples were by no means ignorant of their past, traditional knowledge about which was often preserved and orally transmitted through several generations, albeit not infrequently subject to change – conscious or unconscious – in the light of contemporary circumstances. Further clues about the non-literate African past can be obtained from studying the distributions and interrelationships of modern languages. Each of these approaches presents its own problems, and has its own potential to illustrate particular aspects of the past.

Each volume in the series is a specialist's attempt to condense, and to order, a large and diverse body of scholarship on a way of life. The series describes both changes and continuities, relating historic processes occurring at all levels of scale, from the domestic to the intercontinental. The changing definitions and self-definitions of peoples, in the light of new communications and sensitive ethnic and national politics, pose difficult problems for theory and description. More often than not it is debatable where, and when, one population ends and another begins. Situating African societies flexibly in time and space, and taking account of continual movements, anomalies, and complexities in their cultures, these volumes attempt to convey some sense of the continent's great variety, to dispel myths about its essential character or its plight, and to introduce fresh and thoughtful perspectives on its role in human history.

PARKER SHIPTON

Glossary

Other specialized words and terms used in *The Egyptians* are explained where they occur in the text.

Abbreviations: Ar. = Arabic; Fr. = French; Gk = Greek; Pers. = Persian; Turk. = Turkish

In a definition, any word in SMALL CAPITAL letters is defined elsewhere in the glossary.

Aga (Turk.)	a chief officer in the Ottoman administration
bey (Turk.)	Turkish governor
boustrophedon (Gk)	alternately from left to right and from right to left: 'as the ox ploughs'
demotic	ancient Egyptian script used from about 700 BC on business documents etc. By the Graeco-Roman period, it had become the ordinary writing of everyday life. The word is derived from Greek *demoticos* meaning common
fellah, pl. **fellahin** (Ar.)	Egyptian peasant
feddan (Ar.)	about 1 acre (0.4 hectare) of land
gebel (Ar.)	mountain
gezireh (Ar.)	sandy spit of land in the cultivation on which Egyptians often built

	Delta settlements to avoid using agricultural land which was, in any case, subject to the Nile flood
hieratic	cursive form of HIEROGLYPHS The word is derived from Greek *hieratikos* (priestly)
hieroglyphs	picture-writing of ancient Egypt. The word is derived from Greek *hieros* (sacred) *glupho* (sculptures)
ibn (Ar.)	son
Khalif (Ar.)	religious ruler; strictly speaking a descendant of the Prophet Muhammad
Khedive (Turk.)	Viceroy of Egypt
Kufic (Ar.)	ancient Arabic script, so-called after KUFA, a town on the Euphrates which was the capital of the Khalifs before Baghdad was built
Kufa	was famous for the skill of its copyists. The Koran was originally written in Kufic script
liwan (Ar.)	vaulted hall, open at one end
madrassa (Ar.)	school or collegiate mosque
Mahdi (Ar.)	Muslim Messiah ('He who is divinely guided')
manara (Ar.)	minaret
mastaba (Ar.)	bench, usually of mud-brick; adopted as description of an ancient Egyptian tomb type
memorial temple	*see* MORTUARY TEMPLE
mihrab (Ar.)	prayer niche (in mosque)
minbar (Ar.)	pulpit
mortuary temple	the term 'mortuary temple', in common use in Egyptology, is misleading. The *Oxford English Dictionary* definition of the noun 'mortuary' is 'building for temporary keeping of corpses'. This is by no means the case with Egyptian 'mortuary temples' which were places in which it was intended

	that the royal cult should be celebrated for ever. Hence the terms 'memorial' or 'commemorative' might be more appropriate; and in this book at least the author intends to use the term 'MEMORIAL TEMPLE'!
obelisk (Gk)	needle-shaped granite monolith
ostracon, pl. ostraca (Gk)	in Egyptological terms, a piece of broken pot, sherd of limestone etc. on which sketches were drawn, notes were written etc.
pasha (Turk.)	high-ranking Turkish military, naval or civil officer
pharaonic	the period between the First Dynasty and the Thirtieth when Egypt was ruled by kings now called Pharaohs
sahn (Ar.)	courtyard (of mosque)
saqiah (Ar.)	water-wheel
satrap (Pers.)	provincial governor
serdab (Ar.)	small room in an ancient Egyptian tomb where a statue of the tomb owner was placed
shaduf (Ar.)	counterweighted pole with bucket used for raising water
Shi'a (Ar.)	The Party: Shi'ite and SUNNI are the orthodox branches of Islam
Sublime Porte (Fr.)	translation of Turkish term *kapi,* the gate of the Topkapi Palace in Istanbul, the seat of government in the Ottoman Period. Eventually synonymous with the Ottoman Government
Sunni (Ar.)	orthodox Muslim
sultan (Ar.)	a sovereign of a Muslim country, especially of the Ottoman Empire
wadi (Ar.)	dry river-bed
zir (Ar.)	large water jar

A Note on Transliteration

From about 3100 BC, the ancient Egyptian language was written in hieroglyphic script, a decorative and complex picture-writing that remained in use for over 3000 years, the best examples being cut precisely in stone using a chisel. From hieroglyphic writing there developed a cursive script known as *hieratic*, a more rounded and abbreviated form of hieroglyphs suitable for writing on papyrus with a reed pen. From about 700 BC, hieratic itself gave rise to a form, *demotic,* that was so much abbreviated that it could be written rapidly, and was thus used for business documents and letters.

In the Graeco-Roman era, the ancient Egyptian language, as expressed in the hieroglyphic, hieratic and demotic scripts, was replaced as the official language of Egypt by Greek, and was lost for centuries until, in AD 1822, Champollion became the first person of modern times to decipher hieroglyphs correctly. The pronunciation of the language recorded in these scripts is not known with any degree of certainty, because the original language, even in its last-known form, Coptic, is used only in the liturgy of the Egyptian Christian church. Arabic, spoken in Egypt today, is a different language altogether, although it has one thing in common with ancient Egyptian: in neither script are vowel sounds written. Although the ancient Egyptian language employed vowel sounds, the position of these vowels is not indicated in the scripts, which consist only of consonants.

For an English-speaker to be able to read any of the ancient Egyptian scripts, the signs have to be turned into an approximation of the English alphabet, that is, transliterated. There are schools of transliteration for ancient Egyptian and for Arabic, with different traditions for inserting vowels: some write Idfu where we write Edfu (Arabic place-name); some write Ra where we write Re (name of ancient Egyptian Sun God), and so on. As a general rule of thumb, English-speaking readers of *The Egyptians* will find it convenient for pronunciation purposes to put an 'e' into ancient Egyptian words wherever it would otherwise be difficult to pronounce a string of consonants. Where this simple expedient of inserting an 'e' between consonants does not work, the work has been rendered into an approximation of English: on page 53, for example, the ancient Egyptian for 'Seizer-of-the-Two-Lands', *iṯt-t3wy*, has been written 'itje-tawy'.

The Egyptians: Table of Dates

Predynastic Period:
in Lower Egypt (i.e. the Faiyum) from *c*.5200 BC
in Upper Egypt   from *c*.5000 BC

Archaic Period: *c*.3100–*c*.2686 BC
Dynasty I *c*.3100–*c*.2890
Dynasty II *c*.2890–*c*.2686

Old Kingdom: *c*.2686–*c*.2181 BC
Dynasty III *c*.2686–*c*.2613
Dynasty IV *c*.2613–*c*.2494
Dynasty V *c*.2494–*c*.2345
Dynasty VI *c*.2345–*c*.2181

First Intermediate Period: *c*.2181–*c*.2040 BC
Dynasty VII *c*.2181–*c*.2173
Dynasty VIII *c*.2173–*c*.2160
Dynasty IX *c*.2160–*c*.2130
Dynasty X *c*.2130–*c*.2040

Middle Kingdom: *c*.2106–1633(?) BC
Dynasty XI *c*.2106–1963
Dynasty XII 1963–1786
Dynasty XIII 1786–1633 (?)

Second Intermediate Period: 1786–1550 BC
Dynasty XIV 1786–*c*.1603
Dynasty XV 1648–1540

Dynasty XVI *c*.1684–1587
Dynasty XVII *c*.1648–1550

New Kingdom: 1550–1070/69 BC
Dynasty XVIII 1550–1295
Dynasty XIX 1295–1186
Dynasty XX 1186–1070/69

Third Intermediate Period: 1070/69–525 BC
Dynasty XXI (at Tanis) 1070/69–945
Dynasty XXI (at Thebes) 1080–945
Dynasty XXII 945–715
Dynasty XXIII 818–715
Dynasty XXIV 728–715
Dynasty XXV (Kushite) 716–664
Dynasty XXVI (Saite) 664–525

The Late Period: 525–332 BC
Dynasty XXVII (Persian) 525–404
Dynasty XXVIII 404–399
Dynasty XXIX 399–380
Dynasty XXX 380–343
Dynasty XXXI (Persian) 343–332

Macedonian Kings: 332–304 BC

Ptolemaic Dynasty: 304–30 BC

Roman Period: 30 BC–AD 395

Byzantine and Coptic Period: AD 395–641

Islamic Period: AD 641 to present
Khalifs AD 641–1258
Mamelukes AD 1258–1517
Ottomans AD 1517–1882
British Occupation AD 1882–1914
British Protectorate AD 1914–1922
Independent Kingdom AD 1922–1953
Republic AD 1953–present

Introduction

Egypt has the longest continuous history of any country. The Nile Valley[1] has been occupied since about 5200 BC, when it was settled by Neolithic societies, though hunter-gatherers are known to have been active on the edges of the Valley in the Palaeolithic Period (*c.*200,000–12,000 BC). Egyptologists set the end of the prehistoric period at about 3100 BC, when the country came under the control of a single ruler; and follow Manetho, a scholar-priest who lived in Egypt in the third century BC, in dividing the succeeding rulers into dynasties, or groups of kings. Hence the historic era in ancient Egypt is termed Dynastic, and the prehistoric age Predynastic.

In his account (the *Aegyptiaca*, in Greek) Manetho categorized the history of Egypt into thirty dynasties, dating from Menes, the founder of the first, to the death in 343 BC of the last native Egyptian king, Nectanebo II. To Manetho's list of dynasties have since been added two more; and all have been subdivided into groups as shown in the table on pages xix–xx. Three of the groups are commonly called 'kingdoms', a term that here means a state unified under one king, and has no reference to geographical boundaries. The rest are known as 'intermediate periods', denoting times that lacked strong central government.

By definition, the prehistoric era had no written language and so no historic framework, such as inscriptions in contexts with well-attested dates, through which cultural developments can be linked. From the end of the nineteenth century, however, the ceramic

---

[1] The valley of the Nile north of Aswan, plus the Delta and the Faiyum Depression.

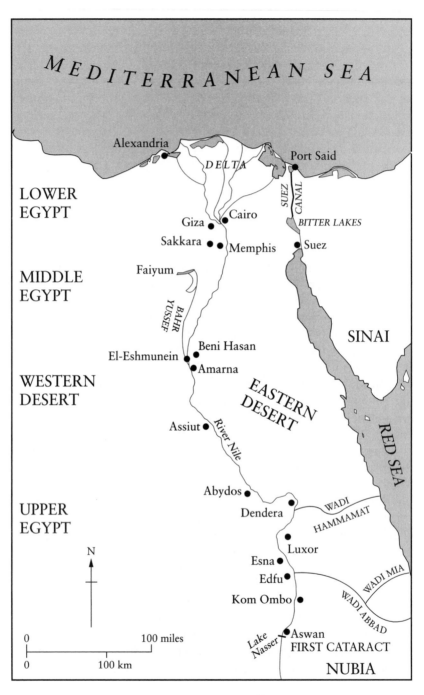

Map 1   Egypt: general map.

objects found in abundance at predynastic sites have been useful as *relative* dating tools. Flinders Petrie was the first archaeologist to employ these objects systematically for the purpose, in a system of seriation which he called Sequence Dating.[2] To each type of pot excavated at sites in southern Egypt he assigned a type number, and placed all objects found in the same stratum as a type-numbered pot in the same historical sequence. This system of seriation is still the basis of dating objects of the predynastic period in southern Egypt, although today it is augmented by more scientific archaeological techniques such as dendrochronology, radiocarbon and thermoluminescence dating, which produce actual, rather than relative, ages.

The ancient Egyptians did not define years from a chronologically fixed starting point, but, in the earliest historic times, named each year after some outstanding event occurring in it; and later, in the last two dynasties of the Old Kingdom, dated years by reference to the biennial cattle census. Otherwise, the regnal year of the reigning king was used, but not uniformly so between different dynasties: in the Twelfth Dynasty, a new regnal year began on New Year's Day; in the Eighteenth it began with the king's accession.[3] Thus, ancient Egyptian chronology does not lend itself to any modern system of arranging years in a continuum.

In theory, a complete list of the kings of Egypt, together with an accurate record of the number of years each of them reigned, would allow us to arrive at the total number of years that represent the span of ancient Egyptian history. Unfortunately, no such complete list is available: we do not even have a copy of Manetho's original work but only an edited extract preserved by Josephus, the Jewish historian (*c.*AD 70), and much-garbled versions by the Christian chronographers Sextus Julius Africanus (early third century AD) and Eusebius (early fourth century AD). Several King-lists, in varying states of completeness, do survive from other ancient sources. The earliest of them is probably the Palermo Stone, originally a free-standing diorite tablet inscribed on both sides with names and year numbers. The Stone is broken, the largest piece, measuring some 48 centimetres high by 30

[2] Petrie, 1901.
[3] See A. H. Gardiner, 'Regnal years and civil calendar in pharaonic Egypt', in *JEA*, XXXI, 1945, pp. 11–28.

centimetres wide, being in the Palermo Museum, with other fragments in Cairo Museum and in University College, London. In spite of its condition, the Palermo Stone provides a continuous year-by-year record starting, it is thought, with Menes, and ending with Nyuserre, the sixth king of Dynasty V. In addition to the name of a king, that of his mother is usually given, together with the height of the Nile Inundation and any outstanding events in the year.

Forty-eight names of kings are legible in the Karnak Table, a chronological list compiled in the reign of Thutmose III (1479–1425 BC), which was carved on a wall in the Temple of Amun at Karnak: it is now in the Louvre Museum. Fifty kings honoured by Ramesses II (1279–1213 BC) are named in a King-list in the Sakkara necropolis inscribed on a wall in the tomb of Tjunery, the king's overseer of works. Seventy-six kings are named in what is perhaps the most famous King-list, that carved on a wall in the memorial temple of Ramesses II's father, Sety I (1294–1279 BC), at Abydos. The Abydos King-list is accompanied by a fine relief showing father and son making offerings to their ancestors; but only those kings who were considered worthy of honour were commemorated in this way. Known names absent from the List include Hatshepsut, Akhenaten and Tutankhamun, all considered noteworthy by modern students of ancient Egypt but not, it seems, by Sety and his son.

The list offering the greatest number of royal names is the papyrus called the 'Canon of Kings', dated to the thirteenth century BC (Dynasty XIX) and now in the Turin Museum. Though this, the Turin Papyrus, was said to be in perfect condition in the last century when acquired in Egypt, it was broken with pieces missing by the time it reached Italy. Nevertheless, what is left of it yields nearly 90 names, together with the length of each reign and the total number of years spanned by each dynasty, all ranged in chronological order from the beginning of Dynasty I to the end of the Second Intermediate Period.

Accuracy in such lists is more or less established by contemporary inscriptions, papyri and monuments (such as stelae) that show the regnal years of currently reigning kings, amplified by coeval events and reigns elsewhere. For instance, Sheshonq I (called Shishak, King of Egypt, in *I Kings*, xiv, 25) invaded Palestine in the fifth year of Rehoboam, which is known to be c.925 BC; and Osorkon IV of Egypt sent a present to Sargon II of Syria in 715 BC, the date established from Syrian sources. From the eighth century BC, when the dates of events in Egypt can be confirmed by comparison with events in other parts of the world, the dates of Egyptian history become firmly fixed. It is also possible to date certain points precisely by using astronomical data and the time framework provided by the lists.

Unlike most ancient civilizations, the Egyptians used a solar, not a lunar, calendar, dividing the civil year into 12 months of 30 days each, with five epagomenal (extra) days added, making 365 days. This year was divided into three seasons of four months each: Akhet or 'Inundation' (mid-July to mid-November); Peret or 'Winter' (mid-November to mid-March); and Shomu or 'Summer' (mid-March to mid-July). The civil year began on the nineteenth day of July (in the Julian calendar), the expected first day of the annual rising of the Nile near Memphis, and the day the Dog Star, Sothis (Sirius), appeared on the eastern horizon at the moment the sun rose – the so-called heliacal rising of Sothis. Each such year, however, was short of a quarter of a day, so that the civil calendar crept ahead of the astronomical calendar by one day each four years. It took 1456 years for the heliacal rising of Sothis to co-incide again with the start of the Egyptian civil year (the Sothic Cycle). This defect in the civil calendar threw the seasons out of joint during the passage of a Sothic Cycle, and the real winter sometimes fell in the summer of the calendar and sometimes vice versa. If an Egyptian text describes an heliacal rising of Sothis, events can be dated within a margin of four years. Given the time taken to complete a Sothic Cycle, this has not happened often, but such a confluence of contemporary observations and an astronomical date took place in 1317 BC and AD 138.

In the seventh century BC, Egyptian independence was compromised by four Assyrian invasions.[4] After the Persians invaded in 525 BC, the country became a province of their empire. Alexander the Great conquered Egypt in 332 BC; and it was ruled by Macedonian Greeks from then until, in 30 BC, it merged with the Roman Empire. Egypt had converted to Christianity in its own Coptic form long before AD 383, when the Emperor Theodosius closed all the 'temples of paganism' throughout his domains. When, in AD 395, the Emperor divided his territories between his two sons, he placed Egypt under the authority of Constantinople, and thus annexed it to the Byzantine Empire, an event that signals the final date of what we know as ancient Egyptian history.

[4]   Kitchen, 1986, pp. 391–3.

The Arab Conquest of AD 641 brought the Byzantine era in Egypt to an end, and the country became part of the Islamic Empire. The first four Khalifs immediately succeeding Muhammad were followed by the 'Umayyad Khalifate of 661–749 and the long Abbasid Khalifate of 750–1258. Mamelukes ruled from then until 1517, succeeded by the Ottoman Turks to 1798, when Napoleon occupied the country for a short time. Though nominally under the suzerainty of the Ottomans, Muhammad Ali became undisputed ruler of Egypt in 1805. From 1882 the country was occupied by the British until, in December 1914, it became a British Protectorate. Some eight years later it was re-established as a sovereign kingdom, securing full independence after nearly two- and-a-half thousand years of foreign dominance. The Republic of Egypt was declared on 18 June 1953, and its king went into exile.

1

The Land and its People

Geography

Egypt lies on the eastern edge of the Sahara, today the vast, empty and arid region whose very name is Arabic for 'desert'. Satellite pictures, however, have established that a network of old river beds exists below its surface; and cave-paintings in places such as Tassili[5] have proved that, as recently as 4000 years ago, at least parts of the Sahara were fertile areas with rivers and green valleys teeming with a rich variety of fish and animal life. Towards the end of the last European ice age (about 10,000 BC), north Africa became hotter. It seems that this did not immediately lead to a period of unremitting desiccation: instead, there were times during which rain was fairly abundant. The first of these periods of increased precipitation appears to have been between 9200 and 6000 BC, the second began about 5000 BC and the third some time after 4000 BC. Northern and eastern Egypt enjoyed considerable rainfall until about 2350 BC, by which time aridity had reached a level that has persisted to the present.[6]

Modern Egypt has a total area of some 1,002,000 square kilometres, of which the greater part is desert: less than 40,000 square kilometres of land is cultivable and habitable,[7] most of it lying in the area immediately adjacent to the Nile, in the Faiyum depression and the oases in the Western Desert, and above all in the Delta. The Nile has played a vital part in the creation of Egypt, a

[5] Lhote, 1958.
[6] Butzer, 1971, p. 584.
[7] *The Europa World Year Book*, 1994.

process which started about five million years ago when the river began to flow northwards into Egypt from twin sources in Ethiopia (the Blue Nile) and Uganda (the White Nile). The two streams converge at Khartoum in the Sudan and from there flow as a single river for some 3170 kilometres to the Mediterranean. About 300 kilometres north of Khartoum the river is fed by a major tributary, the Atbara. The flow of the river is interrupted at intervals by six cataracts, the name given to areas where the river flows over outcrops of rock. They are numbered from north to south, the first being at Aswan, the sixth nearly 1000 kilometres above it, in the Sudan.

The Egyptian section of the Nile – the 1250 kilometres from the First Cataract to the Mediterranean – was, in its formative stage, much wider than it is today, and bordered by marshland and swamps. Gradually, the river bed cut deeper and the Nile narrowed, flowing through terrain that was rocky and barren. The land sloped very gently to the north,[8] and large quantities of the gravel, sand and silt carried by the river were deposited at its mouth to form a delta, later to become one of the most fertile areas of Egypt. In addition, large amounts of detritus sank to the bottom of the river so that, over the millennia, it aggraded: the different levels of the river bed are still visible, in the form of cliffs and terraces on the east and west sides of the Nile Valley.

The cultivable land that now borders the river owes its existence to the material washed down from the Ethiopian plateau by the rains that produced the annual flooding of the banks of the Nile (the 'Inundation'), leaving behind alluvial silt and mud on the river banks as the flood waters receded. At first, there was a tendency for the mud to be deposited close to the bank, creating an embankment or levee. The resulting rise in the height of the river bank increased the velocity of the water running down its slope so that less sediment was deposited at the top of the levee and more at its base, gradually enlarging the area covered by alluvium and creating a flood plain on which grew thickets of trees such as tamarisk, sycamore and acacia. Today, the river banks slope towards the desert irregularly, on average about 19 centimetres to the kilometre; at the edges furthest from the river, the ground

[8] Today, Aswan is 113 m above sea level, Luxor 79 m, Assiut 55 m and Cairo 37 m, a rate of decline of 1 in 11,000 or about 9 cm to the kilometre.

remains moist enough in places to support a variety of grasses and other vegetation.

The deposition of alluvium is thought to have begun about 8000 BC and continued for nearly 10,000 years until, in the 1960s, the construction of a hydroelectric dam at Aswan (*see* page 307) brought it to an end. Up to that time, however, the alluvium accumulated at a maximum rate[9] of about 10 centimetres a century until it reached an average depth of 9 metres. It is clear that originally all cultivable land in the Nile Valley owed its existence to the actions of the Nile, giving rise to Herodotus' famous observation that Egypt 'is, as it were, the gift of the river'.[10] With negligible rainfall in the north, except on the Mediterranean coast, and virtually absent in the south, the Nile also provides Egypt with most of its drinking and irrigation water. Despite the dictum of the Roman poet Tibullus: 'Father Nile . . . because of thee Egypt never sues for showers',[11] there have been times of hardship in Egypt whenever the Nile flood was abnormally low. Pliny the Elder estimated that an Inundation of 5.5 metres left the Egyptians starving while 7 metres gave a bumper harvest.[12]

Egypt's southern border was traditionally set at Aswan; but, in very early times, the effective southern boundary seems to have been 75 kilometres further north at Gebel Silsileh. In modern times, northern Nubia has become part of Egypt, so that the boundary is now set a few kilometres north of Wadi Halfa in the Sudan, though the land south of Aswan is still known as Nubia and not Egypt. Egypt, which the ancient Egyptians called Ta-meri [Land of the River Bank(s)], is composed of two distinct parts: the north or Lower Egypt, consisting of the Delta and a small part of the Nile Valley south of its apex; and the south or Upper Egypt, comprising the rest of the Valley to Aswan. The ancient Egyptians called the north Mehu and the south Shemau: together they were known as the Two Lands. The fertile alluvium deposited as the Inundation receded inspired another ancient name for Egypt, Kemet (Black Land). In contrast, the desert area untouched by the flood was called Deshret (Red Land).

9 Butzer and Hansen, 1968, pp. 276–8.
10 Herodotus, *The Histories*, Book 2, 4.
11 Tibullus Book I, vii, 24–25.
12 Pliny, *Natural History*, 5, 58.

There are marked geographical dissimilarities between the two halves of the country. In Upper Egypt, the arable land is never more than 14 kilometres wide and the desert is ever-present: in Lower Egypt, the Nile opens out into the wide Delta and disgorges its silt-laden water into the Mediterranean along 200 kilometres of coastline. The Delta, which has an area of some 15,000 square kilometres, is the most productive region in Egypt, a place where fertile land seems to stretch as far as the eye can see.

Natural Resources

Egypt has two principal natural resources. One is Nile alluvium, the basis of its agriculture, and until modern times an inexhaustible and annually renewed source for the manufacture of the mud bricks which for millennia have been the basic component in Egyptian architecture. The other natural resource is stone, available in such quantity and variety that it is an admirable medium for building and for artistic purposes. Except for the mountains in the Eastern Desert, the land surface of Egypt, from the Mediterranean to the area south of Luxor, is limestone; from Gebel Silsileh to Aswan, some 63 kilometres to its south, there is a belt of sandstone; and at Aswan, the limestone and sandstone layers have eroded to reveal the igneous rocks of the old continent – granite, diorite and dolerite. Limestone cliffs stretch from a point south of Luxor to Cairo. The limestone was formed from the skeletons of marine organisms that abounded in the Tethys[13] and hardened to form thick layers of sedimentary rock as the Tethys receded. A large proportion of these creatures was a type of foraminifera which, because of their coin-shaped shells, have been given the name nummulites, from the Latin *nummus* (coin): hence the limestone is largely nummulitic. Several other types of stone were available to the Egyptians, notably greywacke, obtained from the Eastern Desert near Coptos, quartzite from Gebel el-Ahmar, north-east of Cairo, and calcite (and gypsum) from Hatnub, north of Assiut, and from the Wadi el-Garawi, south of Cairo.

Gold, copper and iron are the only metals native to Egypt. In ancient times, the rift mountains of the Eastern Desert were rich in gold: for centuries the mines at Coptos were worked and, as these

[13] The name given to the ocean (a forerunner of the Mediterranean) that covered a large part of Egypt between 60 and 30 million years ago.

became exhausted or too difficult, mining activity was transferred to Lower Nubia. Copper was obtained from the Sinai peninsula, Lower Nubia and the Red Sea area of the Eastern Desert. Though deposits of iron occur at Aswan, the ancient Egyptians seem not to have been aware of them, and iron was imported into Egypt from about 1000 BC. Lead is found at Aswan, tin and lead in the Red Sea area of the Eastern Desert. The same area produces emerald, Egypt's only precious stone; and beryl, feldspar, jasper and porphyry. Amethyst and steatite are found near Aswan; and malachite in the Eastern Desert, Lower Nubia and the Sinai Peninsula. Sinai is also a source of turquoise. The Western Desert is a source of alum, gypsum and, above all, natron, the carbonate of soda vital to the practice of mummification.

Flora and Fauna

Egypt is deficient in wood, though trees were probably not so scarce in pharaonic times as they are now. Several species of tree have been introduced in modern times, notably *Casuarina*, or she oaks, native to Australasia, which are planted as windbreaks and along the sides of roads, and, being quick growing, are a useful source of timber. Indigenous Egyptian trees include the Egyptian willow (*Salix subserrta*), tamarisk (*Tamarix nilotica*), and two oil-producing trees, moringa (*Moringa peregrina*) and acacia (*Acacia nilotica*). The sycamore-fig tree (*Ficus sycomorus*)[14] was not native to Egypt but has been cultivated at least from the First Dynasty, as has the vine for the production of wine: Egypt is still a wine-producing country. Attempts to cultivate olive trees were made in the Eighteenth Dynasty, but olive oil was imported until the Ptolemaic Period, when large numbers of olive trees were planted in the Faiyum. Since ancient times, dom-palm (*Hyphaene thebaica*), the nuts of which are used to make drinks, and date palm (*Phoenix dactylifera*) have been grown. The date palm needs artificial pollination; and hand pollination seems to have been practised from early dynastic times. Today, there are some 30 different kinds of dates, ranging from very sweet to dry. Palm has been commonly used for roofing, but otherwise the quality of

---

[14] Not be confused with the European sycamore (*Acer pseudoplatanus*) a maple tree; or with the North American sycamore (of the genus *Platanus*), a plane tree.

Egypt's timber is poor and largely useless for building or artistic purposes. What the country lacked in trees was compensated for by the plant *Cyperus papyrus* which, in ancient times, grew in abundance in the marshes of the Nile Valley and the Delta although it no longer does so (*see* page 309). Almost every part of the papyrus plant was utilized: ropes, mats, boxes, sandals and even boats were made from it. Above all, the stalk, sliced into thin sections that were laid side by side and crosswise, then pressed into sheets and dried in the sun, formed an unsurpassed writing material.

In ancient times the tree- and grass-covered upland areas of the steppes to the west of the Nile Valley and in the northern Red Sea hills supported large numbers of rhinoceros, elephant, giraffe, deer, ibex, antelope, gazelle, wild ass and cattle and ostrich, which were hunted. It was once thought that increasing aridity in the steppes that bordered Egypt forced the movement of the hunter-gatherers who inhabited the area into the Nile Valley. It is now known, however, that there was no such climatic deterioration. Instead, around 6000 BC, it seems that a reasonably moist climate facilitated the movement of groups of people into and through what is now a desert[15] and finally into the Nile Valley, where they found a proliferation of the same variety of fauna as that in the uplands. In addition, there was a river in which there were many varieties of fish – a boon somewhat offset by the presence also of crocodiles and hippopotamuses. Such favourable conditions encouraged them to stay in the Nile Valley, where they developed from nomadic hunters into sedentary agriculturalists.

The two main food crops grown by ancient Egyptians were barley (*Hordeum vulgare*) and emmer wheat (*Triticum dicoccum*). Yeast (*Saccharomyes winlocki*) was used for fermentation. Pulses, especially beans and lentils, onions, garlic, lettuce and celery were, and still are, widely grown, as were herbs such as fenugreek, thyme, marjoram, liquorice and mint, used for both culinary and medical purposes. Sugar cane and rice, unknown to the ancient Egyptians, are two of modern Egypt's major crops, and potatoes, introduced in the last century, are grown in great quantities for home consumption and for export. Indian corn (maize), also introduced in the last century, and lucerne, or Egyptian clover (*Trifolium alexandrinum*, in Arabic – *bersim*), brought from the

[15]   Trigger et al., 1983, p. 9.

Balkans during the Byzantine Period, are both used as animal fodder.

The Egyptians

The racial typing of the earliest Egyptians is a vexed question.[16] They were certainly people of north-east Africa but, whether this means, as some claim, that they were black is open to question. One has to define what is meant by 'black', the popular conception of which is the physical type that is today found typically in West Africa. The writer, Gustav Flaubert, admirably expressed the futility of assigning a uniform appearance to all black peoples: 'I became convinced that the Negro race is even more varied than the white race.'[17] Judging from the skeletal remains excavated at several sites in the Delta and in southern Egypt, the best that can be said is that the inhabitants of southern Egypt were largely small and fine boned, with long narrow skulls and dark wavy hair; and the people of the Delta taller, of a more sturdy build, with broader skulls. It is probable that the early inhabitants of the Delta were in contact with south-western Asia and that intermarriage modified their appearance. Centuries later, Libyans from the west and Nubians from the south added to Egypt's racial mix, and later still, Greeks and Romans did likewise. In modern Egypt there are both Arab and Turkish elements in the population. The language spoken by ancient Egyptians is classified by linguists as 'Afro-Asiatic' (or Hamito-Semitic) and, as much as the racial origins of the Egyptians, is the subject of argument.[18] Ancient Egyptian has been replaced in modern times by a Semitic language, Arabic.

Geographical differences had a profound effect upon the inhabitants of the Two Lands: Upper Egypt developed in a different way from Lower Egypt. Throughout Egyptian history the two regions have been distrustful of each other. Ancient Egyptians were all united, however, in their common scorn of anyone not fortunate enough to live in Ta-meri. Shut in by deserts or sea, with high cliffs on either side of the Nile Valley limiting their physical, and seemingly their mental, horizons, the Egyptians had a sense of being a race apart, superior to all others.

[16] Vercoutter, 1978.
[17] G. Flaubert, *Correspondence* (Paris, 1973), vol. 1, p. 655.
[18] Trigger et al., 1983, pp. 11–12.

The geographical situation of Egypt made it a land ideally suited to civilizing forces. Surrounded by a combination of desert and sea, it was not prey to easy attack from outwith its borders. On the other hand, it was not completely cut off from outside influence: it could be reached by way of the Fertile Crescent or through the deserts to the east and west or along the edge of the Delta, and was thus open to stimulus from other cultures. Though plentiful, Egypt's natural resources were not so superabundant as to induce sloth. The ancient Egyptians' sense of superiority seems to have limited their achievements, however: in some directions, these were considerable; in others, much less than one might have expected. If we imagine the world they knew, we must conclude that they made great innovations, but only within the Egyptian context. This said, however, it cannot be denied that they created one of the world's greatest civilizations.

The hallmark of the civilization of ancient Egypt is the attention paid to the dead. Wherever possible, the Egyptians occupied sites close to the Nile and its life-giving water, building their houses of perishable materials such as mud-brick. In contrast, they buried their dead in tombs and graves meant to last for for eternity – the ancient Egyptian word for tomb (*pr nḥḥ*) means 'house of eternity'. They did not waste arable land by burying the dead in it, but used the arid cliffs and desert land on the edges of the Nile Valley, at a distance from habitation sites. The dryness of the atmosphere aided the preservation of graves and tombs, and of their contents, so that burial sites and buildings associated with them, such as mortuary chapels and temples, have become the basis for Egyptian archaeology.

The conviction that there was life after death, and that a secure tomb was essential to support it, formed the foundation for the cultural beliefs of the ancient Egyptians, and caused them to devote a large part of their resources to funerary practices. What remains of their culture is largely concerned with death and preparations for the dead; and the archaeological sites of ancient Egypt give some people the impression that the Egyptians took a very unhealthy interest in death, almost to the extent of being in love with it. That this was not the case is evident from papyri and other sources such as reliefs and inscriptions in tombs, which portray tomb-owners enjoying life, particularly hunting in the marshes and the desert; and attending parties, accompanied by their pet monkeys and cats, at which guests, plied with food, drank to get drunk, listened to music and were entertained by dancing girls.

Far from being morose, the ancient Egyptian, like his and her modern counterpart, displayed an engaging and irreverent sense of humour.

Daily life

The family in ancient Egypt was as closely knit as it is in Egypt today. It was the custom to represent not only a man on his tomb stele but also his wife, his children, his parents and, often, his grandparents. A man's mother was given a more prominent position than his father because descent was traced through the female line. In spite of the many love poems that have come down to us, it seems probable that most marriages were arranged with an eye to social and financial advantages. Marriage between cousins was then as now the ideal (*see* page 314); and it was not unusual for marriages to take place between uncle and niece,[19] for reasons of family property. By modern Western standards, ancient Egyptians matured early and many marriages took place at a young age – 15 for boys, 13 for girls; but, until quite recently, marriage at these ages has not been uncommon among the *fellahin* (peasants).

Taking a wife appears to have been synonymous with setting up a house. A man was expected to love his wife, as the following exhortation from the sage, Ptah-hotep, makes clear: 'Love your wife, feed her, clothe her and make her happy . . . but don't let her gain the upper hand!'[20] Another sage, Ani, proffered a recipe for a happy life: 'Don't boss your wife in her own house when you know she is efficient. Don't keep saying to her, "Where is it? Bring it to me!", especially when you know it is in the place where it ought to be!'[21]

As with today's Muslims in Egypt, there was no marriage ceremony, the marriage itself being enacted by the bride simply entering her husband's house. Marriage is a contract between a man and a woman, freely entered into. A marriage deed that binds two equal parties allows both to state their conditions. In ancient Egypt, at least among the propertied classes, there was a marriage settlement, usually drawn up between the prospective husband and the bride's father, although a woman was herself often the

[19]   Pestman, 1961, p. 7
[20]   Lichtheim, 1975, p. 69.
[21]   Lichtheim, 1976, p. 143.

contracting partner. The settlement stipulated the bride's dowry and the marriage gift due to her from her husband.

In normal circumstances, an ancient Egyptian man had one wife, although others might be taken with the agreement of earlier spouses. A Muslim Egyptian today may have four wives, but only with good reason, and provided he treats them all exactly the same. Polyandry was not and is not practised! It was and, for Muslims, still is possible to divorce with relative ease, the most common reasons for divorce being barrenness, or a man's desire to take another wife against the wishes of the first, or simply because a wife had ceased to please her husband. A Muslim Egyptian man may divorce his wife by repeating 'I divorce thee' three times before male witnesses. Men have been known to divorce their wives without their knowledge, to avoid financial penalties. This has brought problems when a husband dies, the divorced wife being surprised to discover that she has no rights of inheritance.

In ancient Egypt, a woman was entitled to initiate divorce: and often came out of the marriage with more security than many modern women. A man who divorced his wife had to return her dowry, give her the marriage gift agreed to in the marriage settlement, and pay her compensation. A woman who divorced her husband was given back her dowry; and usually a share of any property that had accrued since marriage. After a divorce, both parties were free to remarry.

In ancient Egypt a woman enjoyed the same rights under the law as a man. What her *de jure* rights were depended upon her social class not her sex. All landed property descended in the female line, from mother to daughter, on the assumption, perhaps, that maternity is a matter of fact, paternity a matter of opinion. A woman was entitled to administer her own property and dispose of it as she wished. She could buy, sell, be a partner in legal contracts, be executor in wills and witness to legal documents, bring an action at court, and adopt children in her own name. An ancient Egyptian woman was legally *capax*. In contrast, an ancient Greek woman was supervised by a *kyrios* (guardian); and many Greek women who lived in Egypt during the Ptolemaic Period, observing Egyptian women acting without *kyrioi*, were encouraged to do so themselves. In short, an ancient Egyptian woman enjoyed greater social standing than many women of other societies, both ancient and modern.

Mothers have always been revered in Egypt. The sage, Ani, enjoined a man to take care of his mother, in repayment of the care she had taken of him as a child. All children, whether boys or girls, were welcomed at birth by ancient Egyptians, but boys especially so. It was expected that a girl would marry and leave the paternal home, whereas a boy would remain and in due course be responsible for the upkeep of his father's tomb. In the same way, a modern Muslim Egyptian wishes for his first child to be the son who will say prayers for his father after his death.

In ancient Egypt, formal education was not usually given to girls or peasants. Boys attended schools, which were either attached to temples or run by government departments, from the age of four or five until 15. At school, emphasis was placed on discipline, good manners, honesty and humility. Education in modern Egypt is compulsory for both sexes from the age of six to 14. State education is free, and there are many private, fee-paying schools. In some areas, the number of children of school age demands that the school day be run in two shifts. Tertiary education is available in 13 universities. In ancient Egypt, the majority of the population was illiterate. In modern Egypt, the adult illiteracy rate averages just under 50 per cent.

Food

The basic diet of an ancient Egyptian peasant was probably similar to that of a modern *fellah*: bread, onions, cheese and chickpeas or beans, supplemented with Nile fish and wildfowl. The daily bread was made from emmer wheat ground to flour with a stone pestle and mortar or on a saddle quern. Dough was made into round, flat loaves and baked, unleavened, on hot stones or on the outside of a stove. The stove was about a metre high, conical in shape and open at the top, and made of Nile mud. The fire lit inside it made the exterior of the walls so hot that pats of dough could be stuck to them until they were cooked, at which time they fell off. Today, *fellahin* eat *eish baladi* (village bread) made in a similar way.

Bread was the staple food even among the rich in ancient Egypt. The most common sort was called *ta*, but in the Old Kingdom there were at least 15 different kinds, and in the New Kingdom over 40 varieties of bread and cake. Bread took many sizes and shapes, and honey, fruit or spices could be added to the basic dough. Generally speaking, young Egyptians, ancient and modern, possess good teeth. The teeth of ancient Egyptian mummies do not exhibit dental caries, perhaps because of the lack of sugar in the diet, but in many older people they are worn and pointed. The pointing was perhaps due to the intrusion of particles of sand into their food; but Egyptians owed worn teeth to the fact that much of their bread was made from flour produced from grain threshed on a stone threshing floor and ground on a stone quern. Over the years, the small stones that were an intrinsic part of the bread played havoc with teeth! The teeth of upper-class Egyptians do not exhibit the same amount of wear, presumably because they did not eat so much coarse bread.

Beer was made from barley dough, first prepared and set to bake in clay pots as if for bread. When part baked, it was crumbled into a large vat and mixed with water, sometimes sweetened with date or pomegranate juice. This mixture was left to ferment, which it did rapidly, and the liquid strained from the dough into a pot. The beer went flat very quickly. It was drunk in great quantities, in preference to water: a reasonable habit, since pure drinking water is a luxury of modern, industrialized countries or mountainous regions. Alcohol is forbidden to the Muslims of modern Egypt; but the Nubians make a beer, usually from barley but sometimes from wheat or millet, that is similar to that of ancient Egypt. It is called *boozah*.

Beef was the most popular meat in ancient Egypt, but mutton and goat meat were also eaten, as well as the flesh of gazelle and antelope. Peasants could not afford meat: even today beef is prohibitively expensive (*see* page 312 note 299). Though the ancient Egyptians considered pork and fish 'unclean', presumably because they went off so quickly in the hot climate, and a strict taboo forbade anyone who took part in religious rituals to eat fish, peasants especially could not afford the luxury of eliminating such 'unclean' meat from their diets. Today, Muslim dietary laws forbid the consumption of pork and certain other foods: the meat most readily available is lamb. Cheese was made from the milk of goats, sheep or cows, probably in the same fashion as it is sometimes made in Egyptian villages today, when milk is placed in an animal skin (usually goat) strung on a frame, and rocked back and forth until churned to cheese.

Many foodstuffs grown in Egypt today – rice, potatoes, lemons, oranges, bananas, tomatoes, almonds, mangoes, peaches, for example – were introduced in modern times. Sugar, now one of the staple crops, was unknown to the ancient Egyptians: they, being as sweet toothed as their modern descendants, used honey as a sweetener. The poor foraged for wild honey in the desert, the rich obtained their honey from bee-keepers: the production of domestic honey was an important industry in ancient Egypt.

Health

There is a marked similarity between the ailments suffered by ancient and by modern Egyptians. This should come as no surprise: in rural Egypt living conditions are much the same now as they have always been. The damp, to which mud-brick houses are susceptible, is injurious to health; contaminated water and lack of hygiene lead to intestinal disorders, bilharzia, skin diseases, worms, boils and sores. Infections and diseases of the eye are especially prevalent. In World War II, British soldiers in Egypt were appalled by the terrible effects of trachoma, particularly on children's eyes. 'Golden Eye Ointment', readily available from chemist shops in Britain, was a simple remedy; today, tetracycline or chloramphenicol are the preferred antibiotic treatments. Infant mortality was high, largely from lack of hygiene during birth; and later from the baby's living conditions. Large numbers used to die from the effects of infant diarrhoea until, a few years ago, a programme was introduced to teach mothers simple rehydration methods.

The sources for the study of diseases in ancient Egypt are medical papyri; sculptures, paintings and reliefs; and mummies and skeletal remains. Clement of Alexandria (AD 200) claimed that there were 42 Egyptian books containing the sum of human knowledge: of these, six dealt with medicine (anatomy, diseases, surgery, remedies, diseases of the eye, diseases of women). No exact examples of these papyri have survived, but a number extant deal with medical matters, the largest and most significant being the Ebers Papyrus, written *c.*1550 BC and named after the German Egyptologist, Georg Ebers, who purchased it in Luxor in 1873. The Ebers Papyrus deals with diseases of the stomach, the action of the heart, the surgical treatment of boils and carbuncles, and gynaecology. The oldest papyrus, the Kahun, written *c.*1880 BC and named after the site where Petrie discovered it, deals with diseases of women, and also has a veterinary section. A manual of surgery is the subject of the Edwin Smith Papyrus, written *c.*1880 BC and named after the American dealer in antiquities who purchased it and the Ebers papyrus in Luxor in 1862. These, and another six major papyri, provide evidence that, among other ailments, the ancient Egyptians suffered from trachoma, seasonal ophthalmia, hernia, skin disease, haemorrhoids and ear infections.

Artistic representations show examples of achondroplastic dwarfism, bilateral dislocation of the hip, atrophied limbs due to poliomyelitis and pituitary disorder. Skeletal remains and mummies, examined using radiography, macroscopy, endoscopy and histological techniques such as light, polarizing and electron microscopes, show evidence of congenital diseases such as achondroplasia, acrocephaly, hydrocephaly, hip-joint dysplasia, cleft palate and osteoporosis symmetrica; and of acquired diseases such as osteoarthritis, middle-ear infection, tuberculosis, gout and osteoporosis. Schistosoma (bilharzia) and tapeworm, kidney and gall stones seem to have been common; as were respiratory diseases such as pneumonia, bronchitis and, not surprisingly in the conditions that prevailed, emphysema and sand pneumoconiosis. There was gonorrhea, but no tumours and very little cancer – possibly because few lived long enough to succumb. There was no leprosy until Roman times; and no epidemic diseases such as plague or cholera, although there is thought to have been a smallpox epidemic in Dynasty XX. Because of the sunlight there was no rickets. Thirty per cent of Egyptian mummies examined indicate a generally poor state of health in childhood and adolescence, as indicated by Harris's lines, transverse lines on the tibia shown up by X-ray, and caused by intermittent disease or malnutrition.

It was once thought that scientific medicine began with Greeks such as Hippocrates and Galen, and that medicine as practised in ancient Egypt was but a hotch-potch of magic and superstition. It is now clear that this was not so, that Egyptian medicine was based on a body of knowledge already developed some 2000 years before the first Greek physicians. Advanced modern medicine has been available in Egypt for some time: but it is salutary to think that a plentiful supply of clean water for both drinking and washing purposes does more to counteract disease and promote essential hygiene. Though tourists find picturesque the sight of village women filling their pots from the Nile and washing pans and clothes at the river's edge, these practices are clearly not conducive to good health.

2

The Earliest Egyptians

The Stone Age

In recent years, attention paid to palaeolithic sites has produced evidence of hunter-gatherers inhabiting the gravel terraces on the high fringes of the Nile Valley. This evidence consists chiefly of primitive stone tools, such as hand-axes, chipped roughly into shape from cores of flint. Excavations at Nag Ahmed el-Khalifa, south of Abydos, for example, have yielded primitive hand-axes dating to the mid-Pleistocene Period (c.200,000 BC). Some time after 100,000 BC, stone tools were being made by flint-knappers to any shape desired, using the so-called Levallois technique. These early tools were made only from stone occurring in readily available cores; but evidence from Nazlet Khater, south of Assiut, shows that c.33,000 BC, more elaborate flint-mining was practised. Trenches were cut into the ground until a stratum of flint was reached, usually about 2 metres down, along which miners tunnelled. With the stone obtained by these more advanced methods, flint-knappers produced flaked tools that were much more refined than the primitive hand-axes.

Late palaeolithic sites have mostly been found in Upper Egypt, notably at Shuwikhat, near Qena, the site of a hunting-camp dating to 25,000 BC, where fine flint tools were discovered; and at Kubbaniya, near Esna, where, c.20,000 BC, there was a fishing-camp. The large quantity of fish bones found at Makhdama, near Qena, proves that fish was an important part of the diet of the hunting community living there c.12,000 BC; and the amount of carbon found at the site suggests that fish were dried over fires. At present, evidence of human activity taking place in the Nile Valley

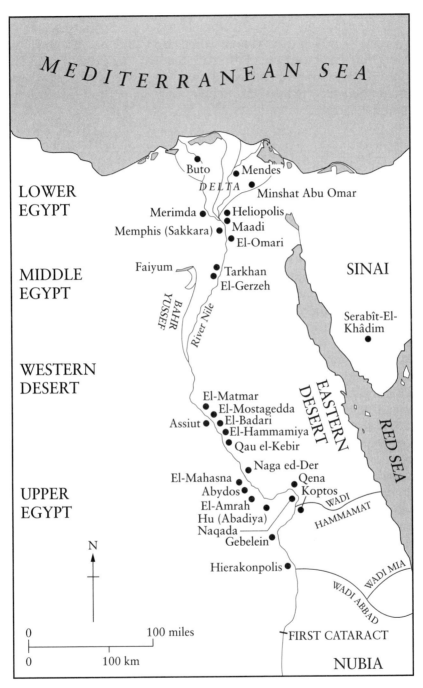

MEDITERRANEAN SEA

LOWER
EGYPT

MIDDLE
EGYPT

WESTERN
DESERT

UPPER
EGYPT

SINAI

EASTERN
DESERT

RED SEA

NUBIA

Buto
Mendes
DELTA
Minshat Abu Omar
Merimda
Heliopolis
Memphis (Sakkara)
Maadi
El-Omari

Faiyum
Tarkhan
El-Gerzeh

BAHR YUSSEF
River Nile

Serabît-El-Khâdim

El-Matmar
El-Mostagedda
Assiut
El-Badari
El-Hammamiya
Qau el-Kebir

Naga ed-Der
El-Mahasna
Qena
Abydos
Koptos
El-Amrah
Hu (Abadiya)
Naqada
Gebelein
WADI HAMMAMAT

Hierakonpolis
WADI MIA
WADI ABBAD

FIRST CATARACT

N

0   100 miles
0   100 km

Map 2   Map of Egypt showing sites of the Predynastic and Archaic
Periods.

between 11,000 and 8000 BC is lacking, possibly because remains are covered by alluvium; but at the end of this period, signs of human occupation re-emerge, showing that the Nile Valley was still inhabited by palaeolithic people, who hunted and fished from seasonal camps.

Predynastic Egypt

Until AD 1895, the prehistory of Egypt was unknown, but in the winter of that year Flinders Petrie began excavating at a site in Upper Egypt near the village of Naqada. He uncovered huge cemeteries in which the graves contained objects, notably clay pots, of unfamiliar types. Initially, he assigned them to the First Intermediate Period; but in 1898–9, Petrie's excavations of similar cemeteries at Abadiya and Hu, a short distance to the north of Naqada, convinced him that all these sites predated the dynastic period; and in the years that followed, other predynastic sites came to light.

The study of predynastic Egypt was complicated by a convention that gave the different stages of cultural development the names of the sites of discovery. Thus, Petrie named three stages of the Predynastic Period, Amratian (after a site in Upper Egypt called el-Amra), Gerzean (after el-Gerza near the Faiyum), and Semainian (after es-Semaina), though the objects found at this site were later assigned to the First Dynasty. The first two of these names came to be used as alternatives for Naqada I and Naqada II respectively. In 1957, the German Egyptologist, Werner Kaiser, proposed that Naqada, as the site from which the culture spread, should give its name to a new system in which stages would be designated Naqada I, Naqada II and, for the first time, Naqada III. Although it is realized that there was a certain amount of overlap between stages, Kaiser's system stresses the continuity of the Naqada culture, and is used with subdivisions for a more accurate record of its development.

Early in the twentieth century, many more predynastic sites were excavated, particularly around the Faiyum. An important discovery near the village of el-Badari, near Assiut in Upper Egypt, disclosed a culture older than Naqada I, and later named Badarian. A site predating Badari by several hundred years was found on the edge of the Delta at Merimda. From these it was realized that there were differences between the southern cultures and that of Merimda in the north, suggesting that the two areas developed separately. Badari and Naqada, the Upper Egyptian sites, give their names to other sites identified as having the same culture; but so far the same convention has not been applied to Lower Egyptian sites, each being treated as a separate entity.

In the last 20 years or so, archaeological excavations, notably at Hierakonpolis in Upper Egypt, in the Faiyum and in the Delta, have thrown new light on predynastic Egypt. For many years it was believed that in late prehistoric times the Nile Delta was a vast, uninhabitable swamp. Consequently, excavators did not look for early settlements except on its edge or at its apex, where they succeeded in locating Merimda, el-Omari and Ma'adi (*see* below). When eventually it was realized that the Delta had not been so inhospitable a place (*see* page 27), it was concluded that its major predynastic sites must have been situated in the inner Delta because, in later times, this was a key area of settlement. Its topography and continued occupation were thought to preclude excavation, with most of the sites destined to remain covered by Nile alluvium or to lie beneath more recent settlements.

Since the 1970s, many predynastic sites have been discovered all over the Delta. Merimda remains the best excavated, although drilling at Minshat Abu Omar[22] in the eastern Delta has turned up pottery, flint and faunal remains; and potsherds have been found below a layer of organic-rich mud that has enabled them to be radiocarbon dated to 4700 BC. The terrain in the Delta makes excavation difficult – Minshat Abu Omar lies 6 metres or more below the present water-table – although the Ma'adi site is more accessible and has yielded remains dated to 3500 BC.

In recent years, the chronology of the Faiyum has been revised. Egyptologists first excavated in the Faiyum in the 1930s,[23] and named its culture Faiyum A. Another culture, Faiyum B, was said to be a later development. In the 1960s, the first radiocarbon dates for the Faiyum[24] proved that Faiyum B (Qarunian) was palaeolithic and about 1000 years older than Faiyum A, which was dated to about 5000 BC.[25] Since then excavators have further

---

22 Krzyzaniak, 1992, pp. 151–55.
23 Caton-Thompson and Gardner, 1934.
24 Said et al., 1972.
25 Wendorf and Schild, 1976.

divided the Faiyum A culture into an earlier phase, called Fayumian; and a later phase, the Moerian.[26]

Lower Egypt in the Predynastic Period

The Faiyum

The earliest neolithic settlements in Lower Egypt, which date back to about 5200 BC,[27] are in the Faiyum, a large depression in the Western Desert about 60 kilometres to the south-west of Cairo. Some time during the early Palaeolithic Period (perhaps some 70,000 years ago),[28] the Nile broke through the strip of desert between it and the Faiyum and flooded the depression. The lake thus formed is thought to have covered an area of at least 2800 square kilometres,[29] to a height of between 42 and 44 metres above sea-level. Over the millenniums, its level has lowered and risen several times and it has become smaller, so that today the Faiyum lake (Birket Qarun), in spite of being fed by the Bahr Yusef, the only true side-branch of the Nile in Egypt, occupies an area of about 200 square kilometres and is some 45 metres below sea-level.

When the surface of the lake stood about 10 metres above sea-level, a neolithic pastoralist-agriculturalist tribe (or tribes) arrived in the Faiyum and began the cultivation of emmer wheat and six-rowed barley. Since these grains were native to western Asia, it has been suggested that the settlers must have had some contact with that region. Fourteen settlements have been located along some 60 kilometres of the northern and north-eastern shores of the lake. Although numerous cooking-hearths have been found near the fertile soil at the edge of the lake, there is a lack of evidence concerning the structure of the dwellings to which they were attached; and it is assumed that the earliest Faiyum settlers lived in reed or matting huts. They cut wheat and barley with sickle-shaped flints set into wooden handles, and stored grain in communal underground granaries, of which over 160 have been located,

[26]   Ginter, 1982.
[27]   Hassan, 1985.
[28]   Ball, 1939, p. 190.
[29]   ibid., p. 191.

dug in high ground far enough away from the lake to keep their contents dry.

While these early Faiyum settlers were clearly agriculturalists, they were evidently still reliant on hunting – elephant, hippopotamus, gazelle, antelope and even crocodile made up part of their diet, supplemented by fish and mussels taken from the lake. The animals were killed with small spears and concave-based arrowheads; the fish seem to have been trapped in reed baskets, there being no evidence that fish-hooks were used. The bones of sheep, goats, oxen and pigs have been found in the settlements but whether any of these were domesticated is unclear. Like the emmer and barley, the sheep and goats had a western Asiatic origin.

The Faiyum people cultivated flax and spun it on a spindle to produce a thread from which they wove coarse linen to wear. For ornament they used sea shells obtained from the Mediterranean and from the Red Sea. They used straw and reeds to make baskets of a high standard; and lined their granaries with straw matting. Coarse clay, with chaff as filler, was used to hand-make pots, which were mainly small bowls and cups, deep bowls, and cooking bowls and pots, with an occasional pedestalled cup, a cup with knobbed feet and a rectangular dish. Most had a plain rough surface but some were overlaid with a burnished red slip.

The Delta

The Nile Delta in its present configuration was formed between 6500 and 5500 BC, during a deceleration in the rise of sea-level.[30] In the last ice age, from about 16,000 BC, global sea-level rose rapidly to over 100 metres above its glacial minimum height; but, by 8000 BC, it had begun to recede, reducing the gradient of the Nile and allowing alluvium to accumulate. The Delta thus became suitable for farming, a vital step in the development of civilization, just at the time when hunter-gatherers were migrating from the Western Desert into the Nile Valley. The new conditions in the Delta may also have encouraged the introduction of domesticated cereals, and possibly livestock, from the Near East.

[30] Stanley and Warne, 1993.

Merimda

A fully sedentary village life in the Nile Valley first occurred at Merimda, which lies on the western edge of the Delta some 90 kilometres north of the Faiyum. The village, estimated to have covered about 180,000 square metres, is the oldest-known neolithic site in the area, first settled *c.*5000–4900 BC[31] and inhabited for some 600 years. Stone artefacts from Merimda resemble those of the Faiyum, although they are of more varied shape and more elaborate decoration, and it is possible that the Merimda culture is related to Faiyum neolithic.

The Merimda inhabitants appear at first to have lived in scattered shelters made of wood, later building oval-shaped adobe houses, partly sunk below ground level and possibly with wattle superstructures. These houses had neither hearths nor door openings at ground level. Entrance holes were probably set high up in the wall at its junction with the roof, a method still used by the Nuba tribe in the Sudan. None of the Merimda houses is more than 3 metres in diameter, room enough for only one adult, perhaps a woman, and her children. This type of single-adult dwelling, arranged in clusters, each house inhabited by a member of a close family group, is found today in sub-Saharan Africa, and may at one time have been prevalent from Palestine to north-east Africa.[32]

Some of the houses at Merimda were arranged unevenly on either side of what appears to be a straight street, although they may be the remnants of a double ring of houses.[33] Each house had a granary consisting of a basket or clay jar three-quarters buried. Apart from the evidence of a primitive form of town-planning at Merimda, there are also signs, for the first time, of an organized community life, most notably in the circular, clay-lined threshing floors. The artistic achievements of the Merimda culture are best illustrated by the stone vases and pear-shaped mace heads, made in ever-increasing number, and by the burnished black pots excavated from the upper layers of the site.

[31]   Hassan, 1985
[32]   Flannery, 1972, pp. 23–53.
[33]   Vandier, 1952, pp. 117–19.

El-Omari

From about 4100 BC, a group of settlements known collectively as el-Omari grew in and around the mouth of the Wadi Hof, some 50 kilometres south of Merimda, on the east bank of the Nile. The houses were mostly oval, constructed from poles and wicker matting, although several seem to have been semi-subterranean huts;[34] and their granaries consisted of pits lined with basketwork or matting. Domestic animals appear to have been kept in large pens surrounded by reed fencing. El-Omari pottery was predominantly red or black, mostly undecorated, and more elaborate, with many lipped and vase-shaped vessels, than that of Merimda. On the outskirts of the settlement was a flint-knapping area, where flake and blade tools were manufactured.

Ma'adi

Ma'adi, some 10 kilometres north-west of el-Omari, flourished for several hundred years from 3800 BC. It is a large site, covering about 18 hectares, and may have been surrounded by a defensive palisade and ditch. The houses, grouped together in the middle of the village, were mostly oval huts made of wattle and mud, many with grindstones and storage jars or storage pits, some of them indoor. There were also numbers of subterranean dwellings, circular or rectangular in shape, spacious and dug to a depth of about 2 metres. They were entered from above by means of stairways; inside each was a hearth. One rectangular structure with reed and straw walls, and another constructed from logs laid horizontally, may have been the houses of the village headmen.

In the southern part of the settlement were numerous storage pits, with sloping or vertical sides, some of them lined with mud or basketwork. Although their purpose was to store grain, some housed valuable items such as carnelian beads and basalt vases. A special storage area on the north side of the village consisted of pottery jars, each about a metre in height, buried up to the neck in the ground.

At Ma'adi, agriculture replaced gathering; and the keeping of herds diminished the importance of hunting, which was

---

[34] ibid., p. 156.

apparently limited to ibex, hippopotamus, turtles, fish and molluscs. There was a great advance in craftsmanship, Maʿadi being the first place in northern Egypt at which copper was used to make tools and weapons. Its location, lying at the mouth of the Wadi Digla, an important route into Sinai and beyond into Syria-Palestine, meant that the village became a centre for Egyptian trade with those areas. Both Maʿadi and el-Omari made some cultural contact with southern Egypt.

Funerary practices in predynastic Lower Egypt

The predynastic inhabitants of Lower Egypt early on displayed a belief in some sort of existence after death, a belief which informed so much of later culture. It led to the practice of interring the dead in graves equipped with objects for use in an afterlife. At Merimda, it was the custom to bury at least some of the dead in spaces between houses, the bodies randomly orientated and without grave goods. At el-Omari, the dead, provided with a few grave goods, were buried within the settlement, the later burials in the granaries of earlier periods. At el-Omari, bodies were usually laid on the side, heads to the south and faces to the west, perhaps because even at this early date the west had been identified as the abode of the dead. At Maʿadi, burials within the settlement were largely of stillborn and very young children, and a few women; otherwise, the dead were buried outwith the village. There were three sorts of cemetery: in the earliest, the graves were simple, oval pits dug in the sand; in the other two sorts, they were roofed with stone slabs. Bodies were laid with heads to the south, but, in contrast to the custom at el-Omari, on their right sides, accompanied by an increased number of high-quality grave goods.

Upper Egypt in the Predynastic Period

The predynastic cultures of the northern part of the Nile Valley[35] seem to have developed in isolation from the southern, with the oldest of the known Lower Egyptian cultures, Merimda, predating the oldest in Upper Egypt by about 700 years; but even when

---

[35] Note, this does not include the Faiyum.

cultures were flourishing contemporaneously in both parts of the land, they seem to have had little contact with each other.

The Badarian Culture

The oldest predynastic culture in southern Egypt, the Badarian, flourished between 4300 and 3800 BC, although it began at least as far back as 5000 BC. The principal Badarian sites so far identified, el-Matmar, el-Mostagedda, el-Hammamiya, Qau el Kebir and Tasa, all cluster round el-Badari, the village giving the culture its name. Although the cemeteries at el-Badari and el-Mostagedda between them contain over 600 graves, suggesting that Badarian occupation of the region was fairly dense, it is possible that Badarian settlements were built as far south as Hierakonpolis; and that some of them, as yet undiscovered, were far larger and more advanced than those around el-Badari. The origins of the Badarians are unclear. They were not expert at flint-working: their failure to make use of the high-quality flint found in the cliffs near their settlements has been taken to mean that they did not appreciate its importance, having migrated into Egypt from an area further to the south, where there was no flint-bearing limestone, which occurs only north of Esna.[36]

The Badarians appear to have had a semi-sedentary way of life. No house remains have been found, so they may have lived in tents or huts of perishable materials. They grew barley and wheat, from which they made bread; and produced oil from castor seeds, which were probably wild. Bones of cattle, sheep and goats have been found at the settlements, but whether any were domesticated is not certain. Although the Badarians seem to have done a certain amount of fishing and hunting, using perforated fish-hooks of ivory, flint arrowheads and throwing sticks, they probably relied less on wild animals and birds for food than did their contemporary northern counterparts.

Most clothing was made of linen, although animal skins and leather were also used. Bone sewing-needles have been found, but only in the graves of men, so the making of clothes is assumed to have been a male occupation. Kilts were worn, and robes or large shirts; and in some graves, the position of pieces of linen suggests that they may have been turbans. Men wore bead girdles; and

---

[36] Brunton and Caton-Thompson, 1928, p. 75.

three amulets have been found, two in the shape of hippopotamuses, the third a bone-carving of the head of a gazelle, all
probably used as hunting charms. Bangles of bone, horn or ivory
were worn on the forearm.

The Badarians buried the dead in cemeteries located in the
desert, not far from the settlements, most in oval pits roofed over
with matting and sticks, though some graves, many of them for
women, were rectangular and larger than the rest. The reasons for
these differences in shape and size are not known. A grave usually
contained one body, lying in the foetal position, head to the south,
face to the west, and either wrapped in matting or hides or placed
in a straw hamper. Bodies were buried with hands, containing a
few grains of cereal, cupped in front of mouths in preparation for
the first meal in the afterlife. The cemeteries also contained animals, buried in the same sort of grave as the humans, possibly an
early example of the burial of sacred animals which became the
custom in dynastic Egypt.

Grave goods, consisting of food, cosmetic palettes (*see* below),
small stone vases and ivory objects, such as ornamental combs,
spoons and vases, as well as clay or ivory figurines, were placed in
the graves. Because these grave goods were similiar in quantity and
type for most burials, they give no clue to distinctions in wealth or
social position. The cosmetic palettes, which were an essential part
of predynastic funerary equipment, are rectangular and made of
stone, and, with the spoons and vases, were used to prepare face
paint. Malachite was ground on a palette, mixed with fat, and
used as eye paint by both sexes, not simply for decoration but also
as protection, as the fat caught grains of sand and dust before they
could lodge in the eye, and the green colour of the malachite
deflected the sun's rays.

Malachite was probably obtained from the Eastern Desert.
Copper tools found in graves indicate that the Badarians knew
how to smelt malachite ore to obtain copper. No trace of the metal
has been found in contemporaneous northern settlements, which
suggests that the Badarians were the more technologically advanced. Beads made from steatite, covered with a glaze coloured
blue-green with malachite, are commonly found in their graves
and are a further demonstration of their technological development. In one grave, a magnificent multi-stringed belt made from
such beads was found around a man's waist.

*Plate 2.1   Predynastic bowls from the Badarian and Naqada II periods.
(Courtesy of the Petrie Museum, University College, London.)*

Badarian pots are generally simple in shape, with semicircular bowls the most popular. Everyday pots are either smooth or rough brown; others demonstrate a sophisticated technique in their making, some being red, with a black interior and lip, an effect probably produced by placing the pot lip down into carbonizing material immediately after removing it from the kiln.[37] The fine ware is either black or red in colour, burnished before firing, its surface often combed into a ripple effect. The Badarians valued this ripple-ware so highly that they repaired broken bowls by threading the broken pieces together with wet thongs which, as they dried, pulled the sherds together. The best-quality pottery is thinner than any manufactured in any other era in predynasic Egypt. Stone vases have rarely been found in their graves, which suggests that the Badarians were not adept at stone working. Their tools were simple: sickle-stones, a few bifacial saws with serrated cutting edges and small push-planes.

Nothing is known of their political or social organization. Few weapons have been found, only arrowheads without bows, which suggests that they were not warlike and perhaps had no need to be.

---

[37]   Lucas and Harris, 1962, pp. 377–81.

The religion of the Badarians can only be deduced, mostly from their burial customs. There is no sign that they had shrines for their gods, or that they had images of them. The interment of sheep, cows and jackals in the same cemeteries and in the same manner as humans may indicate that animals were worshipped as deities. Even at this early stage, rams may have become synonymous with virility, as they were in dynastic Egypt. Cows may already have represented a great mother goddess, worshipped in dynastic times as Bat or Hathor; and figurines of naked women found in graves at el-Badari and el-Mostagedda[38] were probably votive statuettes for her. The jackal, later worshipped as Anubis, Lord of the Necropolis, may already have assumed this role in Badarian times.

Naqada I

The Badarian culture in predynastic Upper Egypt gave way to one in which the standard of living was higher, with an increased use of metal and a more highly developed artistic sense. This later culture, dating to about 4000 BC, originated in the region of modern Luxor and spread northwards into the Badarian area and southwards to the First Cataract and beyond into Nubia. El-Amrah, near Abydos, was once adopted as its type-site, but to-day it is named after Naqada, a village on the west bank of the Nile just north of Luxor. Although the Naqada I (Amratian) culture was much wider spread than the Badarian, its main sites are concentrated between el-Mahasna, north of Abydos, and Gebelein, south of Luxor.

The one Naqada I settlement where houses have been identified with any certainty is el-Hammamiya, where the remains of nine huts have been found, all of them circular and between 1 and 2 metres in diameter, with walls, about 30 centimetres thick, made from mud mixed with limestone chips. The inner faces of the walls are coated with smooth mud which merges unbroken with the beaten mud of the floors. There are no door openings and entrance can only have been effected as at Merimda (*see* page 28). Roofs were probably made of straw or some other perishable material but no trace has survived. Not all of the hut-circles were dwellings: only one has a hearth; and the desiccated remains of

---

[38] Brunton and Caton-Thompson, 1928, pl. xxiv, 3 & xxv, 3, 4, 6, 7.

dung found in another indicates that it may have been used as an animal pen.

The Naqada I economy seems to have been much the same as the Badarian, with hunting, fishing and farming its mainstay. There was, however, a striking improvement in flint-working in the Naqada I period, producing fine flint knives, pressure flaked into swallow-tailed and rhomboidal shapes, which could have been made only by specialist craftsmen, an indication that the economy was buoyant enough to support people who were not engaged in the production of food, the main activity of the community. The stone pots made by the Badarians were small and crude; the Naqada I craftsmen became adept in the working of hard stone, their finest productions being maces with disc-shaped heads of hard limestone, calcite or black-and-white porphyry. Their pottery is not of such high quality as that of the Badarians, but it has a greater variety and range in shape, decoration and use. Early in the Naqada I period, ripple-ware died out and the quality of black-topped pots declined. Burnished red pots, however, remained popular; and a new form of decoration emerged, consisting of red, or occasionally black, burnished pots painted with white or cream cross-lines and decorations featuring natural elements such as hills and animals, and more rarely boats and human figures.

The burial customs of Naqada I were similar to those of the Badarian culture. Linen and animal skins have been found in the graves of the period, but it has not been possible to reconstruct the style of clothing for which they were used. Long, ivory hairpins, either plain or with an incised pattern, and sometimes with a decorative knob at one end, seem to have been in fashion, as were carved ivory combs very like those of the Badarian period but smaller. The cosmetic palettes of Naqada I were often carved in the shape of Nile turtles, birds or hippopotamuses; and some are impressively large, measuring 42 centimetres and more in length.

The social and political organization of the Naqada I period remains a matter of conjecture. The community was larger and richer than the Badarian, lived in towns which may have been fortified and based its economy mainly on farming and hunting. There were few weapons, and the fine flint knives were probably for ritual use only. It is likely that the maces were not so much weapons as symbols of power, because the haft-holes drilled in the mace heads are so small that a haft narrow enough to pass through would snap when a blow was struck.

Little can be said with certainty about the religion of the period. A belief in magic is revealed by the use of protective amulets, most frequently shaped like hippopotamuses and worn as prophylactics by the hunters who killed the animals for their ivory. Designs on pots occasionally depict male and female figures in what seems to be a ritual dance. Cosmetic palettes, decorated for the first time with the horns and ears of a cow, suggest that the cow goddess continued to be important. A haircomb from a woman's grave at el-Mahasna[39] is carved with what is thought to be the earliest representation of the god Seth; and the hippopotamus, later associated with Seth, may already have been an object of worship, hence the depictions of it painted on many bowls and modelled round the rim of a dish from the grave at el-Mahasna.

For the first time in Egypt, the mining and flaking of flint became an industry. The absence of gold, of which there is no trace, may be accounted for by grave robbery, because it seems likely that the men who mined for flint in the Eastern Desert also found the gold we know was there. The original name of Naqada, *Nbt*, is taken from the ancient Egyptian word, *nb* (gold), so that *Nbt* means 'Gold Town'. If *Nbt* was named 'Gold Town' during the Naqada I period, then gold was the probable source of its wealth, enabling the people of the period to import luxuries such as turquoise and lapis lazuli. More importantly, it was perhaps their trading activities, facilitated by their gold, that exposed them to new ideas from outside Egypt.

Naqada II

From about 3600 BC, the Naqada I culture began a change so rapid that archaeologists once claimed that it was due to foreign invasion, a theory no longer accepted for lack of evidence of any such invasion. There is, however, abundant evidence of contacts with south-west Asia[40] which probably contributed to the great advances apparent by 3500 BC. The main cultural centre of Upper Egypt was still Naqada, but eventually its influence spread southwards as far as Lower Nubia and northwards into the Delta and

[39] Ayrton and Loat, 1911, pl. xii, 2.
[40] Trigger, 1983, pp. 32–3.

the Faiyum. Gerzeh, near the Faiyum, was once considered to be the type-site, but the culture is now known as Naqada II. There is no reason to assume that there was a complete break between Naqada I and Naqada II – religious beliefs, for instance, are similar – but the Naqada II (Gerzean) culture advanced so much that it is now seen to be the precursor of ancient Egyptian civilization.

The two principal Naqada II settlements are Naqada itself and Hierakonpolis, some 90 kilometres to its south. Houses at these two sites were rectangular and made largely of mud-brick. The so-called South Town at Naqada, which was surrounded by a wall some 2 metres thick, contains the remains of several houses dating to the Naqada II period. At Hierakonpolis, the best example of a Naqada II house, which was burned down in predynastic times and therefore preserved by being carbonized, measures 4 metres by 3.5 metres. The lower part of its walls is mud-brick intermingled with pottery sherds; the upper part is no longer there but was probably made of wattle and daub. Wooden posts still *in situ* would once have supported the roof of a porch of which the hearth and partly sunk storage jar are still in place. It is possible that single-roomed rectangular houses, each with an enclosed courtyard, were those of the richer members of the community.

The graves of the Naqada II period reflect an increasingly stratified society. The earlier burials were in oval or circular pits, a type of grave that continued in use for the poorer sections of society throughout dynastic times. Later in the period, the more affluent members of society were interred in larger and deeper rectangular graves, the earliest examples lined with matting, later graves with brick or wooden planks. Some had special niches for grave goods or for the bodies of the dead. Later graves, each clearly marked by a tumulus, were equipped with roof supports or roofing of timber. Bodies, wrapped in mats or placed in baskets, but never wrapped in hides, were buried in the foetal position, with no consistent direction for the placement of the head. In late graves, the bodies were in wooden or pottery coffins. In richer burials, a pattern for the arrangement of grave goods became established: personal items such as jewellery, cosmetic palettes and small stone jars were placed near the head; and large storage jars, essential to a burial at this time, at the feet. Some jars contained aromatic fat or unguent; others the remains of funerary feasts.

At Hierakonpolis and in Cemetery T at Naqada, there are several brick burial chambers, each rectangular in shape, with a single or double room, and a courtyard. They are reminiscent of the houses of the period, and are perhaps the earliest manifestations of the ancient Egyptian conviction that a tomb, *pr nḥḥ* or *pr ḏt*, both meaning 'house of eternity', was a house for the dead. The interior of the Hierakonpolis tomb[41] was plastered and painted with scenes of men, desert animals and boats, all in red, black and white on a yellow background. It has been suggested that these tombs were for predynastic royalty.

The economy of the Naqada II period was based not only on farming but also on well-developed flint, metal, stone and pottery industries. Tools and methods had increased in number, variety and efficiency: Naqada II was the zenith of the flint-knappers'art; and stone-workers had perfected their metallurgical talent to produce and work-harden copper tools. Stone-workers of the period invented the bow-drill, a tool to which so much importance was attached that, when the ancient Egyptians began to write, it was an ideogram of a stone-worker's drill that was used to mean 'craftsman'. With these tools, and using wet quartz sand as abrasive, they were adept in working even the hardest stone.

Artefacts of copper became more common: knives, adzes, axes, spearheads, fish-hooks, harpoons, needles, small ornaments and finger-rings were beaten and cast from the metal. The repertoire of weapons was added to in the form of pear-shaped mace heads, made from a variety of stones. When the haft was removed and replaced by a leather thong, these maces could be used very effectively in the manner of the medieval ball and chain. Gold was worked, and the rims and handles of cosmetic jars were often covered in gold foil. Egypt has no silver deposits, but the metalsmiths of the Naqada II period worked with a rare native alloy of gold and silver called *ḥḏ* (white gold or electrum). Electrum, an import from Nubia, was prized for its rarity.

Naqada II pottery, found at sites throughout the whole of Egypt, takes such standard forms that it can have been produced only at a very small number of centres. Much of it was utilitarian, made, in the usual way, from clay obtained from the banks of the Nile; but, in this period, potters began mixing clay with calcium carbonate, most of it obtained from around Qena and el-Ballas,

[41]   Case and Payne, 1962; Kemp, 1973.

where limestone (calcium carbonate) rubble is washed out of the cliffs bordering the Nile Valley. The process produced a buff clay, which they formed into jars that were left unburnished but decorated with geometric patterns, boats, birds and animals painted in red. They also produced buff jars with wavy handles, a type that is thought to have been influenced by the pottery of the Early Bronze Age I culture of Palestine.[42]

Their artistic talent found further expression in cosmetic palettes of slate cut into the shapes of animals, fish and birds; and in stone vases of many designs, from tall jars with tubular handles, to globe-shaped, open bowls, cut from stone such as breccia, porphyry, diorite, serpentine, limestone and calcite. Some stone vases were copies of pottery originals; others took the form of animals, or of frogs fashioned from an appropriate green stone such as serpentine. Great quantities of beads were produced, some made from gold or 'silver' (white gold), most from hard stone such as lapis lazuli or obsidian. Amulets were also made from lapis and obsidian, neither of which occurs in Egypt and must, therefore, have been imported.

The production of relatively large numbers of luxury items shows that Naqada II was not only a period of technological and artistic advances, but was able to support a society in which not everyone lived at subsistence level, and some were in a position to obtain and enjoy such items. Much of the pottery found within the settlements differs from that found in tombs, indicating that certain kinds of pottery, and some of the luxury goods, were specially made for funerary use. A cult which attaches importance to funerary goods tends to stimulate their production, and it is probable that it was the funerary customs of the Naqada II period that gave impetus to the production of luxury goods, and contributed to the formation of an increasingly stratified society.

The predynastic cultures of Upper Egypt progressed more rapidly than those of Lower Egypt, where artistic achievements and cultural developments appear less advanced because the impetus for change was less. The reason for this lies probably in the nature of the land: the Delta area of Lower Egypt was very fertile, and enjoyed a maritime climate wetter and less harsh than that of the Nile Valley. The comparative ease with which the predynastic inhabitants of the Delta could make use of its natural resources

---

[42]   Trigger, 1983, p. 32

was not conducive to innovation. In contrast, life in Upper Egypt was harder: the desert was ever-present on the near horizon, threatening to engulf the narrow strip of fertile land which the Nile flood occasionally failed to irrigate. The Upper Egyptian farmer had to be inventive and, at an early date, learned to co-operate with his neighbours in harnessing the river water through the building of irrigation canals and drainage ditches.

The Nile flowed through Upper Egypt as a single, navigable stream, easing contact between one area and another. In contrast, the Nile in predynastic times flowed through the Delta to the Mediterranean by way of several large branches and many rivulets, dividing the Delta into small areas of land. Nothing is known of the political organization of Lower Egypt but, presumably, each village was responsible for its own affairs and, because of the difficulty of communication, had little contact with neighbouring villages. Such isolation would have hampered the interchange of ideas. Thus, it was the predynastic Egyptians of Upper Egypt who played the greater part in laying the foundations of a lasting political and socio-religious system which persisted, with some fluctuations, over the three millennia up to the Roman conquest.

The eastern Delta, being nearer to south-west Asia, was the route by which imports and ideas from the Near East filtered into Egypt: in late predynastic times, Maʿadi, in particular, was an important entrepôt through which Near Eastern materials gained access to the Nile valley. But it was Upper Egypt and its promise of gold that was a magnet for foreigners, and their ideas. Whether they arrived in Egypt in such numbers as to constitute an invasion is doubtful. It was once thought that a new ethnic group, the so-called Armenoid or Gizeh race, entered Egypt by way of the Delta towards the end of the Naqada II period, a theory now discounted in favour of one that assumes it was a short period of either direct or indirect contact with Mesopotamia that gave the impetus leading to the remarkable advances made in Egypt at the end of the predynastic period.

Much of the evidence of Mesopotamian influence in Egypt[43] lies in the style and design of its art and architecture. Recessed and panelled brick, for example, typical of Mesopotamian monumental architecture, began to appear. Mesopotamian motifs, such as

[43]   Kantor, 1959, pp. 239–50.

pairs of entwined animals or composite animals, especially griffins and serpent-necked felines, decorate knife handles and votive palettes. A hero dominating two lions, another typical Mesopotamian motif, appears in the painted tomb at Hierakonpolis and on the handle of a knife found at Gebel el-Arak,[44] which is notable for its depiction of details of the hero's musculature. Other Mesopotamian peculiarities of style on knife handles and palettes include antithetical groups, animals shown in long files, sometimes in rows one above the other and sometimes *boustrophedon*; and groups of carnivores attacking a passive prey. On the Gebel el-Arak knife, the hero wears Mesopotamian costume; and on the knife, in the Hierakonpolis tomb and on vases, Mesopotamian ships are depicted.

The engraved cylinders used as personal seals by Mesopotamians have been found in Egypt, and may have been the principal means by which writing, their most important contribution to Egyptian culture, was introduced. This seems to have occurred at the very end of the predynastic period;[45] and from the outset, the style of writing was typically Egyptian, taking the form of hieroglyphs, or sculpted figures, more suited to cutting on stone surfaces than the cuneiform script of Mesopotamia, which was impressed into soft clay with reed styluses. The objects depicted in the hieroglyphs were typically Egyptian, though some of the signs appear to have been invented by Semites and may indicate that a Semitic language was in process of being imposed upon the original African language of the Egyptians.

Naqada III

From about 3250 BC, Upper Egypt entered a transitional period, the Protodynastic or Naqada III. This period lasted for less than two centuries, during which centres of predynastic culture, notably Naqada, Hierakonpolis and This, or Thinis, the cult centre of the god Anhur, which is thought to have been located at Mesheikh on the eastern bank of the Nile opposite Abydos, began to develop into powerful city states. The first two were aided in their progress by easy access to, and control of, the Eastern Desert with its wealth of gold and other mineral resources. Naqada lay on

44 Benedite, 1916.
45 Watterson, 1993, pp. 34–5.

the west bank of the Nile almost opposite the western end of the Wadi Hammamat, a major route into the Eastern Desert and thence to the Red Sea; Hierakonpolis, also on the west bank, lay opposite its twin city, el-Kab, located at the western end of a similar wadi. For much of the Naqada III period, southern Egypt seems to have been ruled by kings based in Hierakonpolis; but, by the end of the period, the rulers of Abydos had brought Upper Egypt under their control.

The population of Upper Egypt[46] increased during the Naqada III period, and new settlement areas were sought. The fertile north was attractive, and recent excavations at Minshat Abu Omar (*see* page 25) have unearthed grave goods that are in the classic Naqada III style. With trade with the Levant increasing, the rulers of Upper Egypt may have decided to extend their hegemony to Lower Egypt to control the trade routes through the Delta. The first attempt to conquer Lower Egypt was probably made by the last king of the Hierakonpolis dynasty, Scorpion, but it was another 100 years or so before the kings of Abydos succeeded in unifying all Egypt.

The Archaic Period: Dynasties I and II

History

The legendary founder of the First Dynasty of kings of a united Egypt was Menes, who is thought to have commemorated the event by adopting the title, *nbty* or 'Two Ladies', that is, Nekhbet, the vulture goddess worshipped in the Upper Egyptian city of el-Kab and Wadjet (Edjo), the cobra goddess of the Lower Egyptian city, Dep, thus symbolizing the unification of Upper and Lower Egypt. According to Herodotus, it was Menes who founded a city near the border between Upper and Lower Egypt, on land that had been drained by diverting the Nile. Greeks called it Memphis, although its Egyptian name was *'Inb-Ḥd* (White Wall), probably a reference to the fortified royal residence which would have been built of whitewashed mud-brick. Although Abydos, and to a lesser extent Hierakonpolis, remained centres of power, Memphis became the political capital of the united Egypt.

---

[46] By about 3000 BC the population of Egypt is estimated to have numbered between 100,000 and 200,000: Butzer, 1966, pp. 210–27.

Menes may be identified with the king called Narmer who appears on the votive palette from Hierakonpolis that bears his name. On one side of this palette, Narmer is shown wearing the White Crown of Upper Egypt, and about to club a prostrate enemy from the Delta; on the other, he is wearing the Red Crown of Lower Egypt, and inspecting two rows of the decapitated bodies of his northern enemies. The palette was probably made to celebrate the unification of the Two Lands (Egypt), seen by all subsequent generations of Egyptians to be an ideal, but which in practice was achieved only during the times when a strong central authority ruled. It is a salutary fact that in the 2575 years of its history, from the Unification (about 3100 BC) until the Persian conquest (525 BC), when Egypt succumbed to successive world empires, nearly a third of the time was spent under fragmented governments during the so-called Intermediate Periods (*see* page 1).

Narmer's queen, Nithotep, may have been a northern princess whom Narmer married to strengthen his claim to Lower Egypt. When she died, she was buried in a magnificent tomb at Naqada in the south, which may indicate that Narmer's hold on the north was unsure. For Narmer himself, the only tomb so far known, which is at Abydos, is so much smaller than Nithotep's monument that it must be a possibility that it was constructed for Narmer when he was king only of Upper Egypt, and that his real tomb is yet to be found. Narmer's successor, Aha, consolidated his work in Egypt, and may have conducted military campaigns in Nubia and in Libya. Another northern princess, Merytnit, seems to have played an important role in maintaining the political balance in this part of the dynasty, and she may even have been queen regnant. Whatever her role, at this stage in the unification of Egypt the outcome remained uncertain. The probability that in the early years of the First Dynasty conditions in Egypt were turbulent is perhaps reflected in the aggressive names given to the kings: Aha, meaning 'Fighter', Djer, meaning 'Stockade', and Djet, meaning 'Cobra', which was thought to have the ability to annihilate the enemies of the king. The fifth king of the dynasty was Den, whose name means 'Killer'.

Djer, Djet and Den, however, are best known for peaceful activities. Djer's greatest claim to fame is the tradition that he wrote a treatise on anatomy; but he also founded the royal palace at Memphis, and much artistic progress was made during his reign. Djet has become known chiefly for the fine artistic work of his time. Den was an energetic ruler whose reign was the most prosperous of the Dynasty. He conducted a military campaign in Sinai, but he also encouraged artistic activities and advanced the administration of the country. For the first time, the name of a chief minister of Egypt is known – Hemaka. Den was the first king to style himself *nsw-bit*, that is, King of Upper and Lower Egypt; and, during his reign, there is the earliest authenticated celebration of a jubilee or Sed-festival (*see* page 79).

Den was succeeded by his son, Adjib, who, after a short reign, was perhaps overthrown by his half-brother, Semerkhet. We do not know how the First Dynasty, which lasted for just over 200 years and had eight kings, came to an end: so little has come to light concerning political events in the early years of Egyptian history that we often do not even know the reasons for dynastic changes. The Second Dynasty, like the First, had eight kings and lasted for a similar length of time but, when it ended, a unified state with a strong centralized government had emerged, and Memphis was firmly established as the capital city of Egypt. These two factors, and important cultural advances, brought Egypt to the brink of its first golden age, the Old Kingdom.

Government and administration

By the end of the Second Dynasty, the political structure of Egypt was established and the basis for its administration laid. Unfortunately, detailed knowledge of the administration is extremely limited: information comes largely from inscriptions on wood and ivory labels, seals and seal impressions, containing the names and titles (which can often be interpreted as job descriptions) of the owners of the objects to which they were attached. By their very nature, these inscriptions cannot give a balanced picture; and in any case, the script in which they are written is archaic and presents difficulties in translation. It is clear, however, that even at this early period Egypt was an extremely hierarchical society, perhaps best, and appropriately, described as pyramid shaped. At the apex of the pyramid was the king, a divine being, the earthly embodiment of the god Horus, whose name was an element in the royal titulary. Another name, the *nbty* (*see* page 67), associated the king with the goddesses Nekhbet and Wadjet, and, together with the title King of Upper and Lower Egypt, proclaimed the duality of the country. The supreme function of the king was to maintain this duality, to ensure that Upper Egypt was never sundered from Lower Egypt. Below the king in the pyramidal society were the nobles and high officials; beneath them, the lesser officials and members of the court; and beneath them, the artisans and craftsmen. At the base of the pyramid were the peasants, the agricultural workers whose labours were at all times of paramount importance to the country.

Economy

In the early dynastic period, as throughout later Egyptian history, the bureaucracy seems to have been large and efficient, its chief function the collection of taxes from all parts of the country. Taxes were paid in kind, mostly in the form of grain and other foodstuffs that were gathered in government storehouses, ready for distribution to the recipients of royal largesse or to pay for state (that is, royal) undertakings. The height of the Inundation, carefully monitored, was used in assessing the annual taxation on agricultural products. With surplus food and manufactured items, the Egyptians traded with the Lebanon and Syria for good-quality wood, and with Palestine for olive oil. Trade with these countries was direct; but goods from further afield, such as lapis lazuli from Afghanistan, came through intermediaries. The need to keep records of administrative activities ensured that the development of writing proceeded apace.

By the beginning of the dynastic period, the natural resources of the country had enabled the Egyptians to develop a stable and successful society which produced much more than was required for subsistence, so that there was no need for territorial expansion. Surplus production was not wasted on the financing of war but, given the ancient Egyptian belief that houses for the dead should be more permanent than those for the living, was lavished on building the great funerary monuments that were to be the glory of ancient Egyptian civilization.

Cultural achievements

The royal court at Memphis employed many craftsmen so that it might enjoy luxury goods for daily and for funerary use. They were gathered together in one place, and employed full time, which brought a great advance in standard and technique, and eventually established a distinctive art-style. Clay pots were still mass produced, as they had been in the late predynastic period; but they were no longer decorated, which suggests that they were strictly for utilitarian use and not regarded as vehicles for artistic expression. The most spectacular vessels of the early dynastic period were of diorite, basalt, brecchia, quartz, alabaster and other kinds of stone, and of a standard never to be matched.

The proliferation of copper tools aided the development of bas-relief and stone sculpture, and improved the handling of large blocks of stone: at Abydos, for example, a chamber in the tomb of Khasekhemwy, the last ruler of the Second Dynasty, is lined with limestone, expertly cut into blocks. A greater variety of tools advanced the craft of carpentry, and led to innovative techniques such as the mortise-and-tenon joint, and a new facility in the carving and inlaying of wood. Wooden beds, stools, chairs and chests, all with bovine-shaped legs, became the fashion. Metal workers made great advances, producing vessels such as bowls and ewers of beaten and cast copper; and decorating knife handles and other objects with sheet gold. Lapis lazuli, turquoise, carnelian and other semiprecious stones were used alongside gold in the making of high-quality jewellery; and the pilasters of one tomb chamber at Sakkara[47] were inlaid from floor to ceiling with gold, an indication that large amounts of the metal were readily obtainable in the early dynastic period.

Sculpture

In the reign of Khasekhemwy, there was marked progress in technical achievement. The finest examples of sculpture from the early dynastic period are the two statues of the king, one in schist and the other in limestone, found at Hierakonpolis. They show him seated on a low-backed, cube-shaped throne, wearing the Upper Egyptian crown and wrapped in a cloak, his right fist clenched upon his right thigh, his left arm crossed in front of his body, hand resting on the right forearm. These two statues established the conventions for depicting the royal figure that were to endure for thousands of years.

[47]   Emery, 1961, p. 228.

Royal tombs

Funerary monuments belonging to Queen Merytnit, all the kings of the First Dynasty, and two, Peribsen and Khasekhemwy, from the Second Dynasty, have been located in the Umm el-Qaab area of the necropolis at Abydos. However, funerary structures from the reigns of Merytnit and all the First Dynasty kings, with the exception of Narmer and Semerkhet, have also been found at Sakkara, the Memphite necropolis, leading to speculation about the actual place of burial. The Sakkara tombs are twice the size of those at Abydos, which may indicate that the kings preferred to be buried near their new capital city, Memphis. On the other hand, Abydos was their ancestral home. On balance, opinion favours Abydos, because several large structures identified as funerary palace complexes have been found there. That there are two royal burial sites is consistent with the concept of the duality of Egypt; and at this early date, kings would have found it politic to give recognition to both halves of the land by building funerary complexes in Lower and in Upper Egypt.

In the first two dynasties, a royal tomb consisted of a burial chamber and several subsidiary rooms, constructed below ground level, surmounted by a rectangular superstructure made of mud-brick, usually between 40 and 60 metres long, 15 to 20 metres wide, and up to 8 metres high. It was slightly larger than the substructure, and honeycombed with cells in which grave goods were stored. The outer walls, sloping in towards the top, were built in the form of panelled projections alternating with recesses – the palace façade design thought to have originated in Mesopotamia (*see* page 40). This type of tomb is known as a *mastaba*, from the Arabic word for the rectangular, mud-brick bench that it is thought to resemble.

Perhaps the most important *mastaba* is that of King Den at Sakkara (number 3035). The superstructure of this tomb, which measures 57.3 metres by 26 metres, contains 45 storage cells. Cut into the rock below it are three small rooms, and a burial chamber, measuring some 10 metres by 5, and originally roofed in wood, which was entered by means of a descending stairway that starts some 9 metres outside the tomb's eastern façade. This stairway was blocked in three places by limestone portcullises lowered into place after the burial. When Den's *mastaba* was excavated in 1936, some of the storage cells were found still intact: the 60 wooden tools, 305 flint tools, 493 arrows, 362 jars of alabaster, crystal and schist, not to mention over 700 wine jars and miscellaneous items such as ivory gaming pieces, that were found in them form the largest single known collection of early dynastic objects.

The royal tombs at Abydos are surrounded by rows of smaller graves belonging to courtiers and other members of the royal entourage, large numbers of whom appear to have died at the same time as the king. The inescapable conclusion is that they were put to death, or perhaps chose to die, to accompany their royal master into the Afterlife. Many of the graves contained the bodies of women, others those of men who had been minor court functionaries and artisans. The practice of sacrificial subsidiary burial culminated in the reign of Djer, around whose tomb nearly 600 people were buried, but then decreased, the tomb of the last king of the First Dynasty, Qa'a, having less than 30. It was perhaps realized by this time that the loss of trained personnel was a drain on the economy. Djer's tomb became famous when the Egyptians came to believe that it was the burial place of Osiris, the God of the Afterlife, who from the the Sixth Dynasty was one of the most popular gods in Egypt. Pilgrims to the tomb left behind so many pieces of pottery dedicated to Osiris, that they inspired the Arabic name for the site, Umm el-Qaab, 'Mother of Pots'.

3

The Era of Pyramid-builders

The era of pyramid-builders lasted for nearly 1000 years. It began in the Third Dynasty and, if the art of building pyramids is regarded as the prime expression of economic and cultural achievement, reached its apogee in the following Dynasty. The rest of the Old Kingdom, and the First Intermediate Period, were times of weak central government and disharmony, resulting in a decline in pyramid-building. In the Middle Kingdom, former patterns of strong central government were regained, so that in the Twelfth Dynasty, pyramid-building flourished, as did sculpture and literature. The Middle Kingdom was followed by another era of internal strife exacerbated by weak government, resulting in a decline in economic and cultural activities; and in the Second Intermediate Period, the era of pyramid-building in Egypt came to an end.

History

The most successful king of the Third Dynasty was Djoser (c.2667–2648 BC), during whose reign confidence in the use of new building materials and in the ability to construct large monuments grew to such an extent that the king's tomb at Sakkara (the Step Pyramid – *see* page 77) is one of the most innovative monuments in the history of architecture. The last king of the Dynasty, Huni, was succeeded by Sneferu (c.2613–2589 BC), who may have been Huni's son by a minor queen, and was the husband of Hetepheres, the daughter of Huni and his chief queen. A powerful and active king, Sneferu initiated the golden age of the Old

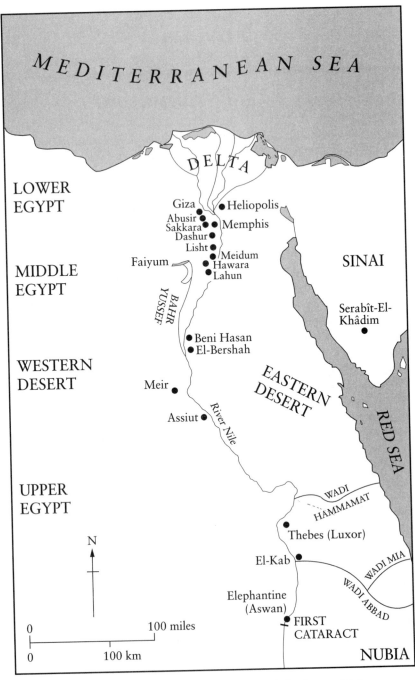

MEDITERRANEAN SEA

DELTA

LOWER
EGYPT

Giza • • Heliopolis
Abusir • •
Sakkara • • Memphis
Dashur •
Lisht •
• Meidum
Faiyum • Hawara
Lahun

MIDDLE
EGYPT

SINAI

Serabît-El-
Khâdim

BAHR YUSSEF

• Beni Hasan
• El-Bershah

WESTERN
DESERT

Meir •

River Nile

EASTERN
DESERT

RED SEA

Assiut •

UPPER
EGYPT

WADI
HAMMAMAT

N

• Thebes (Luxor)

El-Kab •

WADI MIA

WADI ABBAD

Elephantine
(Aswan)

0   100 miles
|————————————————|

0   100 km

FIRST
CATARACT

NUBIA

Map 3   Map of Egypt showing sites of the Pyramid Age.

Kingdom, his most notable achievements being the two pyramids built for him at Dahshur (*see* page 82).

Annals of several years of Sneferu's reign have been preserved on the Palermo Stone (*see* page 3). He led military expeditions to Sinai to protect Egypt's interests in the turquoise mines, and to northern Nubia and Libya, bringing back from Nubia 7000 prisoners and 200,000 head of cattle, and from Libya 11,000 prisoners and 13,100 head of cattle. The prisoners were probably used to augment the work-force in quarries. In succeeding generations, Sneferu acquired the reputation of being beneficent and liberal, and, according to a story recounted in the Westcar Papyrus,[48] capable of the common touch in addressing one of his subjects as 'my brother'. The story tells how a bored Sneferu goes boating with the most beautiful women in his palace, dressed by his command in nothing but fish-netting.

Sneferu's son, Khufu (*c*.2589–2566 BC), was the first of the three kings of the Fourth Dynasty who built their pyramids at Giza. He, Khafre and Menkaure are better known today by their Greek names, Cheops, Chephren and Mycerinus, their pyramids, recognized by the ancient world as one of its Seven Wonders, making a deep impression on popular imagination ever since. Little is known about Khufu. In contrast to his father, he was viewed by later generations as oppressive and autocratic. The Westcar Papyrus[49] portrays him as careless with life, ordering a magician to demonstrate his ability to reunite a severed head with its body on a live prisoner. Herodotus related in a scurrilous story that Khufu was so eager to complete his pyramid that he sent his daughter to a brothel with orders to demand payment in stone for her services.[50]

To associate the royal family with the solar cult, Sneferu appointed his son, Rehotep, as 'Greatest of the Seers', the high priest in the temple of Re at Heliopolis. The influence of Re grew during the Old Kingdom as the king became closely identified with the god. The shape of the royal tomb was based on the *benben*-stone, the sacred fetish representing the primeval island of creation that was worshipped in the temple at Heliopolis, a link reinforced in the Fourth Dynasty when one of the components of the royal

---

[48]   Lichtheim, 1975, pp. 216–7.
[49]   Lichtheim, 1975, p. 219.
[50]   Herodotus, II, p. 152.

titulary,[51] the *nsw-bit* (King of Upper and Lower Egypt) name, was occasionally written inside a cartouche, thereby signifying that the king ruled over everything that the sun's disc, or Re, encircled. The use of the cartouche became normal in the Fifth Dynasty, when kings adopted the title 'Son of Re'. In previous dynasties, kings were deemed to be the earthly manifestation of the god Horus: but, in adding the new title to the royal titulary, they reduced their status from god to son of god. The king's divine authority was further eroded in the Fifth Dynasty, when temples were erected at pyramid sites not, as before, for the worship of the king, but for the celebration of the cult of Re.

Towards the end of the Sixth Dynasty, royal power declined rapidly, due largely to the unsustainable charge on the royal exchequer of maintaining the funerary monuments of previous kings, and making gifts to nobles of mortuary equipment and endowments of offerings (known as *ḥtp di nsw* – 'a gift given by the king'). The endowing of mortuary priests who served increasing numbers of tombs transferred wealth away from the king to the priesthood. At the same time, the power of provincial governors grew until they became barons of their own fiefdoms. Things were brought to a head during the reign of Pepi II (*c.*2269– 2175 BC), who came to the throne as a child and died a very old man, incapable of exercising royal authority with the required assurance. He was succeeded by Nitocris, a female ruler, whose brief reign of less than two years was followed by a half-century in which royal authority was much diminished.

The loss of central authority during the First Intermediate Period should have led to a breakdown in social order, but Egyptian society remained hierarchical, with local governors taking over as leaders of society. In the period following the end of the Old Kingdom, people of quite low status in society owned tombs, hitherto restricted to the privileged, often employing local craftsmen of limited talent to build them. Most of these tombs, being made of mud-brick, have disappeared: but many of the stone funerary stelae associated with them have survived.[52] The stelae are engraved with short biographies of the occupants, men proud of their own localities and intensely loyal to the local rulers, who, during the First Intermediate Period, provided for their welfare while maintaining social order.

---

[51] Gardiner, 1966, pp. 71–76.
[52] For examples *see* Lichtheim, 1975, pp. 83–93.

In 2106 BC, one of the local barons, Mentuhotep of Thebes (modern Luxor), proved more powerful than the rest and declared himself king of a united Egypt, the first of the Eleventh Dynasty. Thebes became the royal capital. It was not, however, until the reign of Mentuhotep II (2033–1982 BC), the fifth king of the dynasty, that Egypt was brought fully under administrative control. Mentuhotep II, who was viewed as a second Menes, was an active king who developed foreign trade and brought renewed prosperity, although at times prosperity was marred by severe famine.[53] He renewed interest in Nubia, enabling his country to benefit from Nubian resources and labour.

Less than 20 years after the death of Mentuhotep II, Amenemhat, the chief minister of Egypt, led an expedition of 10,000 men to the Wadi Hammamat to quarry stone for Mentuhotep IV. Rock inscriptions in the Wadi[54] record that the mission was very successful, completing its work in less than a month, after a gazelle gave birth upon a block of stone suitable for the lid of the royal sarcophagus, thus bringing it to the attention of the working-party. A well found full to the brim with sweet water was seen as a miracle. It seems, however, that Mentuhotep IV made use of his sarcophagus sooner than he would have wished, for less than four years after his return from the Wadi Hammamat, Amenemhat had become king, the first in the Twelfth Dynasty.

Amenemhat I (1963–1934 BC) established his capital, now called Lisht, near the Faiyum, naming it *Amenemhat-itje-tawy* (Amenemhat-Seizer-of-the-Two-Lands). In spite of the bravura of the city's name, Amenemhat's seizure of the throne seems to have met with some opposition, culminating in a failed plot against the king's life (*see* page 95). In the twentieth year of his reign, Amenemhat I set a pattern for the dynasty by associating his son on the throne as ruler with him, a strategem partly designed to allow the older king to delegate the more strenuous royal duties, such as military campaigns, to a younger man, but more importantly to ensure a smooth transfer of power on his death. It is possible, however, that when he died nine years later (*see* page 95) Amenemhat's foresight failed to prevent political troubles.

The kings of the Twelfth Dynasty, active in promoting Egyptian interests in Nubia, adopted an aggressive policy from the outset.

---

[53] James, 1962.
[54] ARE, II, 439–43; 452–3

This may have been forced upon them, conditions in Nubia having undergone a change when warlike tribes (the so-called C-group) entered the country some time after the end of the Old Kingdom. Provided the Nubians did nothing to hinder them in reaching their objective, the mining of gold, however, the Egyptians had no wish to exterminate them. Amenemhat I dispatched several military

Plate 3.1   Senwosret III (1862–1843 BC).
(Courtesy of the Trustees of the British Museum, London.)

expeditions to Nubia; and in the reign of his son, Senwosret I (1943–1898 BC), fortresses were built south of the Second Cataract. Some 50 years later, however, Egyptian authority in Nubia needed to be re-established.

Senwosret III (1862–1843 BC), the real conqueror of Nubia, set up a system of 11, great, mud-brick forts in the area round the Second Cataract, blockading the river to safeguard Egypt's southern frontier in Nubia. His proud boast was: 'I made my boundaries further south than those of my fathers', which indeed he did by establishing a fort at Semna only 61 kilometres north of Wadi Halfa. The purpose of the forts, and Senwosret's contempt for the Nubians, is made clear by the inscription on a stele set up in the sixteenth year of his reign at Semna Fort:

> The Nubian hears only to fall at a word . . .
> If one is aggressive towards him it is his back that he shows . . .
> They are not people of much account . . .
> The southern boundary was fixed in Year 8 . . . in order to prevent any Nubian passing it when travelling northwards by land or by boat; nor any flocks belonging to the Nubians: except for any Nubian who may come to trade in Iken (Mirgissa), or with a message – anything which may be transacted lawfully with them but without allowing a Nubian ship going north ever to pass by Heh (Semna).[55]

The forts were not intended primarily to guard Egypt's frontier or to subjugate the local population but to maintain an Egyptian trade monopoly on goods such as ivory, gold and animal skins from Africa.

In the reign of Amenemhat III (1843–1789 BC), Egypt was at a peak of unity, prosperity and prestige. Provincial nobles were no longer a threat to central government, Nubia was completely under control, and Egyptian suzerainty was acknowledged by many rulers in western Asia. There is little sign of any serious decline in the reign of his successor, Amenemhat IV (1798–1789 BC) but, within three years of his death, the Twelfth Dynasty had come to an end – like the Sixth Dynasty, with the reign of a queen, Sobekneferu. According to Manetho, the Thirteenth Dynasty (1786–1633 BC) consisted of 'sixty kings of Diospolis (Thebes).' The throne appears to have changed

<hr>

[55]   ARE, I, 653–60.

hands on average every two-and-a-half years, and never handed on from father to son: in fact, there seems seldom to have been any relationship between a king and his successor, its absence often emphasized by naming non-royal parents on monuments. A noted exception to this was the 'mini dynasty' of three brothers, Neferhotep I (*c.*1730–1720 BC), Sihathor and Sobekhotep IV.

In contrast, a viziership (*see* page 61) in the Thirteenth Dynasty seems to have become an hereditary office monopolized by the same family for generations, and so capable of surviving the rapid succession of kings. Real power, therefore, lay not with the king but with the vizier, and it is possible that there was an elective kingship in which puppet rulers were controlled by viziers. Respect for the authority of central government was, on the whole, undiminished, and, until the late eighteenth century BC, Egyptian prestige in western Asia continued largely unabated.

Inevitably, the instability of the royal succession eventually had an adverse effect; and the end of the Middle Kingdom, like that of the Old Kingdom, was marked by a decline in court culture and the fragmentation of central authority. An outcome of the breakdown in central control was the neglect of Egypt's eastern border, across which, in the last years of the Thirteenth Dynasty, groups of people, known to us by the Greek word, Hyksos, but whom the Egyptians called ʿAamu ('Asiatics'), began to infiltrate the eastern Delta:

> ... and unexpectedly from the regions of the East invaders of an obscure race marched in confidence of victory against our land. By main force they seized it easily without striking a blow; and having overpowered the rulers of the land, they then burned our cities ruthlessly ... and treated all the natives with a cruel hostility.[56]

This, according to Josephus, was how Manetho, writing more than 1000 years after the event, described the Hyksos invasion of Egypt which began *c.*1650 BC. The truth was probably somewhat less dramatic. The invaders, whom Manetho referred to as 'shepherds' or 'shepherd kings', were, according to the Egyptians, *ḥḳ3w ḫ3swt*, which means simply 'rulers of foreign lands' and is so imprecise that it tells us nothing about the Hyksos except that

---

[56] Josephus, *Against Apion.*

they were not Egyptian. The Egyptians made a distinction between them and the large numbers of ʿAamu assimilated into Egyptian society during the late Middle Kingdom; and in the Turin King-list, the names of the Hyksos kings, which were not written in cartouches, were marked by a hieroglyphic sign meaning 'foreign'.

The names of the Hyksos kings imply that they were of Semitic origin, but there is no known Hyksos race or people. Neither was there a great invasion of Egypt by a Hyksos army: instead, there was probably a gradual infiltration from the east, which culminated in Hyksos control over Lower Egypt and the Delta, except for Xois where the native Fourteenth Dynasty retained its independence. It seems that the Hyksos made no attempt to conquer Upper Egypt, leaving the Thirteenth Dynasty to continue ruling from Thebes, but treating it as a vassal state from which they levied tribute. There were two groups of Hyksos: the major group, Manetho's Fifteenth Dynasty, established its capital at Memphis; an offshoot, the so-called Sixteenth Dynasty, was based at *Ḥwt-wʿrt* in the north-eastern Delta.

Ḥwt-wʿrt (Greek: Avaris) has been located at Tell ed Dabʿa on the Pelusiac branch of the Nile. In the last few years, excavations undertaken at Tell ed Dabʿa by Manfred Bietak of the University of Vienna have established that the site had successive periods of occupation, beginning in the Twelfth Dynasty, followed by a Canaanite presence, then the Hyksos followed by the Eighteenth Dynasty. In the Nineteenth Dynasty, the place became Pi-Ramessu, capital of Ramesses II (*see* page 151). The most startling finds from Tell ed Dabʿa are thousands of fragments of painted decorations from the floors and ceilings of a 'citadel' dating to the Hyksos period. The paintings, which are Minoan in character, may have been produced for the Hyksos by itinerant Minoan artists, but it is possible that there was a Minoan settlement at Avaris which outlasted the Hyksos. Ironically, fragments of pumice found at Tell ed Dabʿa may be the tephra from one of the eruptions of Thera (Santorini), the volcano thought by some to be responsible for the destruction of Minoan Crete.

The Hyksos took over the existing machinery of administration, only gradually filling posts with Semites, who worked alongside Egyptians. Their rule seems not to have been unduly oppressive, although heavy taxes were imposed upon the native population. Hyksos rulers borrowed extensively from Egyptian culture, writ-

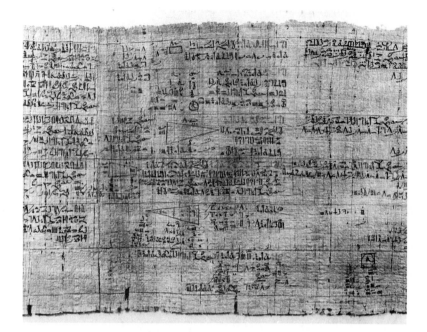

Plate 3.2   *The Rhind Mathematical Papyrus, written in the reign of
the Hyksos king, Apopi I (c.1600 BC).
(Courtesy of the Trustees of the British Museum, London.)*

ing their names in hieroglyphs and adopting throne names and
titles. The number of statues and reliefs which they either usurped,
or imitated from good Middle Kingdom originals, bears witness to
their admiration of Egyptian art. They had copies made of famous
Egyptian literary and scientific works – the Rhind Mathematical
Papyrus and the Edwin Smith Surgical Papyrus are two that have
survived. In return, the Hyksos may have introduced into Egypt
such cultural innovations as the lyre, the vertical loom and even
the *shaduf*, a frame that supported a pole with a weight at one end
and a bucket at the other, which eased the lifting of water for
irrigation.

Towards the end of the reign of the Fifteenth Dynasty Hyksos
king Apopi (*c.*1580 BC), the Egyptians began to reassert themselves. Inspiration for the revolt came from a line of princes ruling
the area around Thebes, notably Seqenenre Tao II ('the Brave');
and his son, Kamose, the last two kings of what became the
Seventeenth Dynasty. The only known account of the events lead-

ing to Seqenenre's challenge to the Hyksos was not written until over 300 years later,[57] and may not be historically accurate; but, for what it is worth, the story of King Apopi and Seqenenre tells of how Apopi sends a messenger to Thebes, saying: 'Come away from the hippopotamus pool. Its noise keeps me from sleeping by day and by night; its noise is in my ear' – not a very convincing excuse for a confrontation since Apopi, in Avaris, was over 800 kilometres from Thebes. In the ensuing war, Seqenenre was killed. His mummified body, now in Cairo Museum, is badly mutilated, its head showing terrible wounds made by clubs and axes.

Seqenenre's mother, Tetisheri, was later revered as the founder of the royal line. His wife and sister, Ahhotpe, was an equally remarkable woman, for, on a stele erected at Karnak by her younger son, Ahmose, she is praised as:

> one who cares for Egypt. She has looked after its soldiers, she has guarded it, she has brought back its fugitives and collected together its deserters. She has pacified Upper Egypt and expelled rebels from it,[58]

which suggests that at some critical moment, possibly when Seqenenre died, Ahhotpe restored order and enabled her elder son, Kamose, to continue the struggle against the Hyksos.

Accounts of Kamose's deeds were inscribed on two stelae,[59] which tell of how Apopi made an alliance with the king of Nubia and tried to outflank Kamose by means of a pincer movement; but his message to the Nubian was intercepted by the Egyptians and the strategy failed. Kamose eventually sailed to Avaris, where, he says:

> I caught sight of his womenfolk upon his roof, looking out of their windows towards the river-bank, their bodies frozen at the sight of me. They looked out with their noses on their walls, like young mice in their holes, crying, 'It's an attack!'

Having triumphed, Kamose sailed back to Thebes. When he died, after a short reign of about three years, he had control of Upper

---

[57] In Papyrus Sallier I (British Museum, 10185), dating to Merenptah (1213–1203 BC).

[58] ARE, II, 29–32.

[59] Habachi, 1972; excerpt quoted here translated by author.

Egypt and may have taken Memphis. It was left to his brother, Ahmose, the founder of the Eighteenth Dynasty, to complete the conquest of the Hyksos; and, in the eleventh year of his reign (1539 BC), he became the first king for over 250 years to rule over the whole of Egypt.

Hyksos rule in Egypt lasted just over 100 years, not the unmitigated disaster proclaimed by the native historians of later periods, but the catalyst that impelled Egypt into its imperial age, providing it with the incentive for expansion and, more importantly, the means with which to achieve it. The shock of the Hyksos invasion had had a salutary effect upon the Egyptians, who looked upon other nations with scorn. The Egyptian word for 'mankind' (*rmt*) referred only to Egyptians; they spoke of other ethnic groups in derogatory terms – 'the vile Kushites', 'the wretched Asiatics'. The Hyksos had destroyed their age-old sense of security, for the first time bringing home to them that they were not inviolable. The Hyksos, being from western Asia, however, brought the Egyptians into contact with the peoples and the culture of that region as never before, and introduced them to the horse-drawn war chariot; to a composite bow made from wood reinforced with strips of sinew and horn, a more elastic weapon with a greater range than their own simple bow; to a scimitar-shaped sword, called the *khopesh*; and to a bronze dagger with a narrow blade cast in one piece with the tang. The Egyptians developed this weapon into a short sword. From the Hyksos invasion came the realization that, if a second invasion were to be prevented, a buffer state in western Asia must be created; and in fulfilment of this policy, the early rulers of the Eighteenth Dynasty took the measures that enabled Egypt to embark upon its imperial age.

Government and Administration

By the beginning of the Third Dynasty, Egypt had become a mature, well-administered state, the governing of which was founded on a court culture headed by a king considered to be a god. The largest section of society was made up of peasants; above them a narrower stratum of professional classes – the scribes, artisans and merchants, although, as no standing army was formed until the New Kingdom, there was no professional military class; then the nobility, that is, the holders of the great offices of state and the high officials who served the temples.

From an early date, administration seems to have been highly compartmentalized into financial, religious, judicial, military and civil departments, and into those connected with the king and his activities; and the organizational skill needed to marshal the men and materials to build the Old Kingdom pyramids gives an indication of its efficiency. The titles of the nobles, recorded in their tombs, provide invaluable information about the administration of Egypt, and shed light on the intricacies of court etiquette. The fact that men such as Kanefer (*see* below) held many titles – in Kanefer's case, 47 – indicates that often the title was merely nominal and that the real work was done by bureaucrats. Each holder of an administrative office was called 'Seal Bearer of the God' [*sd3wty ntr* – *ntr* (god) meaning the king], although another title, 'Seal Bearer of the King of Lower Egypt' (*sd3wty bity*) rapidly became honorific, held, for example, by leaders of quarrying expeditions.

The head of administration was the vizier (*t3ty*). From Sneferu's time onwards, the viziership was the most important of the offices of state, its holder second only to the king. Several of Sneferu's sons by minor wives became viziers, which suggests that, as a matter of policy, he rewarded capable men who might have had some claim to the throne with the viziership, thus keeping them loyal. Neferma'at, a vizier who may have been a son of Sneferu's father, Huni, was succeeded by Sneferu's son, Kanefer, who in turn was succeeded by Neferma'at's son, Hemiunu. Another of Sneferu's sons, Ankhhaf, became vizier years later. Throughout the pharaonic period, the vizier was the intermediary between king and bureaucrats. He was also chief architect and minister for works, with special responsibility for the building of temples and royal tombs and the ordering of royal statues. In addition, a vizier was often Chief Justice.

Next to the vizier in importance was the chancellor (*sd3wty*), in charge of a Treasury divided into two halves, one for Upper Egypt (*pr hd* – the White House), the other for Lower Egypt (*pr dšr* – the Red House), and responsible for the collection and supervision of the national revenue. Taxes were paid in kind, largely in the form of cereals, oils and wine which were collected and stored in depots situated in the capital and in the provinces.

The need for capable, practical men to supervise the many great building and trade projects undertaken during the Old Kingdom meant that public office could be attained by men of ability rather than of noble birth. Sneferu's policy of filling the most important administrative posts with members of his immediate family, however, was so successful that it was adopted by the kings who followed him. In the Fourth Dynasty, in particular, the king's favour was reserved for members of the royal family.

Throughout the Fifth Dynasty there was a decline in royal power. Authority was increasingly delegated away from the centre and many of the high offices of state ceased to be held by members of the royal family. Local provinces, whose governors had always been appointed by the king, began to exert a greater degree of independence, and the office of provincial governor gradually became hereditary, leading to lines of independent rulers.

Amememhat I, the founder of the Twelfth Dynasty, relied upon support from district governors to attain the throne, but once installed as king, he took steps to limit their powers and to foil any ambitions they had to be kingmakers. He made no attempt to abolish the office, however, allowing governors to set up miniature courts of their own and granting them permission to raise troops and collect taxes. At the same time, he prevented rivalry between governors and attempts at territorial expansion by making regular tours of inspection. He retained the right to appoint governors, and one who died was usually replaced by a man from another district, who was sometimes the son of a governor. Amenemhat, and his successors, were thus able to take advantage of family traditions without making the mistake of allowing the post of provincial governor to become hereditary.

Economy

The economy of Egypt stayed predominantly agricultural, with the breeding and raising of stock playing an important part. There was no coinage: transactions were carried out through barter, with payment made in kind. At the beginning of the Old Kingdom, all land belonged to the king. Kings, however, did reward nobles and temples with gifts of land, large or small, temporary or permanent, so that over the generations they grew steadily poorer in land with a resultant decline in royal power. Initially, Egyptian peasants had been free men, many renting royal land and working it on their own behalf, others working it for a wage or hiring their services to non-royal landowners. As royal power decreased, the position of the peasants became precarious: they were forced to accept stricter terms of service and longer contracts, so that the peasantry, once independent, entered into semi-serfdom.

They did not, however, become slaves. Herodotus claimed that the Great Pyramid at Giza was built with the labour of 100,000 slaves working in three-monthly shifts,[60] a charge that cannot be substantiated. Much of the non-skilled labour on the pyramids was undertaken by peasants working during the Inundation season when they could not farm their lands. In return for their services they were given rations of food, a welcome addition to the family diet.

The First Intermediate Period is remarkable for the number of contemporary references to famine in Upper Egypt, some claiming that it was linked to low levels of the Nile. In contrast, Middle Kingdom graffiti at Semna, dating to about 1770 BC, record several years when there were abnormally high levels; and a stele in the temple of Amun at Karnak refers to the flooding of the temple. These freak Nile levels adversely affected Egypt's capacity to be self-sufficient in food and so reduced the surplus with which luxuries were obtained that the stability of the government came frequently under threat.

In the Twelfth Dynasty the need for more agricultural land led to the development of the Faiyum (*see* page 25), an area that had never been fully exploited although Amenemhat I established his new capital city, Lisht, at its edge. Amenemhat III reclaimed a large part of the Faiyum, increasing the amount of cultivable land by some 450 square kilometres. The Faiyum lake's feeder-stream, which branches off the Nile at Assiut, and is known today as the Bahr Yusef or Joseph's Canal, was kept free of silt so as to increase the supply of water.

At the start of the Old Kingdom, with internal strife at an end and no threat from abroad, the rulers of Egypt were ready to take full advantage of natural resources by exploiting, in particular, quarries and mines in Sinai and the Eastern Desert for copper, turquoise and gold. In the Fourth Dynasty they began amassing wealth by trade. The Palermo Stone (*see* page 3) records that Sneferu sent trading missions to the Lebanon seeking cedar wood,

[60]   *ibid.*, p. 151.

continuing the contact with Byblos first established in the Second Dynasty by Khasekhemwy. Forty shiploads of cedar were brought to Egypt,[61] some for making doors and statues for a palace, the rest to build ships. Sixty small vessels were constucted from the wood and two large ships, each 100 cubits (46 metres) long, presumably as sea-going vessels for the Byblos trade. The Fifth Dynasty was a time of growth in general prosperity, boosted by trade between Egypt and Nubia, Punt (*see* page 101), and Byblos. In the Middle Kingdom, trading contacts were established with Crete, and, for the whole of the Twelfth Dynasty, relations with Byblos were so close that there may have been an Egyptian governor there.[62]

Temples endowed with estates proliferated, playing an important part in the economy. The Palermo Stone records that in the Fifth Dynasty the cult of the sun-god, Re, received substantial gifts of land, and that the cults of Hathor, Ptah, Nekhbet and Wadjet were also the recipients of donations. The size of a temple's estate varied greatly, from 1 to over 50 hectares, but it was a major source of income for the temple, which could either work the estate itself or rent it out. Endowments, or pious foundations, were established for the statues of kings and of private individuals. In the Twelfth Dynasty, for example, the local governor of Assiut, Hapdjefa,[63] signed ten legal contracts which stipulated that at least one statue of himself should be housed in the local temple of Wepwawet, where he was high priest. In return for their services, which included making offerings to Hapdjefa's statue on certain days, the temple staff, most of whom were members of the local community who served in the temple part-time, were granted a regular income from Hapdjefa's own estate. The patronage of Hapdjefa, and other governors like him, brought great benefit to the local economy.

Religion

By the beginning of the Old Kingdom, the fundamental religious beliefs of the ancient Egyptians had been formed. There is, of course, no written evidence of religious development in the prehis-

---

[61]   ARE, I, 4, 66; 39, 30; 41, 236–7.
[62]   Kitchen, 1967.
[63]   Reisner, 1918.

toric period, but in Badarian times the Egyptians were evidently animists, believing that certain animals, birds, stones and natural phenomena were imbued with magical forces, some with the capacity for harm and others for good. One of the most ancient deities was the god known in dynastic times as Min: his fetish, thought to be a fossil belemnite, a cigar-shaped cephalopod related to the cuttlefish, is found on decorated vases of the Naqada period. Min was worshipped as the god of fertility *par excellence*; and his fetish can be seen as a phallic symbol.

Well before the dynastic era, religion had begun to find expression in the worship of sacred animals, each locality having its own tribal god whose earthly manifestation was in the form of a particular mammal, bird or reptile. The Egyptians chose their sacred animals from among the creatures with which they were in daily contact, venerating them out of admiration or fear engendered by some quality they possessed – fecundity, perhaps, or strength, or speed, or ferocity. Thus, the cow became a fertility goddess, the ram or bull a god of virility. It was not until the dynastic era that cosmic gods such as the moon, storm, wind and, especially, the sun, were added to the pantheon. They represented a more advanced form of divine being, the comprehension and worship of whom demanded a greater intellectual effort than had been needed with the more tangible fetish- and animal-gods of earlier times.

In the dynastic period, sacred animals and objects were often represented as statues in human form. Housed in shrines, they were cared for by priests whose duty it was to mediate between deity and worshippers. There are, however, difficulties inherent in the worship of inanimate objects and animals in that they are unable to communicate. The priests seem to have solved the problem by donning masks fashioned in imitation of the heads of the animal-gods, from within which they themselves gave voice to the gods' wishes, a practice that resulted in the noted Egyptian custom of depicting gods with human bodies and animal heads.

In the dynastic period, Egypt was divided into 42 administrative districts (*separt*, perhaps better known by a Greek word, *nome*), probably predynastic tribal areas, each with its own individual characteristics. Communication between towns and villages tended to be so poor that customs peculiar to them developed, with each locality having its indigenous deity who was often provided with his or her own mythology and manner of worship.

The same outward form – bull, cow, or ibis, for example – might be worshipped at many different places under many different names, so that hundreds of deities came to be recognized.

Before the Old Kingdom, Egypt had enjoyed the benefits of political unification for over 400 years, reaching during this time a marked degree of religious conformity. The deities of certain localities, notably those with royal connections, became pre-eminent, achieving the status of state gods. Their fame brought such distinction, and perhaps more importantly, such economic advantage, to their home towns that other, less fortunate, places sought to associate themselves with them, either by introducing a state god into their own temples; or by conveniently identifying their own god with the state god. This practice of syncretism led to that degree of tolerance which was the hallmark of ancient Egyptian religion, marred only by attempts made to impose a solar monotheism in the Fifth and Eighteenth Dynasties (*see* pages 51 and 111). Solar monotheism, however, failed because it made no appeal to the populace in general, being too cerebral, too remote from everyday life, and unacceptably intolerant.

Among the deities of the Old Kingdom who achieved the status of universally worshipped state god were the cow-goddess known in dynastic times as Hathor, the jackal-god, Anubis, Ptah of Memphis, and several sun-gods. The sun was worshipped in many places as the source of light and life, but, from the Second Dynasty, it was the deity worshipped at Iunu (Heliopolis) in Lower Egypt who became predominant. The sun was personified in several forms: the young sun was Khepri, represented as a scarab beetle; the midday sun was Harakhty, a falcon or falcon-headed man; the evening sun was Atum, the primeval deity at Iunu. As an indication of his venerable age, Atum, revered as a great creator-god, was often depicted in dynastic times as an old man leaning on a stick.

Early in the Old Kingdom, Atum was replaced as the chief deity of Iunu by Re, often called Re-Atum or Re-Harakhty and represented either as the sun-disc itself, or as a man with the disc on his head. He was thought to sail through the sky every day in a celestial boat,[64] and at night to sail through the Underworld, where he was the great Judge of the Dead. Re, like Atum, was a creator of gods, but he was also a creator of mankind. Both Atum

---

[64] *mˈn_dt*, 'barque of the morning', often translated as 'solar boat'.

and Re were said to have fathered Shu, the god of air, and Tefnut, the goddess of moisture. They in their turn bore Geb, the earth god, and Nut, the sky goddess, who were the parents of Osiris, Haroeris, Isis, Seth and Nephthys. These descendants of Re-Atum made up the nine deities of the Heliopolitan Ennead.

Hawks were worshipped in many places as sky gods: but even before the Unification the falcons worshipped at Pe in Lower Egypt and Nekhen in Upper Egypt had eclipsed other hawk-gods and, as Horus, become the royal god *par excellence*. This was achieved by virtue of the fact that Pe and Nekhen were important centres of power for the rulers of northern and southern Egypt. Thus, Horus became patron deity of both lines of kings and, after the Unification, became the first state god of Egypt. The reigning king, referred to as 'the Living Horus', was considered the god's earthly embodiment, the Horus Name in the royal titulary being symbolic of the king's role as Horus incarnate.

Another name in the royal titulary, the *nbty* (Two Ladies), was written with hieroglyphic signs that represented a vulture and a cobra – the two ladies of the title. Vultures and cobras were worshipped under different names in several parts of Egypt but, in this instance, the vulture was Nekhbet and the cobra, Wadjet. Nekhbet was the local goddess of Nekheb, one of the most ancient cities of Egypt, sited on the eastern bank of the Nile opposite Nekhen (Hierakonpolis). The economic importance of a city that controlled the routes to the Red Sea and areas of the Eastern Desert rich in tin, flint, gold and lead, and was, in addition, near Nekhen, gave Nekhbet pre-eminence. In dynastic times, she was elevated to the position of protectress of the King of Upper Egypt. Wadjet, her Lower Egyptian counterpart, was worshipped in the Delta city of Dep, which lay so close to Pe (*see* above) that, by the New Kingdom, the two cities had merged. The *nbty*-name, first used in Dynasty I, symbolized the Unification of Egypt.

During the Sixth Dynasty, the importance of Osiris, a hitherto obscure deity, grew with the expansion of funerary provisions for the dead. In the early part of the Old Kingdom, Re had been chief judge of the dead, and ruled an Underworld in which the promise of an afterlife was at first held out only to the king, and eventually to a privileged few. The myth of Osiris presented the god as a beneficent king of Egypt, the shepherd of his people who was murdered by Seth, his jealous brother. With the aid of Isis, his faithful wife, Osiris was resurrected to rule over the Underworld, where he replaced Re as judge of the dead. The story of Osiris naturally evoked sympathy, but his cult spread until he became one of the most popular deities in Egypt largely because he democratized the Underworld, holding out the promise of eternal life to everyone. According to tradition, his head was buried at Abydos, in the tomb that actually belongs to the First Dynasty king, Djer, but which had, by the Sixth Dynasty, become the focal point of the pilgrimage to Abydos that every devout worshipper of Osiris endeavoured to make.

Funerary beliefs and practices

Funerary practices were an essential part of Egyptian religion. The basic beliefs and practices that were to last until the Christian period had already evolved by the end of the Old Kingdom. The rich were buried in tombs, the poor in graves dug in the desert sand, but both were equipped with grave goods for use in an afterlife that all believed they would attain. Reliefs which decorate the walls of non-royal tombs from the Fifth Dynasty onwards show that the Afterlife was imagined to be a more perfect version of life on earth, except for the poor, who, it seems, were translated after death to the sky where their souls, housed in little boats, became 'imperishable stars'. The poor do not seem to have been resentful of the fact that their afterlife was not going to be as enjoyable as that of the rich; but perhaps the deep peace of the 'imperishable stars' was attractive after a hard life of labour.

For tomb-owners, the care given by servants was continued after death. In the Old Kingdom, models of servants were placed in the tomb, either as single figures or in groups performing the tasks of everyday life, such as brewing, baking, weaving and ploughing. It was believed that servant statues, having been brought to life by magic spells, worked for the deceased in the Afterlife; thus the need to kill servants and bury them with their masters was avoided – a kinder way of solving the servant problem in the Afterlife! In the Middle Kingdom, it became the fashion to replace servant-models with statuettes known as *ushabties*, a practice that was continued by later generations. The word *ushabti* is derived from the ancient Egyptian verb, *wšb*, which means 'to answer': thus the role of a *ushabti* was to answer on behalf of the deceased should he be called upon to work in the Afterlife.

The ancient Egyptians believed that the persona of a man or woman comprised two spiritual forms, the *Ka* and the *Ba*. The *Ka*, sometimes translated as double or twin, came into existence at the moment of birth; and when a man died, it was his *Ka* that lived on in the Afterlife. The *Ba*, usually represented as a human-headed bird, stayed behind on earth, able to leave the tomb during the day, but always returning to it at night. The purpose of the tomb and the offerings that were made there was to ensure the well-being of the *Ba*, for if the *Ba* died then, it was feared, the *Ka* could no longer go on living in the Afterlife.

The ideal site for burials was traditionally on the west bank of the Nile, for the West, the place where the sun set, or died, was considered to be the abode of the dead. Only when the terrain on the east bank was more suitable for burial were the dead buried there. In the Predynastic Period, most bodies were buried in pits dug in the porous sand of the desert, through which the fluids of decomposition drained away. At the same time, the heat of the sun penetrated the sand, desiccating the body rapidly and preserving it. But then the Egyptians began to bury their dead in tombs, the elaborate superstructures of which proved counterproductive because they shielded the bodies they contained from the effects of sun and sand, thus becoming instrumental in the destruction of the very things they were intended to protect. Perhaps because of seeing bodies preserved through natural desiccation whenever Predynastic graves were disturbed, the Egyptians came to believe that the preservation of the body was necessary for the enjoyment of an afterlife. Attempts to accomplish such preservation by artificial means were made as early as the First Dynasty, when limbs were wrapped in layers of fine linen impregnated with resin in an effort to maintain the shape of the human body. The technology of true mummification – the evisceration of the body to inhibit the process of decomposition, followed by rapid desiccation brought about with chemicals – took time to develop, but had done so well before the end of the Old Kingdom. The earliest truly mummified body known is that of Nefer,[65] who lived in the Fifth Dynasty and still lies in his tomb at Sakkara.

---

[65]   Hart, 1991, p. 175.

Domestic Life

Housing

Few ancient Egyptian houses have survived. Built of materials such as mud-brick, reed and a little wood, old buildings were quickly reduced to rubble and became the foundations of new houses. They were situated in cities, towns and villages continually being rebuilt in the same place; and today, many of the ancient sites lie beneath the cities, towns and villages of modern Egypt. In the Delta, houses had to be built on dunes (*gezirahs*), dykes and artificial mounds so as to be out of reach of the Inundation. Even in the Nile Valley, where towns and villages could be expanded beyond the cultivation into the desert, the people working the land did not willingly build their houses far away from the work-place. Building land was therefore at a premium.

Most evidence on the appearance of Old Kingdom houses comes from the so-called 'soul-houses' such as those found at Rifa, near Assiut (*see* below). Towards the end of the Old Kingdom, it became the custom to place at the northern end of a grave a pottery offering-table in the shape of a house. Each offering-table was a model of the type of house lived in by a petty official or a small trader. These houses were single or double storeyed, the former with three rooms and a veranda, the latter with six rooms, a roof loggia, and a staircase on the outside wall, both having a front courtyard. Flinders Petrie, who excavated Rifa in 1906,[66] said of its 'soul houses' that they gave him a better idea of the layout and details of ordinary ancient Egyptian houses than any of the actual remains, and that in most respects they closely resembled Egyptian housing in his own time, an observation as true today as it was then, for the basic house type of the Old Kingdom period has persisted throughout Egyptian history, and, only slightly modified, can be seen in villages today.

The simplest mud-brick house of the Old Kingdom was a single-roomed, flat-roofed structure, square or oblong in shape, with its entrance on the north side facing the direction of the cool evening breeze. A sort of awning over the entrance offered shade for the housewife who, like her modern counterpart, sat there cooking or spinning or performing other tasks. In front of the house was a

[66]   Petrie, 1907, p. 20.

courtyard where animal fodder and many of the animals themselves were kept. The house was mainly a sleeping-place, and at night animals and owners shared it, the animals gaining protection from predators, the human beings warmth from the animals. The ancient Egyptians lived in as close a proximity to their livestock as the *fellahin* do today. Needless to say, such houses were dark, smelly, lice ridden, cramped and without privacy. During the First Dynasty, sleeping quarters for the head of the house were sometimes provided by dividing off part of the interior, at first with animal skins or woven cloths, later with a lattice partition. By the Old Kingdom, mud-brick was being used for partitions, and, once the idea of subdividing the interior of a house by means of a mud-brick wall had taken hold, progress to more complex and varied architecture ensued.

Eventually, the awning at the front of the house became a more solid structure, a veranda, with a reed or matting roof supported by pillars made of reeds or wood. Although the roofs of houses were normally flat, they were sometimes barrel vaulted or dome shaped. As today, a flat roof was often used to store fodder, which functioned as insulation from heat and cold. In hot weather, it was cooler to sleep on the roof, and so a parapet of reeds or wood was built for privacy. A light wooden pavilion was sometimes erected. This developed into a second storey, or at least a loggia, access to which was by outside stairs – an interior staircase, which would take space from what was already a small area, was seldom constructed.

The daylight was so bright that a small window set high in the wall let in enough light, and, with no window glass in ancient Egypt, less dust and fewer insects. A cool, dim interior was preferred, and all but the poorest had roll-up blinds made of papyrus matting, often patterned and very colourful. Houses of the rich boasted stone window-gratings; and gardens with flower-beds and pools. From at least the beginning of the Old Kingdom, richer Egyptians used lamps at night in the form of pottery or stone bowls filled with animal fat or castor oil, in which floated a wick of twisted grass or linen. Otherwise, lives were regulated by the sun: peasants rose just before dawn, worked during daylight hours, and went to bed soon after sunset.

No matter what the size of the house or the social position of its owner, the basic building materials were the same. Houses were constructed largely of sun-dried mud-brick, and in most the floors were made of beaten earth. Wood was used only for columns, ceiling beams, stair supports and bonding for the top and outside edges of walls. Wood was also used as a sort of damp course: wooden poles, set at intervals along the upper part of a wall, kept the mud-brick dry by allowing moisture to permeate through them until it reached the outside air. Large trees were scarce in Egypt; stone was not. Nevertheless, stone was used only for the frames and thresholds of house doors, and for the lintels of windows. Because ancient Egyptians regarded their houses as temporary homes on earth, they were content to build them of the cheapest, simplest materials to hand, and the tomb-owning classes preferred to lay out their wealth on tombs which, as the Egyptian term for tomb, *pr nḥḥ*, 'house of eternity', suggests, were meant to last forever.

Much valuable information about Middle Kingdom housing comes from excavations at el-Lahun, also called Kahun.[67] This site, named *Ḥtp-Snwsrt* (Senwosret-is-satisfied), was a town specially built for the officials and workers engaged in the construction of royal tombs. Begun by Senwosret II (1868–62 BC) for the men who were building his pyramid, and their families, it was afterwards occupied for over one-and-a-half centuries by the workers who were employed in building the pyramids of Senwosret's successors. The houses in *Ḥtp-Snwsrt* were erected on a virgin site to a preconceived design, not randomly in the usual Egyptian way on the remains of older structures.

El-Lahun, the earliest-known example of town planning, is rectangular, walled and divided into two parts. Its eastern section, nearly three-quarters of the area of the village, housed its wealthier inhabitants, the officials who were in charge of building the royal tombs, and the scribes and foremen who were the more important members of the work-force. The much smaller western part contained the houses of ordinary workers. The streets, especially those in the west section, were straight and crossed each other at right-angles – an example of a grid system re-invented over 1000 years later by Hippodamus of Miletus. Down the centre of every street ran a shallow stone channel, a little over half a metre wide, which functioned as a gutter.

Along the northern edge of the wealthier part of the town, situated where they might take full advantage of the cool north

67   David, 1986.

wind, were five large houses, one detached, four in a terrace, but all conforming to the same plan. Each house, or mansion, measured 42.06 metres by 60.35 metres, or about 25 times the area of a worker's house, and contained a maze of rooms and passageways, about 70 in all. The sole entrance from the street was a small door set in the southern side, opening on to a narrow passage and overlooked by a doorkeeper's room. Each mansion was a single-storeyed building, divided into four sections, in effect making four separate houses, each section having a central court and direct access through one or two passages to the main entrance corridor.

These mansions were imposing buildings, with large, airy living quarters. The four sections comprised the master's apartments, quarters for women and for servants, and kitchens, granaries and offices. The master's quarters contained a court, open to the sky in the centre and surrounded by a colonnade, in which a stone water-tank let into the floor afforded a cool, refreshing central area and a place for bathing. Similar, but smaller, tanks were let into the mud floors of even some of the poorer houses. The master's bedroom, the largest bedroom in the house, had a raised alcove at its southern end for the bed.

Some rooms were barrel vaulted in brick, others had ceilings of wooden joists covered with thatch. Ceilings were sometimes supported by wooden columns set into stone plinths, or by columns of fluted or ribbed stone, occasionally with palmiform capitals. Doorways were arched, and thresholds and doors were of wood. Doors were set into stone pivots, in some cases worn through constant use, thus needing the insertion of a washer to lift the door up to fit into the doorway: the favourite material for the washer was a piece of leather cut from an old sandal. A surprising quantity of wood was used in the construction of the mansions and some of the smaller houses, much of it conifer, an imported wood. Many rooms in the mansions were decorated with a dado consisting of a band of dark-brown paint running round the bottom 30 centimetres of a wall, above which was a second band, about 12 centimetres high, of vertical stripes of black, white and red. The rest of the wall was coated with limewash in pale buff. In some rooms, the walls sported frescos.

Most of the worker's houses were ranged along 11 streets in the western section of el-Lahun, although several larger houses in the eastern section were for workers. The smaller houses are about

95 square metres in size, with four rooms; the larger dwellings have on average seven rooms and measure 169 square metres. Each house was flat roofed and single storeyed, with an outside staircase up to the roof and a central courtyard, which may have been covered, surrounded by rooms which were generally roofed over with beams of wood interspersed with lath (reed) and plaster (mud). Worker's houses seem not to have had separate kitchens; and hearths, and even grain silos, have been found in living rooms.

Palaces

The palaces of the older period of Egyptian history have either disappeared completely or what remains of them has not yet been found. However tempting it may be to assume that the kings who built the pyramids lived in splendid palaces constructed from the finest materials, the likelihood is that they regarded their palaces in much the same light as their subjects viewed their own houses, for use in this life only and therefore built largely of perishable and cheap materials. Most royal palaces were probably very large versions of the private houses, suitably modified to accommodate royal receptions and audiences, and with separate quarters for the king, his chief queen, his children, and his secondary wives.

The rich decoration in Middle Kingdom palaces is hinted at in a description[68] of the palace of Amenemhat I (1963–1934 BC) as a house decked with gold, with ceilings of lapis lazuli, floors of silver, the roof of sycamore, and the doors of copper, with bolts made of bronze. This description is a little exaggerated, as the gold was gold leaf or gold paint, the lapis lazuli blue paint, and the doors were of wood overlaid with sheet copper. Nevertheless, all of these materials were costly.

Furniture

It was the practice to put favourite pieces of furniture into a tomb for use in the Afterlife. Sadly, most of what was placed in Old

[68]   Lichtheim, 1975, p. 137.

Kingdom tombs has been plundered, but enough remains, added to evidence from tomb-reliefs showing scenes of everyday life, for a complete conspectus of the kinds of furniture available to the more prosperous Egyptian. The elegance and refined taste with which Sneferu furnished his palace can be judged from the funerary equipment taken from the tomb of his wife, Hetepheres (*see* page 83). The queen's two armchairs, her bed, canopy frame, curtain box and carrying chair, all in wood with decorations of gold sheet, are of superb design and craftsmanship. One of the chests found in the tomb contained a headrest, for use as a pillow. Headrests were made of wood or stone, and usually had a curved headpiece supported by a short column set into a solid base. They were widely used throughout Egyptian history, and are still in use in Kenya and other parts of Africa, although to Europeans they appear extremely uncomfortable.[69]

In the earliest period of Egyptian history, only the nobility possessed wooden furniture. Gradually, however, other classes were able to afford it. The basic designs were similar for both king and commoner, although royal furniture was made of more expensive materials and was richly decorated. Certain items which are in use today, such as a double bed, a wardrobe or cupboard, a large dining table or a sofa, have not been found among examples of ancient Egyptian furniture; but couches, stools and chests were in use from an early date, as were single beds with wooden frames filled in with string or leather webbing. There were no mattresses. Furniture legs were usually carved to resemble the legs or feet of animals such as lions or bulls. The royal family, at least, possessed chairs with arms and backs, a particularly fine example, belonging to Queen Hetepheres, being a chair with high back and arms, which, like the rest of her furniture, was overlaid with sheet gold. From the Third Dynasty, nobles and their wives used wooden chairs with very low backs, seats of plaited leather and legs carved in imitation of animal paws.

Stools, in fairly common use, were made of wickerwork or wood, and usually seated with plaited leather. They were either three or four legged, and some were for one person, others for two, presumably a man and his wife. Chests, made of wood or

---

[69] Headrests might perhaps be better described as neckrests because the most comfortable way to use one is as a support for the neck, thus lifting the head clear of the mattress and allowing air to circulate round the head and keep it cool.

cheaper materials such as wicker or plaited reeds, housed clothing, linen, and objects to be kept tidy or secure. Some were large, others more in the nature of small boxes. Most Old and Middle Kingdom houses were probably sparsely furnished, with only a pot-stand and one or two small wicker work chests. The master of the house, and his guests, sat on cushions on a mud-brick divan or bench built along a wall in the main room, although his wife may have had a wickerwork stool. Most houses also had a mud-brick bench outside the front door, similar to the benches or *mastabas* still found in some Egyptian villages.

The craft of furniture making was advanced by the invention of mortise-and-tenon jointing techniques which replaced thonging at a very early date, and by the adze, the chief woodworking tool of ancient Egypt, used instead of a plane which was then unknown. But without copper tools, fine wooden furniture would not have been made. A hoard of such tools, consisting of several hundred knives, awls and engraving tools, 7 saws, some with the handles still intact, 51 chisels, and 98 adzes of different shapes and sizes, was discovered at Sakkara in Tomb 3471 which dates to the early part of the First Dynasty and belonged either to an overseer of woodworkers or to a high official in charge of the manufacture of

Plate 3.3   The Step Pyramid of Djoser, Sakkara (c.2650 BC). Note outline of original mastaba at base.

copper tools. With tools like these, the woodworkers of so early a period achieved a high degree of skill.

Cultural Achievements

Architecture: royal tombs

From early in the Old Kingdom to the end of the Second Intermediate Period, complexes of buildings centred on the royal tomb gave monumental expression to the cult of divine kingship. Royal tombs, all situated in the western desert to the north and south of Memphis, were pyramidal and of two basic types: the stepped pyramid and the true pyramid. Work on his tomb began as soon as a king ascended the throne, and those kings who had short reigns had perforce to be buried in uncompleted pyramids.

The first attempt to build a pyramid-tomb was undertaken on behalf of the Third Dynasty king, Djoser, whose stepped pyramid at Sakkara is the world's earliest-known monumental building to be constructed of dressed stone. The architect of this remarkable structure was traditionally the king's chief minister, Imhotep who was, in later times, revered by the Egyptians as a sage and physician, and then by the Greeks, who identified him with Asclepius for his skill in medicine. Confirmation of his profession is on the base of a contemporary statue discovered near Djoser's tomb, where an inscription describes him as: 'Chancellor of the King of Upper and Lower Egypt, the first after the King of Upper Egypt, Administrator of the Great House, hereditary noble, Greatest of the Seers (High Priest) in Iunu, Imhotep, the builder, the sculptor'.

The Step Pyramid of Sakkara underwent several changes in the course of construction, some demonstrable others hypothetical. There seem to have been five main stages, the first of which was the sinking of a 7-metre square shaft nearly 30 metres into the limestone bedrock. At the bottom of this shaft was constructed a burial chamber some 2 metres in height and width and about 3 metres long, lined with pink Aswan granite, entrance to which was effected at the northern end through a circular opening in the roof. After burial, this opening was stopped up by a granite plug, 2 metres thick and 1 metre in diameter, weighing about 3.5 tonnes. About 20 metres from the tomb-chamber and roughly parallel with its sides are four long galleries hewn into the bedrock and connected with one another by passages. All the galleries may have been lined with faience tiles; and blue-glazed tiles have been re-covered from the east gallery, the panelling of which is interrupted in three places by limestone reliefs of the king.

As nucleus, the superstructure of the pyramid contains an 8 metres high *mastaba* of unique shape, in that its ground plan is square. The *mastaba* was faced with an outer layer of fine, dressed limestone from the Tura quarries, east of Cairo; its core is coarse rubble set with clay mortar. Originally nearly 64 metres long on each side, after its completion it was extended by just over 4 metres on each of its four sides and a second facing of dressed limestone was added. The height of the extension is 60 centimetres lower than the original, making the structure a stepped *mastaba*. Along its east side 11 shafts were sunk, each 32 metres deep and ending in horizontal galleries some 30 metres long, running under the superstructure. These were the burial places of Djoser's family.

The burial-shafts for the family necessitated an enlargement of the *mastaba* on its east side to cover the entrances. Hence, the third building stage added nearly 9 metres to the east side of the *mastaba*, and made its shape oblong. From this part of the Step Pyramid were recovered not only two fine alabaster sarcophagi, one containing a coffin once covered with gold in which the remains of a young child were found, but also a store of over 30,000 hard stone and alabaster vases.

At this point, Imhotep seems to have decided on an entirely different design, and the next stage saw the emergence of a four-stepped monument, formed by increasing the height of the core *mastaba* and adding an accreting series of three walls round it, each higher than the one on its outside. This resulted in the first known stepped pyramid, the entrance to which was on the north face. In the fifth and final stage, two more steps were added. The resulting six-stepped pyramid, which has a rectangular base measuring 120 metres from west to east and 108 metres from north to south, is just over 60 metres high and was cased in Tura limestone. It is the focal point of a complex of buildings, the whole assembly enclosed by a 10-metre high perimeter wall over 1.5 kilometres in length. This enclosure wall is of limestone and modelled in the palace façade design, possibly in imitation of the mud-brick walls of the capital city, *Ineb-hedj* (Memphis).

Within the enclosure wall, subsidiary buildings, most of which are without any known precedent, include the so-called 'South Tomb' just inside the southern enclosure wall, a suite of chapels connected with the celebration of Djoser's *Heb-sed* Festival or Jubilee, a memorial temple and a *serdab* (*see* below) built against the north face of the pyramid. The memorial temple (*see* Glossary), a development of the offering niche or chapel in *mastabas*, was the place where funerary offerings for the dead king were made; and the *serdab* (Arabic for cellar) was a sealed chamber with two small holes cut into its front wall, through which the life-sized limestone statue of Djoser housed within might, by magical means, partake of the offerings. Although several statues have survived from earlier periods, it is not known if they were originally placed in *serdabs*, and Djoser's *serdab*-statue is the first to have been found in position. The remains of several more large statues of the king were found in his Jubilee court.

The 'South Tomb' may have been a cenotaph, to represent Djoser's acknowledgment that his ancestors had been buried in Upper Egypt; or it may have been connected with the *Heb-sed* or Jubilee Festival. This was a ceremony that seems to have had its origins in a far earlier time when a king was ritually slaughtered after a certain period of rule, to ensure the continued prosperity of his people and the fertility of the land. The purpose of the *Heb-sed* in the dynastic period was the renewal of the king's powers through magic to avoid killing him. One of the rituals in the ceremony seems to have been a race run round the walls of Memphis, represented at the Step Pyramid by the enclosure wall. The Jubilee chapels were for the re-enactment of Djoser's coronation.

Although Djoser's pyramid seems to have been a radical departure from the traditional *mastaba* form, it is probable that its design was the outcome of previous customs in the building of royal *mastabas*. Inside several of the late First Dynasty *mastabas* at Sakkara there is a mound of sand overlaid with mud-brick,[70] with four sides that rise in steps reminiscent of the hieroglyphic sign for a double stairway, ⌂. They performed no architectural function, nor were even visible once the outer walls of the *mastaba* had been built, and must, therefore, have had a religious, magical purpose.

Clues to what this might have been are found in the Pyramid

---

[70] Emery, 1961, p. 84.

Texts (*see* page 92). These Texts were chiefly to ensure that a dead king should find his rightful place among the gods and become as one with Re, taking his place beside him in the celestial boat. They refer to methods by which a king might reach the sky, one of which was by means of a staircase.[71] The brick-covered mounds found inside *mastabas* might have represented this celestial staircase. With its resemblance to a gigantic flight of steps, the Step Pyramid, designed by a high priest of Re, must surely have represented the means by which Djoser magically ascended to the Sun God.

The Step Pyramid complex is notable for displaying a number of architectural innovations, among which are fluted columns and imitation doors made from stone rather than from the traditional reeds and wood. It has been doubted that such a high degree of architectural and technical achievement could have been arrived at without a long process of development, although there is no evidence that stone had ever before been used to such an extent. Many features of the complex, however, suggest that its builders lacked experience in the use of stone. Small blocks were used, probably because they were easily handled, and because the masons were unable to quarry and transport larger blocks. Engaged columns were preferred, not for reasons of artistic taste but because of doubts that free-standing columns of stone would be as stable as those of reed or wood. The patterns chosen for decoration were copied from materials used in earlier buildings, the stone of roofs carved to imitate palm logs, the columns made from drums of stone carved to imitate bundles of reeds. The Step Pyramid complex shows that forms more suited to stone rather than to traditional materials were yet to evolve.

Royal burial complexes similar to Djoser's were begun by two of his successors, who did not live to see them completed. The next advance in the architectural development of pyramids, therefore, was at Meidum, some 55 kilometres south of Memphis, in the reign of Huni (*c*.2637–2613 BC), the last king of the Third Dynasty. The Meidum pyramid underwent several changes in design during construction, beginning as a seven-stepped pyramid, later enlarged to eight. It was formed from a central core of masonry around which was built a series of accretion walls, each higher

[71] Faulkner, 1969, p. 183 (Utterance 508 and 1108) and 196 (Utterance 523 and 1231).

than the wall on its outside. The stone blocks of the accretion walls, inclining inwards at an angle of 75°, were not bonded together but depended on friction at the chosen angle of incline, the method of construction used in other Third Dynasty pyramids. The Meidum pyramid was 93.5 metres high and cased in Tura limestone. Having collapsed, probably at some time during the New Kingdom, it now looks like a high tower standing on a mound of rubble, and is known locally as 'the false pyramid'.

The Meidum pyramid was surrounded by a wide pavement of mud plaster, bordered by a low wall. On its south side, between pyramid and wall, lay a small, subsidiary pyramid, analogous to the 'South Tomb' of the Step Pyramid; and on its east side a memorial temple. In earlier pyramids, the memorial temple, like the entrance to the pyramid, had been on the north face: its position at Meidum divorced it from the pyramid entrance but allowed it to be connected by a causeway to the edge of the cultivation, where there was a temple in which the king's body was prepared for burial. This, the valley temple, was reached by canal from the Nile, along which the king's funerary cortège would have sailed. Both it and the causeway are the earliest known examples of such structures, and they, together with the other ancillary

Plate 3.4   Meidum Pyramid (c.2600), east face and causeway.

buildings around the pyramid, made up what was to become the standard layout of a pyramid complex. Each complex provided for the burial of nobles in *mastabas*, the position of which in relation to the pyramid reflected a noble's status: the closer to the king's tomb, the greater the status.

The last stage in the building at Meidum brought a transformation to a geometrically true pyramid. The steps were filled in and cased to produce a straight-sided, smooth-faced pyramid. The masonry in-filling the steps was laid in horizontal courses, a different method of construction from that used in the rest of the pyramid but one which became standard in the Fourth Dynasty, perhaps indicating that the Meidum pyramid underwent its final change during the reign of Huni's son, Sneferu. From graffiti in the small memorial temple, one of which refers to a visit made in 1438 BC by a scribe named Aa-Kheper-Re-Soneb to 'the beautiful temple of King Sneferu', it seems that Egyptians in the New Kingdom accorded Sneferu the credit for the whole building.

Two pyramids, each originally about 104 metres high, were built for Sneferu himself at Dahshur, some 48 kilometres north of Meidum. The earlier inclines to 43°40′, shallower than the later norm of 52° or so, and perhaps a sign of caution on the part of the builders. It is the first true pyramid known to have been completed according to design, and the first to be given a contemporary name, 'The Shining Pyramid', today known as the Red Pyramid. South of it is 'The Southern Shining Pyramid', the only known monument of its type, which has its lower portion inclined at a little over 54° but its upper half at 43°22′. Hence it is known today as the Bent Pyramid. The change in angle was perhaps due to the haste with which it was finished. Certainly, the masonry in the upper part is less carefully laid than that in the lower.

The Bent Pyramid, uniquely, has two entrances: one, in the usual position on the north face, leads to a passage slanting down to two chambers cut into the bedrock; the other, cut high in the west face, leads by way of a sloping corridor to a corbelled chamber. This corridor and the chamber lie entirely within the superstructure, a new design in pyramid architecture which, perhaps because of a perceived need to reduce the weight of masonry borne by the corbel vaulting, could have been responsible for the change in angle. The pyramid is cased in Tura limestone laid, not in horizontal, but in sloping courses angled inwards towards the centre in the Third-Dynasty style, a technique ensuring such cohesion that most of the casing is still in place, making it the best preserved of any pyramid. The pyramid complex contains a causeway, over 700 metres long, which leads down to a large valley temple once decorated with reliefs. The memorial temple consists only of an open offering place with an altar and two limestone stelae. Sneferu's pyramids are innovative but perhaps their importance lies chiefly in the fact that they represent the experimentation from which the true pyramid evolved.

The true pyramid was an architectural development that retained a mythological significance, its precursor, the stepped pyramid representing a ladder to heaven, the true pyramid evoking the spreading rays of the sun and recalling the *benben*-stone. The finest examples of the form are the pyramids of Khufu (in Greek, Cheops), Khafre (Chephren) and Menkaure (Mycerinus) which dominate the Giza plateau, being ranged along its edge from north-east to south-west in descending order of size. So much has been written about the Great Pyramid of Khufu that little need be said here. It is the largest pyramid ever built, so large that it was named 'The Horizon'. Its original height was 146 metres (the top 9.5 metres are now missing) and it covered an area of over 5 hectares. Because it was constructed on a core of rock, it is not possible to ascertain how much hewn stone went into its building, but it has been estimated to consist of some 2,300,000 blocks of limestone. The weight of individual blocks ranges from 2.5 to 15 tonnes; and it has been said that if they were to be cut up into 30-centimetre cubes and laid in a row, they would extend two-thirds of the way round the world at the equator. The pyramid, which was originally cased in Tura limestone, has three chambers, one cut into the bedrock and two within its superstructure. Entrance to the uppermost chamber is gained by means of an ascending corridor, some 46 metres of which was enlarged to form a magnificent corbel vault over 8 metres high – the Grand Gallery – which leads to the granite-lined burial chamber.

Khufu's pyramid was probably designed by the vizier, Hemon, his cousin and Master of Works. Most of its complex has disappeared, but one subsidiary burial is of particular interest. Khufu's mother, Hetepheres, was first buried near her husband at Dahshur; but some of her grave goods, mostly jewellery and furniture (*see* page 75), and her embalmed viscera, but sadly not her body, were found over 4500 years after her death at the bottom of a shaft some 30 metres deep near the Great Pyramid at Giza.[72] It has been postulated that Khufu, hearing that his mother's tomb had been robbed, had her reburied more safely near his own. Her jewellery was plundered, except for pieces of four silver bracelets inlaid with carnelian, lapis lazuli and turquoise in the shape of butterflies, of the same understated elegance as that of the gold cosmetic jars and toilet implements buried with her, which have also survived. The discovery of Hetepheres' viscera was an important landmark in the study of mummification, proving that even at this early date their removal was recognized as a necessary stage in the preservation of the body.

Around the base of Khufu's pyramid are five boat pits, two of which, when discovered in AD 1954 and 1987, contained dismantled wooden boats. One pit has been left unopened, but the other contained a cedar-wood vessel, dismantled into 651 pieces of timber, that has now been reassembled. This magnificent boat, 43.5 metres long, with elegant lines, carried Khufu's body to his tomb. It is the oldest large boat so far found anywhere in the world. The significance of the boats that were once in the other three pits is unclear, but it was probably mythological, two being the solar barques in which Khufu sailed with Re across the sky each day and through the Underworld each night, the other the vessel in which the king made eternal pilgrimages to Abydos.

Despite its ancient name of 'The Great Pyramid', the pyramid of Khafre (c.2558–2533 BC) was a little smaller than Khufu's monument, with an original height of 143.5 metres. Its lowest course of casing is of granite rather than limestone and its complex is remarkable chiefly for the granite valley temple built at the end of the causeway. This temple is an austere building devoid of decoration, its walls made from blocks of granite, or limestone faced with granite, its floors paved with calcite. The granite blocks are so large that it is tempting to think that the builders were trying to show what they could do with this hard stone, using the tools available to them: work-hardened copper chisels and hard stone pounders. Granite is not only much more difficult to work than the softer limestone but could not be obtained locally. It had to be brought from the Aswan quarries, some 1000 kilometres to the south, and floated down the Nile on rafts made of papyrus. Near the temple, a knob of limestone too friable to be cut into building blocks was fashioned into a lion's body with a king's head,

72   Reisner and Smith, 1955; Johnson, 1995.

probably a portrait of Khafre. It was worshipped as the god, Horemakhet (Horus-on-the-Horizon) and, as the Great Sphinx, has become a widely recognized symbol of ancient Egypt. The smallest of the Giza pyramids (its height 65.5 metres, less than half the size of the other two) belongs to Menkaure (*c.*2533–2505 BC). 'The Divine Pyramid', as it was called, is cased in limestone except for the lowest 16 courses which are in red Aswan granite. A basalt sarcophagus, decorated in the palace façade design and found in the burial chamber, was lost at sea while being shipped to England in the nineteenth century. The pyramid complex seems to have been finished in haste: the memorial temple was begun in limestone with granite facing but completed in mud-brick. The mud-brick valley temple, however, has yielded several superb royal statues (*see* page 90). With Menkaure, the golden age of pyramid-building came to an end.

Much smaller pyramids were built for the kings of the succeeding dynasty, at Sakkara and Abusir. They range in height from 43 metres to 70 metres, and may reflect a belief that magic should prove more effective than size, which had failed to protect the bodies of their predecessors against the depredations of tomb robbers. The outstanding monument belongs to the last king of the Fifth Dynasty, Unas (*c.*2315–2345 BC), who was buried at Sakkara in a pyramid named 'The (Most) Beautiful of Places', a landmark in the history of ancient Egypt, for it is the earliest pyramid to have inscriptions in its interior (*see* page 93).

The kings of the Eleventh Dynasty obviously felt no obligation to build their tombs near Memphis, in their time only an administrative centre. Instead, they elected to be buried at home, on the west bank of the Nile at Thebes. Mentuhotep II chose an embayment in the cliffs at Deir el-Bahri as the site for one of the most unusual of Egypt's funerary monuments. His tomb was integral with its memorial temple, which was a *mastaba*-shaped structure surrounded by a colonnade, the whole being set on a terrace fronted by columns and approached by a ramp.

Twelfth Dynasty kings resumed the practice of pyramid-building. At Lisht a pyramid complex was constructed for Amenemhat I, similar to those of the Old Kingdom. The pyramid, set on a pavement of limestone blocks, was originally 55 metres high and cased in fine white limestone. Its builders looked to the Old Kingdom for more than inspiration, for in the pavement and the core of the pyramid are set many decorated limestone blocks stolen from Old Kingdom tombs at Giza, Sakkara and Dahshur. Lisht is also the site of the pyramid of Senwosret I, which had an original height of 61 metres and a unique internal construction: its superstructure consisted of a framework of eight walls running from its centre, four to the corners and four to the mid-points of the sides, further divided by cross-walls and filled in with rubble. The memorial temple, which is the best preserved of the Twelfth Dynasty, housed large limestone statues of Senwosret I, many of which still survive, and nine small pyramids were provided for the burial of royal ladies.

Amenemhat II (1901–1866 BC) was buried at Dahshur, but his successor, Senwosret II (1868–1862 BC), chose a site on the edge of the Faiyum, at El-Lahun. His pyramid was only 48 metres high, its lower courses of stone, the rest of mud-brick. But its builders introduced two new features: an entrance on the south face rather than the north – perhaps an attempt to foil tomb-robbers – and a superstructure, built round a core of rock some 12 metres high, first quartered then divided into eighths, by limestone and mud-brick walls, into compartments filled with mud-brick. For the rest of the Middle Kingdom, pyramids including those of Senwosret III and Amenemhat III at Dahshur, were built of mud-brick cased in limestone. These were larger than other Middle Kingdom pyramids, being 78.5 and 105 metres high respectively, with concealed entrances and complex internal arrangements designed to protect them against robbery. They were the last pyramids of any consequence to be built during the Middle Kingdom. A second brick pyramid was built for Amenemhat III at Hawara, near the Faiyum. It has elaborate internal structures, but its chief claim to fame was its memorial temple which, according to Pliny,[73] boasted 3000 apartments, half of them underground, and was the original Labyrinth.

Architecture: private tombs

The custom for nobles to be buried in *mastabas*, a tomb form forsaken by kings in favour of pyramids, was in place by the end of the Third Dynasty. At Meidum, a necropolis to the east and north of the pyramid contains large mud-brick *mastabas*, of which

[73] Pliny, xxxvi, 13.

two Fourth Dynasty examples are noteworthy, one belonging to Rehotep (*see* page 89) and his wife, Nefert, the other to Neferma'at and his wife, Itet. They are famous because of what was found in them: in the one, life-size statues of Rehotep and his wife, and in the other, part of one of the earliest painted plaster reliefs, in which several geese are depicted in a well-observed and naturalistic way. The Meidum geese, as they are known, were originally part of a large scene in which Itet's two sons were shown catching fowl in a clap-net, an activity that was to become an essential theme in later tombs, for it not only depicted one of the country pursuits of which Egyptians were so fond but also had ritual undertones of the struggle against harmful manifestations.

Khufu and Khafre turned the area around their pyramids into a veritable city of the dead, where members of the royal family and favoured members of the court were buried in neatly arranged parallel rows of *mastabas*. These *mastabas* consisted of a solid core of coarse, local stone cased in fine limestone – from this time onwards, mud-brick was used only for less important burials – and the interior walls of many were covered in reliefs depicting scenes from the daily lives of their owners, of a quality

Plate 3.5   Mud-brick mastaba tomb (No. 17), Meidum.

that was equalled only in the Fifth and Sixth Dynasty *mastabas* at Sakkara.

Khufu buried three of his queens in small pyramids, but Khafre's queens and children were buried in tombs cut into the cliff faces created during the quarrying of stone for his pyramid. These rock-cut tombs are the earliest of their type at Giza, and at Sakkara, and because there are few real cliffs in the area around these relatively flat plateaux, they were a novel idea. On the other hand, such cliffs abound along much of the length of the Nile to the south, and, by the end of the Old Kingdom, powerful local governors were being buried in ever more elaborate tombs cut into cliff faces at places such as Aswan and Khokha, on the west bank of the Nile at Thebes (Luxor).

The tombs of local governors at Beni Hasan in Middle Egypt are cut high up in the cliff face, with the pit burials of their retainers in the scree at its foot. These tombs, which date from the First Intermediate Period to the late Twelfth Dynasty, consist of tomb chapels with burial shafts sunk into their floors; and they develop from a type that consists of a simple square room, to one that has a large hall with columns, fronted by a pillared portico similar to that found in front of a house. Paintings on the walls of several chapels, notably those of Khnumhotep and Amenemhat, depict in lively detail scenes of daily life; and similar scenes in tombs at Assiut and Meir are executed in finely carved relief. The construction of large, well-decorated rock-cut tombs came to an end following the reign of Senwosret III, however, when economic pressures prevented the great provincial governors from building them.

Sculpture

It was not until the First Dynasty that the Egyptian practice of sculpture proper began. Although some figurines and votive statuettes had been produced in the predynastic period, the art of sculpture developed over the first two dynasties so that, by the beginning of the Old Kingdom, the principles which were to guide ancient Egyptian sculpture for nearly 3000 years had evolved. The best Egyptian sculpture conformed to three ideals – simplicity, dignity and durability; and even during periods of decline, sculpture is dignified and simple in line, and only occasionally overloaded with detail.

The art of sculpture was so highly advanced during the Old Kingdom that it seems almost to be the culmination, rather than the beginning, of development. That such a high standard was reached at this early date is largely thanks to the belief that the preservation of the body was necessary to ensure a continued existence in the Afterlife. Statues, therefore, were not designed to be admired as objects of beauty, but to be substitutes for a dead body should it be damaged or lost, and were placed out of public view in temples, chapels and tombs. In addition, good quality stone was readily available to the ancient Egyptian sculptor, who was more fortunate in this respect than his Mesopotamian counterpart, for the stone he used had to be imported, forcing him to produce only small statues. Egyptian experience in monumental building had led to expertise in cutting large blocks of stone, which in turn led to the use of the cubical statue form. The cubical form itself allowed the Egyptian sculptor to specialize in the large-scale statues which became one of the chief characteristics of Egyptian sculpture.

Two early masterpieces illustrate the classic Old Kingdom style of sculpture: the life-sized limestone statues of Rehotep and Nefert, which were found in the *serdab* of their *mastaba* at Meidum (*see* page 89). The figures are painted, as was the norm with limestone statues; the flesh tones are natural, with the red-brown of Rehotep's skin indicating that he spent time in the open air, the pale cream of Nefert's that she was a lady who lived her life largely indoors. Each is seated on a block of stone that resembles a high-backed chair, their bodies carved in one piece with the chair so that the essential cube form is maintained.

Few statues have survived from the time of Khufu, a notable exception being the life-sized, limestone statue of Hemon (*see* page 83), found in the *serdab* of his *mastaba* at Giza, which shows him as a corpulent, middle-aged man. During Khufu's reign, tomb statues gave way to so-called 'portraits' or 'reserve heads', made of limestone, which were placed in the burial chamber, and were perhaps intended to be death masks. In Khafre's reign, statuary was reserved for members of the royal family, perhaps because Khafre was jealous of the privileges of the throne. There were life-sized statues of Khafre himself in his valley temple, of which only one has survived more or less intact. Sculpted from diorite gneiss, and polished rather than painted, its austerely majestic depiction of Khafre makes it a masterpiece of Egyptian art. The valley temple of Menkaure has yielded several magnificent statues: of these, four are slate triads, each depicting the king with the goddess, Hathor, and a personification of one of the Egyptian provinces; and one, the earliest of its type, a double statue in schist of Menkaure standing with his queen (probably Khamerernebti II) by his side, her arm encircling his waist.

The most accomplished private sculpture of the Old Kingdom comes from the Fifth and Sixth Dynasties. A life-sized wooden statue of Ka-aper, known since its discovery as the 'Sheikh el-Beled', or village headman, because of its uncanny resemblance to a modern *fella* of a certain age and (well-fed) standing, is one of the finest examples, as is a painted limestone group of the dwarf Seneb with his wife and children. Seneb sits, short legs akimbo, on a block with his wife beside him, her arm protectively around his waist in a manner reminiscent of Khamerernebti (*see* above). His two children stand in front of him in the place where the legs of a man of normal size would be, thus cleverly maintaining the balance of composition.

From the Middle Kingdom, the best art, not surprisingly, is in royal sculpture, in which a distinctive style developed in the Twelfth Dynasty. In the Old Kingdom, the king was regarded as a god, and his statues depicted him as such: he was never portrayed as less than regal, but as an awesome and aloof being. In the Middle Kingdom, the concept of monarchy changed: the kings of the Twelfth Dynasty, founded by a usurper, had to live with the facts of their mortality and vulnerability. Royal statues reflect these aspects: they were carved in a simple, traditional style, except for the heads, which were modelled in a realistic and eloquent way, and portray kings as serious, even dour, their faces often lined with worry, sickness, age or disillusionment. Many of the statues were placed in temple forecourts, an indication that in the Middle Kingdom, royal sculpture had lost its purely funerary purpose and had become commemorative. From thenceforward, many royal statues were designed for public viewing.

Painting and relief

Carvings in relief were closely linked to architecture, with compositions being executed on the walls of temples and tombs. Like sculpture, painting and relief were not merely for decoration but had a religious and magical purpose. In temples, reliefs represented the link between king and cosmic forces; in tombs, scenes of activities enjoyed in this life by the tomb owner were intended to ensure that he would go on enjoying them after death.

The highly distinctive Egyptian style in relief seems to have appeared out of nowhere; and from the beginning of the dynastic period the human figure was formally depicted with head in profile but with eye full-face; shoulders to the front, stomach three-quarters turned. From the waist down the body was depicted in profile. Ideally, sculptured relief was embellished by paint, the paint being given shading by the modelled surface underneath. Painting on a flat surface was never considered an art in itself and therefore a separate technique was never developed: such painting consists merely of outlines filled in with a flat tint.

A painter had seven basic colours at his disposal. Blue was made either from azurite or from an artificial frit made from heating together silica, calcium carbonate (chalk) and a copper compound (probably malachite). Yellow was made from an ochre coloured by hydrated oxide of iron, or orpiment (natural sulphide of arsenic). Green was made from powdered malachite, or from a frit similar to that from which blue was made but with yellow ochre added. Brown and red were made from ochres (hydrated oxides) or iron oxide. White was made either from calcium carbonate or from calcium sulphate (gypsum). Black was made from carbon. Black and white were sometimes mixed to make grey. Brushes were made from reeds frayed at the ends; and paint was applied with gum arabic. The finished painting was sometimes coated with beeswax, but no other form of preservative was used. The fact that many of the reliefs have lasted until today with their colours as bright as when they were first painted is due almost entirely to the dry atmosphere.

The Old Kingdom artist sometimes began work with a freehand sketch but, in general, he needed guidelines, commonly a vertical line around which to draw his figure. With a standing figure, the line ran in front of the ear, down half-way between the legs, and crossed the near foot. Horizontal lines were drawn at fixed places. Although normally a figure in a relief was arranged without regard to others above or below, sometimes the vertical lines were used to align one figure with another. From the Twelfth Dynasty onwards, a canon of proportion was employed: black or red paint was used to rule off small squares over the surface of a wall, to serve as guidelines for the proportions of a figure. In the classical canon (Dynasties XII–XXVI), the height allotted for a standing male figure was 18 squares from the sole of the foot to the hairline, the knee at the sixth square and the shoulders at the sixteenth.

From the outset, Egyptian art, whether sculpture or relief, was meant to be informative rather than impressionistic: thus perspective was not used and there was no attempt to convey an aspect from any one angle. Instead, characteristic attitudes at the most perfect moment were depicted. Plants and fruit were shown in the freshest condition, humans in the prime of life: when one considers that a statue of a tomb owner might have to take his place in the Afterlife, it is not surprising that he should want to go there as a virile young man rather than an impotent old one!

Relief was not often used in the royal tombs of the Old and Middle Kingdoms – it comes as a great disappointment to many that even the great pyramids at Giza are undecorated inside. Presumably it was not considered necessary, or even proper, to show a king carrying out his daily activities. Private tombs, on the other hand, especially those of the earlier period at Giza and Sakkara, are often resplendent with sculptured relief. At Sakkara, the *mastabas* of Ti and Ptah-hotep in particular are decorated with beautifully executed reliefs which depict scenes of country life in the Fifth Dynasty, as are many walls in the *mastaba* of Mereruka, vizier under the Sixth-Dynasty king, Teti.

In the private tombs of the Middle Kingdom, sculptured relief was either out of fashion, or unaffordable. At places such as Meir, el-Bershah and Beni Hasan, however, tombs were decorated with scenes painted on a flat surface, a style that was considered inferior. Paintings in some tombs at Beni Hasan (*see* page 88) are indeed inferior in execution and proportion, perhaps due to the fact that Beni Hasan was 'provincial', but they are, nevertheless, full of life, with many innovative themes, such as wrestling, battles and siege warfare, not to mention scenes of children's games and complicated dances, and are justly celebrated today.

Literature

Magical texts of very ancient origin were preserved for posterity as inscriptions within five pyramids dating to the end of the Old Kingdom. The collection is known today as the Pyramid Texts.

Out of a possible total of more than 700, 228 spells are carved in vertical columns of hieroglyphs on a white background, each sign filled in with blue pigment so that it stands out clearly, in the burial chamber and its antechamber in the pyramid of the Fifth Dynasty king, Unas (*see* page 85). They comprise the oldest body of religious literature in the world. The purpose of such texts was to provide a king with written descriptions of the offerings that would be made for him at his tomb and in his memorial temple, and with all the information he needed concerning the Afterlife and how to reach it.

In the Sixth Dynasty, it became the custom to carve biographical inscriptions on the walls of the tombs of nobles, recording details of their lives and careers. One of the most interesting careers was recorded in the Abydos tomb of Uni, who lived in the reign of Pepi I (*c.*2332–2283 BC).[74] At one time or another during his career, Uni was Inspector of Prophets (priests) in the king's Pyramid City, a judge who conducted an inquiry against the king's wife, and a general contractor who undertook four expeditions to acquire building materials for the king – one to Tura for limestone, one to Aswan for granite, one to Hatnub for alabaster, and finally, one to Nubia for acacia wood which was to be made into ships for transporting granite. This expedition was accomplished 'in only one year' thanks to the five canals that were excavated by Uni's men to take the ships round the First Cataract! The versatile Uni also conducted a campaign against the nomads of the northeast, using forces raised from all parts of Egypt, supplemented, for the first time, by conscripts from Nubia. Although Uni claimed a great victory, it later became necessary to mount another expedition to quell an uprising among these 'sand-dwellers'. He next organized an expedition in southern Palestine during which troops were transported by ship to a place called Gazelle Nose, probably part of Mount Carmel, the first known combined land/sea operation.

The Sixth Dynasty was an age when the local rulers of Elephantine (Aswan) opened up adjacent parts of Africa, thereby becoming powerful. According to the biographical inscriptions on the walls of their tombs, however, their African exploits were not without danger. Sabni, the overseer of Upper Egypt during the long reign of Pepi II (*c.*2269–2175 BC), recorded that he had the

74 ARE, I, 4, 134, 140 and 146; 41, 98.

unhappy task of mounting a swift expedition into Nubia, to bring back the body of his father, Mekhu, who had been killed on the Upper Nile. Pepynakht, also called Hekayib, Pepi II's overseer of foreign troops, recorded that he had to send a force to southern Nubia, to quell inter-tribal fighting, and another to the Red Sea to fetch back the body of an officer who had been killed by nomads while supervising the building of ships for an expedition to Punt.

The most famous explorer of the dynasty was Harkhuf, another overseer of foreign troops, who had begun his career in the reign of Pepi II's grandfather. As a professional leader of caravans, like his father before him, Harkhuf made at least four journeys into Africa. His account[75] of the fourth is most touching, relating how he sent a letter to King Pepi II, then a boy of about nine years old, to tell him that he was bringing back a dwarf (possibly a pygmy) to Egypt. In his letter of reply, the little boy's excitement breaks through the stilted phraseology expected of a king as he begs Harkhuf to hurry to the court with the dwarf, setting a guard on him in the boat lest he fall into the water, for 'My Majesty longs to see this dwarf more than any of the products of Sinai or Punt'.

The Middle Kingdom was a productive period for literature, largely because of the circumstances in which the Twelfth Dynasty had been established (*see* page 53). When Amenemhat I came to the throne, he had two immediate concerns: the legitimacy of his dynasty, and the creation and training of a loyal and efficient bureaucracy to replace that lost during the First Intermediate Period. He initiated the policy for which the Twelfth Dynasty is noted: the use of literature as propaganda for the furtherance of political ends. This policy heralded the proliferation of literary works written on papyri.[76] One, entitled 'The Tale of Neferty', purports to have been written in the reign of Sneferu and tells of the sage, Neferty, who describes Egypt in a state of chaos; and foretells the advent of a saviour called Ameny, from Khen-Nekhen (southern Upper Egypt), son of a woman of Elephantine. Coincidentally, Amenemhat's mother, Nefert, came from Elephantine and he was born in Khen-Nekhen. Ameny is not too dissimilar from Amenemhat – retrospective prophecies should not be word

[75] Lichtheim, I, pp. 23–7.
[76] For translations of all the works mentioned below, *see* Lichtheim, 1973.

perfect if they are to be credible! By means of this Tale, Amenemhat's seizure of power was given legitimacy through the claim that his coming to the throne had been foretold; and his name was cleverly linked with that of Sneferu, who had a reputation as a wise and humane king.

A dynastic crisis seems to have inspired the 'Instructions of Amenemhat I', a manual of advice to his son, later King Senwosret I, presenting Amenemhat as a beneficent and successful ruler, deserving of loyalty. In it, the king describes how an attempt was made to assassinate him as he lay asleep in his own bedchamber, and bitterly advises his son never to trust a subordinate. Senwosret has a part in what is claimed to be the first novel ever written, but which is in any case a work that is one of the most accomplished pieces of narrative prose in Egyptian literature. It narrates the tale of Sinuhe, a courtier on campaign in Libya with Senwosret when the king dies. After receiving the news of his father's death, Senwosret hurries back to Egypt, but Sinuhe overhears a message being given secretly to another of Amenemhat's sons and, fearing lest he might become implicated in the plot, flees into exile in the desert. After many years of colourful adventures, Sinuhe is finally granted a royal pardon and returns to Egypt to a warm welcome from the royal family. 'The Story of Sinuhe' was extremely popular, even many hundreds of years after it was written; and, in portraying Senwosret I as a magnanimous monarch and conveying the message that loyalty pays, proved an effective piece of propaganda.

Two papyri, the 'Book of Kemyt' and the 'Satire of the Professions', were produced as aids for recruitment to the bureaucracy. The former is a manual of scribal good practice; the latter contrasts every other profession, to its disadvantage, with that of scribe. Scribes were indeed powerful: they claimed that it was they who directed the work of everyone else, not least because most Egyptians were illiterate. Literary works, whether propaganda or simply entertaining stories, were disseminated through professional storytellers. In the Middle Kingdom, these storytellers might choose from many tales, the best being the three tales of wonder recounted in the Westcar Papyrus; the 'Story of the Eloquent Peasant', in which the eloquent tongue of a peasant enables him to right a wrong done to him; the 'Story of the Shipwrecked Sailor', an adventure story wherein a sailor finds himself on a magical island ruled by a kindly serpent; and the 'Dispute of a Man with his Soul', a masterpiece in which a man, longing for death, tries to persuade his soul not to desert him. The Middle Kingdom was a golden age of literature, and thanks to this literary output, it became the classic period of the ancient Egyptian language.

4

The Imperial Age

The Theban rulers who drove out the Hyksos founded the New Kingdom, Egypt's imperial age. The kings of the early Eighteenth Dynasty were quick to realize that if the indignity of another foreign incursion into their territory were to be avoided, then Egypt must become the dominant international power. Accordingly, they initiated a policy whereby, first through war and then by diplomacy, they colonized Nubia and established protectorates in western Asia, thus forming a great empire under Egypt's sovereignty.

Imperial ambitions necessitated a radical change in army policy. In the Old Kingdom, there had been no need for a standing army, because there was no serious threat to Egyptian interests beyond its borders. It had been necessary, occasionally, to mount brief punitive forays into western Asia but, otherwise, troops took part in quarrying and trading expeditions, and it was the responsibility of local governors to raise recruits as and when needed. Middle Kingdom policy required an efficient body of troops to be permanently stationed in Nubia but, in Egypt itself, there does not seem to have been a professional military class.

In the Eighteenth Dynasty, the Egyptian army developed, on a national basis, into a well-organized service in which military officers were professional soldiers rather than nobles co-opted *ad hoc*. The main body of the army was recruited by conscription; and training, which seems to have consisted of drill practice combined with physical punishment, was carried out in special camps. For the first time, the army included infantry and chariotry, with the chariotry,[77] the elite corps, being equipped with the type of

[77] Hansen, 1994.

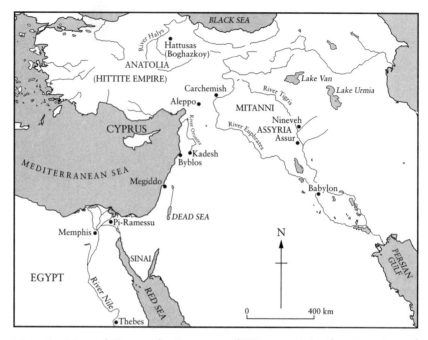

Map 4   Map of Egypt, the Levant and Western Asia showing sites of
the New Kingdom.

horse-drawn vehicles that had been used against the Egyptians by
the Hyksos. At this stage, the navy was employed primarily in
transportation, troops and chariots travelling on the Nile in the
type of boat that had been in use since predynastic times. The
army had three or four divisions, each of about 5000 men under
the control of a general, usually one of the king's sons. There were
20 companies to a division, and normally five platoons, of 50
infantrymen each, in a company. Officers of many ranks, supported by a plethora of scribes, made up a complex hierarchy.
Uneducated men of ability were often able to work their way up
through the ranks, though officers were usually recruited from
men of standing. The commander-in-chief was, of course, the king
himself.

History

At the beginning of the Eighteenth Dynasty, control of Nubia was
regarded as the essential preliminary to aggressive wars in western

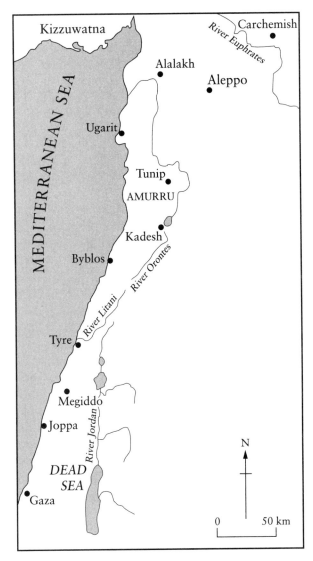

Map 5   Map of the Levant in the New Kingdom.

Asia. Apart from a brief foray into Phoenicia, Ahmose (1550–1525 BC) concentrated on safeguarding the back door into Egypt by establishing his hegemony as far south as Buhen (Wadi Halfa), and, for the first time, appointing a viceroy, the so-called 'King's Son of Kush', with sole responsibility for governing Nubia. In the 33 years after Ahmose's death, his successors conducted campaigns aimed at 'pacifying' the Nubians. Graphic accounts of these campaigns were given by a doughty ship's captain named Ahmose, in the autobiographical inscription in his tomb at El-Kab,[78] in which he recorded that he served with distinction in Nubia, first under Amenhotep I (1525–1504 BC) and then under Thutmose I (1504–1492 BC) who, according to Ahmose, sailed back to Thebes at the conclusion of his Nubian campaign with the dead body of a defeated Nubian chieftain hung upside down from the prow of his ship. The marine Ahmose also recorded his part in King Ahmose's sieges of Avaris and Sharuhen, a description that is of particular historical importance because his is the main account, apart from those given by Kamose (*see* page 59), of the expulsion of the Hyksos. In the year of Thutmose I's death, there was a revolt in Nubia that was put down with great ferocity by his son, Thutmose II (1492–1479 BC), after which there was no need for further campaigns in Nubia until 1436 BC when the Egyptians under Thutmose III reached Napata (Sudan).

As early as the reign of Thutmose I, Egyptian ambitions were firmly directed towards western Asia. Thutmose I boasted that the northern boundary of his empire had been set at the Euphrates, which would seem to indicate that his predecessor, Amenhotep I, the son of Ahmose, had undertaken a considerable amount of preliminary skirmishing in the area. Thutmose II conducted a punitive expedition in Palestine, but his son, Thutmose III (1479–1425 BC), was only a child when he came to the throne, and imperial ambitions were set aside when his stepmother, Hatshepsut, who had acted as regent for two years, declared herself Female King of Egypt, initiating an era of peace which lasted until her death some two decades later.

Hatshepsut (1479–1457 BC) was the daughter of Thutmose I by his Great Royal Wife, Queen Ahmose, herself the daughter of a king. Hatshepsut's husband, Thutmose II, was also a child of Thutmose I, but by a concubine. Hatshepsut bore her husband a daughter, Neferure; but Thutmose II's son, Thutmose III, was, like his father, the child of a concubine. Hatshepsut's move to claim the throne of Egypt for herself, relegating Thutmose III to a secondary role, was bold, but she seems to have regarded the fact

---

[78] Lichtheim, 1976, p. 12ff.

that her lineage was superior to that of her husband and his son as ample justification for it. The move was also successful, due partly to her own personality and partly to support from a powerful group of courtiers, notably the vizier, Ahmose; the High Priest of Amun (*see* page 135), Hapu-soneb; and, above all, Senenmut (*see* page 129).

The great achievements of Hatshepsut's reign were architectural (*see* page 160) and commercial. Of her commercial ventures, the most lucrative was an expedition by sea to Punt, probably located in the east Sudan bordering on northern Eritrea/Ethiopia,[79] which Hatshepsut claimed was the first of its kind, despite the despatch of ships to Punt in the Old and Middle Kingdoms. Five ships[80] set out from a port on the Red Sea (possibly Quseir) to journey southwards to Suakin, where the expedition disembarked. The voyage had taken between 20 and 25 days, covering on average about 50 kilometres a day, with the ships hugging the coast rather than risk the dangerous deep water of the Red Sea.[81] From Suakin, the route to Punt was overland through the Red Sea hills. Reliefs at Deir el-Bahri (*see* page 161) show the Puntites living in houses set on stilts, and their chief, Perehu, as tall and thin, in striking contrast to his obese and sway-backed wife, Ese. In return for a modest present of a few Egyptian weapons and some trinkets, the Puntites gave their visitors sacks of aromatic gum, gold, ebony, ivory, leopard skins, live apes and incense trees (*see* page 162).

Hatshepsut was, in theory, commander-in-chief of the Egyptian army but, towards the end of her reign, Thutmose III took charge. One can only speculate about his frustration at being prevented from exercising his military prowess while his stepmother was on the throne, because he was later to prove a great general. During

---

[79] Kitchen, 1971, p. 188.

[80] Most Egyptian boats were unsuitable for sea voyages, although in Dynasty VI, Uni (*see* page 93) took troops to Palestine on *nmiw*, translated as 'travelling-ships'. In general, sea-going boats were called *kbnt*, a term derived from the Egyptian word for Byblos, *kbn*, though whether this means that the boats were built there, or that the cedar wood for their construction came from Byblos, or refers to Byblos as a familiar trading destination, is not clear, but, probably by the New Kingdom, the Egyptians were building their own sea-going boats on the old Byblos patterns.

[81] Kitchen, 1971, p. 196ff.

Hatshepsut's reign, the petty kingdoms of Syria-Palestine, which were weak, posed no trouble but, early in the Eighteenth Dynasty, the Mitannians, a Hurrian[82] people, had begun to move into Naharin, a stretch of land lying in the bend of the Euphrates, and, by the time of her death, they were attempting to progress south to Egypt. Thanks to Hatshepsut's policies, Egypt was prosperous and well organized, enabling Thutmose to lose no time in marching into Syria-Palestine to meet the challenge of the Mitannians, fighting the first of the 17 campaigns[83] which, over the next 32 years, established an Egyptian empire in western Asia and made him the epitome of the warrior pharaohs who were such a distinguishing feature of the New Kingdom.

In 1458 BC, Egypt's enemies in western Asia had made an alliance. Mitanni was its chief supplier of men and equipment, but the confederation was led by the ruler of Kadesh,[84] a city on the River Orontes in Syria. Kadesh, therefore, had to be dealt with before Mitanni. In his first campaign, Thutmose III launched an attack across Sinai into Palestine and led an army up on to the ridge of Mount Carmel (near Haifa). Meanwhile, one of his generals, Djehuty, laid siege to Joppa (modern Jaffa), which, according to legend,[85] he took by smuggling his men into the city like Ali Baba's, but inside baskets rather than jars. Once in Palestine, Thutmose made plans to capture the key city of Megiddo,[86] consulting his war council on the choice of routes into the city. There were three: the usual route, through Dothen; the western approach; and the Aruna road, through a defile in the hills, which the war council dismissed scornfully, saying, 'How can we go upon this road, which threatens to be narrow? . . . Will not horse come behind horse and man behind man likewise? Shall our advance-guard be fighting while our rear-guard is still standing in Aruna, waiting to fight?' Thutmose, however, was set upon taking the Aruna road, lest the enemy think him too afraid to do so; and naturally his army had no choice but to follow as he led them through the defile, to take Megiddo by surprise.

[82] Although Hurrian, the ruling dynasty adopted Indo-Aryan names.
[83] The campaigns are recorded in the Annals carved on walls in the Temple of Amun at Karnak. For translations, see ANET, p. 234ff.
[84] Tell Nebi Mend, some 30 km south-west of Homs.
[85] Erman, 1966, pp. 167–9.
[86] Biblical Armageddon: 150 km north of Gaza.

The Egyptians routed the enemy which retreated in disarray. The gates of the city were barred and the escaping soldiers had to be hauled up by their clothing over the city walls, vulnerable to further attack. Alas, as the Egyptian chronicler ruefully noted:

> If only the army of his Majesty had not decided to plunder the enemy's possessions, they would have captured Megiddo at this moment . . . its champions lay stretched out like fish on the ground, while the victorious army of his Majesty went round counting their portions.

As it was, there was a siege of seven months before Megiddo finally fell, but from this one city, the Egyptians took an enormous quantity of spoil:

> 340 living prisoners; 83 hands (cut off dead bodies); 2041 mares, 191 foals, 6 stallions; a chariot wrought with gold, as was its pole (property of the ruler of Kadesh); a beautiful chariot wrought with gold (property of the ruler of Megiddo); 30 chariots belonging to other chiefs plus 892 chariots belonging to his wretched army; a fine suit of bronze armour belonging to that enemy (the ruler of Kadesh) and 200 suits of armour belonging to his wretched army; 502 bows; 7 poles made of *mry* (a kind of wood) wrought with silver belonging to the tent of that foe; 1929 large cattle [oxen?], 2000 small cattle [sheep?], 20,500 white small cattle [goats?].

After the fall of Megiddo, Thutmose III went on to capture three other cities to its north, which were given to the Temple of Amun at Karnak, taking captive 38 lords and 87 children belonging to the chiefs, and nearly 2000 slaves and their children. The booty consisted of:

> flat dishes of costly stone and gold, a large two-handled vase of Kharu work, miscellaneous dishes and drinking vessels, 3 large kettles, 87 knives. Gold and silver rings, a beaten-silver statue, 6 chairs of ivory, ebony and carob-wood with 6 footstools, 6 large tables of ivory and carob-wood. A sceptre-shaped staff of carob-wood wrought with gold and costly stones belonging to that enemy, a statue of that enemy wrought with gold, the head of which was inlaid with lapis-lazuli. Bronze vessels; and large amounts of clothing belonging to that enemy.

At the conclusion of this first campaign, Thutmose returned to Egypt to celebrate his victory in the Temple of Amun. The following year, he made a progress through Palestine and southern Syria, receiving tribute from the conquered rulers – cattle, slaves, chariots, a bronze corselet inlaid with gold and a gold horn inlaid with lapis lazuli, not to mention the daughter of a chief. Presents sent by Assyria, including a large amount of lapis lazuli, were recorded in the Annals as tribute, implying, wrongly, that Egypt had conquered Assyria. After the campaigns of 1455 and 1454 BC, no more than promenades through Palestine to confirm Egypt's hold, Thutmose remained in Egypt for three years. Realizing that, if he were to make any advance against Mitanni, he needed to do more than hold Palestine, he set out on his fifth campaign (1451 BC) to obtain a foothold in Phoenicia, with such success that, by the end of it, he had established land bases, capturing several ports and a number of Phoenician ships. He was now in a position to sail to a port near his main target, Kadesh.

In 1450 BC, Thutmose III sailed up the Phoenician coast to the port of Simyra, and thence to Kadesh, which he overthrew, taking hostage the children of its chiefs. They were sent back to Egypt but, in due course, 'the son of whosoever died amongst these chiefs was allowed by his Majesty to succeed him'. A year later, during the seventh campaign, Thutmose sailed up and down the Phoenician coast, forcing submission, taking supplies to his garrisons and laying in supplies for future operations. Then, in 1447 BC, he fought the eighth and greatest of his campaigns. Thutmose sailed to Byblos and marched through the Lebanese mountains to the Orontes valley, taking with him boats on carts which were dragged overland by oxen. Having defeated the King of Mitanni at Aleppo, Thutmose chased the Mitannian army across the Euphrates, and then sailed with his troops up and down the river in boats that had been dragged from Byblos via Aleppo, a journey of over 400 kilometres. Settlements on the banks of the Euphrates were attacked but the Egyptians did not venture into the interior of the country.

During the journey back to Egypt, Thutmose found time for some big-game hunting, and at Niy, in northern Syria, he encountered a herd of 120 elephants. The ensuing slaughter was not without its dangers to Thutmose, for the largest tusker turned on him and he was saved only by the prompt action of Amenemhab, one of his officers, who leaped forward and cut off the elephant's trunk, thus saving the king for further campaigns! The incident, which was recorded in Amenemhab's tomb at Thebes,[87] was not the only example of the officer's resourcefulness. In the last campaign, the prince of Kadesh let loose a mare in front of the Egyptian army, with the intention of unsettling the stallions in the chariotry. Amenemhab saved the day by chasing her and slitting open her belly, after which he cut off her tail and presented it to his king. Neither was the elephant hunt at Niy the only example of Thutmose's hunting prowess: on a stele at Armant,[88] it is recorded that he killed seven lions 'in the twinkling of a eye', overcame 'twelve wild bulls in an hour', and brought down a rhinoceros while hunting in southern Nubia.

Although Thutmose's eighth campaign did not result in the conquest of Mitanni, it did cut the country off from its Syrian allies, encouraging other powers, notably the Hittites of Anatolia, to move to the attack. It also brought renown to Egypt so that, in 1447 BC, Babylon and Assyria sent presents. According to the Annals, which are much more concerned with listing amounts of tribute than with describing the details of Thutmose's campaigns, Hatti (the land of the Hittites) sent 400 *deben* (36.5 grams) of silver, and Cyprus a large weight of lead and copper. For nine years after his attack on Mitanni, Thutmose III simply went on tours of inspection, receiving tribute from an empire which stretched from Egypt to the banks of the Euphrates, with only the occasional skirmish. In 1438 BC, however, Kadesh revolted, and Thutmose, no longer a young warrior pharaoh but a man in his fifties – old by the standards of the time – was forced to go to war again. Kadesh resisted his attack but eventually it fell, and, inevitably, it was Amenemhab (*see* above) who was first to breach the defences. Equally inevitable was the vast amount of tribute exacted by the Egyptians.

Thutmose III, a man of diverse abilities and talents, excelled as general and as administrator. His policy of educating in Egypt the children of captured foreign princes, so that they were not only held hostage to their fathers' good faith but brought up as Egyptians, demonstrated his far-sightedness. When these children succeeded to their fathers' offices, they remained loyal to Egypt.

---

[87] Tomb no. 85.
[88] Mond and Myers, 1940.

Plate 4.1   Festival Hall of Thutmose III (1479–1425 BC), Precinct of
Amun, Karnak.

Thutmose seems to have been an accomplished horseman, archer
and athlete; but he also encouraged and promoted art and
architecture, his buildings being models of restraint and good
taste. He was unusual for his time in that he took an interest in
natural history, and ordered a vestibule in his memorial temple at
Karnak to be decorated with reliefs depicting the 'plants that his
Majesty encountered in the land of Syria-Palestine'. The flora and
fauna carved on the walls of the vestibule – now called 'the
botanical garden' because of them – had evidently made a deep
impression on Thutmose, who insisted that 'all these things really
exist . . . my Majesty has made (the reliefs) to enable them to be in
the presence of my father, Amun'. One of the most interesting
references in his Annals is to 'a bird that lays an egg every day'
(thought to be a hen) which he had received as part of his Asiatic
booty. Sadly, Thutmose seems not to have appreciated the possi-
bilities of hens, and it was not until the Persians imported them
into Egypt 1000 years later that the Egyptians ate eggs other
than those laid by waterfowl. The reign of Thutmose III was
singularly free from acts of brutality, except for one occasion in
Mitanni, when he ordered barley to be pulled up and crops to be

destroyed.[89] For all his achievements, Thutmose was a modest man, his inscriptions being much less bombastic than those of less-accomplished rulers.

Thutmose III's death, on 17 March 1425 BC, was the signal for revolt in the Asiatic empire, put down by his son and successor, Amenhotep II (1427–1393 BC), who captured Tahsi (near Kadesh) and made an example of seven enemy princes, whom he claimed to have slain with his own mace. He ordered them to be hung upside down at the prow of his ship, afterwards hanging six of them in front of the walls of Thebes, while the remaining 'fallen one' was 'taken upriver to Nubia and hanged on the wall at Napata in order to display His Majesty's triumph'.[90] After this vindictive episode, Amenhotep II was not called upon to emulate the military exploits of his father, but instead made much of his military training. Near the Great Sphinx at Giza, a stele[91] was erected on which his prowess was recorded: by the time he was 18, he had mastered the arts of war, and had such a profound understanding of horses that his father put him in charge of the royal stables, where he handled horses so skilfully that they were able to run long distances without sweating – how this was achieved is not explained! Amenhotep gloried in his strength, claiming that, on one occasion when in a boat with 200 rowers who had become tired, he seized an oar himself and rowed six times as far as they had done. A cynical interpretation of this feat might suggest that the 200 oarsmen had rowed upstream but that Amenhotep had only wielded the rudder-oar, steering downstream with the current. He tested 300 strong bows and then, mounted on his speeding chariot, shot at four copper targets, his arrows hitting them so hard that each target was pierced through to the back. This feat was recorded in granite, in a relief in the Temple of Amun at Karnak, and now in the Luxor Museum, on which the inscription states that Amenhotep insisted that the targets be copper rather than the normal wood because, as he was so much stronger than ordinary men, his arrows pierced wood as though it were papyrus.

The power of the Hittites grew in the reign of Amenhotep II's son, Thutmose IV (1393–1383 BC), and to contain it he made an alliance with his grandfather's old enemy, Mitanni, asking the

[89]   ARE, ii, 461, 465.
[90]   ANET, pp. 247–8.
[91]   ANET, p. 244.

Plate 4.2   Amenhotep II (1427–1393 BC) shooting arrows at a copper target. Granite slab from Temple of Amun, Karnak.

Mitannian king, Artatama I, for his daughter's hand in marriage. Thutmose IV's outstanding achievement in the field of foreign relations was his marriage with this Mitannian princess, but he had to go to considerable lengths to achieve it, making his request six times before Artatama agreed to the match. Then, for nearly 40 years, there was peace in the Asiatic empire, the warrior pharaohs of the Eighteenth Dynasty having established Egypt as the dominant power in the Near East, with diplomacy taking the place of warfare as the method of maintaining supremacy.

Egypt was at the peak of political power and cultural development as Amenhotep III (1383–1345 BC), known as 'the Magnificent', came to the throne. He had a penchant for opulence and display which he was not slow to indulge, and throughout his reign pursued all manner of worldly pleasures. He undertook a programme of self-glorification second to none, to which end he had temples built in Egypt and Nubia, and favoured sites, particularly in Thebes, rebuilt and embellished. In the first 12 years of his reign, he informed the world at large of his activities by issuing what amounted to public relations bulletins, copies of which have been found as far south as Soleb in the Sudan and as far north as

Ras Shamra in Syria.[92] These bulletins, unique to Amenhotep III, take the form of large stone scarabs,[93] each with a flat underside containing a short inscription commemorating an important event: in one series, the killing of 96 wild cattle during a hunt held in his second regnal year is described;[94] in another, of which over 40 examples survive, '102 fierce lions'[95] shot by his own hand during his first ten years are recorded.

The first series of these scarab-bulletins was issued at the beginning of Amenhotep III's reign, to announce his marriage to 'the Great Royal Wife, Tiy, whose father's name is Yuya, and whose mother's name is Thuyu'. That the parents of Tiy are referred to without any title that would link them to the royal family has often been taken to mean that she was a commoner, and that her marriage to Amenhotep was a love match. Sadly, love can have played little part in the marriage of Tiy, who was a child at the time, and the arrangement, therefore, must have been engineered by her father. Yuya was no nonentity: he was the King's Lieutenant of Chariotry and Master of the Horse, signifying influence at Court, and held important priestly offices in the temple of Min in his native city, Akhmim, the capital of the ninth province of Upper Egypt. Moreover, it has been suggested that Yuya was the brother of Mutemwiya, Amenhotep's mother.[96] Amenhotep held him in such esteem that he allowed a tomb[97] to be made in the Valley of the Kings for him and Thuyu, a rare honour indeed because burial in the valley was normally restricted to kings and their consorts.

In making Tiy his Great Royal Wife, Amenhotep III flouted tradition. A Great Royal Wife (*ḥmt nsw wrt*), as a chief queen was called, was usually a princess, a royal heiress[98] through whom a king might legitimize his claim to the throne, because all landed property passed through the female line. Tiy was not a princess

---

[92] Krieger, 1956.
[93] Drioton, 1947; Lansing, 1936; Shorter, 1931.
[94] Newberry, 1906.
[95] Breasted, 1906, sect. 865.
[96] Aldred, 1972, p. 71ff.
[97] Quibell, J. E., 1908.
[98] Some scholars dispute that this was so. For a discussion for and against the existence of a royal heiress *see* G. Robins, 'A critical examination of the theory that the right to the throne of ancient Egypt passed through the female line in the 18th Dynasty' in *Goettinger Miszellen*, Heft 62, 1983, pp. 67–77.

but, thanks in part to her own personality and in part to the affection in which she was held, first by her husband and then by their son, Amenhotep IV (*see* page 111), she exercised great influence during the reigns of both kings. Honoured to an even greater extent than illustrious queens such as Tetisheri, Ahmose and Ahmose-Nofretari, Tiy was the first queen to appear regularly on public monuments by the side of the king, and the first whose name was linked with his in official inscriptions. Her knowledge of foreign affairs was recognized by King Tushratta of Mitanni, who wrote two letters[99] after the death of Amenhotep III in which he sought her good offices in his dealings with her son.

Marriage to Tiy was not the only instance of Amenhotep's willingness to flout tradition. He was deified in his own lifetime, being worshipped in Nubia in the temple at Soleb; Tiy was similarly honoured in a temple her husband had built for her at Sedeinga. At some time before the thirty-first year of his reign, Amenhotep married Sitamun, his daughter by Tiy, and had children by her. More conventionally, he saw marriage as a means by which to cement alliances with foreign potentates, and arranged several diplomatic marriages for himself. The first was made, in the tenth year of his reign, to a daughter of King Shuttarna II of Mitanni, Gilukhepa, who arrived in Egypt with a train of 317 ladies-in-waiting. The event was announced, inevitably, through a series of scarabs,[100] issued jointly by Amenhotep III and Tiy, whose name, even after ten years as queen, is followed by 'whose father's name is Yuya, whose mother's name is Thuyu'. Amenhotep later married another Mitannian princess, Tadukhepa,[101] a daughter of King Tushratta; and also the sister and daughter of King Kadashman-Enlil of Babylon.

In the latter part of his reign, Amenhotep III was forced to take steps to reduce the power of the priesthood of Amun (*see* page 135). In spite of his efforts, however, the priesthood continued to present a major threat to the throne, a situation exacerbated by events abroad. In the Asiatic empire, the Hittites under King Suppiluliuma had become more powerful, as had the Assyrians; and Egypt's ally, Mitanni, was engaged in an increasingly

---

[99]   Moran, 1992.
[100]   Engelbach, 1941.
[101]   Gelb, 1944, p. 76ff.

desperate struggle to fend them off. Moreover, there were intrigues among the petty princelings of Syria-Palestine. It is reasonable to say that only another Thutmose III could have dealt with the situation: but Amenhotep III and his son and successor, Amenhotep IV (?1353–1337 BC), were not warrior pharaohs.

Instead of taking measures to safeguard his empire, Amenhotep IV concentrated on attempts to counter the power of Amun by promoting the cult of Aten (*see* page 138). In the fifth year of his reign, he changed his name from Amenhotep (Pleasing-to-Amun) to Akhenaten (Glorious-Spirit-of-the-Aten), having the name of the god written inside a cartouche in the manner of an earthly king. Thenceforward, great emphasis was placed on this kingship of Aten, and upon the indivisibility between the two kings, Akhenaten and Aten, and the two gods, Aten and Akhenaten. Existing colossi of Akhenaten depict him as an hermaphrodite, as a god who was both father and mother. In Akhenaten/Aten, the cult of divine kingship, long since a part of Egyptian culture, was taken to extremes.

In the sixth year of his reign, Akhenaten began to build a new city some 330 kilometres north of Thebes: it was to be called Akhetaten (Horizon-of-the-Aten), better known today as Amarna. There, Akhenaten lived with his wife, Nefertiti, and their six daughters. Nefertiti was probably the daughter of Tiy's brother, Ay, and so Akhenaten's cousin.[102] Akhenaten also married two of his own daughters, Meritaten and Ankhesenpaaten, and had children by both. Courtiers moved with him to the new city and were rewarded with lavish gifts and tombs, which are largely decorated with scenes of the royal family out and about among its loyal and adoring retainers, the nobles for whom the tombs were built. They are cut into the cliffs that border the desert edge to the east of the city, and thus symbolically removed from the aegis of Osiris, God of the West.

By the ninth year of his reign, Akhenaten had proscribed the old gods of Egypt, and ordered their temples to be closed, a very serious matter, for these institutions played an important part in the economic and social life of the country. Religious persecution was new to the Egyptians, who had always worshipped many deities and were ever ready to add new gods to the pantheon. Atenism, however, was a very exclusive religion confined to the

[102]   Aldred, 1972, pp. 73–4.

royal family, with the king as the only mediator between man and god.

Meantime, large sections of the Asiatic empire were being lost. Many requests for help were sent to Akhenaten, who either ignored them or perhaps was not permitted by over-zealous officials to see them. Egypt's most loyal ally seems to have been Ribaddi of Byblos, who sent over 50 letters[103] to Akhenaten seeking help against Abdiashirta of Amor, and later against Abdiashirta's son, Aziru. Ribaddi warned that 'Abdiashirta is a cur and he is aiming to capture all the cities of the king' and claimed that Akhenaten's inaction was allowing Byblos 'to go out of his hand', all for the lack of a pitifully small amount of aid:

> May it seem good to my lord, the Sun of the Lands, to give me twenty pairs of horses. Entreat the king to give you 300 men: thus will we be able to hold the city.

Alas, Ribaddi was not heeded, possibly because Akhenaten's minister of protocol, the chamberlain Tutu,[104] was on Aziru's side.

About a year before his death, Akhenaten appointed one Smenkhkare[105] as his co-ruler, giving Meritaten (see page 111) to him as wife. But a short time later Smenkhkare, also, had died, to be succeeded by Tutankhaten, who changed his name to Tutankhamun and married Ankhesenpaaten (see page 111). She, too, dropped the 'Aten' element from her name, becoming Ankhesenamun. Tutankhamun (1336–1327 BC) was a child when he came to the throne and reigned for only nine years. Probably on the advice of his ministers, he moved back to the old state capital, Memphis, and reinstated the cult of Amun at Thebes. He was said to be a king who 'spent his life making images of the gods', and it was during his reign that work on the colonnade in Luxor Temple (see page 167), with its superb scenes of the Opet Festival,[106] was

---

[103] Moran, 1992.

[104] Though unfinished, Tutu's tomb (no. 8), is one of the most architecturally elaborate at Amarna.

[105] Smenkhkare was probably the brother of Tutankhamun; see Harrison et al., 1969. They may have been sons of Amenhotep III either by Tiy or by his eldest daughter, Sitamun; or of Akhenaten by a minor wife named Kiya.

[106] The Opet Festival, which took place in the second month of the Inundation season, celebrated the divine union of Amun and Mut, and was the time in which the statue of Amun was taken in procession from Karnak to Luxor Temple (see page 167).

undertaken. A year before the king's death, his treasurer, Maya, carried out a fiscal inspection of the temples of Egypt, from Aswan to the Mediterranean. As far as the modern world is concerned, however, Tutankhamun has been the best known of Egypt's kings since AD 1922, when his tomb was found almost intact.

Tutankhamun was succeeded by Ay (*see* page 111), but not before his widow, Ankhesenamun, had persuaded Suppiluliuma, the king of the Hittites, to send her one of his sons to be her consort as king of Egypt. The chosen prince, Zananza, was killed, possibly on the orders of the Egyptian general, Horemheb, and Ankhesenamun was forced to marry her grandfather-great uncle, Ay, who became king but only for the next four years. Ankhesenamun's fate is unknown. Horemheb inherited the throne, perhaps because he was married to Mutnodjmet, Ay's daughter, and Nefertiti's sister, but more probably because the army had decided that it was time to intervene before the whole Asiatic empire was lost, an early example of the military exceeding their remit so as to replace what they perceive to be failed civilian powers.

Horemheb (1323–1295 BC) proved an effective king. His family came from Herakleopolis, a provincial town near the Faiyum, where the ram-headed god Herishef was worshipped. No record has been discovered that Horemheb's forebears served in the Herishef cult, which may indicate that they were not a sufficiently prominent family, and it seems likely that Horemheb enjoyed a spectacular rise through the ranks of the army. A magnificent tomb was built for him at Sakkara[107] in the reign of Tutankhamun, a fitting acknowledgement of his successes as military commander in campaigns in Syria, Nubia, and possibly Libya: even before he became king, Horemheb had made attempts to regain the empire.

His death in 1295 BC brought the Eighteenth Dynasty to a close. Having no lineal successor, Horemheb left the throne to his vizier, Pa-ramessu, evidently an army colleague and the scion of an old Delta family with an attachment to the god Seth. Pa-ramessu's wife, Sitre, bore him a son, named Sety after his paternal grandfather, and it was presumably because of this son that Horemheb felt confident that the throne of Egypt would be in safe hands. Paramessu became the first king of the Nineteenth Dynasty and adopted the new name of Ramesses I. He reigned for only 16

[107]   Martin, 1991.

months before being succeeded by Sety I (1294–1279 BC), who continued Horemheb's policy of restoring the *status quo ante* the Amarna period.

It was Sety I who succeeded in restoring Egyptian authority over Syria-Palestine, through campaigns against the Hittites in which Kadesh was recaptured. Egypt and Hatti had been diplomatic enemies for years, but had never before come face to face in war. Sety 'made a great slaughter among the wretched Hittites', rampaging among them, 'slaying their chiefs, overthrown in their own gore, charging among them like a tongue of flame, annihilating them', until he could secure a peace treaty. His campaigns were recorded on the north and east exterior walls of the Hypostyle Hall of the Temple of Amun at Karnak.[108] Unlike records of earlier campaigns, such as the Annals of Thutmose III, Sety's campaigns are set down in a mixture of hieroglyphic inscriptions and reliefs depicting the king's activities, and initiated a new form of Egyptian art, namely the depiction of historical events.

Sety I was succeeded by his son, Ramesses II (1279–1213 BC), who is known today as Ramesses the Great. To what extent that epithet is justified is debatable: he has a reputation as a vainglorious boaster, and might be better described as incredible, even preposterous! A comparison of his mummy, which has survived, with his statues shows that he was handsome and physically imposing. When he died, he was over 90 years old and had reigned for 67 years, a term out-matched only by Pepi II. He was a prolific procreator: 49, possibly 50, of his sons and 38 of his daughters are known by name, and they are not the total number. He had several Great Wives (queens-in-chief), at least four of whom were his daughters. In addition to his own building activities, Ramesses usurped the monuments of previous kings, expunging their names in inscriptions and inserting his own. His name, therefore, is ubiquitous, and, under his throne name, *User-maat-Re*, corrupted by the Greeks into Ozymandias, Percy Bysshe Shelley credited him with the evocative invitation: 'Look on my works, ye Mighty, and despair!'[109]

---

[108]   The Sety I war-reliefs were published in full, with translations, in 1986 by the Oriental Institute, Chicago, as *The Battle Reliefs of King Sety I*. See also Kitchen, 1993, p. 6ff.

[109]   Shelley, *Ozymandias*.

For the first three years of his reign, Ramesses II seems to have been occupied with domestic affairs, until, in his fourth year (1275 BC), he made his first foray into western Asia, an event commemorated on a stele erected at Nahr el-Kalb (Dog River) in the Lebanon.[110] A year later, he set about trying to capture Egypt's lost possessions in Syria. At this time, the Egyptian army was divided into its customary four divisions, each with 5000 men, a combination of chariotry and infantry, and all named after gods as the divisions of Pre, Ptah, Sutekh and Amun. Ramesses himself led the last. For Thutmose III, the king whom Ramesses was eager to emulate, the main enemy had been Mitanni, the capture of Megiddo the key to his success; for Ramesses II, the enemy was Hatti, the key city Kadesh.

At the start of his Kadesh campaign,[111] Ramesses took the main body of the Egyptian army north along the Bekaa valley towards Kadesh, at the same time despatching a seasoned fighting force up the Phoenician coast, which was largely controlled by Amor, with orders to show the flag there, then turn inland to rendezvous with him at Kadesh. Ramesses made camp overnight about a day's march from Kadesh, and then pushed on until he was about 13 kilometres south of the city, his way blocked by the River Orontes, which could, however, be crossed at the Shabtuna ford. Before the crossing had commenced, two captured bedouin were brought into camp and questioned. They informed Ramesses that the Hittite army, consisting of 18,000 to 19,000 infantry and 3500 chariots manned by 10,500 men, was not at Kadesh but some 200 kilometres to the north at Halab (Aleppo). Ramesses took this information at face value and ordered his division to cross the ford immediately. He then hurried on with just this one division, leaving the Division of Re still negotiating the ford, and made camp to the north-west of Kadesh.

At this point, two Hittite spies were brought in, and they revealed that the Hittites were not at Aleppo at all, but in hiding to the north of Kadesh. Ramesses immediately sent messengers to the Division of Re with orders to advance at speed, but, before it could reach him, the Hittites attacked, emerging from the southern

---

[110] PM, 1951, p. 385.
[111] Descriptions of the Kadesh campaign are inscribed in the temples of Karnak, Luxor, Abydos, the Ramesseum and Abu Simbel. For translations *see* Gardiner, 1960.

side of Kadesh and cutting through the middle of the division, catching it unawares, not yet drawn up for battle. The remnants of the Division of Re dashed into Ramesses' camp, where he was sitting with his officers upbraiding them for what had happened. The camp was thrown into panic, especially when the Hittites arrived in pursuit. Ramesses, surrounded by Hittites with only his bodyguard to protect him, charged out of camp through the enemy lines, and was saved by the cupidity of the Hittite army which, like that of Thutmose III at Megiddo, stopped for plunder.

At this point, the force Ramesses had sent to Amor arrived. They tackled the Hittites in the camp while Ramesses rallied the remains of his two divisions for an attack. The Egyptians joined battle with the Hittites six times, and the Hittite commander launched a further 1000 chariots, but to no avail: they were driven into the Orontes. The battle lasted over three hours and, in that time, the Division of Ptah made up ground and was able to come charging to the rescue. The Division of Sutekh never arrived, and what Ramesses said to its commanding officer is not recorded. Once darkness fell, the fighting was over. The Hittite king, Muwatallish, had kept in reserve between 8000 and 9000 foot soldiers, presumably because he believed that the failure of Ramesses to keep the Egyptian army divisions together was part of an elaborate trap.

According to one Egyptian account, the Hittites asked for a truce. Ramesses was lucky to escape with his life and to have the chance to declare, at the time, that the battle was a draw. Strategically, the result of the Battle of Kadesh was a defeat for the Egyptians: Ramesses failed to capture the city and was forced to return to Egypt with nothing to show for his efforts. Of course, he did not proclaim this to be the case. Instead, for the 62 years that remained of his reign, accounts of the Battle of Kadesh and of how he had won it, almost single-handed, formed a constant refrain on his public monuments. In the twenty-first year of his reign, a peace treaty was drawn up between the Hittites and Egypt, copies of which were inscribed at Karnak and the Ramesseum. The Hittite version has been found in their capital city, Boghazkoi, in Anatolia.[112] The treaty, which included a mutual peace pact, the

---

[112]   Now in the Archaeological Museum at Istanbul: see Alpay Pasinli, Istanbul Archaeological Museums, Istanbul, 1989, pp. 94–5. For a translation of the treaty see S. Langdon and A. H. Gardiner in *JEA*, 6, 1920, p. 179ff.

renunciation of all territorial ambition and a defence pact, also made the first-known provision for the exchange of political refugees. For the rest of Ramesses' reign, relations between Hatti and Egypt were good: the two kings, and their queens, wrote to each other; the Hittite king, Hattusil, even contemplated a state visit to Egypt; and when Ramesses was in his mid-sixties, a daughter of Hattusil was sent to Egypt to be his bride. A few years later, he married a second Hittite princess.

Ramesses II outlived several crown princes and was succeeded by his thirteenth son, Merenptah (1213–1203 BC), who was already well advanced in years when he came to the throne. During his father's old age, vigilance on the western frontier slackened, and the chain of forts[113] along the coastal road to Cyrenaica, designed to safeguard against Libu (Libyan) raids, let fall into disrepair. At the beginning of Merenptah's reign, the Libu were attempting to invade the western Delta. Two clans, the Meshwesh and the Kehek, formed a coalition with the so-called Sea Peoples[114] from the coasts and islands of Asia Minor and the Aegean: the Akawasha, the Lukka, the Tursha, the Sherden and the Sheklesh, some of whom were the tribal ancestors of nations well known to history. The Akawasha are probably identifiable with the Achaeans of Mycenaean Greece, the Lukka with the Lycians of western Anatolia. The Tursha are said to be the ancestors of the Etruscans, the Sherden of the Sardinians and the Sheklesh of the Sicilians.

By the fifth year of Merenptah's reign, the Libu, led by king Mauroy, and the Sea Peoples, were at the gates of Memphis, bringing their families and all their possessions with them, a clear indication of their intention to settle in Egypt. That they were driven by hunger is made clear in the text of a great commemorative inscription[115] at Karnak: 'they spend the day roaming the land and fighting to fill their bellies daily; they have come to the land of Egypt to seek food for themselves'. The Egyptians defeated the coalition in the Delta, in a six-hour-long battle in which 6359 Libu and at least 2370 of their allies were killed, or so the Egyptians claimed. Many prisoners, and much booty, were taken; and King Mauroy ran away. The relief felt by the Egyptians at the averting of a great danger is apparent in the lyrical tone of the inscription

---

113   *See* Kitchen, 1982, pp. 67, 71–2.
114   Onom., i, 196*.
115   ARE, iii, 569ff.

on a granite stele[116] erected in Merenptah's memorial temple at Thebes, extracts from which are quoted below:

> Great joy has come to Egypt, rejoicing comes forth from the towns of Ta-meri (Egypt)... Sit down happily and talk... The strongholds are left to themselves... Messengers can wait by the battlements, shaded from the sun, until the watchmen wake up. The soldiers can lie sleeping... The herds in the fields can be left without herdsmen... There is no shout of alarm in the night... He who plants his crop can be sure of eating it.

Defined in the inscription is the Egyptians' scorn for the wretched Mauroy who 'fled under cover of night alone without a feather on his head, barefoot, his wives seized before his eyes, the meal for his food taken away and without water in the waterskin to keep him alive'; and the fate that had befallen the enemies of Egypt:

> Tjehenu (Libya) is destroyed, Khatti is at peace. Canaan has been cruelly plundered, Ashkelon is carried off, Gezer is captured, Yenoam is annihilated, Israel is laid waste and has no seed, Khor (Palestine and Syria) is widowed because of Ta-meri.

It is, of course, the phrase 'Israel is laid waste' that has made the stele famous and given it the name, the Israel Stele,[117] by which it has, in modern times, become known. The mention of Israel on this stele is the only known instance in any Egyptian text, and, on its discovery in AD 1896,[118] it excited scholars who had always assumed that Merenptah was the pharaoh of the Exodus, whereas this inscription implied that Israel was already a people settled in Canaan in Merenptah's time.

In the 20 years following Merenptah's death, several weak rulers occupied the throne. The six-year-long reign of Merenptah's son, Sety II, was interrupted for a short period by a usurper, Amenmesses, who may have been a son or grandson of Ramesses II. Sety II's son and successor, Siptah, also reigned for six years before dying in his early twenties. He is said to have suffered from poliomyelitis, the cause of the deformed foot revealed by his

[116] ANET, pp. 376–8.
[117] Now in Cairo Museum.
[118] Petrie, 1897.

mummy,[119] and was thus hardly an ideal choice for the position of 'warrior pharaoh'. He seems to have been a puppet of Bay (*see* page 120) and Sety's queen, Twosret; and, at Siptah's death, Twosret, like Hatshepsut, became Female King, with her own large tomb in the Valley of the Kings. This tomb was later taken over by Setnakhte, first king of the Twentieth Dynasty XX. In AD 1898, a coffin inscribed with Setnakhte's name, but containing the mummy of a woman, was discovered, stored in the tomb of Amenhotep II. It is tempting to surmise that the woman was Twosret. Ironically, although Setnakhte may have evicted her from her tomb, she is the one whose mummy has survived. The occupation of the throne by a female, following on a usurper king and a weak king supported by an ambitious foreigner, were all irregularities so little to be countenanced that all three were disregarded by the following dynasty. But the decline in royal power and prestige that finally led to the political fragmentation of Egypt and the disintegration of the traditional style of government had begun.

The Great Harris Papyrus,[120] prepared in the reign of the Twentieth Dynasty king, Ramesses IV (1153–1147 BC), to glorify the memory of his father, Ramesses III, and now in the British Museum, describes the parlous state of Egypt in the last years of the Nineteenth Dynasty. Found at Deir el-Medina, it was probably once in the library of Ramesses III's memorial temple, Medinet Habu. Of all Egyptian state archives, it is the most magnificent, over 40 metres long and 0.5 metre high, with 117 columns of hieratic writing. It exaggerates, perhaps, to draw a contrast between the new dynasty and the old, but is probably correct in claiming that the country was in the hands of local chieftains, every man a law unto himself, plundering or killing his neighbour with impunity, neglecting to dedicate offerings to the gods, and, worse of all, 'Irsu, a certain Asiatic was with them as chief, having put the entire land into subjection before him'. Irsu was probably Bay,[121] who may have been a Syrian. He boasted of having been 'the great chancellor of the entire land' and had a tomb in the Valley of the Kings which, although small and undecorated, was evidence of his privileged position because burial in the Valley was

---

[119] But *see* Dodson, 1993, for a claim that it was due to cerebral palsy.
[120] *See* ARE, iv, 151–412 for a complete translation.
[121] Gardiner, 1961, p. 282.

not usually accorded to commoners. His name translates as 'self-made man'. According to the Papyrus, eventually the gods themselves intervened: the land 'was put into its proper state' and 'they established their son, namely Setnakhte, upon their great throne.' The origins of the new king, Setnakhte (1186–1184 BC), are unknown but, in his brief reign, he began the task of setting Egypt in order. His son, Ramesses III (1184–1153 BC), succeeded him and restored prosperity and prestige to the land.

Reliefs carved on the walls of Medinet Habu temple (*see* page 164) depict Ramesses III's military campaigns, and record that, in the fifth year of his reign, he went to war against the Libyans. For several years before Ramesses came to the throne, there had been a steady and unhindered infiltration into Egypt of Libyans, driven by the lack of food in their own land to the tempting granary of Egypt. The Libyans, whose pretext for war was the claim that Ramesses had interfered in the affairs of the Tjemehu clan by nominating a child as chief, were repelled in the first campaign, but six years later they returned. This time, the problem was exacerbated by an attack made three years before from the northeast, by a new coalition of Sea Peoples. Nomads from the Russian steppes had begun a migration southwards and westwards that was to change the ethnic and political structure of Anatolia, Syria and Palestine.

A confederacy of Sheklesh, the same tribe that had been routed by Merenptah over 30 years before, Peleset, Tjekker, Danuna and Weshesh destroyed the Hittite empire and marched down into Syria. Like the Sea Peoples of Merenptah's time, they brought their women and children and all their possessions with them, proof again that they were not an army so much as an invasion force, intending to settle in a new homeland if they could find one. Ramesses mobilized the Egyptian army and ordered it to halt the invaders in Djahi (Syria-Palestine). It seems that the Egyptians accomplished this but, meanwhile, a second arm of the invasion force was approaching by sea. Ramesses trapped the enemy fleet in the mouth of the Nile, where he trounced them in the first naval battle to be properly recorded. The Weshesh disappeared from history, but the Danuna were in all probability the Danaoi of the *Iliad*. Two of the other invading tribes stayed on in the Middle East: the Peleset, who became the Philistines who conquered and were conquered by the Israelites, giving their name to Palestine;

and the Tjekker, who settled on the coast of Palestine at Dor, and later, perhaps, became the Barbary pirates.

In the eleventh year of Ramesses III's reign, the Libyans returned, only to be defeated again, with over 2000 killed, and many prisoners and cattle captured. At the end of the Great Harris Papyrus, Ramesses' version of events is recorded:

> I turned them back from trampling Egypt. I carried away those whom my sword had spared as numerous captives pinioned like birds before my horses, their wives and children by the ten thousand, their cattle by the hundred thousand. I settled their leaders in strongholds called by my name. I gave to them captains of archers and chief men of the tribes, branded and made into slaves, stamped with my name, their wives and children being dealt with likewise.[122]

Among these captives was Mesher, chief of the Meshwesh, for whose life his father, Keper, appealed in vain.

For the rest of Ramesses III's reign, Egypt was at peace. The king, however, may have won the battle against the Sea Peoples but, in doing so, he lost the war, for some of them took over Egypt's empire in western Asia, and with it access to a major source of iron, the metal that was to revolutionize the first millennium BC. While the rest of the civilized world moved into the Iron Age, Egypt remained lodged in the Bronze Age. Obviously, this was not apparent at the time and, in Ramesses' reign, Egypt enjoyed a period of prosperity, the extent of which is indicated by the long lists of donations to temples recorded in the Great Harris Papyrus. Ramesses also commissioned much building work, notably the sandstone temple at Karnak dedicated to the Theban triad of Amun, his wife Mut, and their son, Khonsu, and his own vast memorial temple at Medinet Habu.

The temple library at Medinet Habu may once have housed a papyrus, now in Turin Museum, which contains the record of an attempt to murder Ramesses III known as 'The Harem Conspiracy' because it was initiated in the women's quarters. The chief conspirator was Tiye, one of Ramesses' lesser wives, who intended to replace Ramesses with her son, but failed in the attempt. The Turin Judicial Papyrus,[123] which is one of the very few records

---

[122]   ARE, iv, 405.
[123]   ARE, iv, 416ff., or A. de Buck, *JEA*, 23, 1937, pp. 152–64.

extant to throw light upon crime and punishment and the conduct of the law in ancient Egypt, provides an account of how they were brought to trial. In it, the son is called 'Pentewere, who bore that other name'; and the names of several of the other accused were changed because components of their original names were considered too auspicious. Thus, one of the men on trial is called Mesedsure, meaning 'Re hates him', his real name presumably being Mersure, 'Re loves him'.

Mesedsure, a royal butler, and Paibekkamen, major-domo of the palace, were Tiye's chief accomplices. They brought into the plot Pere, an overseer of the treasury, Peyes, an army commander, ten harem officials of various ranks, four royal butlers, and three royal scribes. A captain of archers in Nubia, Binemwese, his name changed, as it means 'the wicked man in Thebes', was suborned by his sister, one of Ramesses III's concubines. It is clear that the conspirators intended to back up the assassination within the palace by a rebellion outside it, for the wives of six of the officers of the harem gate sent messages to the outside world; and Binemwese's sister wrote asking him to 'stir up the people, make enmity and come to make a rebellion against your lord'. If the plot had succeeded, a rebellion in Nubia fomented by Binemwese would have been a serious matter, but it failed, despite Paibekkamen's attempts to work magic against the king by means of wax figurines.

There were four trials. In the first, Paibekkamen, Mesedure, Binemwese and the six gate-keepers' wives figure among the 22 people of whom the Papyrus simply records that 'they brought their punishment upon themselves', a punishment that was certainly death. In the second trial, Peyes and five other people were condemned, and 'took their own lives' without leaving the court. In the third, Prince Pentewere and three others were found guilty: as punishment, they 'left him in his place. He died of his own accord', as did the three others, presumably of starvation. The fourth trial was for those arraigned on non-capital charges, among them five of the judges who had conducted the three previous trials, arrested for carousing with the women prisoners! The punishment for minor charges in the Harem Conspiracy brought the cutting off of ears and noses. Of Queen Tiye, there is no mention. Interestingly, several names, of both judges and accused, were those of foreigners: Ba'almahar is a Semitic name, Peluka a Lycian; and Inini is actually called a Libyan.

Ramesses III was the last of the great warrior pharaohs who made the New Kingdom a period of military achievement and territorial expansion, leading to unprecedented prosperity. By the reign of Ramesses XI (1099–1070/69 BC), however, Egypt was in a desperate state. In dynastic times, the linchpin of its society was the king, who was not only mortal but a living god. Kingship was said to have had its origin in the time when the sun god, Re, came to earth, bringing with him his daughter, Maat, the personification of Truth and Justice. Thus, the creation of the earth was synchronous with the establishment of kingship and social order; and, although the king was a god, he was expected to act under the law. The king was central to society because he was divine, primeval and inextricably bound up with justice: Hatshepsut summed up her own position in the declaration 'I am God, the beginning of existence.'

A king's title to the throne had to be legal. Normally, he would inherit it as the eldest son of the reigning monarch; and could reinforce his claim by marriage to that monarch's eldest daughter. There were, however, other means by which the throne could legally be gained. The succession to the throne of Egypt reflected the story of the god Horus and his father, the murdered god-king Osiris, whom he buried. The king of Egypt, considered the living Horus, could justify his claim to the throne by burying his predecessor, as Horus had buried Osiris. Normally, it would be the son and natural heir who buried his father; but sometimes, as in the case of Ay and Tutankhamun, it was the act of burial that conferred legitimacy upon someone who might not otherwise have legally been king. Kings who did not inherit the throne in the regular way took pains to prove their legitimacy by claiming divine birth, Hatshepsut being one example; or by means of oracles, Thutmose III being selected to be king through the actions of the statue of Amun. Thutmose IV claimed to have had a dream in which the great Sphinx at Giza promised him the throne, in return for clearing away the sand that had engulfed it.[124]

For centuries respect for kingship survived changes in dynasty and even the trauma of the Amarna period, until, in the last years of the Nineteenth Dynasty, royal power and prestige began to wane, with royal authority fragmenting by the end of the Twentieth. The reasons for this are not known, but one important factor

[124] ARE, ii, 510–15.

was the person of the king himself. The role a king of Egypt was expected to play required him to be vigorous, preferably both mentally and physically. The ideal pattern of succession was for a king to come to the throne while still relatively young, to rule for a number of years and then to hand on his throne to a son in the prime of life. In the Twentieth Dynasty this pattern was broken by the unusual number of kings coming to the throne as elderly men and ruling only briefly: seven of the ten kings in the Dynasty each ruled for less than seven years.

Even under Ramesses III, royal power was weakening. As the king's power waned, so that of the priesthood increased, and, by the end of his reign, the temple authorities owned a third of the cultivable land of the country, tenanted by a fifth of the population. About three-quarters of this property belonged to the estate of Amen-Re of Thebes. In his position as head of this estate, the High Priest of Amun enjoyed enormous temporal power, the more so since the estate was exempt from taxation. By the late Twentieth Dynasty, the position of High Priest of Amun had fallen into the hands of a powerful family of officials, when Ramesses-Nakht, appointed by Ramesses IV, was succeeded by his son, Nesamun, who was succeeded by his brother, Amenhotep. In a relief at Karnak, Amenhotep is shown receiving rewards from Ramesses IX (1126–1108 BC), both figures carved on the same scale. It was a convention of Egyptian art that the most important figure in a relief was depicted on a larger scale than others: the Karnak relief, therefore, is eloquent testimony to the power that the High Priest of Amun had attained, in Thebes at least.

By the nineteenth year of the reign of Ramesses XI (1099–1070/ 69 BC), Thebes had a new high priest. Herihor (1080–1074 BC) seems to have been of humble origin, though his wife, Nodjmet, may have been a sister of Ramesses XI; but he was also ambitious, not only becoming high priest but also general-in-chief of the Egyptian army and Viceroy of Nubia. For the first time, the Theban high-priesthood, governorship of Nubia and wide military powers were united in one man, and it was but a short step to create a dynasty of priest-kings at Thebes. In the north, supreme executive power was exercised on behalf of the king by one Smendes, who may have been Herihor's son,[125] so that Ramesses XI had to accept a division of Egypt in which Smendes ruled the

[125] See E. F. Wente, JNES, 26, 1967, p. 174.

north and Herihor the south, although the king remained titular head of both. When Herihor died, Piankh, possibly his son-in-law, succeeded him as high priest and military commander. Piankh, however, seems to have died about the same time as Ramesses XI. His position of power was assumed by his son, Pinudjem I; but in the north it was Smendes I (*see* page 174) who succeeded Ramesses XI as king, founding the Twenty-first Dynasty, which ran concurrently with the dynasty of high priests at Thebes.

Government and Administration

In the Eighteenth Dynasty, the foreign tribute which, from the reign of Thutmose III, percolated down to large numbers of temples, created a powerful priesthood which played a vital part in the civil administration (*see* page 139). With the new standing army, a powerful and privileged military class arose; and throughout the New Kingdom, Egypt was governed by a bureaucracy whose members were often drawn from its ranks. Army officers and men were handsomely rewarded for devotion or bravery on the field of battle, the most prestigious decoration being the 'Gold of Valour', which could take the form of a large (and valuable) gold collar. All military ranks shared in booty won from captured cities and their rulers. When stationed in Egypt, troops and their families lived in comfortable barracks. Veterans were settled with grants of land and cattle, often gifted from the king himself. Such gifts remained in a veteran's family as long as any of his direct descendants served in the army, so that military service tended to become hereditary, with ever larger numbers of the population dependent on it. The appeal of a military career alarmed the bureaucracy to such an extent that diatribes against it became a regular part of a boy's school exercises.[126]

By the reign of Amenhotep III, many prisoners of war from Syria, Libya and even Hatti had been allowed to regain their

---

[126] Schoolboys practised writing by copying out model letters. Such letters were often used as propaganda (or brainwashing!) – copying out exhortations, such as 'Let me tell you how wretched a soldier's life is' followed by examples of the many miseries a soldier supposedly endured, were designed to persuade a boy that the life of a scribe was preferable. For examples of model letters *see* Erman, 1966, p. 194ff.

freedom, but on condition that they served in the Egyptian army. Conscripts from Nubia had been employed since early dynastic times; and the Medjay, a nomadic tribe from the eastern desert of Nubia, had for over 100 years been used as scouts. In the Eighteenth Dynasty, Medjay were used for desert patrols and as frontier guards; but some of them became the 'policemen' who kept law and order in Egypt, with special responsibility for the cemeteries. For much of the New Kingdom, it is probable that most of these 'policemen' were actually Egyptians, but the term 'Medjay' was applied to them all. The commander of all the police forces was called the Chief of the Medjay, and any sizeable town or district had its own company of Medjay whose captain was of some importance in the community.

Despite the army's new standing, the most important office of state was still, as it had been since the Fourth Dynasty, that of vizier. Deciding not to entrust such a powerful position to any one individual, Ahmose divided it, creating a vizier for Lower Egypt who probably resided in Memphis which remained the administrative capital of Egypt, and another for Upper Egypt who had his headquarters in Thebes, the new religious capital. In the Old Kingdom, the vizier had regularly been a son of the king; in the New Kingdom, the post was awarded to a nobleman of outstanding ability, whose responsibilities, however, remained much as they had been in the earlier period.[127]

The vizier was custodian of the archives, and responsible for justice, provincial administration, finance, public works and agriculture. During the New Kingdom, he appointed the special group of officials who were dedicated to the manning, equipping and provisioning of the army and navy. As was usual with holders of high office in Egypt, the vizier was not necessarily an expert in any one field: instead he relied on knowing where to secure the expertise needed. He was the intermediary between the King who, whenever possible, received him in audience, and his people: all royal commands passed to the vizier and he in turn passed them on to the scribes of his bureau. It was the vizier who sent messengers (*wḥmw*: literally, 'heralds') with royal commands for the governors of towns and provinces. When a vizier presided in court to hear petitions and make judgements in civil and in criminal cases, he prided himself on being accessible to everyone, even the

[127]   Hayes, 1962, pp. 47–8.

most lowly; and, as inscriptions in the tomb of Thutmose III's vizier, Rekhmire,[128] make clear, when giving audience, he sat in state:

> in a chair with a back, a reed-mat on the ground, wearing a chain of office, a skin at his back, another under his feet, a matting cape upon him, a baton beside him, and forty papyrus-rolls spread before him.[129]

In the New Kingdom, the law seems to have been an expression of the king's will, made known through royal edicts which either superseded or enlarged upon the laws laid down by his predecessors. The rolls referred to above may well have contained a code of law that seems to have existed as early as the Twelfth Dynasty.[130]

Other departments of the government that were under the general control of the viziers but enjoyed independent organizations included the treasury, the national granary and the state herds. Of these, the most important was, as it had been in the Old Kingdom, the treasury (*see* page 61) which, in the New Kingdom, was controlled by two chancellors, matching the two viziers, all cooperating in receiving and accounting for a vast income from many different sources including taxes, trade and tribute from the empire. The national granary, with branches throughout the country, was administered from a central office by an overseer of the granaries of Upper and Lower Egypt, responsible for the recording and storage of the annual harvest. The state herds, which included cattle and other farm animals, were administered centrally by an overseer of cattle who conducted an annual cattle count. The men responsible for individual herds and stables, either as herdsmen or scribes, reported to the overseer or, in provincial towns, to his deputies. There does not seem to have been a minister of works. Instead, activities connected with royal building projects and quarrying operations were undertaken by a variety of officials, from viziers to mayors to scribes, who were rewarded with the title of overseer of works.

The provincial administration, like the national government underpinned by a vast army of scribes and bookkeepers, was

[128] Davies, 1943.
[129] For the duties of and procedures for a vizier *see* Van den Boorn, 1988.
[130] Hayes, 1955.

largely made up of the mayors of the major towns. The authority of a mayor (*ḥ3ty-ᶜ*) extended beyond his town into the surrounding rural district; his chief responsibility was the collection of grain and other goods in and on which taxes were paid, for which he answered directly to the vizier. An offical called the 'Scribe of Fields of the Lord of the Two Lands' took charge of the measurement of fields for taxation purposes. A mayor was responsible for the support of local temples, and would sometimes serve in the local law court (*ḳnbt*), which functioned as a tribunal for cases not important enough to be referred to the vizier.

The bureaucracy governing Egypt was a complex network of officials, who often held public office and positions in the households of the king and his family. Office-holders in the royal household were, naturally, men of power and prosperity. The personal estates of the king were administered by his high steward, his appointment a mark of royal favour, sometimes after a distinguished military career. At the beginning of the Eighteenth Dynasty, the administration of the palace was in the hands of the royal chancellor who, in addition to administering the palace exchequer and the granaries, and organizing royal trading and mining expeditions, was responsible for the education of the king's sons. During the Eighteenth Dynasty, the high stewards began to take over many of the functions of chancellor, and, in the reigns of Amenhotep II and Amenhotep III, two high stewardships were created, one based in Thebes, the other in Memphis. There were, in addition, other high stewards, for example, of cities such as Memphis and Thebes, and of the major temples.

In the palace, the living quarters of the king and his family were managed by a chamberlain responsible for the storage and preparation of food and drink, and for an army of underlings and servants. In all royal palaces, the women's quarters had an overseer, part of whose duties was to supervise the commercial activities undertaken by the women – the grinding of flour and the weaving of cloth – which supplemented the palace exchequer. The royal entourage consisted of courtiers, known as 'royal acquaintances' (*rḫw-nsw*), some in special posts such as the king's cupbearer, the royal herald, the royal scribe, the holder of the king's sunshade, and the fan-bearer (*bḥs ḥbt*). The last two offices, usually held by Nubian or Syrian servants, were functional: the *bḥs ḥbt*, for example, actually waved the fan that cooled the king, and may best be compared to a punkah-wallah in India. By the early Eighteenth Dynasty, however, the office of 'Fan-bearer on the King's Right Hand' (*t3i ḫw ḥr wnmy nsw*) had become purely honorific, the perquisite of only the highest officials. It was considered to be a sign of royal favour, coveted even by high stewards, for the bearer, after all, stood next to the king in a good position to gain his ear. Cupbearers, of course, served the king personally; and many examples are known of such men becoming royal confidants, entrusted with royal commissions.

From Hatshepsut's time onwards, kings adopted a policy of promoting court favourites, and many of the highest offices of state were held by men closely associated with the king, either brought up with him as royal companions, or married to ladies of the court (known as Royal Ornaments), or their daughters, or having served with the him in the army. Thus, Sennefer, mayor of Thebes in the reign of Amenhotep II, was the son of a Royal Ornament; and his own daughter became a Royal Ornament. Ramose, a relative of Amenhotep-son-of-Hapu (*see* below), married a Royal Ornament and became vizier under Amenhotep III. It was also possible to gain high office through talent. Senenmut, for example, though of undistinguished birth – his father and mother having no titles – enjoyed a most remarkable career. He may have joined the army as a young man, possibly in the reign of Amenhotep I,[131] and in time came to the notice of Thutmose II, who appointed him steward, first to the queen, Hatshepsut, and then to her daughter, Neferure. During Hatshepsut's reign, Senenmut amassed many more offices of state, 91 of which have so far been identified,[132] and he was undoubtedly one of the most powerful men in Egypt.

A further example of how, in the Eighteenth Dynasty, men of talent not related to the royal family might rise to positions of power, is Amenhotep-son-of-Hapu, who belonged to an obscure family from Athribis in the Delta but who, in the reign of Amenhotep III, rose to become overseer of all the King's works, royal scribe, scribe of recruits and steward of the estates of the princess, Sitamun. Much of the credit for the great buildings erected during Amenhotep III's reign must go to his namesake, who was honoured with a memorial temple on the west bank at Thebes that was comparable to the royal temples nearby, and for

---

[131]   Meyer, 1982, p. 274.
[132]   Dorman, 1988, p. 203ff.

whom a statue was erected within the hallowed precincts at Karnak. Amenhotep-son-of-Hapu, who lived to the age of 80, was revered by later generations; and in the Ptolemaic period he was worshipped as a god of healing, with a sanctuary at Deir el-Bahri. Neither he nor Senenmut was vizier, yet there can be little doubt that they were even more influential than those holding the office that was, in theory, the most powerful after the kingship.

Until the end of the New Kingdom, the administration of Egypt continued to be in the hands of a bureaucracy comprising priests and palace officials: though from the Nineteenth Dynasty, royal princes figured prominently in important offices. In the Twentieth Dynasty, the army was supplemented by foreign conscripts, including Sherden, once part of the alliance of Sea Peoples that fought Merenptah. Many of these conscripts, recruited throughout the reign of Ramesses III in large numbers, were settled on government land in Middle and Lower Egypt, ready to be called up in times of need.

Economy

Thutmose III's Asiatic exploits had a profound effect on the economy of Egypt, and also on its society. The minds of those Egyptians who were brought into contact with the world outside were broadened, and they became less inward-looking and more willing to accept new ideas. Great numbers of foreigners arrived in Egypt, either as conscripts in the army or as merchants and settlers, bringing with them foreign customs and styles of dress, and even new foreign words, which were incorporated into the language. The great wealth coming into the country from the conquered Asiatic states brought Egyptians of all classes above the peasant level unprecedented prosperity. A taste for luxury developed, and the exotic goods pouring into Egypt from western Asia and Nubia, from Crete and from Mycenae, not only found a ready market among the newly rich Egyptians but exposed Egyptian craftsmen to new artistic forms.

As in all periods of Egypt's history, most of the population was engaged in agriculture and stock farming, the mainstays of the economy. Each year, the damage wrought to river and canal banks by the Inundation had to be repaired, and fields and boundaries to be marked out anew, a cause of much friction when neighbours disagreed on the exact location of the boundaries of their fields. In addition, new land was needed to support the rapidly growing population, and had to be reclaimed from the desert. After the Inundation, water had to be raised to irrigate the fields. Although the introduction of the *shaduf* (*see* page 58) helped greatly, agricultural labour involved many hours of backbreaking work. In spite of this, the peasants who worked the land, legally free men and women, were subject to corvée labour whenever large gangs of workmen were needed for specific projects such as digging major canals and irrigation ditches, constructing revetments and dykes for controlling the Nile, quarrying stone for royal building enterprises.

Gold still played an important part in the Egyptian economy. Although the mines in the Eastern Desert were worked, the richest sources in the New Kingdom were found in Wawat in northern Nubia. According to the Annals of Thutmose III, gold imported from Nubia and the Sudan averaged 280,000 grams a year;[133] in the reign of Amenhotep II, 150 men were needed to carry one shipment of Nubian gold.[134] Work in the mines seems to have been carried out by prisoners of war and criminals; and the appalling conditions endured by the goldminers of the Eastern Desert were described by the geographer, Agatharchides.[135] Even the journey through the desert to the mines was difficult, as noted by Sety I:

> How miserable is a road without water! How shall travellers fare, for surely their throats will be parched and what will slake their thirst? Home is far distant and the desert is wide. Woe betide a man thirsty in the wilderness![136]

In the interest of desert travellers, and so that they might bless his name, Sety ordered the digging of a well some 60 kilometres east of Edfu in the Wadi Abbad.

Inscriptions in the temples and tombs of the New Kingdom refer to produce brought into Egypt from Crete, Cyprus, Asia Minor, Mesopotamia and Africa, unfailingly claiming that it was tribute. Because it is doubtful that Egypt was ever in a position to exact

[133] Vercoutter, 1959, p. 135.
[134] ibid.
[135] As quoted by Diodorus Siculus (iii, 12–14).
[136] Inscription of Year 9 in Wadi Abbad temple; *see JEA*, iv, p. 241ff.

tribute from most of these places, their produce must have been obtained through trade. Egypt possessed more gold than anywhere in the ancient world, so it is not surprising that gold was the chief means of payment for trade goods. Egyptian grain, papyrus, linen and leather were much sought-after commodities. Except for certain foreign manufactured goods, especially vases from Crete and metal weapons from Syria, which were readily imported into Egypt, the policy was to import as few raw materials as possible – only oils, resins and wine from Syria, oak, cedar and other coniferous woods from Asia Minor and Lebanon, copper from Cyprus and silver from the Aegean area, which were either not available in Egypt or found only in small quantities.

Trade with Africa flourished in the New Kingdom. Links with Punt (*see* page 101) by way of the Red Sea were re-established; but it was the Nile that was the main highway into Africa. Ahmose and his successors recognized the importance of Nubian raw materials to the Egyptian economy, and made the re-conquest of Nubia proper (Wawat) a priority. Thutmose I extended Egyptian control into Kush (Sudan) as far south as the Fourth Cataract, for the first time bringing Egypt into direct contact with the negro peoples of central Africa. Thus, the Egyptians had access to elephant ivory, ebony, gums, resins, ostrich plumes and eggs, leopard and panther skins, giraffes, apes, African cattle and hunting dogs, not to mention a reservoir of humans. In the Eighteenth Dynasty, in particular, large numbers of Nubians and Kushites were brought captive to Egypt, and once there, played an important part in Egyptian economic and military life as servants, soldiers and police (*see* page 126). Many seem to have achieved the status of free citizens, and one or two moved into high positions, a notable example being Mahirpre,[137] fanbearer to the king (probably Thutmose IV), who was even honoured with a tomb in the Valley of the Kings.

During the New Kingdom, there was a marked increase in the caravan trade between Egypt and the oases of the Western Desert, with large trains of pack animals plying between Siwa, Bahriya, Farafra, el-Khargah and el-Dakhla. A similar caravan trade operated between Egypt and western Asia across the Isthmus of Suez. Most of the caravans were owned by the king: for much of the New Kingdom, trade by land and by sea was a state monopoly, controlled by him or his representatives. The pack animals were

[137] Forbes, 1993.

donkeys, asses and mules; horses, which had been introduced into Egypt by the Hyksos, were employed exclusively in drawing chariots, usually for war or hunting purposes, but occasionally for inspecting the estates of rich landowners. Camels were not used in Egypt until the Graeco-Roman period. They may have been known from predynastic times, but a pottery camel found in the predynastic cemetery at Abusir el-Melek, east of the Faiyum, is unique.

In the New Kingdom, small-scale commerce within Egypt was carried out in the traditional way, either in town markets, where excess produce could be bought and sold, or between individuals. Since coinage was not invented until the seventh century BC, in Lydia in Asia Minor, a system of barter had long been in use: in the New Kingdom, in a simplified procedure. The worth of standard goods was expressed against fixed values of copper, silver, grain and gold. Values in metal were expressed as units of weight – 91 grams was one *deben*, a tenth of a *deben* (9.1 grams) was a *kite*. The use of silver as exchange was so common that the word for silver, *ḥḏ*, became almost synonymous with 'payment'. Grain was measured in *khar* (a sack containing 2 bushels), with 1 *khar* being equivalent to 2 *deben* of copper. Gold was reckoned to be twice the worth of silver, and silver 100 times more valuable than copper. Typically in the late New Kingdom, a linen tunic was valued at 5 *deben* of copper, a prime bull at 130 *deben* and a calf at 30 *deben*.[138]

Items for sale were not always bought with actual metal or grain, but could be exchanged for agreed equivalents in a variety of other commodities, usually those which the prospective purchaser happened to have available or could obtain, perhaps by means of further barter. Thus, in one Nineteenth-Dynasty transaction, a Syrian servant girl was valued at 4 *deben* and 1 *kite* of silver but purchased with 6 bronze vessels, 10 *deben* of copper, 15 linen garments, 1 shroud, 1 blanket and a pot of honey.[139] Interestingly, one-twelfth of a *deben* was represented in the form of a flat, round piece of metal which might be stamped either with its weight or with the name of the issuing authority, and was for all intents and purposes a coin.[140]

After the death of Ramesses III in 1153 BC, there was a marked

[138] Černy, 1954, pp. 908–10.
[139] Černy, 1954, p. 907
[140] Černy, 1954, p. 912–13.

decrease in temple-building, an indication perhaps that royal economic power had waned, for it was the king who initiated such projects and paid a large part of the costs. The loss of empire would account for a huge fall in revenue, but there was also a fall in the rents and taxes that were the other major economic resources available to him. Although in theory the king owned all the land in Egypt, over the years so much of it had been given away in donations to temples and individuals that, in practice, much of it was in other hands. Ramesses III, for example, flooded the coffers of Amun with '86,486 serfs, 421,362 head of cattle, 433 gardens and orchards, 691,334 acres of land, 83 ships, 46 workshops, 65 cities and towns, plus gold, silver, incense and other valuables in unmeasured amounts.'[141] In any case, the efficient collection of taxes was necessary for the smooth running of the administration, and, in the years after Ramesses III's death, there was a breakdown in local government which impaired the process. The already miserable economic situation deteriorated in the reign of Ramesses V (1147–1143 BC), when there was a smallpox epidemic; and under Ramesses VII (1136–1129 BC), there were times of famine, and grain prices were unprecedentedly high.

Economic depression in the reign of Ramesses IX (1126–1108 BC) led to an alarming increase in the pillage of royal tombs. Strenuous efforts were made to protect them, and the necropolis priests succeeded in saving the royal mummies from destruction, but only after regalia and funerary equipment had been plundered. Tomb robbers were caught and brought to trial; and records of these events have been preserved on several papyri.[142] In 1110 BC, the mayor of eastern Thebes, Paser, realized that tomb robbery was rife in the Theban necropolis. Unfortunately, it was the mayor of western Thebes, Pewere, who was responsible for the necropolis; and Paser suspected that Pewere himself was not entirely innocent. Paser managed to arrest a suspect, who made a confession, the record of which[143] gives a fascinating insight into the style of royal burials, and illustrates the fate of the mummified body once robbers had broken into a tomb:

> We searched and found the tomb of the king and the royal wife, Nub-khas. It was protected and sealed with plaster but we forced it

---

[141] Papyrus Harris; *see* ARE, IV, sect. 156ff.
[142] Peet, 1930.
[143] Papyrus Amherst and Papyrus Abbott, in the British Museum.

open. We opened their coffins and the cloth in which they were wrapped, and we found the noble mummy of the king equipped like a warrior. There were many eye-amulets and ornaments of gold at his neck and a mask of gold upon him. The noble mummy of the king was completely covered with gold and silver, inside and out, and with inlays of all kinds of precious stones.

The robbers stripped the mummies of the king and his wife of all their golden ornaments and divided the spoil among themselves.

Armed with the confession, Paser went to the vizier, Khamwese, and asked him to conduct an examination of the royal tombs. Pewere, however, seems to have had friends in high places, because the ensuing investigation of the royal necropolis concluded that all was well – except, of course, for the tomb of Nub-khas and her husband, King Sobekemsaf. Pewere then made a counter-attack on Paser, complaining that he had been interfering in affairs beyond his authority; and the necropolis workmen, in a great display of injured innocence, staged a 'spontaneous demonstration' against Paser. It was not until two years later, under a new vizier, Nebmare-nakht, that Paser was vindicated. Nebmare-nakht arrested 45 men and instituted the first of several full-scale trials. In what seems to have been the normal practice in ancient Egyptian justice, the accused were encouraged to confess by being 'examined' with a stick applied to the hands and to the soles of the feet, followed by an 'examination' with the birch and the screw. The papyri do not record the outcome of the trials; but some of the accused had sworn oaths, saying, 'If I lie, may I be mutilated and placed on the stake' or 'If I lie, may I be mutilated and sent to Nubia', perhaps the very fates they suffered.

Religion

The conquest of Syria-Palestine in the Eighteenth Dynasty introduced the Egyptians to foreign deities such as Baal, Anat and Astarte, who were quickly assimilated into the Egyptian pantheon. But in the Eighteenth Dynasty, two gods above all came to prominence. They were Amun and Aten.

Amun, whose name means 'the Hidden One', was originally a relatively unimportant god, probably to be identified as one of the eight primeval deities worshipped at a town in Middle Egypt called *Khemenu*. The name of this town was derived from the ancient Egyptian word for eight, ḫmn, and means 'the Town of the Eight Gods'; and its modern name, el-Eshmunein, is derived from the Arabic word for eight. The Greeks named the town Hermopolis after another of its deities, Thoth, the god of wisdom and scribe of the gods, whom they identified with Hermes; and referred to the eight deities as the Ogdoad of Hermopolis.

The cult of Amun was introduced into Thebes at the end of the First Intermediate Period, but, in the Eighteenth Dynasty, after the princes of Thebes had made themselves rulers of Egypt, he was elevated from local to state god, in which capacity he was syncretized with the great sun god, Re. Under the patronage of Hatshepsut and Thutmose III, who both professed great devotion to him, Amun became Amen-Re, King of the Gods. An inscription[144] in the Temple of Amun at Karnak records that, when Thutmose III was a child, the statue of Amun sought him out and led him to stand in the place in the temple normally occupied by the king, an indication that the priesthood of Amun had made the young prince their protégé, engineering a divine oracle to proclaim him the next King of Egypt. Thutmose repaid them by pouring an enormous amount of the wealth gained from the empire into the treasury of Amun; and his immediate successors did likewise.

Amun's status was lowered in the reign of Thutmose IV, who favoured the cult of the sun god, Re of Heliopolis. According to a stele[145] erected between the paws of the Great Sphinx at Giza, Thutmose once had a dream in which Re-Harakhte promised him the throne in return for clearing sand away from the Sphinx. It seems clear from this that Thutmose was not the crown prince, but gained the throne with the backing of the priesthood at Heliopolis, and was thus in its debt. Amenhotep III not only favoured Re but made a determined move against Amun by establishing another sun god, Aten (see below), as chief deity of the empire. He also took steps to reduce the influence of his current High Priest of Amun, Ptahmose, who held not only the offices of high priest and overseer of the prophets (priests) of Upper and Lower Egypt, but also the Theban vizierate, an unacceptable combination of temporal and spiritual power. The king first stripped Ptahmose of the vizierate and restricted him to religious duties, and then replaced him as high priest with an obscure official named Meryptah. The

144 ARE ii, 131–66.
145 ARE, ii, 810–15.

Plate 4.3 Stele from the Temple of Amun, Karnak, showing Thutmose III making offerings to Amen-Re, King of the Gods.

post of overseer of prophets was handed to the new vizier, Ramose.

Ramose and Meryptah were of Memphite origin. Memphis was reinstated as *de facto* capital of Egypt in the reign of Thutmose I, whose palace there, 'Per-Akheperkare' (the House of Akheperkare),[146] became in effect the seat of government. The city was prestigious and had the advantage of being cooler than Thebes in summer; but more importantly, it was a better place from which to send expeditions to western Asia. In practice, Memphis remained the capital city of Egypt thereafter, except briefly during the reign of Akhenaten, though later dynasties favoured their own home towns in the Delta as summer residences. Amenhotep II and Thutmose IV maintained close relations with Memphis, the one because he was born in the city, the other because he was brought up there. Amenhotep III found it politically expedient to favour Memphis, sending one of his sons to be high priest of its chief god, Ptah, and appointing to posts in Thebes men from Memphite families who had no loyalty to Amun.

During the reign of Akhenaten, Aten eclipsed Amun. Aten is today associated with the king who is popularly credited with having invented him, but it is probable there was a sun god called Aten at least as early as the Middle Kingdom. In the reign of Thutmose IV, he was thought of as a war god, but his aspect as sun god was stressed by Amenhotep III, one of whose epithets was *Tehen-Aten*, 'Radiance of the Aten', a term also applied to a town, a lake, the royal barge and a company of the royal bodyguard. It was, however, Amenhotep IV-Akhenaten who developed the worship of the god. In his reign, a new iconography was adopted, in which Aten was represented as a sun disc with many rays emanating from it, the rays terminating in hands, some of which hold the *ankh* signs (♀) that symbolize the giving of life.

Akhenaten's Aten was the pivotal agency of the Amarna Period, those few years of Egyptian history, less than two decades, that are a byword for religious revolution. Many modern scholars have viewed Akhenaten as a mystic, as the first monotheist in history, who bravely chose to wean the polytheistic Egyptians from their ancient deities to the worship of the one true god, Aten. Under Aten, much emphasis was placed on living according to *maat* (Truth): but today, it is generally accepted that the 'truth' of the

---

146   Akheperkare was Thutmose I's throne name.

so-called Amarna revolution is that it was of a political rather than a religious nature, promulgated to distract attention from what was happening in the empire (*see* page 112), and as a means by which to counter the power of Amun and his priesthood. It was short lived, dying even before Akhenaten himself, and Amun was quickly restored to his former pre-eminence.

The failure of Atenism was inevitable. It was a very exclusive religion, with only the king and the royal family ever being depicted worshipping Aten; only the king and the royal family ever receiving the signs of life from the hands of the god. Egyptians, as a whole, were expected to accept Akhenaten as their personal god through whom they could worship Aten. The Egyptians, however, were more at home in the worship of their own local gods, and believed that Osiris offered them the hope of eternal life. When Akhenaten swept away Osiris and the other gods, he left the Egyptians with nothing, and, by closing down all temples save those of the Aten at Amarna, he not only damaged an important part of the national economy but also removed a vital strand in their social life.

Cult temples were important to local communities. They were not, however, used as places of worship for the ordinary Egyptian. Egyptian temples were not intended to be religious centres where congregations could meet to worship or to pray; most Egyptians were never permitted to enter the innermost precincts. Certain areas of a temple were open to the public who could, and did, enter them; otherwise, the most popular form of access to a god was through 'Ear Chapels',[147] the special shrines, usually situated on the exterior walls of a temple, where the carving of an ear was the orifice into which members of the public could whisper prayers to the deity. Ordinary Egyptians also worshipped at the minor shrines they themselves set up (*see* page 149).

An Egyptian temple was regarded as the private house of a god or of a goddess. Only on great festival occasions, when the deity's statue was carried out in procession, did Egyptians have a chance to see the god in person. Temples were, however, great estate owners, renting most of the land to peasant farmers. Within the temple precincts were schools which produced scribes, doctors and artists, and offices where the services of scribes were sought by the local population, most of whom were illiterate, when they had

147   Sadek, 1988, p. 245ff.

need to draw up wills, to write legal documents, to compose letters, and even to write love poems. Physician-priests were based in the temple precincts where they offered a rudimentary health service. Akhenaten's closure of institutions which played such an important part in the economic and social life of the community must have inflicted great hardship on the Egyptians.

The ancient Egyptian terms for temple were *ḥwt ntr*, which means 'mansion of the god', or *pr*, which simply means 'house'. Because each temple was the home of a god, it is not surprising that the services enacted in it were reflections of daily life. During the morning service, the god, represented by his cult statue, was washed and dressed for the day and given his breakfast which afterwards reverted to the priests of the temple. During the evening service he was given his evening meal and prepared for 'bed' – in other words, shut up in his shrine. Only the high priest of the temple – in theory the king himself – was authorized to enter its innermost sanctuary. The temple was also regarded as a representation of Egypt, wherein it was the duty of the king, as its high priest, to ensure that offerings were made correctly so that the god of the temple would aid him in the constant struggle to defend Egypt against the forces of chaos.

Funerary beliefs and practices

The walls of the royal tombs of the New Kingdom are decorated with texts and pictures from the funerary literature of the period, with surrealistic drawings of the journey through the Underworld, and with scenes of meetings between kings and deities. The styles of decoration vary. In the Eighteenth Dynasty, line drawings were favoured, and the walls on which they appear were painted to resemble a huge, unrolled funerary papyrus. In the Nineteenth Dynasty, the preference was for bas-relief, and a technique often used in the Twentieth Dynasty was to raise into relief the background to a figure so that the figure appears to be sunk into it: both kinds were painted.

The funerary literature depicted on the walls of Eighteenth Dynasty tombs is usually the Book of *Amduat* and the Book of Gates. The *Amduat* (What is in the Underworld) shows the journey through the Underworld and is divided into 12 sections, corresponding to the hours of the night. The Book of Gates is similar, except that the hours of the night are separated from each other by gates. Both Books depict the journey of the sun through the Underworld at night, a dangerous and difficult journey that was, nevertheless, always completed successfully so that each morning the sun might rise. The dead king, whose fate was inextricably linked with that of the sun, accompanies the sun god on his journey, helping him to fend off the attacks of the evil demons who inhabit the Underworld, notably the serpent, Apophis, who attacks the sun's boat at dawn. At this point in ancient Egyptian history, the Underworld was thought to be ruled by Osiris and not Re. On his journey through the Underworld, therefore, Re was considered to be in effect dead and therefore an Osiris; and was thus equated with the dead king, also an Osiris.

In the Nineteenth and Twentieth Dynasties, the *Amduat* and the Book of Gates remained popular themes in the decoration of the royal tombs, but they were supplemented by the Book of Day and Night which shows the daily and nightly journeying of the sun, and by extracts from the Litany of Re which, as its title implies, is

Plate 4.4   The Book of the Dead prepared for the scribe, Ani (Dynasty XVIII), showing Ani and his wife, Tutu, standing by the scales in which his heart is being weighed against a feather (representing Truth). The jackal-headed god of the Underworld, Anubis, supervises the scales; the ibis-headed god of writing, Thoth, records the verdict. Only if Ani's heart does not weigh down the feather will Ani be declared 'true of voice' and admitted into the presence of Osiris, ruler of the Underworld. (Courtesy of the Trustees of the British Museum, London.)

a hymn to the sun. In the complete version of the Litany, the sun has 75 different names or forms. Some tombs of this period are decorated with the Book of Caverns, which divides the Underworld into six sections, and in which the divine scarab, the god Khephri, is depicted pushing the sun's disc in much the same way as a real scarab beetle rolls the ball of dung in which it has laid its eggs. It is the emergence of the newly hatched beetles from the seemingly lifeless dung that associated the scarab with resurrection in the minds of the ancient Egyptians. The Book of Caverns, like the Book of Gates, contains a scene devoted to the hall of judgement, in which the deceased appears before Osiris and makes what Egyptologists call 'the Negative Confession', so called because every line begins with the words 'I did not' steal, lie, and so on. The judgement of the dead forms part of the Book of the Dead (see below) also.

An essential part of the funerary equipment of a New Kingdom noble was one or more papyrus rolls containing selections from the magical and religious texts known as *The Chapters of Coming Forth by Day*. These had their origins in the Pyramid Texts of the Old Kingdom which, in the breakdown of central authority that occurred in the First Intermediate Period, had been usurped for more widespread use. Suitably adapted and enlarged for their new purpose, which was to form the basis of inscriptions on Middle Kingdom coffins, they became the Coffin Texts. In the New Kingdom, texts inscribed on coffins gave way to texts written on papyrus rolls – *The Chapters of Coming Forth by Day*, today called the Book of the Dead. Copies of the Book of the Dead were placed in the tomb to provide the deceased with the magic spells that would enable him to enjoy a happy life after death and his *Ba* (*see* page 69) to leave the tomb at will; and extracts from it appear on the walls of royal tombs also.

Mummification

Royal mummies, of the New Kingdom in particular when the art of mummifying reached its peak, have excited much wonder since their rediscovery in modern times. The techniques used in mummification are still not fully understood: there are no contemporary accounts of how the process, a strictly guarded secret, was carried out. Instead, we have to rely on the evidence of surviving mummified bodies, and on information given by Herodotus[148] and Diodorus Siculus,[149] who were writing at a very late date. In recent years, several Egyptologists, in partnership with scientists and doctors, have undertaken experiments to ascertain the validity of the classical accounts.[150]

According to Diodorus Siculus, writing in the first century BC, the Egyptians were offered three types of burial, at differing prices: the most expensive, and therefore the most effective, one talent of silver, the second 20 monoe, and the third 'very little'. Herodotus agrees that there were three methods in use. Diodorus states that the men who performed the mummification had learned their trade from their fathers, and were highly esteemed, associating with priests and being allowed into temples without hindrance. The man who made the first incision in the body, however, using an 'Ethiopian stone' (flint knife) to cut into the left side of the abdomen, was ritually chased away, clear proof that to open a human body was considered impious.

Herodotus, writing some 400 years before Diodorus, gives the fullest account of the procedures, but it is clear that he misunderstood some aspects. He says that the brain was removed from the skull by means of an iron hook, which drew most of it down through the nostrils, the rest being removed with an infusion of drugs. The use of an iron hook was unlikely, given the lack of the metal in Egypt, and the hook was probably of copper or bronze. The use of drugs to clear the skull pan is not thought to be possible, and, in any case, many mummies still contain remnants of brain within the cranium. Diodorus agrees with Herodotus that a sharp Ethiopian stone was used to make the first incision in the body, and because, at this date, knives of copper and bronze were available, flint was probably preferred for some religious reason.

The contents of the abdomen were removed. Diodorus says that the heart and kidneys were left behind. The embalmers may have left the kidneys in place because they were unable to free them from the body without damaging it, but it has been suggested by several surgeons that they may have been unaware that the kidneys were there. The heart was left in place because it was

[148]   Herodotus, II, 85–8.
[149]   Diodorus Siculus, I, 91.
[150]   David and Tapp, 1984.

considered to be the seat of life and intelligence. A term used in Ptolemaic times to mean 'heart' was *ḥry mkt.f* which translates as 'what is in its proper place', the proper place for a heart seemingly being within the body, not pickled with the rest of the internal organs for which there were four special containers, now called canopic jars because Egyptologists found the first examples at Canopus in the Delta.

The vital part of the process, one which is not really understood, came next. This was the rapid desiccation of the body. Herodotus says it was 'cured' in natron (sodium bicarbonate) for 70 days. It was once thought that Herodotus was referring to liquid natron, but current opinion is that dry natron was tightly packed around the body to extract all moisture. Seventy days was actually the maximum time allotted by religious tradition between the day of death and the day of burial, so the desiccation process must have lasted for less than this time. The body was then wrapped in layers of specially made linen bandages. Many aromatics, such as myrrh and cassia, but not, according to Herodotus, frankincense, were used in the preparation of the body, and scores of religious amulets, often made of gold, were placed on it and between the bandages. The largest amulet was a scarab, placed over the heart, and it and the other amulets became targets for tomb robbers.

For the less expensive method of mummification, Herodotus claims that oil of cedar was injected through the anus into the body cavity, and that when, after 70 days, the oil was let out, it brought the dissolved internal organs with it. Oil of cedar is not thought to have the effect he describes, however. For the cheapest method, Herodotus states that the abdomen was cleared with a 'purgative', which he does not identify. None of the methods was cheap enough for the poorer sections of society to avail themselves of them but their bodies, buried in sand, desiccated naturally.

Many mummies, especially those from the Ptolemaic and Roman eras but some from as early as the reign of Ramesses II,[151] were coated with a black substance, once thought to be a resin, blackened with time, that had been used in an inferior method of mummification. Recents studies have shown that the resin is bitumen from the Red Sea[152] and from the region of Hit-Abu Jir in

[151] Connan and Dessort, 1991.
[152] Connan and Dessort, 1989.

Iraq.[153] To import the substance into Egypt was costly, and it would seem that mummies were coated in bitumen not for cheapness but for religious reasons – black, the colour of bitumen, was also the colour of the alluvial soil of the Nile and was a symbol of rebirth. In addition, bitumen was thought to have great antiseptic and preservative properties. The most famous source of the substance in the ancient world was the 'Mummy Mountain' in Persia; and it is from the Persian word for bitumen, *mumia*, that the word 'mummy' is derived.

Domestic Life

Housing

A major source of information about housing in the New Kingdom is Akhetaten (Amarna), constructed on a virgin site, built very rapidly, inhabited for only a few years and, on the death of Akhenaten, abandoned, its walls left to crumble away and be covered by the sand which swept in from the desert, so that its remains can clearly be traced.

The central city at Amarna contained over 500 houses, their sizes varying greatly. The variety depended on the social status of an owner, with over half of the population living in small, cramped houses, another 30 per cent or so – the middle classes – occupying larger, more comfortable dwellings, and the top 10 per cent – the upper classes – living in sizeable mansions or villas. The larger houses, regardless of size, are markedly similar to one another. All reveal a rectangular ground-plan and a square living-room, around which other rooms are grouped. The houses of the more prosperous have more rooms, but each has a living-room, sleeping room(s), a kitchen and an outside staircase leading to a flat roof. Each of the larger houses, or villas, fronts on to the main street of the city and was originally surrounded by a high wall. They are single-storey buildings from 90 to 185 metres square. The main unit of the house consists of a portico, a garden-court and a main hall in the centre, and bedrooms surrounding them. There was a loggia or sitting-room on the roof. Behind the villa

[153] Connan and Deschesne, 1991.

were servants' quarters, kitchens, stables and grain silos, and in front was a garden, a pool and a private chapel.

In a fold of the hills at some distance from, and out of sight of, the main city of Amarna is the village constructed for the workers who prepared tombs in the nearby cliffs for Akhenaten and his court. The workers' houses were inferior to those in the city, as might be expected, with partition walls only one brick thick, and thin interior walls. There was very little in the way of painted walls or ceilings; and the pottery found was utilitarian. It is probable, however, that the workers of Amarna lived in houses that were typical of those of the artisans of the time, and significantly better than those of the peasants.

The village, in which there were about 80 houses, was surrounded by one wall and divided into two unequal sections by another. There were no wells, so that water had to be brought from the river, some 3 kilometres away. With the exception of one large building presumed to have belonged to an overseer, the houses were all alike in size and layout, each some 5 metres wide and 10 metres long, the ground floor divided into four sections: an entrance hall, which led to the living-room, behind which were two small rooms, a bedroom and a kitchen. The roof was flat, with a loggia of wood and matting. The door to the house worked on a pivot, and was wooden and fastened by a latch that could be worked from outside by a cord. When closed, the door could be secured on the inside by a wooden bar fixed between sockets on either door jamb. The architect seems to have overlooked the need for stairs, for no space was left for them on the outside, where staircases would normally have been placed. Instead, they were crammed into entrance halls, taking up half the area; or sometimes into kitchens, leaving no room for kitchen activities, which had perforce to be carried out behind a screen in the entrance hall.

The workers' village at Amarna was cheaply built. Although a certain amount of wood was used – for doors, for example – scarcely any stone was employed for door jambs and lintels. Recent excavations at the site by the Egypt Exploration Society have revealed that the houses were constructed of two types of brick: one, the normal kind made of Nile mud mixed, in this instance, with gravel; the other made of the marl (limestone mud or shale) found in the hills around the village. It has been suggested that, at the beginning, the village was supplied by the government with regular bricks, and possibly with a surveyor to demonstrate how to lay out the foundations of a house, but that, later, the villagers were left to complete their houses themselves, which they did with the marl that was nearer to hand than Nile mud, and with stones.

Much of our information on housing in the Nineteenth and Twentieth Dynasties is gleaned from the houses of the workmen who constructed the royal tombs at Thebes.[154] They and their families lived in isolation in a depression in the hills at the southern end of the Theban necropolis, in a village which today is called Deir el-Medina. The site was once a track in the Theban hills which, according to tradition, was chosen by Amenhotep I (1525–1504 BC) to be the place where the workers in the Theban necropolis should live. The village has one street running through its centre from north to south, originally 85 metres long and now 123 metres. It is very narrow – at times, barely a metre wide. Amenhotep I's son, Thutmose I, surrounded the 12 or so houses that existed in his time with a wall, leaving space within it for expansion, though it was not until some 250 years later that the village reached maximum capacity.

The breadth of the whole village was about 50 metres. Into this area some 70 houses were eventually crammed, most of them sharing a common partition wall; all of them either fronting the main street, or an even narrower side street. Over the years, some of the houses in the village became the property of long-established village families, and unavailable to new workers. Thus, nearly 50 houses were built outside the village wall; and in later times, the descendants of the owners of houses within the wall seem to have considered themselves superior to those whose ancestors had lived outside it.

The earliest houses at Deir el-Medina were built of mud-brick and without foundations; later buildings had cellars of stone, and the bottom courses of the house walls were also of stone, the rest being mud-brick. In all the houses, which were single storey and flat roofed, the floors were made of beaten earth. There are several large houses, such as that identified by an inscription on the column in its large living-room as belonging to 'the chief of the gang, Kaha', but the dwelling of an ordinary worker was small. The decoration and the comfort enjoyed within a house depended to a large extent on the income of its owner. A typical dwelling

---

[154] Černy, 1975.

had four compartments: a front vestibule, behind which was a living-room, which in turn led to two smaller rooms, used either as bedrooms or for storage. The ceiling of the living-room, which was higher than that of the vestibule, was supported by one or two columns; and against one wall was the typical mud-brick bench made comfortable for sitting on with cushions. The room was lit by small windows, set high in the wall and equipped with reed blinds. The walls, inside and out, were often whitewashed, and, in the houses of the more affluent, interior walls sometimes had painted frescos. The columns, and the door- and window-frames, which were made of stone or wood such as acacia, sycamore and date palm, were painted, yellow and blue being the favourite colours. Front doors were often painted red.

At the rear of the house was a walled yard with an oven, an open hearth, storage bins and an area for grinding grain. All cooking was done in this yard, from which a staircase led up to the roof. Occasionally, a staircase was placed in one of the inside rooms, taking up valuable space. Occasionally, too, a house was subdivided and rendered even smaller. Deir el-Medina has no wells, and every drop of water used by the villagers had to be fetched from the Nile, over 1.5 kilometres away. Special water carriers were employed. They used donkeys supplied to them by the workmen, and were accountable for them. Water was kept under guard in a large stone tank outside the northern gate of the village and issued in strictly rationed amounts. It was then kept in tall pottery jars at the doors of the village houses, a custom still practised by many Egyptians who have outside their houses large pots, called *zirs*, in which the water is kept cool through evaporation. If the women of the village wished to wash clothes in the traditional way, at the river bank, they had a long way to walk, though, fortunately, the workmen themselves were officially supplied with washermen.

By modern standards, the houses at Deir el-Medina were small, dark and cramped, with no gardens and little shade. By ancient Egyptian standards, however, living conditions at Deir el-Medina were good, and reflected the fact that the workmen there were skilled and highly valued craftsmen. The domestic life of the community is revealed in records written on stone and papyri, some by the villagers themselves. It is clear that they enjoyed a remarkable degree of self-government in civil and in religious affairs. The village was ruled by a tribunal (the *ḳnbt*) whose representatives were usually a foreman, a scribe and several work-men or their wives, chosen from among the village inhabitants. It settled disputes, and sat in judgement in law cases. When it found an accused person guilty, it could impose punishment, but not the death penalty, which was the preserve of the vizier only.

Judging from the number of small shrines built in the hills to the north and west of the village, the inhabitants of Deir el-Medina were pious. Many of these shrines have votive stelae, inscribed, unusually, with prayers[155] for forgiveness and penitential state-ments, which is in contrast to the Negative Confession (*see* page 142) in which nothing is admitted to! Hathor was particularly venerated; but so was Amenhotep I, together with his mother, Ahmose-Nofretari, the patron deities of the Theban necropolis and its workers. Amenhotep's shrine has not been identified, but several feasts were celebrated in his honour, notably 'the festival of the seventh month' which was called *p3 imn-ḥtp* (the (feast of) Amenhotep), from which is derived the name of the Coptic month, Baremhat. In the Nineteenth Dynasty, when Deir el-Medina reached its apogee, Sety I built temples in the religious area to the north of the village, one for Amenhotep I and another for Hathor; and Ramesses II built a temple for Amun. Several New Kingdom shrines were later covered in the Ptolemaic era by a large temple dedicated to Hathor, and the Theban triad of Amun, Mut and Khonsu, presumably the deities of the original buildings. It was the villagers themselves who acted as priests in these temples, carrying out the daily ritual. They celebrated many festivals and arranged for oracles to be consulted, an activity particularly popular at this period throughout Egypt. A consultation took place when the statue of a deity was carried in procession out of the temple in its portable shrine. Questions were submitted in writing; and were answered with a 'yes' or 'no' by movements of the statue.[156]

The workmen of Deir el-Medina were paid weekly in kind in the form of grain, vegetables, fish, and wood for fuel, supplemented with occasional rations of oil, fat and clothing. Amounts were distributed in quantities that varied according to the status of each workman: for example, the foreman received five-and-a-half *khar*[157] of emmer wheat and two *khar* of barley for making bread

---

[155] For a selection *see* Lichtheim, II, p. 104ff.
[156] Černy, 1962, pp. 44–5.
[157] 1 *khar* equals 76.56 litres.

and beer respectively; a scribe received two-and-three-quarter *khar* of emmer and one *khar* of barley; on average, the ordinary workman received four *khar* of emmer and one-and-a-half of barley. The peasants who lived in the Theban district supplied the grain through their taxes, which were paid in that commodity, while numbers of the peasants living on the plain between the Theban necropolis and the Nile were conscripted to supply the other provisions. Necropolis officials contracted a wood-cutter, who was expected to supply 500 pieces of wood each ten days; and a fisherman, who supplied 200 *deben*[158] of fish, the quantity and quality of which was strictly monitored. These supplies were distributed between groups of 30 workmen, the ratio being set as for the grain. From time to time, extra gifts came from the king – wine, imported Asiatic beer which was stronger than Egyptian beer, salt, meat, and the natron used as soap. In the Twentieth Dynasty, the workmen had on occasion to complain about the late, or non-delivery of their supplies, and, when their complaints were ignored, they went on strike, the first sit-in strike in history being staged at Medinet Habu.[159]

Palaces

In contrast to earlier periods of Egyptian history, quite well-preserved remains of several New Kingdom palaces have survived, notably three from the Eighteenth Dynasty: the palace – now called Malkata – constructed for Amenhotep III to the south of his great memorial temple on the west bank at Thebes (Luxor); and two of the five palaces built for Akhenaten at Amarna – the Great Palace and the Northern Palace where Nefertiti lived. From the Nineteenth Dynasty, we have the palace of Merenptah at Memphis, of which a fine painted throne-room has been excavated recently by the University of Philadelphia; and from the Twentieth that of Ramesses III at Medinet Habu.

As in the Middle Kingdom, royal palaces far outstripped the house of even a great nobleman, but only in size and decoration. A king could afford to decorate his house more sumptuously than a commoner; and it is clear that the queens' quarters were

---

[158] 1.82 kilograms.
[159] Edgerton, 1951.

as lavishly decorated as those of their husbands. At Amarna, the floors of several of the rooms in the palaces were painted: the pavement from the main hall in the women's quarters in the Great Palace, for example, is richly painted to represent a garden pool with fish, duck and lotuses, and shrubs round its borders. It was usual in ancient Egypt to decorate only the top or bottom of an interior wall, but in the Northern Palace at Amarna, the entire wall surface of what is now called 'the green room' was painted, the bottom of each wall to represent sparkling blue water with floating lotus pads and flowers, its middle with reeds and grasses at the water's edge, and the rest with flowering shrubs and birds.

The royal residence at Malkata seems to have been called Tehen Aten, 'Splendour of the Aten', and appears to have been designed to accommodate not only the royal family and its retainers, but also the guests from all over the then-known world who assembled at Thebes to take part in the three Sed Festivals or Jubilees celebrated by Amenhotep III. The main palace, called Per Hai, 'The House of Rejoicing', covered over 32 hectares and, sited within it, were a large temple dedicated to Amun, an audience pavilion, servants' quarters, residences for officials, women's apartments, kitchens, storerooms and three palaces, the largest of which was for the king. The royal apartments were built on an especially grand scale: the king's bedroom, for example, measured nearly 8 metres by 5, and this excludes a raised recess to house the royal bed. The floor in the great hall of the king's palace was painted to represent a pool in the marshes, and that in the palace next door a pool with plants and waterbirds. The entire ceiling of the great hall was patterned with flying vultures; that of the king's bedroom with a row of vultures inside a border of rosettes and a band of chequers. The ceilings of many rooms in the palace were painted with spirals and interweaving designs, combined with naturalistic forms such as flying birds; and dados, door-frames and borders at the tops of walls were decorated in a mixture of geometric patterns and birds.

The splendours of the palaces in which Ramesses the Great lived have largely to be left to the imagination. His principal royal residence, which was in Pi-Ramessu, the city constructed for him in the Delta, has largely disappeared. Contemporary descriptions written by court poets indicate, however, that the palace of Ramesses II was of unrivalled size and splendour, the beauty of its

decorations beyond description; and certainly the evidence of archaeological excavations, which have revealed innumerable varieties of very fine faience tilework,[160] indicates that the poets did not
exaggerate.

Perhaps the finest example of an ancient Egyptian palace is that
built for Ramesses III next to his memorial temple at Medinet
Habu. The ground plan of this palace indicates that it was similar
to the one built for Ramesses II next to the Ramesseum. Ramesses
III's palace was superimposed on an earlier building, in which
there were two distinct sections: an outer palace built against the
south wall of an inner palace, which itself abutted the south wall
of the temple. The outer palace was a row of six two-roomed
apartments; the inner palace a vestibule, a throne-room and several side-chambers. The ceiling of the throne-room, which was
square with a dais at one side for the throne, was supported by
four columns. The vestibule, abutting the south outer-wall of the
first court of the temple, was an imposing, 12-columned room, its
north wall dominated by the short flight of stairs that led to the
'Window of Appearances', at which the king appeared before his
subjects assembled in the first court. This Window of Appearances, the only complete example known (though traces of others
have been found in Eighteenth Dynasty memorial temples at
Thebes), was flanked by two doorways which were the only means
of access to the inner palace. A third door, set in the south wall of
the second court of the temple, led to a corridor which, in turn, led
to the outer palace: there does not seem to have been any direct
means of communication between the two palaces, which could
not be entered except through the first and second courts of the
temple. The awkwardness of this arrangement may be explained
by the false door behind the throne, through which the king
expected to visit the palace from the Underworld after death; and
this in its turn suggests that the earlier palace at Medinet Habu
was designed more for ritual than for living.

The later palace at Medinet Habu, the ground plan of which has
now been built up, so that visitors to the site can obtain a clear
view of it, is very different from the earlier structure, and seems
to have functioned as an official residence, albeit a small one. Its
front wall lay parallel with the south wing of the pylon (monumental gateway) of the temple, and entrance could be gained

160   Hayes, 1937; Bietak, 1975, p. 23.

through a doorway set against the pylon. This doorway led to a small reception room, beyond which was a six-columned hall where perhaps the king received visitors, though the hall lacks a throne dais. This appears instead in a two-columned room to the south which seems to have been part of the king's living quarters for, to its east, is a bedroom with a raised dais, just large enough (2 metres long by 1.15 metres wide) to accommodate a bed the size of that found in the tomb of Tutankhamun. To its west is a bathroom, or rather, a shower-room, in that its bathing arrangement consists of a square stone trough draining into a stone basin below. The six small apartments of the earlier outer palace were turned into three suites of rooms, each consisting of a small living-room and a larger bedroom with an *en-suite* bathroom and a small service chamber.

The later palace at Medinet Habu once had a second storey, but nothing of this now remains. Although built mostly of humble mud-brick, some limestone was used, and the decoration throughout was glazed tiles, some of which are displayed in the Cairo Museum. Like other, similar residences, such as the palace attached to the Ramesseum, it was not equipped with kitchens, servants' quarters, animal pens or other service areas. There was no need for them: these palaces were used infrequently, on fleeting state visits to Upper Egypt. During a visit, the king's needs, and those of his retinue, would be supplied by those responsible for the day-to-day running of the temple.

Furniture

Tomb paintings and reliefs and some actual examples found in many tombs show that the Egyptians of the New Kingdom used much the same types of furniture as their predecessors, with some modifications. Judging from the furniture in Tutankhamun's tomb, which contained a large number of different pieces, royal furniture of the period resembled that of the middle classes. Other than several thrones, the king's furniture differed only in the quality of its woodwork and the splendour of its decoration, which was often of gold leaf, coloured glass and veneers of rare woods.

Stools were still the most widely used form of seat, and even the poorer sections of society were able to afford simple three-legged versions made from offcuts of wood. They were often made with four round legs, but the most popular was the so-called lattice stool, which had four thin square legs jointed at the top and bottom into cross rails, with two vertical struts and two angled braces running between the cross rail and the seat on each of the four sides. Folding stools came into use. Folding stools, then in a simple design of two pairs of uprights, each crossed about half-way down and joined together with a bronze pivot, first appeared in the Middle Kingdom; in the New Kingdom, however, they were more elaborate, the foot ends often carved in the shape of ducks' heads, inlaid with ivory and ebony, mortised into the floor rail as if the bills were gripping it.

Chairs, owned only by the wealthy, often had straight backrests inlaid with ivory and ebony, and seats made from rush weave. Cushions were sometimes placed on their seats; and footstools used, which, in the case of the king, were decorated with figures of his enemies, so that he might symbolically trample them underfoot as he sat. Beds, also, were the preserve of the wealthy, the most novel so far discovered belonging to Tutankhamun: a folding camp-bed made of lightweight wood painted white. In design, this camp-bed is similar to an ordinary bed, but equipped with three pairs of feet, one pair at either end and the third a third of the way along from the footboard. It can be folded to a third of its length by means of heavy bronze hinges.[161]

Chests were sometimes made from sycamore, often painted, or sometimes of the more expensive cedar wood, which had to be imported from the Lebanon, or of ebony, inlaid with ivory and other materials. Most, however, were still made from cheaper materials such as wicker or plaited reeds. The lids of early chests were detached but, from the Eighteenth Dynasty on, they were equipped with hinges. Metal locks and keys were unknown before the Roman era, lids being fastened by thongs twisted around two knobs.

An example of each type of furniture in use in ancient Egypt, and now in the Museo Egizio at Turin, was originally placed in the tomb of Kha at Deir el-Medina (see page 147), excavated in 1906 by E. Sciaparelli. Kha, overseer of works during the reigns of Amenhotep II, Thutmose IV and Amenhotep III,[162] was not a poor

---

[161] Carter, 1972, p. 198.
[162] These kings reigned between 1427 and 1345 BC.

man, and had had a long time in which to amass worldly goods. The 32 pieces of furniture in his tomb consisted of small tables with reed tops, chests, a chair and stools of every kind. A hole was cut out of the seat of one stool to make a lavatory seat, under which a pan of sand would have been placed to catch the night-soil.[163] There were two beds, one for Kha, and one for his wife, Meryt, with blankets made of woven pile, proof that the night air was often cold. Linen was stored in five painted chests; and other chests housed Kha's clothes – 26 shirts, 17 tunics and 50 loin-cloths, all of them monogrammed. A toilet box contained his razor and tweezers. When found Meryt's wig rested on its stand, and her headrest was wrapped in linen, perhaps in an attempt to make it more comfortable!

Cultural Achievements

Architecture

Royal tombs

In the Old and Middle Kingdoms, royal tombs were pyramids, a tradition with which the first kings of the Eighteenth Dynasty broke for two main reasons: a change in the state god and the new capital city, Thebes. Pyramids were associated with the sun god, Re but, in the New Kingdom, Amun replaced Re as state god. Though the west bank of the Nile was still the favoured side for the burial of the dead, at Thebes there are no large plateaux, such as those at Giza and Sakkara, on which to construct pyramids of a size considered fitting. The terrain on the west bank at Thebes consists of high limestone cliffs and valleys; and the kings of the New Kingdom chose to be buried in large, rock-cut tombs hewn into the face of the cliffs. The tomb of Ahmose, founder of the Eighteenth Dynasty, is as yet undiscovered, and it is his son, Amenhotep I, worshipped after his death as one of the patron deities of the Theban necropolis, who was perhaps the first king to start the new trend.

Most of the kings of the New Kingdom were buried in a desolate valley in the limestone cliffs behind Deir el-Bahri (*see*

[163] The earliest-known lavatory seat was found in the house of Nakht at Amarna.

page 160) known as *st wrt*, 'the Great Place', today called the Valley of the Kings. In the Eighteenth Dynasty, queens were buried with them but, in subsequent dynasties, queens and some of their children were interred in a separate valley nearby – *st nfrt*, 'the Place of Beauty', now called the Valley of the Queens. The site chosen for the kings' tombs was probably selected because it is dominated by a pyramid-shaped mountain, known to the ancient Egyptians as *mrt-sgr*, 'She-who-loves-silence', and worshipped as a form of the goddess, Hathor. Over 60 tombs have been discovered to date in the Valley of the Kings, the majority of them royal although a few commoners – Mahirpre,[164] the Nubian soldier who was a companion of Amenhotep II (*see* page 132), Yuya and Thuyu (*see* page 109), and Bay (*see* page 119) – were buried in small tombs in the Valley, a signal honour. The earliest royal burial in the Valley so far identified with certainty is that of Thutmose I (1504–1492 BC).

The basic plan of a typical royal tomb of the early Eighteenth Dynasty consists of a long, descending entrance corridor cut into the rock, with a bend or a right-angled turn in it, and one or more halls, some of them large and pillared in an architectural device derived from pillar-and-stall mining technique. From the late Eighteenth Dynasty to the end of the New Kingdom, the corridors are straight, and some very long, Horemheb's extending for 105 metres. The entrance corridor leads to a burial chamber containing a sarcophagus or large rectangular coffin made of stone, the favourite material being quartzite. Sometimes, as in the case of Thutmose II and III, the burial chamber is oval in shape in imitation of the royal cartouche. From Thutmose II, the entrance corridor had a well sunk into its floor, with a twofold purpose: as deterrence to tomb robbers; and as a sump to collect water from the flash floods that occasionally cascaded from the desert over the cliff edge, causing damage to the lower parts of the tomb. Some tombs have unusual plans: that of Sety I, for example, has a seemingly normal layout of entrance corridor leading to a large chamber; but it also has a second descending corridor, opening out of the left-hand wall of the chamber, and leading steeply to the burial chamber. When Giovanni Belzoni excavated the tomb in 1817, the entrance to this corridor was hidden by a decorated false wall.

[164]   Romer, 1981, p. 171ff.; Forbes, 1993.

In the New Kingdom, at least, the construction of a royal tomb seems normally to have been planned at the beginning of a king's reign by a committee consisting of the vizier and several officials. In the case of Ramesses IV, however, it was only in the second year of his reign that the vizier Neferronpe and two royal butlers, Amenka and Hori, 'went up to the Valley of the Kings to search for a place for cutting the tomb of Usermare-setepen-Amun (Ramesses IV)'. The site once selected, a plan was drawn up showing the design and measurements of the proposed tomb: the plan of Ramesses IV's tomb was drawn on a papyrus, now in the Turin Museum;[165] that of Ramesses IX was drawn on an ostracon, now in the Cairo Museum.[166] Presumably the king then had to give his approval so that work could commence. An inscription in the tomb of Ineni, in which he claimed that he had supervised the construction of the tomb of Thutmose I, 'no one seeing, no one hearing', once led to the assumption that a royal tomb was prepared by slaves who, once the project had been completed, were put to death, so that its whereabouts remained secret in extravagant waste of skilled labour. Evidence from Deir el-Medina gives the lie to this belief, however, proving that, far from being slaves, the men who built the royal tombs were skilled and valued craftsmen, who not only enjoyed a privileged lifestyle by ancient Egyptian standards but were well able to express discontent when they felt like it (*see* page 150).

The workmen of Deir el-Medina normally numbered 60, but were doubled by Ramesses IV presumably to make up for lost time (*see* above). The men formed a gang, divided into two halves, 'right side' and 'left side', the men on the right side working only on the right half of the tomb, those on the left side on the left half. Only rarely did a man change from one side to the other. The number of men in each side was not always equal, an indication that, if a man took time off, sick perhaps, there was no replacement for him. Each side was under the control of a foreman and his deputy. Many of the posts held by workmen were passed from father to son, and some can be traced through several generations: the post of scribe, for example, is known to have been held by members of one family for six generations, spanning nearly the whole of the Twentieth Dynasty.

165   Carter and Gardiner, 1917.
166   Daressy, 1901.

The initial cutting of the tomb out of the rock was performed by a few men only, due to lack of space. The work was comparatively easy because the limestone was soft, although the rock-cutters would occasionally encounter a seam of hard flint, and the cutting of a tomb seems never to have taken more than two years. During this work, the rest of the gang removed the rubble and carried it away from the site in baskets. Scribes noted the number of baskets carried away as a means of keeping a check on the rate of work, and from time to time measured progress on the tomb with a cubit-rod.

After a tomb was cut, its walls were smoothed and overlaid where necessary with plaster. They were then ready for decoration, which consisted largely of excerpts from funerary literature (*see* page 140), the king presumably choosing which excerpts should be used. Initially, draughtsmen outlined figures on the flat wall surface in red, correcting them in black. Sculptors then carved the reliefs with chisels, and finally the reliefs were coloured with paint supplied from the royal storehouse, a magazine situated in the Valley. Decorating a tomb took far longer than cutting it and, in some cases, it was unfinished at a king's death. Work on the tombs continued all year round and, once the workmen had finished a king's tomb, they moved on to his queen's, and occasionally to that of a favoured nobleman.

There was a nine-day working week; and in every month of thirty days, the tenth, twentieth and thirtieth were rest days. During the working week, the workmen lived in huts in the Valley of the Kings but, at 'weekends' they returned to their village. They also had time off for festivals. The work day seems to have been about eight hours long, with a break in the middle for rest and food. A scribe kept a record of the names of workmen as they reported for duty, noting the absentees and their excuses. They also recorded progress, and kept a note of tools issued to the workmen. These tools, mostly chisels and adzes, were made of copper, a soft metal which becomes work-hardened during use, making a well-used implement the more valuable. Thus, as each workman was issued with a copper tool, his name was recorded on a stone replica that was stored in its place. Accountability for the copper tools was strict. When the tomb was deep enough for artificial light to be needed, lamps were issued. These lamps were made of bowls of baked clay filled with vegetable oil into which a pinch of salt had been sprinkled to prevent the oil smoking, with wicks made from linen rags. The wicks were issued from the royal storehouse, and a careful record was made of the number used (between four and 40 daily). The vizier paid frequent visits to the work site, to check progress and to receive complaints.

Private tombs

The workmen of Deir el-Medina cut very fine tombs for themselves in the steep hill on the western side of the village. Each tomb, though quite small, generally consists of a burial chamber and an upper chapel, the walls of which are covered with brightly coloured paintings. The painted mummy cases, coffins and items of funerary furniture placed in the tombs were of the highest quality.

The New Kingdom officials whose working lives were concerned with Upper Egypt and Nubia, and the priests who officiated in the precinct of Amun at Thebes, naturally chose to be buried in the Theban necropolis on the west bank at Luxor. Thebes was only the religious capital of Egypt, however, the administrative capital being Memphis, and many high officials chose to be buried in the Memphite necropolis at Sakkara. The New Kingdom and Late Period cemeteries at Sakkara have until recently been neglected, but now several splendid examples of New Kingdom private tombs have been uncovered.[167] The walls of their stone-built chapels are decorated with reliefs of the finest quality; and many a Ramesside tomb boasts a small brick pyramid on its roof. A miniature pyramid on top of a tomb chapel was also a feature at Deir el-Medina.

The Theban private tombs, like those of the kings, are rock-cut, but much smaller than those of the royal masters, though the quality of the reliefs on the walls of many is unsurpassed. The style of decoration and architecture varies according to dynasty. The main architectural difference is the size of the tomb and the shape of its halls. Early Eighteenth Dynasty tombs are small, the size being larger in the reign of Amenhotep III. In the late Nineteenth and Twentieth Dynasties, tombs once again became small. The chapels, lying above the burial chambers, are usually T-shaped, with narrow halls, though that of Ramose,[168] the vizier under

---

[167]   Martin, 1991.
[168]   No. 55.

Amenhoteps III and IV, for example, has a large front hall which had originally 32, non-functional, pillars. A burial chamber, normally reached by way of a shaft in the floor, contained the mummified bodies not only of the deceased owner but also of members of his family, each in one or more coffins: the outer coffin might be a wooden rectangular box, highly decorated with magical texts and funerary deities; the inner coffin mummiform, hence sometimes called a mummy-case.

For the decoration of private tombs, the subject matter of reliefs falls into two main categories: the private and public life of the tomb owner, and his death and afterlife. Scenes depicting the Afterlife do not appear in Eighteenth Dynasty tombs except, rarely, on the walls of the burial chamber, and burial chambers are more often undecorated. Scenes showing the funeral procession and related rites prevail throughout the New Kingdom; and scenes of daily life appear on the walls of Eighteenth Dynasty tombs, but, from the reign of Amenhotep III, grow fewer, replaced by scenes of the Afterlife; and by the reign of Ramesses II, such scenes have almost disappeared.

Temples

Memorial temples

The narrowness of the Valley of the Kings prohibited the building of memorial temples, which had to be constructed on the plain between the Valley and the Nile. Thus, for the first time, royal tombs were separated from their memorial temples, though, in theory, each tomb in the Valley of the Kings required such a temple. The purpose of these temples did not alter: they were places in which offerings were made to the dead king. In the New Kingdom, however, several of them were given new purpose and became administrative centres: palaces were built within their precincts (*see* page 152).

The most outstanding of the Eighteenth Dynasty memorial temples extant was built for Hatshepsut at Deir el-Bahri. It was called Djeser-djeseru (Holiest of Holy Places), and Senenmut (*see* page 129), perhaps inspired by the architecture of the nearby memorial temple of Mentuhotep II, is thought to have supervised its construction. Djeser-djeseru is built in limestone in a series of

Plate 4.5 Deir el-Bahri, mortuary temple of Hatshepsut (1479–1457 BC).

terraces and colonnades set against a backdrop of cliffs. The flat roofs of the terraces echo the horizontal lines of the limestone beds of the cliffs above, and the vertical lines of the columns, some of which are fluted, reflect the fissures in the rock behind the temple, making it a building married perfectly to its site. Reliefs depicting important themes from Hatshepsut's life decorate walls in the colonnades: her birth, the transportation of obelisks for the Temple of Amun in Thebes, the great expedition to Punt.

Hatshepsut claimed that even though her mother was the queen of her earthly father, Thutmose I, she, Hatshepsut, was the divine child of the god, Amun, by theogamy justifying her claim to the throne. She marked her divine birth by recording it in reliefs in her memorial temple. To demonstrate her devotion to Amun, she sent Senenmut to Aswan to quarry a pair of red granite obelisks, each over 28 metres high, for the Temple of Amun. A relief at Deir el-Bahri shows that they were brought to Thebes strapped end to end on a huge sledge, which was in turn strapped to an enormous barge, made of sycamore and estimated to have been over 92 metres long with a beam of 30 metres. The barge was towed by 27 ships in three columns, each ship rowed by 32 oarsmen. In the fifteenth year of her reign, Hatshepsut commissioned another pair of obelisks. This time, the steward, Amenhotep, was in charge of the expedition: he completed his task in seven months; and one of the obelisks, 30 metres high, still stands in the Temple of Amun. The expedition to Punt obtained, among other things, 31 incense trees (*Boswellia*) which were transported back to Egypt with their roots planted in baskets, so that they might be planted in the 'garden' (the courtyard) of Hatshepsut's memorial temple.

The design of Deir el-Bahri is unique. The standard design of a New Kingdom memorial temple was based on a rectangular ground plan, with a monumental gateway (pylon) opening into a courtyard, beyond which was a columned hall (hypostyle) leading to a sanctuary surrounded by antechambers and subsidiary rooms. Larger temples had more than one courtyard and pylon. The largest memorial temple ever built belonged to Amenhotep III. Made from 'fine white limestone, wrought with gold throughout', it was embellished with granite statues of the king, 18 of which still survive. Sadly, the temple was used as a quarry in the late New Kingdom and little of it survives. Reliefs showing the divine birth

Plate 4.6   The Ramesseum, mortuary temple of Ramesses II (1279–1213 BC), Luxor. Note fallen granite colossus of Ramesses II on far right.

of a king seem to have been standard in New Kingdom memorial temples, but Amenhotep III recorded his divine birth in Luxor Temple.

The finest example of a memorial temple from the Nineteenth Dynasty is that of Ramesses II, known today as the Ramesseum. Misidentified by Diodorus as 'the tomb of Ozymandyas' (*see* page 171), it was in fact a combination of temple, palace and storage place. The earliest temple on the site was built for Ramesses' mother, Mut-Tuiy, who was not a royal princess but the daughter of a Lieutenant of Chariotry named Raia. Reliefs in the temple of Ramesses depict his divine birth as the son of Amun and Mut-Tuiy; many others depict, inevitably, the Battle of Kadesh. To its rear is a large complex of administrative buildings, priests' houses and vaulted storage magazines which, unlike the temple, are built of mud-brick, and are perhaps the finest surviving examples of their type. A papyrus thought to be the text of a play celebrated for the Jubilee or Heb-Sed of Senwosret I (1943–1898 BC) was found in this area in AD 1895. Because this papyrus, known today as the Ramesseum Dramatic Papyrus,[169] dates to the Middle Kingdom, it may indicate that the temple had a library.

Memorial temples were built for Sety I and his son, Ramesses II, at places other than Thebes. A memorial temple was built for each of them at Abydos which, because of its association with Osiris, was one of the most sacred sites in Egypt. Sety's temple, which was the greatest architectural achievement of his reign, is unusual in two ways: it is L-shaped; and was dedicated to seven deities – Osiris, Isis, Horus, Amun, Ptah, Re-Harakhte, and Sety I himself. The standard of workmanship in Sety's time makes Abydos perhaps the most beautiful of all Egyptian temples. Its walls are decorated with reliefs, of a quality matched only by those in Sety's tomb, which is itself the finest in the Valley of the Kings. In his ten-year reign, Sety commissioned the building of several important monuments, all of them, Abydos included, unfinished at his death and completed in the reign of his son. A temple was built at Abydos for Ramesses himself, but perhaps his most famous memorial temple is at Abu Simbel (*see* page 171) in Nubia, where two imposing shrines were cut into a cliff face, one for the king, the other for his wife, Nefertiri.

The last great memorial temple of pharaonic Egypt was built for

---

[169] Helck, 1954; Fairman, 1974, p. 5ff.

Plate 4.7   Abydos, façade of the mortuary temple of Sety I (1294–
          1279 BC).

Ramesses III. The temple, *Khnemt-neheh* (United with Eternity), is
impressively large but conforms to the standard pattern, and was
built in conscious imitation of the nearby Ramesseum. Constructed of sandstone, it consists of a massive pylon, behind which
are two colonnaded courts leading to an inner sanctuary with
numerous side chambers and chapels. Reliefs on the exterior walls
show Ramesses' battles against the Sea Peoples (*see* page 120). The
martial theme is repeated in reliefs on the interior walls of the
courts, together with scenes recording the great festivals celebrated
in the temple.

The precinct is surrounded by a thick mud-brick wall over 18
metres high. Its main entrance, which is on the east side and was
approached by a canal leading from the Nile, is highly unusual,
being a copy of a Syrian *migdol* or fortified entrance gate. Within
the enclosure wall lie not only two contemporary palaces (*see* page
152) but also the greater part of an early Eighteenth Dynasty
temple dedicated to Amun of *Khemenu* (*see* page 135), and several
small chapels built between the eighth and sixth centuries BC by
the Divine Wives of Amun (*see* page 183). 'United with Eternity'
was more than a temple: it became the administrative centre for

Plate 4.8 Medinet Habu, mortuary temple of Ramesses III (1184–1153 BC): dais in the palace built against the south wall of the temple.

the whole Theban necropolis, and, according to the Harris Papyrus, in its heyday was served by 62,626 serfs. Within the circle of its great mud-brick enclosure wall were administrative buildings (from which, not only the temple, but also its far-flung estates were managed) staff houses, storerooms and workshops in which cult objects for use in the temple were made.

In the last years of the Ramesside era, bands of marauding Libyans roamed the Theban countryside, often forcing the local population to seek refuge within the massive walls of 'United with Eternity', which, in the civil war that raged at the end of the twelfth century BC, was attacked and captured. The cult of Ramesses III did not long outlast him, but the temple of Amun (*see* above) continued in use until the Graeco-Roman period, when it was enlarged. In the early Christian era, local Christians built their houses within the temple precinct, which became the town of Djeme, and erected their church in the second court of Ramesses III's temple. Then, in the ninth century AD, for reasons unknown, Djeme was abandoned. Medinet Habu is the Arabic name for the site, and Habu may be a corruption of the Coptic (*see* page 252) word meaning 'father', a reference to the Christian monks who once had their cells there. Medinet Habu may therefore be translated as the town (*medinet*) of the (Coptic) fathers.

Cult temples

Until the New Kingdom, cult temples were constructed of stone and mud-brick: but growing prosperity and the important part temples played in the economic life of Egypt meant that, from the early Eighteenth Dynasty, the older structures were demolished and replaced with more imposing edifices built entirely of stone. At Thebes, the religious capital of Egypt, temples for Amun and other deities were constructed largely of sandstone originating in the quarries at Gebel Silsilah, some 120 kilometres to the south. Amun's earliest temple at Thebes was a mud-brick Middle Kingdom shrine, but, in the Eighteenth Dynasty, it was rebuilt in sandstone. Over the centuries, from the New Kingdom to the Roman period, the great Temple of Amun was continually enlarged and embellished so that, in time, it, with its associated shrines, formed the largest sacred precinct in the world, containing over 20 temples and other religious buildings. The Egyptians called it *Ipet-swt* ('The Most Select of Places'); today, it is usually referred to as Karnak.

The main body of the Temple of Amun runs from west to east, with the innermost sanctuary on the eastern side. It is approached from the west through a series of six monumental gateways (pylons), before several of which are pairs of obelisks, those of Hatshepsut (*see* page 161) placed between the fourth and the fifth. The construction of the Hypostyle Hall, the splendid columned hall for which Karnak is justly famous, was begun in the reign of Sety I, when 122 sandstone columns, each 15 metres high, were arranged in rows on either side of a huge colonnade of 12 columns. Each column in this colonnade is 22 metres high, its circumference nearly 10 metres, its capital shaped like an open papyrus umbel. In contrast, the capitals of the surrounding columns represent lotus buds. Both types arise from the Egyptian custom of basing architectural patterns in stone on ancient vegetable prototypes. The Egyptians did not use a keystone in their stone buildings, hence they never used a stone arch. Each column in the Hypostyle Hall, therefore, is set at a critical distance from its neighbour, close enough to allow the stone slabs of the roof to be laid on top without cracking under their own weight. The Hall,

Plate 4.9   Temple of Amun, Karnak: forecourt and hypostyle hall.

102 metres wide and 53 metres long, is surrounded by a wall, and, in its original state, would have been in darkness, had not the planned difference in height between the central columns and those on either side allowed for the insertion of clerestory window gratings along the length of the central nave.

Luxor Temple, built in the reign of Amenhotep III, was dedicated to Amun manifested as the fertility god, Min. Called *Ipet-reset* ('The Private Apartments of the South'), it was linked to the Temple of Amun at Karnak, some 3 kilometres to the north, by an avenue of sphinxes. The great colonnade joining the older part of the temple with the courtyard constructed for Ramesses II was decorated, in the reign of Tutankhamun, with magnificent reliefs, and usurped by Horemheb and Sety I. But it is the courtyard of Amenhotep III, with its three double colonnades of columns, each graced with a capital in the shape of an unopened papyrus umbel, that is perhaps the most elegant of all the courtyards in Egypt.

Sculpture and relief

At the very beginning of the New Kingdom, there was an attempt to return to past sculptural styles, but, early in the Eighteenth

Plate 4.10 Luxor Temple, Courtyard of Amenhotep III (1383–1345 BC).

Dynasty, an individual style was achieved. Royal statuary of the period shows stylistic affinities with that of the Middle Kingdom, but it also has a new openness and vitality, even charm. Some of the best extant examples are statues of Thutmose III and Hatshepsut who is usually depicted in male attire. Unlike Old Kingdom statues which emphasize the divine nature of kings, and those of the Middle Kingdom which depict their serious and meditative qualities, statues of Thutmose III emphasize his determination and vitality. From this time on, kings are presented in a pleasant, often smiling, mood, none more so than Amenhotep III, whose reign was the golden age of New Kingdom sculpture and whose statues maintain the trend towards natural and human portraiture.

Naturalism reached its peak in the Amarna style of the reign of Amenhotep IV/Akhenaten. The religious doctrines of the time laid emphasis on Maat or Truth which brought perhaps the only attempt at realism in the history of official art in ancient Egypt. Personalities were no longer depicted in an idealized way but with all their physical imperfections ruthlessly exposed, particularly so with the king himself, who is unflatteringly depicted with a prognathous chin and a flabby body. It is possible that his statues, showing him with feminine hips and heavy belly, may not represent his actual looks but, for religious reasons, his wish to be seen as the female half of the Aten.

The distinctive Amarna art style is seen to greatest effect in the tombs of the nobles buried there. The theme of reliefs is not, as was usual elsewhere, the everyday life of the tomb owner. Instead, they show the royal family out and about on official duties, tomb owner in attendance, his figure in flattering imitation of the deformities of the king. At first glance, the Amarna style seems to be original in the realism and naturalness with which these activities are portrayed, but all the old Egyptian principles and conventions of art remain, notably the use of the canon of proportion and the convention that the most important person in any group should be depicted on the largest scale.

Amenhotep III did not observe the convention that statues should be placed out of sight inside temples and tombs. In his reign, many were intended to be seen, as memorials to the ruler and to impress the population. To this end, some were allied to architecture. The 'architectural statue', which could be impres-

Plate 4.11   Relief from the tomb of the Eighteenth-Dynasty vizier, Ramose: No. 55 at Sheikh 'Abd el-Qurna, Luxor.

Plate 4.12   Akhenaten (?1353–1337 BC): head of painted sandstone colossus from the destroyed Temple of Aten at Karnak. (Cairo Museum; photograph David Couling.)

sively large, was designed to stand before pylons or between columns in temple courtyards. The entrance to Amenhotep III's memorial temple, for example, was flanked by two sandstone seated statues of the king, each some 18 metres high, which are known today as the 'Colossi of Memnon'.

After the upheaval of the Amarna age, the Nineteenth Dynasty needed to reassert the idea of a sacrosanct monarchy. Thus, statues of Ramesses II, in particular one, now in the Turin Museum, large black granite seated statue of him wearing a finely pleated shirt and kilt, demonstrate the ideal of the majesty of power. In the reign of Ramesses II, the architectural statue reached unprecedented degrees of size and magnificence. Colossi of the king were placed before Pi-Ramessu's major temple; and huge, seated, sandstone statues of Ramesses were positioned in front of the pylon of Luxor Temple and at the western end of its great colonnade.

Such statues were often the focus of statue cults for the common people.[170] At Luxor, the large standing statues of Ramesses, which were placed between columns in the outer courtyard, still give the impression that they are ready to stride out from the shadows into the light. Many statues of Ramesses were erected in the Ramesseum, but the granite colossus that now lies in pieces in the first two courtyards was the largest statue in Egypt. Measuring 7 metres from shoulder to shoulder, it is estimated to have been at least 17 metres high, and to have weighed 1000 tonnes; it is said to have been the inspiration for Shelley's poem, *Ozymandias*. Although a high degree of craftsmanship is shown in the bold proportions of monumental sculpture, the little attention that was paid to detail leaves an impression of crudity. Reservations are overcome, however, at Abu Simbel, where the two pairs of colossi of Ramesses II that flank the entrance more than hold their own against the grandeur of the temple's setting.

Literature

Many works of the imagination were written in the New Kingdom.[171] They often refer to foreign places and people, a reflection

---

[170] Habachi, 1969.
[171] For translations of all the works mentioned below *see* Lichtheim, 1976.

of the less insular and more cosmopolitan outlook of the Egyptians of the period. Their language was the vernacular of the time and, where a story demands it, could be coarse. Mythological and religious tales, such as *The Contendings of Horus and Seth*, *The Tale of the Two Brothers* and *The Blinding of Truth by Falsehood*, were popular. The first is a robustly humorous account of the struggle between Seth and Horus for the throne of Egypt, which had belonged to Horus' murdered father, Osiris; the last two are allegories of the struggle. *Seqenenre and Apophis* and *The Capture of Joppa* are lively accounts of historical events, and so is *The Report of Wenamun*, which may or may not be the account of an actual mission to Byblos but certainly depicts a period in the reign of Ramesses XI when he was about to yield power to Herihor in the south and Smendes in the north (*see* page 125).

Just as *The Story of Sinuhe* was the masterpiece of Middle Kingdom literature, so *Wenamun* is its New Kingdom equivalent. The use of language is subtle: for the meeting between Wenamun and the prince of Byblos, the author shows himself to be in command of irony, giving the account great appeal to modern readers. *The Story of the Doomed Prince*, a fairy-tale, also appeals to modern tastes, if only because the prince gains access to his princess, imprisoned in a tower in the manner of Rapunzel, by climbing up the hair she has let down to him; and her threats to her father when he does not agree with her plans are reminiscent of Violet Elizabeth Bott's threats to 'thcream' until she is sick, in the Richmal Crompton 'William' books.

A popular literary genre in the New Kingdom was the Instruction, which could take the form of advice on behaviour – the Instruction of Any, for example; or model letters for schoolboys to copy. Such letters are a form of brainwashing, with exhortations to become scribes and not to be seduced by the seemingly more exciting or rewarding life of the soldier or farmer. Perhaps even more popular were the love poems, written by scribes for illiterate clients, but no less effective for that. There are many, but one I have translated from the Cairo Vase[172] will have to suffice here:

> My mind turned to my love for you
> When my hair was only half plaited.

[172]   Posener, 1972, pp. 43–4.

I came running to find you
Forgetting about dressing my hair; but
If you will let me go,
I will finish doing my hair
And be ready in a minute!

5

The Last Pharaohs

History

Because of the autonomy gained by the high priests, Thebes was lost as a capital city, and the first king of the Twenty-first Dynasty, Smendes I (1070/69–1043 BC), was forced to establish his capital elsewhere. He chose a site in the Delta, using buildings in Ramesses II's city, *Pi-Ramessu*, as a quarry for the construction of temples and palaces in his new city, Tanis. Relations between Thebes and the North remained amicable because, after all, the two lines of rulers were branches of the same family; and they were fostered by marriage, the High Priest of Amun, Pinudjem (1070–1032 BC), marrying Henttawy, a daughter of Ramesses XI. Two of their sons succeeded him as high priest, and another, Psusennes I, became the third king of the Twenty-first Dynasty in Tanis.

Pinudjem took it upon himself to take care of the royal mummies in the Valley of the Kings, having his efforts recorded on their coffins and mummy wrappings. In his sixth and seventh years as High Priest of Amun, he had Thutmose II and Amenhotep I reinterred; in his ninth and tenth years, the mummies of Ramesses III and Sety I were re-wrapped in linen; in his thirteenth, Ramesses III, and in his seventeenth, Ramesses II, were reburied. It is possible that by this time some recycling of wealth had been imposed, on official orders, to replenish the exchequer; nevertheless, such items of funerary equipment as were left, together with the royal mummies, were transferred for safekeeping to the tombs of Amenhotep II in the Valley of the Kings and of Queen Inhapy at Deir el-Bahri, where they remained undisturbed until the nineteenth century AD (*see* page 298).

The kings of the Twenty-first Dynasty maintained normal trading relations with the Levant, and were on friendly terms with the Kingdom of Israel, though when King David seized Edom,[173] its young prince, Hadad, was given asylum in Egypt. The Edomite prince later married the sister-in-law of the Egyptian pharaoh, and it was probably this king, Siamun (978–959 BC), who sent a daughter to be one of Solomon's wives.[174] After Solomon's death, Jeroboam, a pretender to his throne, sought sanctuary in Egypt[175] with a pharaoh whom the Bible names Shishak, a version of the Libyan name Sheshonq.

Throughout the Twenty-first Dynasty, Libyans had been settling in Egypt, some of them very successfully. One, Sheshonq, became so Egyptianized that when his father, Nemrat, died, he had him buried in the Egyptian way, at Abydos, where an inscription[176] records that Sheshonq, the 'great chief of [the Libyan clan] the Meshwesh', had sought permission from the king, Psusennes II (959–945 BC), to do so. Chief Sheshonq's power-base was *Pi-Bast*, 'The House of Bast', known to the Greeks as Bubastis, modern Zagazig, the cult centre of the great cat goddess, Bast (sometimes called Bastet). It was a strategically important town in the eastern Delta, controlling the routes through the Delta from Memphis to Sinai. From *Pi-Bast*, Sheshonq's family forged links with Dynasty XXI, so that Sheshonq became the king's son-in-law, and when, in 945 BC, Psusennes II died, Sheshonq succeeded him as King Sheshonq I (945–924 BC) of the Twenty-second Dynasty. Although Memphis and Tanis continued to be the administrative and political capitals of Egypt, Sheshonq I began to develop his home town, *Pi-Bast* , paying particular attention to the Temple of Bastet.

Sheshonq I was to be succeeded by his son Osorkon I (924–889 BC), but several of his other sons were assigned to such positions as would benefit the regime, the most astute move being to install Iuput as High Priest of Amun at Karnak, an appointment that flattered the Thebans and brought this all-important office under the influence of the king. Sheshonq then tried to curb the power of the high priesthood with a decree that high priests should not be

173 I Kings, xi, 14–22.
174 I Kings, iii, 1.
175 I Kings, xi, 40.
176 *JEA*, xxvii, 83ff.

succeeded by their own sons. No major building work had been undertaken on the Temple of Amun at Karnak after the Nineteenth Dynasty, and Sheshonq favoured it with his attention by commissioning the building of an outer court on the monumental gateway to which Amun is shown presiding over the ceremonial slaughter of the enemies that 'Shishak, king of Egypt'[177] captured during his raid on Palestine. The gateway is known today as the Bubastite Portal.

By the reign of the fifth king of the dynasty, Osorkon II (874–850 BC), the internal stability of the administration was weakening. At Thebes, High Priest Harsiese was succeeded by his son, in contravention of Sheshonq I's decree. Accordingly, on the death of this son, King Osorkon stepped in and appointed his own son, Nimrat, as High Priest, thus reasserting the royal prerogative. Henceforward there was tension between the king and Thebes, which was exacerbated when Takeloth II (850–825 BC) attempted to carry out dynastic policy by appointing his son, crown prince Osorkon, as High Priest of Amun. Prince Osorkon, an army commander and the governor of the south, resided in el-Hiba and visited Thebes only for festivals. Opposition in Thebes to the Bubastite administration became so bitter that, in 836 BC, civil war broke out. The war lasted for ten years, until Prince Osorkon effected a short-lived peace. A year later, Takeloth II died and was buried at Tanis, to be succeeded, not by Osorkon but by Sheshonq III (825–773 BC), his brother. The reason for this is unknown, but it is possible that problems in Thebes so detained Osorkon that Sheshonq buried Takeloth and was thus able to claim the throne (*see* page 123).

Sheshonq III had not reigned for long before a rival claimant to the throne appeared – Pedubast. By the eighth year of Sheshonq's reign, Pedubast had founded a new dynasty, the Twenty-third, based at Leontopolis. The two dynasties ran concurrently, and were recognized as legitimate throughout much of Lower Egypt, though the princes of Herakleopolis and Hermopolis ruled independently. Thus, from 818 BC, authority in Egypt was fragmented, with four rulers, all derived from one original Libyan dynasty, claiming to be kings. The real power in the land, however, was Tefnakhte, prince of Sais in the Delta, the founder of yet another Libyan dynasty, the Twenty-fourth. He began to expand south-

177   I Kings, xiv, 25–6.

wards, capturing Memphis and moving into Upper Egypt. At this stage, Egypt was ripe for intervention; and intervention duly came, but from an unexpected source – Kush (Nubia).

Kush, to the Egyptians long the source of men and materials, had become an independent kingdom, albeit one whose culture had been influenced by Egypt. The Kushites worshipped Amun, and their king, Piankhi, regarded himself as protector of the Thebaid. He saw Tefnakhte as a threat to Thebes, and so, in 728 BC, he marched into Egypt. For over 30 years, Thebes had been ruled by daughters of the ruling royal house, each one holding the position of 'Divine Wife of Amun' (*see* page 183). Piankhi installed his sister, Amenirdis, as Divine Wife Apparent, and then went on to conquer the whole of Egypt. He chose not to stay in Egypt, however, but was content to rule Kush from his capital at Napata, recognized by Thebes as an absent ruler. After his death, his brother Shabaka (716–702 BC) became king, resident in Egypt and true founder of the Twenty-fifth, Kushite, Dynasty.

During Shabaka's reign, Egypt was caught up by events in the Near East. In 712 BC, Sargon II of Assyria attacked Ashdod, whose ruler, Iamani, fled to Egypt. Unfortunately for him, however, Shabaka's policy towards Assyria was one of politeness and respect, and Iamani was duly returned to the Assyrians. Shabaka's successor, his nephew Shabitku (702–690 BC), reversed his uncle's policy so that, when Sennacherib of Assyria invaded Palestine in 701 BC to put down Hezakiah of Juda, he despatched Egyptian troops under the command of his uncle, Taharqa, to reinforce Hezakiah. They were trounced at Altaqa.

Taharqa became king in succession to Shabitku. During his reign, which lasted for 24 years, he initiated a substantial building programme. Karnak received particular attention, but a large cliff temple was erected for him at Napata in Nubia, near his tomb, which, like those of the other Kushite kings, was in the form of a small, brick-built pyramid. At this time, Egypt must have been fairly united and prosperous, but the Assyrians were an ever-present threat and, in 674 BC, led by King Esarhaddon, they attacked and reached 'the river of Egypt', where they were driven back. Three years later, they attacked again and this time Taharqa was routed. The Assyrians occupied the Delta, and set up a puppet ruler, Prince Necho of Sais.

When Taharqa died in 664 BC, he was succeeded by Tantamani (664–656 BC) who claimed that, while he was still in Napata, he was promised the throne of Egypt in a dream. And so he marched north to claim his prize, killing the Assyrian puppet, Necho. The Assyrians, led by their new king, Assurbanipal (*c.*669–627 BC), came back, marching unhindered through Egypt until, in 663 BC, they reached Thebes and sacked the city. Tantamani fled back to Nubia, and the Assyrians installed Necho's son, Psammeticus, as king of Egypt (664–610 BC).

For the first eight years of the Twenty-sixth Dynasty, Psammeticus I accepted Assyrian control, as did other princes in the Delta and Middle Egypt, although Thebes remained loyal to the Kushites. In 656 BC, however, Psammeticus I opened negotiations with Thebes, sealing an alliance by sending his daughter, Nitocris, to be adopted as the next Divine Wife of Amun. A year later, Psammeticus made a treaty with Gyges of Lydia, and declared Egypt independent of Assyria. By this time, Assyria was struggling to keep her empire together, and in no position to challenge Psammeticus. He, however, adopted a conciliatory policy towards Assyria and was even prepared to become her ally against Nabupolassar, the King of Babylon. In 614 BC, Assur fell to the Medes and, two years later, Nineveh was conquered by a coalition of Medes and Babylonians. Assyria, reduced to a small kingdom, vanishes from history after 608 BC.

The Twenty-sixth Dynasty, known as the Saite Period, had begun inauspiciously with Egypt vassal of the Assyrians. Once the Egyptians had succeeded in ridding themselves of their Assyrian overlords, however, there was a revival in national pride and a renaissance in cultural life. Throughout Egyptian history, the underlying desire was for stability, and it was this that allowed the Saite kings to re-establish a centralized government. In what was to be the last great age of pharaonic civilization, inspiration was sought from the earliest periods of Egyptian history. Spells from Old Kingdom Pyramid Texts were copied on the walls of Saite tombs, some of them exact copies of Old Kingdom *mastabas*. Every religious, artistic and architectural device of the Old Kingdom was passionately copied; old forms of hieroglyphic writing and the style of Middle Kingdom literary works were imitated.

During the reign of Necho II (610–595 BC), Egypt and Babylon were rival claimants to Syria. In 605 BC, Nabupolassar of Babylon sent Crown Prince Nebuchadnezzar to fight the Egyptians, and defeated them at Carchemish. Four years later, another major battle took place between the two countries; it is not known where, but it was inconclusive and after it, the Babylonian army needed 18 months to be re-fitted. In the reign of Psammeticus II (595–589 BC), Egypt was neutral, but its next king, Apries (589–570 BC), falling for the blandishments of Zedekiah, last king of Judah, was tempted into Palestine to fight Nebuchadnezzar. He was unable to prevent the fall of Jerusalem, after which the Jews were taken into captivity in Babylon. In time, many of them made their way into Egypt, where they founded a colony at Elephantine (Aswan). In 570 BC, Apries sent his army to Cyrene to help the Libyans against the Greeks. It was defeated, much to the disgust of the Egyptians, who accused the king of sending Egyptian soldiers to their deaths. General Amasis led a successful *coup d'état* against him, and became king. Amasis (570–526 BC) was a shrewd ruler. He soothed national pride by stationing the Greek mercenaries, who were being employed in ever-increasing numbers in the Egyptian army, on the extreme border points of Daphnae (eastern Delta), Marea (western Delta) and Aswan, out of sight of the Egyptians. He also limited Greek traders to Naucratis, the flourishing city in the western Delta founded in the reign of Psammeticus I by Milesians as a commercial centre.

In 550 BC, the Persians under Cyrus II successfully revolted against their Mede overlords, and the two peoples merged. Cyrus began the conquest of western Asia and, in 539 BC, turned his attention to Babylon whose king, Nabu-naid (Nabonidus), spent his time examining ancient monuments, to the detriment of his royal duties. Neither Nabu-naid, the 'archaeologist', nor his son Balshazzar, who saw the 'writing on the wall',[178] were matches for Cyrus the Great, and Babylonia, with Syria and Palestine, were annexed to the Persian empire. Ten years later, Cyrus died and was succeeded by his son, Cambyses, who, in 525 BC, invaded Egypt.

According to Herodotus,[179] the progress of the Persian army was facilitated by Phanes, a Greek mercenary in the Egyptian army. Phanes defected to Cambyses and advised him that the best means of passing through the desert into Egypt would be by a safe-conduct acquired from the king of Arabia. The Persians duly crossed the desert and defeated the Egyptians at the Battle of

[178] Daniel, V, 24–38.
[179] Herodotus, III, pp. 175–8.

Pelusium, but not before the Greek and Carian mercenaries in the Egyptian army had taken their revenge upon Phanes by cutting the throats of his sons in sight of their father, collecting the blood in a bowl and drinking it.

Cambyses went on to capture Memphis and, within six months, the whole of Egypt was under Persian control. He seems to have ruled Egypt firmly. His reduction of temple grants to afford-able levels was bitterly resented by the priesthood. Herodotus claimed[180] that, during one of the fits of madness from which Cambyses suffered, he stabbed the sacred Apis Bull. His reputa-tion was so blackened that, to later generations of Egyptians, his name was a byword for tyranny and incompetence. Cambyses led an army into Nubia but it was so badly prepared that it had to turn back; and the ill-fated expeditionary force he despatched across the Western Desert to Siwa disappeared without trace. There was one Egyptian, however, who sang his praises, Udjahorresne,[181] who had served as a naval officer under Amasis and Psammeticus III and witnessed the destruction of the Saite state by the Persians. Cambyses appointed him priest of Neith at Sais, and also courtier and royal physician. Thanks to the patron-age of Cambyses, Udjahorresne was able to have the Temple of Neith at Sais re-consecrated, and to soften the effects of the Persian invasion on the people of Sais.

In 522 BC, Darius I (died 486 BC), called the Great, succeeded to the throne of Persia. He organized the empire, including Egypt, with consummate skill. Egypt, the oases in the Western Desert and Cyrenaica in Libya formed the Sixth Satrapy (province), from which a tribute of 700 talents, probably equivalent to £500,000 sterling today, was due. The Egyptian fleet and the mercenary army were taken over as they stood and incorporated into the Persian forces, acquitting themselves well in battles against the Greeks. In the last year of Darius' reign there was a revolt against him in the Delta, the after-effects, perhaps, of his defeat at Mara-thon in 490 BC. Order was restored by his successor, Xerxes I (486–464 BC), who reversed Darius' policy of enlightened patron-age, dismissing all Egyptian officials with the exception of army officers, and treating Egypt as if it were a rebellious province. During the reign of his successor, Artaxerxes I (464–424 BC),

180   ibid., p. 186.
181   Lichtheim, 1980, pp. 36ff.; Lloyd, 1982.

Inaros, a princeling of Libyan origin, led a revolt in the western Delta. He defeated and killed the satrap but could not capture Memphis and was unable, therefore, to make progress against Persian rule in the rest of Egypt. In the ensuing stalemate, Inaros appealed to Athens for help. Memphis fell to a combined Libyan-Athenian army, only to be retaken by the Persians in 456 BC.

The revolt shook the solidity of Persian rule: henceforward, Persia controlled Upper Egypt and the eastern Delta, but the western Delta was lost to them. The reign of Darius II (423–405 BC) seems to have been largely uneventful, though there are scarcely any Egyptian records dating to his reign or indeed to the 50 years that preceded it, an indication perhaps that they were times of insecurity and impoverishment. One crisis known to have occurred took place in Elephantine (Aswan) in 410 BC. A Jewish mercenary community was well established there, in a district in which the Egyptian ram god, Khnum, was worshipped. It is probable that lambs were sacrificed in the Jewish temple, a custom that would offend the religious susceptibilities of the priests of Khnum. Local friction between Egyptians and Jews became so bitter that the Egyptians persuaded the local Persian commander to raze the temple of Jahweh.

In 404 BC, Amyrtaios of Sais, sole ruler in the Twenty-eighth Dynasty, raised a revolt in the Delta and captured Memphis and Upper Egypt. The Persians assembled a large army in Persia to deal with it, but internal strife at home prevented it setting out for Egypt. Amyrtaios was replaced by Nepherites (399–393 BC), founder of the Twenty-ninth Dynasty, whose chief concern was to protect Egypt's independence from Persia. Nepherites' foreign policy consisted of taking Persia's enemies as Egypt's friends, and, to this end, he supported Sparta against Persia and its ally Athens. Under Nepherites' successor, Achoris (393–380 BC), Egypt began to grow strong once more, so that when Artaxerxes II marched on Egypt in 385 BC, the country was united and prosperous, with an army under the command of the best general of the day, Chabryias, a Greek. He had set up strong defences in the Delta which the Persians were unable to penetrate during three years on the offensive.

In 379 BC, Nectanebo I came to the throne as the first king of the Thirtieth Dynasty. The Persians attacked the Delta but they were poorly led and, caught by the Nile Inundation, were driven back. Nectanebo instituted a massive building programme, largely in the Delta, most traces of which have long since disappeared. He was succeeded by his son, Djedhor (365–360 BC), who minted the first pharaonic coin. He was pro-Greek but tried to revive Egypt's alliance with Sparta. Fearing a Persian attack, he raised money by every available means to assemble the largest possible army, and led this enormous army into Syria-Palestine, where it enjoyed great success. At home, his throne was seized by his brother on behalf of his nephew, Nectanebo; and Djedhor was forced to go to Sidon to throw himself on the mercy of the Persians. General Chabrias retired to Athens.

Nectanebo II (360–343 BC) was the last native pharaoh of Egypt. During his reign, Egypt prospered, and he was able to institute a large programme of building and sculpture, the quality of which, inspired by the Saite Period, was high. The situation outside Egypt was threatening: Artaxerxes III (343–338 BC) had an overriding ambition, which was to return Egypt to the Persian Empire. In 351 BC he tried and failed, thanks to the Greek mercenaries under the Spartan general, Agesilaos, who spearheaded the Egyptian army. Artaxerxes III then raised a force of 300,000 men and 300 galleys which he pitted against an Egyptian army consisting of 60,000 Egyptians, 20,000 Greeks and 20,000 other nationalities, backed by strong Delta defences. The Persians attacked by land and sea, and Nectanebo interfered with Agesilaos' plans, so that the Persians were able to break through and threaten Memphis. Nectanebo abdicated and fled south, and the Persians installed a satrap in Memphis. Between 343 and 342 BC, Nectanebo survived in Upper Egypt, but, by 341 BC, the whole of Egypt was in Persian hands. Nothing is known of Nectanebo's fate but Egyptian independence was at an end.

Egypt remained under Persian rule until the reign of Darius III (336–332 BC). After Darius' defeats at the hands of Alexander the Great, the Persian Empire dissolved, and Alexander became ruler of the world from Macedon to India. In 332 BC he arrived in Egypt, where he was greeted as a liberator. Egypt, however, was freed of the Persians only to fall into the hands of Macedonians and Greeks.

Government and Administration

Kings from the Twenty-first to the Twenty-third Dynasties met the challenge posed by the fragmenting political system by handing over combined civil, military and religious powers to royal relatives, who, as 'great army commanders', were posted to strategically important places throughout Egypt. Civil bureaucracy declined, as government power was firmly based on military force, and many of the royal relatives set up their own power-bases.

In the Twenty-third Dynasty, Osorkon III devised a way of asserting more control over Thebes. Osorkon, evidently a forceful king, contrived to prevail upon the reigning High Priest of Amun to accept the transfer of the estates and property of Amun to a priestess, who was given the title 'Divine Wife of Amun'.[182] The power of the high priesthood was so diminished that, for the next 200 years or so, the position of each High Priest of Amun at Thebes became that of a mere religious figurehead, the temporal power formerly wielded by holders of that office being exercised by the Divine Wife of Amun.

From Osorkon III's time onwards, the Divine Wife of Amun was a princess who became the consecrated wife of the god. She was expected to reside in Thebes and to remain celibate throughout her life. Each Divine Wife had a second title, that of 'Hand of the God', possibly a reference to one of the creation legends in which the god, Atum, was said to have brought his children into existence by masturbation. She was accompanied by attendants, who were considered to be the concubines of Amun and, like herself, expected to be celibate. Being officially celibate and without children of her own, each Divine Wife ensured the succession by adopting a 'daughter', who was recognized as the heiress presumptive, and who, it has been suggested, bore the title 'Divine Votaress'. The reigning king took pains to ensure that it was one of his own daughters who became the Divine Votaress.

By virtue of their position, the Divine Wives of Amun owned great estates and employed a large number of officials to administer them. Because of their vast wealth, which enabled them to wield temporal power, and their religious position, through which they wielded spiritual power, they also enjoyed great political influence. The authority of a Divine Wife was limited only by the fact that it was not exercised beyond the Theban area. In Thebes, at least, she was regarded as the equal of her royal father and was depicted in temple reliefs making the offerings to the gods, whereas elsewhere, it was the king who was shown carrying out these rituals.

[182] Watterson, 1991, pp. 159–71.

On her succession, a Divine Wife was accorded a formal inves-
titure and a coronation. Because she was the symbolic monarch of
Thebes, she was addressed as 'Your Majesty', though she bore
neither the title of queen nor was given a Throne Name. In
inscriptions, the Divine Wife's name was written inside a
cartouche as though she were a ruling monarch. Her death was
described officially in the same way as that of a king; and she was
accorded a royal burial and a memorial temple in which offerings
were made to her 'throughout eternity'. The most famous of these
temples were built between the eighth and sixth centuries BC, in
the precincts of the great Temple of Medinet Habu.

It is difficult to establish what the duties of the Divine Wife of
Amun were. Stelae recording the adoptions of two of the Wives,
Nitocris and Ankhnesneferibre, make it clear that they had extensive properties and revenues at their disposal. Presumably, it was
expected of the Divine Wives that they use a good part of their
wealth to make certain that Theban officials remained loyal not
only to them but also to the reigning king. In all probability, their
chief duty would have been to make known the will of Amun
through oracular means, just as the high priests before them had
done: and it is not difficult to appreciate that the manipulation of
the Oracle of Amun, enabling the Divine Wife to maintain control
over the devotees of Amun who held important posts in the
Thebaid, made her a valuable agent of her father.

From the reign of Osorkon III to that of Psammeticus III (526–
525 BC), Thebes was ruled by a succession of daughters of the
ruling royal house. The Kushite kings of the Twenty-fifth Dynasty,
who observed Egyptian customs and traditions with fervour, were
not slow to appreciate the advantages of having Divine Wives of
their own at Thebes. Piankhi installed his sister, Amenirdis I, as
the adopted daughter of the current Divine Wife Shepenupet I; and
she in her turn adopted her niece, Shepenupet II, Piankhi's daughter. Some years later, Shepenupet II adopted Amenirdis II, the
daughter of Taharqa (690–664 BC).

For most, if not all, of the Twenty-sixth Dynasty, the central
administration was based in Memphis. In the traditional manner,
the king took an active part in judicial matters, in the appointment
and reward of officials, and in government decision making. As
always, access to the royal presence seems to have been relatively
easy, and gaining the king's ear allowed royal favourites and the
possessors of such old titles as 'king's acquaintance' and 'sole

companion' to exercise a sizeable degree of influence. The title of vizier was still used, but whether a vizier functioned in the same way as in earlier times is debatable. As ever, the mainstay of the economy was agriculture, and it is not surprising that many of the most important posts in the administration were concerned with it. Thus, there was an 'overseer of farmlands', assisted by 'land-measurers'; and an 'overseer of storehouses', assisted by a 'scribe of accounts'. The traditional practice in pharaonic Egypt of non-specialization continued, so that, for example, a high official, such as the overseer of storehouses, could also function as a judge. Military men were often used for police duties, and the whole system was underpinned by an army of scribes.

Under the Persians, the traditional administrative system remained more or less unaltered, with the Persian system, in many respects similar to that of Egypt, superimposed upon the Egyptian with as little disruption as possible. The king was still head of government, the only differences being that he was Persian rather than Egyptian and that his permanent residence was not in Egypt. The king's deputy in Egypt was a satrap (provincial governor) based in Memphis. The satrap was always an aristocratic Persian, often a relative of the king, and was never entirely trusted but kept under surveillance by the Persian secret police (the 'King's Ears'). Collecting taxes continued to be the main preoccupation of the administration, and this was the satrap's chief duty.

Darius I spent some time in Egypt, and sought co-operation from Egyptians by actively encouraging them to take on high offices of state. Over a period of 16 years, he had the laws of Egypt codified and drawn up not only in Aramaic, the official language of the Persian Empire, but also in Egyptian demotic (*see* page 191). Darius supported local cults, providing Udjahorresne (*see* page 180), for example, with the finance to revive the House of Life at Sais, so that medicine, temple administration, ritual and theology might be studied in it as of old.

Economy

In the Twenty-first Dynasty, as Thebes and Memphis declined, the importance of the fertile Delta was reflected in the rise of Tanis, Sais and Leontopolis. Tanis, in particular, as a port well positioned for the lucrative sea trade with the Levant and as the home

town of the rulers of the Dynasty, grew in importance. In the Delta
and Middle Egypt, fortified cities began to proliferate – Piankhi
(see page 177) mentions 19 of them at roughly 14-kilometre
intervals along a 266-kilometre stretch of the Nile in Middle
Egypt, an indication not only of unsettled times but also of an
appreciation of the part the area played in feeding the population
of Egypt, estimated to have been about 3 million in the Saite
period, and, according to Herodotus,[183] at an unusually high level
in the time of Amasis.[184]

The Persians tried to integrate the economic structure of Egypt
into their empire both fiscally, with the payment of an annual
tribute (see page 180) supplemented with salt and Nile water for
the royal table, and physically by means of a new canal. In the
reign of Darius I, a direct sea link between the Nile Delta and
Persia was established by the completion of a canal between the
Nile and the Red Sea that had been started in the reign of Necho
II (610–595 BC). There may have been an attempt to construct a
waterway connecting the Red Sea with the Mediterranean as early
as the reign of Thutmose III; and a relief in the Temple of Amun
at Karnak shows Sety I returning from a campaign in Asia by way
of a canal in the eastern Delta. The modern Suez Canal was
anticipated in 606 BC when the Egyptians started a canal that was
intended to run from the Red Sea, through the Bitter Lakes area
and the Wadi Tumilat, into the Bubastite branch of the Nile
flowing through the eastern Delta into the Mediterranean.

The construction of this waterway would have involved excavating two canals: one, some 20 kilometres long, between the
northern end of the Red Sea and the Little Bitter Lake; the other,
about 15 kilometres long, between the northern end of the Great
Bitter Lake and Lake Timsah. A breech would then have been
made from Lake Timsah into the Wadi Tumilat. According to
Herodotus,[185] 120,000 Egyptians died in the attempt to construct
Necho's canal but, in spite of the high mortality rate, it was
abandoned only when an oracle warned that it would be the
Persians who would benefit from it. Just over a century later,
Darius I ordered work on the canal to be restarted, and Darius'
canal, which ran from the Red Sea to the Bitter Lakes and then

---

[183]   Herodotus, II, 177, 1.
[184]   Trigger, 1983, p. 300.
[185]   Herodotus, II, 158.

westwards to Bubastis, a distance of about 180 kilometres, was completed *c*.490 BC.

The oases in the Western Desert assumed great importance during the Saite and Persian periods. The Saite kings developed those of Kharga and Bahriya, and, for the first time, brought the Siwa oasis under Egyptian control. The earliest temple of the Siwan oracle dates to the reign of Amasis. Egyptian interest in the oases was largely economic, but they were strategically important also: Siwa, for example, was taken over at a time when Cyrene began to threaten Egypt's western frontier. The Persians continued the Saite policy of development of the oases, when Darius I ordered the construction of a temple dedicated to Amen-Re at Hibis at el-Kharga, the only Egyptian temple built during the Persian period. Seth, reviled in the Nile Valley for the murder of Osiris, was worshipped in el-Kharga as the deity who would ensure the fertility of the oasis, and, in a relief in the hypostyle hall at Hibis, a winged figure of Seth is shown slaying the serpent Apophis, a depiction which some scholars claim was the inspiration for the Christian story of St George and the dragon. Communication between the Nile Valley and the oases was improved, possibly because use was made of bedouins and their camels.

Religion

Funerary practices

After the New Kingdom, decorated tomb chapels were rarely built. Instead, the most essential of the funerary scenes and texts were transferred to funerary papyri, to stelae, and above all, to coffins and mummy cases. The study of the hundreds of burials of the temple staff of Amun found at Deir el-Bahri has given a clear picture of the funerary practices of private people during the Third Intermediate Period.

The corpse of a private person of affluence was provided with two wooden mummy cases and a mummy board, the full-length covering, usually shaped like a mummy, that was placed over the top of the body in its bandages. Occasionally, the board represented the deceased as a living person dressed in everyday clothes, as in the case of Isis, wife of Kha-bekhnet, the Nineteenth Dynasty Deir el-Medina workman. Mummy cases were anthropoid and placed one inside the other, their interiors usually coloured dark red and decorated. On the floor of each case, the Goddess of the West, a form of Hathor, or a *djed*-pillar, was often painted. The *djed*-pillar, thought to represent the backbone of Osiris, was a symbol of stability and permanence, particularly appropriate because the backbone of the mummy rested on it.

The exteriors of these cases were highly decorated, with funerary scenes painted in bright colours on a yellow ground, and varnished. Occasionally, the figures on the lids were moulded in plaster, perhaps to imitate raised relief. The cases of men and women were similar, both decorated with figures of the sky goddess, Nut, spreading her wings protectively over the lids, the lower parts of which are decorated with representations of a bewildering variety of gods, religious motifs, funerary scenes and texts, crammed into every available space, in a style typical of the period. The theme of much of the decoration is death and rebirth, with the journey through the Underworld to the Hall of Judgement and Osiris being most common.

In the Twenty-second Dynasty, the old yellow mummy cases were superseded by cases of a new, simpler design. The more affluent were buried in up to three of them, and the mummy board gave way to a cartonnage mummy case. The moulding of a cartonnage case was apparently achieved with layers of gum-soaked linen laid over a plaster-coated core of mud and straw, formed to an average mummy's shape and size. A slit at the back of the case allowed the core to be removed and replaced with the prepared corpse. The decoration of the case, often very attractive, seems to have been carried out only after the mummy had been placed inside.

By the Twenty-fifth Dynasty, funerary furniture had undergone a further change in style. The cartonnage mummy case became less common in favour of one of wood, which was cut into the shape of a mummy standing on a pedestal, its back supported by a column, perhaps in imitation of a statue. The pedestal may have been useful when the case was set into an upright position during the funeral ceremonies, but the case was finally laid to rest in a horizontal position within one, sometimes two, anthropoid cases of the more traditional shape. A new type of outer coffin was introduced at this period, rectangular with a vaulted lid and posts at each corner, the tops of which were flush with the top of the lid, modelled in imitation of a shrine.

Cultural Achievements

Architecture

Royal tombs

The kings of the Twenty-first and Twenty-second Dynasties may have considered the proven impossibility of protecting royal tombs at Thebes as more than justifying their break with tradition in deciding not to be buried there. In any case, the Delta was their home. Thus, the royal tombs of these dynasties are at Tanis, housed safely in the middle of the administrative and religious quarter within the city itself. Their design was determined by the nature of the terrain: there were no cliffs in which to cut them, so they were sunk into the ground as stone-lined chambers. Nothing made from perishable material was buried with the king, because the damp conditions of the Delta would rot anything other than metal or stone; and in Psusennes I's tomb, found almost intact in AD 1940,[186] there were only vessels of gold and silver. The royal tombs at Tanis are largely undecorated, but the royal bodies were interred in magnificent sarcophagi of granite or quartzite, some of them usurped from earlier rulers, and silver mummy cases. Funerary equipment of the time, especially jewellery, was simple and elegant.

Sculpture

The Twenty-first Dynasty saw a marked revival in the arts. Great building schemes undertaken at Tanis, Memphis, Bubastis and Thebes brought a demand for the sculpture needed for the embellishing of temples, much of it derivative, relying on models from the past. Perhaps the most important artistic accomplishment of the whole Libyan Period (Dynasties XXII and XXIII) was the fine bronze statuary, the production of which demanded an impressive degree of technical skill. Gold and silver, semi-precious stones, glass and vitreous pastes were skilfully inlaid into the bronzework, otherwise sombre, adding an impression of warmth.

---

[186] Montet, 1942.

The masterpiece of the era is a bronze statuette, almost 60 centimetres high, now in the Louvre Museum, of Queen Karomama II, the wife of Takeloth II (850–825 BC). Her dress is etched with a pattern of feathers, damascened in gold, silver and electrum. Her facial features are delicate, her limbs slender, and reveal the feminine ideal of the period, which seems to have been inspired by Thutmoside models. Unusually, the name of the man who sculpted this, one of the outstanding works of Egyptian art, is known: Ahtefnakht.

In the era of Kushite rule, there was a surge of activity in the production of statuary. Statues fell into two distinct styles: the priests at Thebes favoured traditional themes with a tendency towards archaism, fine examples being the surviving statues of the Divine Wives of Amun (*see* page 183); and the non-priestly preferred realistic portraiture of individuals, well represented by a dozen or so statues of Montuemhat, high steward of the Divine Wife of Amun *c.*660 BC, rivalled by a magnificent, black granite head of King Taharqa from Karnak. The sculptors of the realistic style did not flinch from confronting reality: they ruthlessly portrayed faces lined with old age, and flabby bodies; but they also represented the wisdom and scepticism that are the advantages of advanced years.

The trend towards archaism found its fullest expression in the Saite era of the Twenty-sixth Dynasty, when the statuary of the Old Kingdom was reproduced to such effect that it is often difficult to distinguish the Saite copy from the original. The Saite era was artistically an age of reproduction, and sometimes what appears to be an Old Kingdom statue betrays its true origin only by its facial expression: Saite artists discovered the 'archaic smile' of ancient Greek sculpture, although it must be admitted that in Saite hands the 'archaic smile' became a simper. Saite sculptors did display some originality, however, and had a preference for materials that were hard and sombre looking.

Literature

Much of the literature of the Third Intermediate Period comprises royal decrees, accounts of royal victories, hymns to the gods and the autobiographies of private individuals. They are written in hieroglyphs in the classic stage of the ancient Egyptian language, known today as Middle Egyptian, though some words and grammatical constructions show interesting traces of the vernacular of the New Kingdom, that is, Late Egyptian. The hieroglyphic inscriptions of the time in general follow the main literary genres of earlier periods. The Victory Stele of Piankhi,[187] with its unusual wealth of detail about Piankhi's campaigns (*see* page 177) and the thoughts and feelings of the king, is an outstanding example of Egyptian historiography. The Kushite king, Shabaka, even seems to have indulged in the forgery of an Old Kingdom work, claiming to have found on a worm-eaten papyrus a version of the 'Memphite Theology',[188] that is, the theology taught at Memphis by the priests of Ptah, and to have ordered it to be copied on stone, the Shabaka Stone now in the British Museum. It seems certain, however, that the inscription on the Stone was composed in the Twenty-fifth Dynasty.[189]

From about 700 BC, records of daily life – contracts, business documents, wills, lawsuits and tax dealings – were written in the demotic script. The term 'demotic', when applied to language or script, is derived from Herodotus, Book II, 36, in which he states that the Egyptians had 'two sorts of writing, the sacred and the common (that is, demotic).' This script, which has been described as resembling a series of agitated commas, is a much-abbreviated form of hieratic, the cursive version of hieroglyphs. Although demotic script normally expressed the vernacular language of the time, it was occasionally employed for monumental inscriptions, of which the Rosetta Stone of 196 BC is the most famous example. Thus far, no love poems in demotic have come to light; and the model letters to schoolboys, so popular in the New Kingdom, seem to have fallen out of favour. Narrative stories and instructions in the pursuit of wisdom were written in demotic: the best examples to have survived date to the Graeco-Roman period.

[187] Lichtheim, 1980, p. 66ff.
[188] Lichtheim, 1975, p. 51ff.
[189] *See* F. Junge, MDAIK, 29, 1973, pp. 195–204.

6

Hellenistic Egypt

With the coming of Alexander the Great, Egypt was drawn inexorably into the Hellenistic world. In his usual manner, he took pains to act in a conciliatory fashion towards a conquered people. In contrast to the Persian Cambyses, who had caused the death of the sacred Apis Bull[190] of Memphis, Alexander sacrificed to it, and to other national gods,[191] and mollified the priesthood by making the arduous journey to Siwa in the Western Desert to consult the Oracle of Amun, whom he seems to have believed to have been his divine father.[192] In return, the priesthood resorted to the old Egyptian tradition of theogamy. Shortly after Alexander's death, possibly even before it, the story was being put about that the last native king of Egypt, Nectanebo II, had assumed the shape of a serpent to impregnate Olympias, the wife of Alexander's earthly father, Philip of Macedon, so that Alexander, the son born of this union, might be seen as the true successor to the native Pharaohs.

He left Egypt in April 331 BC and set out for Mesopotamia where, three months later, he fought his final battle against Darius at Gaugamela. After his death in Babylon on 10 June 323 BC, Alexander's vast empire was divided between his generals who, at first, ruled on behalf of his heirs, his posthumously born son, Alexander IV, and his half-brother, Philip Arrhidaeus. Antipater governed Macedonia, Lysimacus Thrace, Antigonus Asia Minor, Seleucus Babylonia, Laomedon Syria, Meleager Phoenicia, and

[190] Herodotus, III, 27–8.
[191] Arrian, III, 1.
[192] Arrian, III, 3–5.

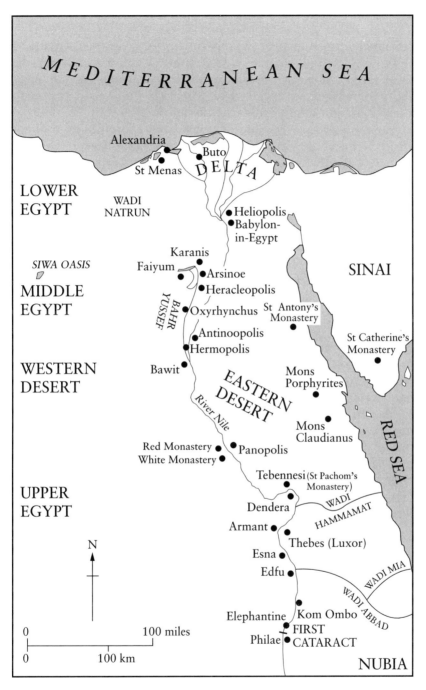

MEDITERRANEAN SEA

Alexandria
Buto
St Menas
DELTA

LOWER
EGYPT
WADI
NATRUN

Heliopolis
Babylon-
in-Egypt

Karanis

SIWA OASIS
Faiyum
Arsinoe

SINAI

MIDDLE
EGYPT
Heracleopolis

BAHR YUSSEF

Oxyrhynchus
St Antony's
Monastery

St Catherine's
Monastery

Antinoopolis
Hermopolis

WESTERN
DESERT
Bawit

EASTERN DESERT

River Nile

Mons
Porphyrites

Mons
Claudianus

RED SEA

Red Monastery
White Monastery
Panopolis

Tebennesi (St Pachom's
Monastery)

UPPER
EGYPT

Dendera

WADI HAMMAMAT

Armant
Thebes (Luxor)

N

Esna

Edfu

WADI MIA

WADI ABBAD

0   100 miles
0   100 km

Elephantine
Philae

Kom Ombo
FIRST
CATARACT

NUBIA

Map 6   Map of Egypt showing sites of the Graeco-Roman Period.

Ptolemy became satrap of Egypt. Ptolemy was the son of Lagus, an obscure Macedonian squire, and Arsinoe, a minor member of the royal family. It had been rumoured that his father was actually Philip of Macedon, and it was true that Philip had taken an interest in the young Ptolemy, making him one of Alexander's Companions, the seven boys of noble birth chosen to be brought up and educated with Alexander. In an astute move, Ptolemy brought back the body of Alexander to Egypt, and, just as a king of Egypt traditionally had legitimized his claim to the throne by acting as Horus to his predecessor's Osiris (*see* page 123), so Ptolemy buried Alexander.

For nearly 20 years, Ptolemy was constrained by his status: he was a satrap not a king. In 317 BC, however, Philip Arrhidaeus was murdered by Alexander's mother, Olympias, and both the young Alexander IV and his mother, Roxane, were put to death by Cassander, son of Antipater, satrap of Macedonia, sometime between 311 and 309 BC; thus, Cleopatra, the aged sister of Alexander the Great, was left as his last remaining blood relative. Ptolemy offered to marry her and, as he had a reputation for honesty, sobriety and generosity, she accepted, setting out for Egypt in 308 BC, only to be murdered at Sardis by Antigonous, the satrap of Asia Minor.

The demise of Alexander's family changed the attitude of his former generals who abandoned their allegiance to his ideals. One by one, Cassander, Lysimachus, Seleucus and Antigonous declared themselves kings. In 304 BC, Ptolemy, at the age of 63, finally felt able to proclaim himself King of Egypt, as Ptolemy Soter (Saviour), so becoming the founder of a line of Macedonian kings who ruled Egypt for nearly 300 years as the Ptolemaic Dynasty.

History

Ptolemy Soter's main concern was the defence of Egypt against the territorial ambitions of his erstwhile companions-in-arms, by creating a buffer state between his territory and theirs. He acquired extensive tracts of land in the Aegean and western Asia, including Cyprus, Palestine and Coelesyria, the fertile valley between Phoenicia and the Syrian desert. Cyrenaica also fell into his hands, after its rulers had asked him for help against rebels: Ptolemy supplied the help and then treated Cyrenaica as a prize of war.

Inevitably, however, he and his successors were drawn into the quarrels and wars between the other former satrapies.

In 285 BC, when Ptolemy Soter was about 80 years old, he retired to become a soldier in the palace guard, leaving the throne to his son. Ptolemy II Philadelphus (285–246 BC), whose wife was Arsinoe I, daughter of Lysimachus of Thrace, marked the beginning of his reign by holding a great pageant in Alexandria, in which images of the deities of Greece and Egypt were carried in procession. The highlight of the display was a parade of birds and animals unknown in Egypt: of buffaloes, gemsbok, gnus, zebras, tigers, a rhinoceros and a white bear. Shortly after the pageant, Ptolemy Soter died. Macedonian veterans insisted that he should be buried in Alexandria in the Sema, the great tomb that had been prepared for Alexander; and the two men were duly reunited in death.

In 281 BC, Lysimachus of Thrace and Seleucus of Babylon, the last of Alexander's satraps, finally contrived to kill each other. Lysimachus' widow, Arsinoe II, Philadelphus' sister, returned to Egypt, and soon had engineered an accusation of treason against her brother's wife, Arsinoe I, who, in 279 BC, was banished to Coptos, where she died five years later. A year or so before the death of Arsinoe I, Arsinoe II married Philadelphus, her brother, a match that was countenanced in Egyptian law but incest in Greek. It was to be a childless marriage which lasted until Arsinoe II's death in 269 BC, but it brought to Philadelphus most of Lysimachus' possessions in the Aegean. Arsinoe II was a woman of great ambition and ability, and, as queen, she exerted a decisive influence on Egyptian politics.

Egypt's formal contacts with Rome began during Philadelphus' reign. In about 271 BC, he refused a request for help from his friend Pyrrhus, the king of Epirus, who had mounted an invasion of Italy, and, at the end of the campaign, sent congratulations to the victorious Roman Senate. A treaty of friendship between Rome and Egypt was concluded; it was to be of utmost benefit to Rome some 60 years later, after Hannibal had been ravaging the Italian countryside for almost a decade, when Egypt supplied her ally with grain.

Ptolemy II Philadelphus died at the age of 63, fat, bald, riddled with gout, and unable to move without assistance. He was succeeded by the son of Arsinoe I, his first wife. A year before his accession, Ptolemy III Euergetes I (246–222 BC) married Berenice

II, the daughter of Magas of Cyrenaica. Though she had been betrothed to Euergetes I in childhood, after her father's death, her mother Apame arranged for her to marry Demetrius, the half-brother of the king of Macedon. Demetrius found life in Cyrenaica very dull and embarked on an affair with his mother-in-law. Finding the pair *in flagrante delicto*, Berenice ordered the palace guards to stab her husband to death. In the heat of the moment, Apame also was killed, despite Berenice's efforts to save her. The court at Alexandria admired Berenice's spirit, and she was extolled by Callimachus, the Cyrenaican poet who became head of the library in Alexandria, in a poem[193] in which he addressed her as a 'stout-hearted girl' whose actions had been 'a splendid crime that won for you your prince'.

Ptolemy III Euergetes I was a successful soldier whose campaigns in Syria added greatly to Egypt's foreign possessions. During his reign, Ptolemaic power was at its peak: the Egyptian empire consisted of Libya, Cyrenaica, Nubia, Palestine, Phoenicia, the Cyclades, Cyprus and large parts of south-western Asia. To control such extensive territories, Euergetes I kept a standing army of 200,000 men, supplemented by a navy of 1500 vessels. By 240 BC, however, he had overreached himself. In a vain attempt to gain control of the coast of Asia Minor, he sacrificed Egyptian possessions in Syria, only to be defeated by a coalition led by the island of Rhodes to protect its trading interests.

Euergetes I returned to Egypt to find the country in the grip of a terrible famine, and ordered wheat and barley to be distributed to the starving from the stocks he had brought back to Egypt from Syria. Berenice, the 'stout-hearted girl' whom he had left in charge of Egypt during his absence, had proved to be ineffectual in alleviating famine and keeping order, instead making daily pilgrimages to Canopus to the temple of Arsinoe-Aphrodite to intercede for the welfare of her husband. A lock of hair which she had dedicated to the goddess disappeared from the temple, and was conveniently identified by the court astronomer, Conon, as a hitherto unobserved cluster of stars, between Leo Virgo and Ursa Major, which he named *Coma Berenices* (Berenice's Curl).

Euergetes I decided to mark the occasion for his Egyptian subjects, and ordered a temple to be built at Canopus larger than that of Arsinoe-Aphrodite. On behalf of himself and his wife, he

---

[193]   *Aetia* (On Origins), Books 3–4.

dedicated it to Osiris, an action that did not win him the plaudits he expected. The Egyptians were not contented that the upstart city of Alexandria had replaced the ancient capital, Memphis, as the seat of government. They also resented the fact that Euergetes had enabled Alexandria to usurp Osiris, the most popular god of Egypt, quite ignoring his restoration of the divine images stolen from Thebes by Cambyses, his contribution to the upkeep of the Apis Bull in Memphis, and even his deliverance of the populace from the recent famine.

In the last ten years of his reign, Euergetes I became a morose and suspicious man, and the reign of a king once driven by reforming zeal ended in a welter of oppression. The first three Ptolemies had achieved many reforms and much progress, but, after the death of Euergetes, incessant civil war and the corruption of the royal family led to the progressive weakening and impoverishment of the country. His son, Ptolemy IV Philopator (222–205 BC), who was about 25 years old at his accession, and a former pupil of Eratosthenes, came under the influence of a Greek courtier, Sosibius, who, in furtherance of his own ambitions to be the power behind the throne, encouraged Philopator to indulge the violent and licentious side of his nature. He provided him with a mistress, Agathoclia, instructing her to persuade her lover to dispose of his mother and co-ruler, Berenice II, because she was reported to be thinking of installing her younger son, Magas, on the throne in place of his brother. Easily persuaded, Philopator had Berenice and Magas murdered.

In 217 BC, Antiochus III of Syria invaded Palestine and marched towards Egypt. Philopator, accompanied by his sister Arsinoe III, crossed Sinai with a cavalry force of 5000 Macedonians and Thessalians, and an infantry of 65,000 soldiers, nearly half of them Cretans, Thracians, Persians, Libyans, Gauls, and, for the first time in the Ptolemaic army, native Egyptians. With him were also 73 African elephants. At Raphia in June 217 BC, Antiochus, with 10,000 fewer infantry but superior numbers of cavalry, and Indian elephants which, though smaller than the African, were more amenable to training, was decisively defeated.[194] After the battle, Philopator married Arsinoe III.

Philopator, a lazy and incompetent administrator, took little interest in the welfare of his people. After a series of low Niles,

---

[194] Polybius, Book V, para. 79ff.

famine threatened, and the Egyptians looked to him to rescue them as his father had done, but to no avail. Agathocles, the brother of the king's mistress, Agathoclia, advised him to leave Egypt to fend for itself, a disastrous policy. Food shortages led to local unrest, and for the last three years of Philopator's reign and for a large part of his successor's, the district of Thebes was under the control, once again, of Nubian kings. Philopator replaced Agathocles with Tlepolemus who ordered savage reprisals against the Egyptians, though he mollified the Alexandrians and kept their loyalty by distributing food in the city. Success in the Battle of Raphia had been a great stimulus to Egyptian nationalism. Agathocles, under whose guidance the Ptolemaic army was reorganized, had initiated a policy of recruiting native Egyptians into it; and the Egyptian soldiers, who believed that the victory at Raphia was due largely to their efforts, resented the fact that they were not given credit for it. This resentment combined with harsh taxation culminated in a long series of native revolts which led, over the course of the next century, to a state of insurrection becoming endemic in Egypt.

Arsinoe III withdrew from court in 209 BC, disgusted at the excesses of her husband. Five years later she was murdered, and Philopator himself died in 205 BC at the age of 39, a victim of his own debaucheries. Their son, Ptolemy V Epiphanes (205–180 BC), was a child of four when he came to the throne, and Sosibius tried and failed to become Regent. Rioting erupted in Alexandria, in the course of which Agathoclia, Agathocles and their mother, Oenanthe, were torn to pieces by an Alexandrian mob. Tlepolemus was appointed Regent, and it was not until 197 BC that Ptolemy, at the age of 13, was crowned. His coronation was performed according to Macedonian practice: the army paraded and, as the young prince passed down the ranks, acclaimed him as king. Spectators applauded and saluted him as Epiphanes – 'god made manifest'. He was also crowned at Memphis, this time in accordance with Egyptian rites. In 196 BC, a stele was erected to commemorate the occasion, the Rosetta Stone, which, because it was inscribed in Greek, demotic and hieroglyphs, was to prove the principal key to the deciphering of hieroglyphs some 2000 years later (see page 297).

In 193 BC, at the age of 17, Epiphanes married Cleopatra, the daughter of Antiochus III of Syria. Cleopatra I, some six years older than her new husband, brought with her as dowry the revenues of Coelesyria, Phoenicia, Samaria and Judaea. Neither the alliance, nor the wealth it brought to Egypt, prevented the loss of most of Egypt's foreign possessions over the next few years, following attacks made by the Seleucids in alliance with Macedonians. Epiphanes was more successful against the rebels in the Thebaid: in the nineteenth year of his reign, his general, Polycrates, at last suppressed the Theban revolt by enticing the rebel leaders to Sais with a promise of negotiation but, once in Sais, putting them to death and causing their naked bodies, tied to the wheels of his own chariot, to be dragged round the city walls.

Epiphanes died when he was less than 30 years old, the cause of death unknown. He left behind his widow, Cleopatra I, two sons, Ptolemy Philometor and Ptolemy Euergetes, and a daughter, another Cleopatra. For four years, Cleopatra I acted as Regent for her son, Ptolemy VI Philometor (180–145 BC), a minor when he came to the throne. Cleopatra I, a capable and intelligent woman, was a fine Regent. She determined to erode the barriers between her Greek and Egyptian subjects and encouraged those who lived outwith Alexandria to work together in their common interest. At her urging, many provincial Greeks married Egyptian wives and assumed an Egyptian way of life so that, gradually, they began to think of themselves as Egyptians. The Greeks in Alexandria were a different matter: they continued to consider themselves superior in every respect to Egyptians.

The objective of Cleopatra I's foreign policy was the maintenance of peace; and as long as her father, Antiochus III, was alive, the treaty between Egypt and Syria ensured her success. But when, in 176 BC, her brother Antiochus IV seized the throne of Syria, Cleopatra I was placed in an invidious position. An Alexandrian lobby for war with Syria grew more vociferous, and Cleopatra I, probably in failing health, realized that she could not ignore it. To safeguard Philometor's position as king should war come, she arranged for him to be crowned, like his father before him, according to Egyptian and to Macedonian rites; and to be married to his sister, Cleopatra II. A few months later, Cleopatra I died.

Since the beginning of the second century BC, Rome had been steadily extending its power eastwards, coming into conflict with one Mediterranean state after another, although remaining on friendly terms with Egypt. By the time of Cleopatra I's death in 176 BC, Rome had become the dominant power in the region, holding out the promise, or perhaps the threat, of a *pax Romana*.

After his mother's death, the young Philometor was encouraged by incompetent advisers to order the army to establish bases in Palestine, with the intention of attacking Syria. The Alexandrians, persuaded that an invasion of Syria would be a simple undertaking, were delighted. Antiochus IV retaliated by claiming that the Coelesyrian revenues had been granted to Egypt for no longer than his sister's lifetime and by repudiating the treaty with Egypt. Each side sent its emissaries to Rome, complaining about the duplicity of the other and appealing for arbitration.[195] Before Rome could respond, war broke out, and the Egyptians were forced to retreat.

Antiochus IV captured Philometor and marched to Memphis, where he claimed that his chief interest was to advise his nephew as a good uncle should, though this did not prevent him from issuing decrees in the name of 'King Antiochus'. The Alexandrians were incensed and elected Philometor's brother, Euergetes, as king, whereupon Antiochus sailed to Naucratis in preparation for an attack on Alexandria. Euergetes II, meantime, was sending out to neighbouring states invitations to attend his coronation. Two triremes dispatched against Antiochus were quick to surrender but, fortunately for Alexandria, Antiochus, reluctant to begin what would inevitably be a long siege of the city and unsure of Rome's reaction, withdrew to Syria, leaving Egypt with a dynastic problem.

Euergetes refused to relinquish the throne, claiming he had been legally elected to it. Thus, for some time, he ruled Lower Egypt from Alexandria while his brother, Philometor, ruled Upper Egypt from Memphis. Trade between Alexandria and Upper Egypt ceased, and prosperity, which had begun to revive after the famines of previous years, came to an end. It was at this point that Cleopatra II, the sister-wife of Philometor and a woman who brooked no opposition in the furtherance of her own ambitions, persuaded her brothers to share the throne with her, and, between 170 and 164 BC, Egypt was ruled by a triumvirate.

This uneasy alliance was forced to maintain its unity by further threats from Antiochus IV. He sent a division of the Syrian army to occupy Cyprus, an Egyptian possession, and marched to Rhinocolura (the modern el-Arish) from where he sent a message to 'the gods Philometores' demanding that they cede to him Cyprus, Pelusium and all the territory bordering the Pelusiac mouth of the Nile. Irritated, the Roman Senate sent its envoy, Popilius Laenas, to deliver the message that 'the Senate would consider whichever party persisted in the dispute to be neither their friend nor their ally'.[196] It was several months before Popilius reached Egypt: he was delayed by a blockade of Delos mounted by a Macedonian fleet, and, only after a battle had been fought at Pydna (168 BC), did he resume his journey. On his arrival in Egypt, he decided to keep Antiochus waiting while he went sightseeing in Alexandria, as an indication of what little importantance Rome attached to the king. When Popilius finally confronted Antiochus, the king was fully armed and very angry. Popilius, in contrast, was dressed in a toga, a light wand in his hand, but vested with the authority of the Roman Senate; and Antiochus decided that a victory over Egypt was not worth the price of making an enemy of Rome. He abandoned Cyprus and returned to Syria.

Rome accepted the joint rule of Philometor and Euergetes II, an arrangement certain to lead to friction. Each had his own following: Philometor supported by provincial Egypt, Euergetes by the Alexandrians who had elected him. When a certain Petosarapis spread the rumour that Philometor had murdered Euergetes, an Alexandrian mob gathered baying for the 'murderer' to be deposed, and the two brothers were compelled to appear together in public to disprove the rumour. Philometor pursued Petosarapis into Upper Egypt to Panopolis (modern Akhmim), where he captured him, had him executed and, for good measure, had the city razed to the ground.

Euergetes took advantage of his brother's absence to gain the sympathy of the Alexandrians, pretending to be in fear of his life and begging his followers to save him from his brother. Thus, when Philometor arrived back in Alexandria, he was not greeted as a returning hero but with suspicion. He travelled to Rome to seek help, and, in 164 BC, Rome adjudicated between the two brothers, awarding Egypt to Philometor and Cyrenaica to Euergetes. The Alexandrians, disillusioned with the decline in prosperity and the rising number of executions in Euergetes' reign, had dubbed him 'Cakergetes' (the Evil-doer) and were glad to see him go.

---

[196] Livy, Book XLIV, Chapter 19.

Once installed in Cyrenaica, he lost no time in trying to add Cyprus to his possessions. Rome ordered Philometor to hand over the island to his brother, and appointed two Roman senators, Torquatus and Merulla, to see that it was done. Euergetes, then in Greece recruiting mercenaries for an invasion of Cyprus, was reminded of Rome's decree that there should be no war, and reluctantly returned to Libya, escorted by Merulla. Meanwhile, Torquatus went to Alexandria, where Philometor had established his court, to advise the king to forgive his brother because, after all, Cyprus was such an unimportant little island. Philometor knew differently: Alexander the Great had believed Cyprus to be the key to Egypt, and, during the Ptolemaic Dynasty, Egypt had drawn its currency largely from the mints in Salamis, Paphos and Ra Citium, so Philometor, much to Egypt's approval, held on to the island.

Hardly had Euergetes arrived back in Cyrenaica than the country rose in revolt, and, for the next few years, he was fully occupied in keeping order. Philometor, aided by his sister-wife Cleopatra II, was able to rule Egypt in his own way. He believed that it was the paramount duty of a king to look to the welfare of his subjects, and he sometimes took a personal interest in the problems of individuals. A benevolent and hard-working king, he treated all his subjects, rich and poor, alike, impartially and fairly. From time to time, he made tours of inspection of the whole of Egypt, accepting hundreds of petitions, all of which he was said to read and answer. He was perhaps deserving of a better epitaph than that given to him by Polybius: 'A man who according to some deserved great praise ... according to others, the reverse', and, damning with faint praise, 'He never put any of his own friends to death on any charge whatever'.[197]

At his death in 145 BC, Ptolemy VI Philometor was succeeded by his son, Ptolemy VII Neos Philopator. Euergetes II, however, returned to Egypt, intent upon taking the throne for himself. He entered Alexandria to the acclamation of the mob, but his sister, Cleopatra II, had already fled, taking with her her son, the young king Neos Philopator, together with the contents of the treasury. She established herself in Memphis, intending to rule Egypt with Neos Philopator and leave Euergetes in possession only of Alexandria. Support for her came from Ptolemais, in Upper Egypt, a city

---

[197] Polybius, Book XXXIX, Chapter 18.

in which Hellenistic ideals were strictly adhered to and therefore a magnet for Macedonian and Greek mercenaries.

Meanwhile, in Rome, Cato's exhortation *Delenda est Carthago* had been acted upon, and, in 146 BC, Scipio Aemilianus Africanus had indeed destroyed Hannibal's city. Emissaries were sent to Euergetes II to enquire whether he wished to retain Cyrenaica in his possession: if not, Rome might add it to Carthage and form a new Roman province. Euergetes would have been prepared to cede Cyrenaica to Rome in return for Rome's support against his sister, but support was not forthcoming and he decided to offer marriage instead. Cleopatra II, who had used every weapon at her disposal against her brother, agreed, and in 144 BC they were married, spending their honeymoon visiting Thebes to admire its ancient glories, and making a tour of inspection of the temple at Edfu, the construction of which, started in the reign of Euergetes I, was now almost complete. Once Euergetes II was certain that Cleopatra II was pregnant with his child, he had her son, Neos Philometor, murdered.

From 144 BC to 116 BC, Ptolemy VIII Euergetes II, was ruler of all Egypt. Cleopatra II must soon have realized her mistake in marrying him: her husband never sought her counsel, nor did he ask for her company, preferring that of his mistress, Irene, a Cyrenaican. Two years after his marriage to Cleopatra, his eye fell upon her daughter, Cleopatra III, who was as ambitious as her mother. By this time, he was a repulsive figure, known to the Alexandrians as 'Physon' (Pot-belly), but Cleopatra, undeterred by his appearance, married him for his throne. It was not a marriage in name only: Cleopatra III bore her husband five children. Euergetes did not divorce his sister-wife Cleopatra II before marrying his niece Cleopatra III, and between 143 BC and 101 BC, all three ruled Egypt together.

In 136 BC, Scipio Aemilianus Africanus visited Egypt.[198] The contrast between the distinguished soldier and his host, the King of Egypt, was marked. The garrulous sovereign, so fat that 'the longest pair of arms could not encompass his stomach',[199] was clad in a diaphanous garment that did not conceal his deformities. Scipio looked to his visit to the Mouseion and the Library in Alexandria to make up for the shortcomings of the king, but he

[198]   Diodorus, Book XXXVII.
[199]   Athenaeus, Book XII, Chapter 73.

was disappointed, for the places of learning were empty of scholars who had abandoned them in the face of Euergetes' proscriptions. Scipio was disgusted by Euergetes II, and so were the Alexandrians who could countenance a marriage between siblings but not between uncle and niece, and who condemned the murder of the child, Neos Philometor, the lawful heir to the throne.

In 132 BC, many cities in Egypt revolted. Euergetes suppressed the rebellious Thebaid with ferocity, putting Hermonthis (Armant) and several other cities to the sword. He then turned on Alexandria, having a large number of youths rounded up and taken to a gymnasium, which was then set on fire. Realizing that he had gone too far, Euergetes fled to Cyprus, taking with him Cleopatra III, their five children, and Memphites, his child by Cleopatra II. Cleopatra II was left as sole ruler of Egypt, but her Greek subjects were reluctant to agree to a woman reigning alone and suggested that she make a dynastic marriage with Apion, the viceroy of Cyrenaica, and bastard son of Euergetes II. She rejected the advice and, in 130 BC, ascended the throne to rule alone. Euergetes had their son Memphites murdered,[200] and on Cleopatra's birthday, he sent her a gift – a box containing the boy's dismembered body.[201]

A year later, Euergetes returned to Egypt and reconquered Alexandria. Cleopatra withdrew to Syria but, by 124 BC, she had returned to Egypt and, until his death in 116 BC, Euergetes ruled with both Cleopatras. In his will, he left all power to Cleopatra III who would have preferred her younger son, Alexander, as co-ruler, but, realizing the army's preference for primogeniture, reluctantly accepted her elder son, Ptolemy IX Soter II, commonly known as Lathyrus (Chick Pea). Soter II (116–80 BC) had already married his sister, Cleopatra IV, before his father died, but their mother, wary of her daughter's ambitions, persuaded Soter to order his wife to leave Egypt whereupon she went direct to Cyprus to raise an army. She offered her hand and her army to Cyzenicus of Syria who was at war with his cousin, Antiochus VIII, the husband of her sister, Tryphaena. Defeated in battle, Cleopatra IV and Cyzenicus, barricaded themselves in Antiochia, where Cleopatra IV sought sanctuary in the temple of Artemis. In vain: she was dragged from the temple and put to death by her sister.

---

200   Diodorus, Book XXXIV, Chapter 14.
201   Justin, Book XXXVIII, Chapter 8.

In 110 BC, Soter II, by then married to another sister, Cleopatra V Selene, was forced by his mother to accept his brother, Ptolemy X Alexander I, as his co-ruler. Cleopatra III died in 101 BC and Alexander I married his niece, Cleopatra Berenice, daughter of Soter II. Alexander I made several vain attempts to wrest the throne from his brother, but, in 88 BC, he died in a naval battle, and left Soter II to reign with Cleopatra Berenice as co-ruler. On Soter's death in 80 BC, the all-powerful Roman general, Sulla, made a minor prince of the Egyptian royal family, and his protegé, King of Egypt as Ptolemy XI Alexander II, forcing him to accept Cleopatra Berenice as his joint ruler. Alexander II married Cleopatra Berenice and murdered her 19 days later, but Alexander, the last legitimate member of the Ptolemaic dynasty, was himself killed by the Alexandrian mob shortly afterwards, leaving a will of doubtful authenticity, in which he bequeathed Egypt to Rome.

The throne was inherited by Ptolemy XII Neos Dionysos (80–51 BC), the son of Ptolemy IX Soter II and a mistress. The Alexandrians called him 'Nothus' (Bastard) until, noting his fondness for playing the flute, they nicknamed him 'Auletes' (Piper). In accordance with what had become Ptolemaic tradition, Auletes married his sister, Cleopatra VI Tryphaena. At this stage in the Ptolemaic dynasty, tenure of the throne depended upon the patronage of Rome, and Auletes needed the Roman Senate to sanction his coronation. He thought to obtain Rome's favour by means of bribery, assuming that Egypt's resources were limitless. He was mistaken: receipts from crown monopolies, such as the gold mines of Nubia and the Eastern Desert, had dwindled; the linen industry was practically moribund; Cyprus was making little contribution to the exchequer; Cyrenaica had ceased to pay tribute; and farmers had become reluctant to send their produce to Alexandria for fear of not being paid.

Fortunately for Auletes, Alexandria grew impatient with the illegitimacy of an uncrowned king and let his coronation proceed. Twenty years later, however, the Alexandrians blamed Auletes for Rome's annexation of Cyprus and, in 58 BC, he judged it prudent to depart for Rome, leaving his wife and children behind in Egypt. In his absence, Cleopatra VI Tryphaena ruled with her daughter, Berenice IV, but within two years, she was replaced by Berenice's husband, Archelaus. Berenice's attempts to reconcile the Egyptians with the Crown, and her husband's start on reforming the army and refitting the navy, were cut short in 55 BC, when the proconsul of Syria, Aulus Gabinius, restored Auletes to the throne. Auletes

imprisoned his daughter and her husband and had them murdered; four years later, he died.

Cleopatra VI Tryphaena had borne Auletes five children in all:
Berenice IV (*see* above), Cleopatra VII, Arsinoe, and two sons,
both named Ptolemy. On Auletes' death in 51 BC, Cleopatra VII
became queen-regnant of Egypt at the age of 18, the last and, in
many ways, the greatest of the Ptolemies. Popular legend spoke of
her as a great beauty, but it seems certain that her beauty lay in her
voice and manner rather than in her face. She had abundant charm
as well as outstanding ability and character, and was prepared
to use her body as an instrument of power politics. Her reign
began inauspiciously. Having made a dynastic marriage with her
brother, the elder of the two named Ptolemy, who thereby became
Ptolemy XIII, she was ousted by the 12-year-old boy and forced
to flee to Syria. In 48 BC, Pompey was defeated at Pharsalus by
his rival, Julius Caesar, and sought refuge in Egypt. Once there,
he was put to death with Ptolemy XIII's approval. When Julius
Caesar himself arrived in Egypt, he was dismayed by the news, but
took no action against the young king, apart from forcing him to
take back Cleopatra in accordance with the testament of Ptolemy
Auletes.[202] Several months later, Ptolemy XIII joined an insurrection against Caesar, was defeated in a skirmish and drowned in the
Nile.[203]

In 47 BC, Cleopatra VII married the younger of her brothers,
Ptolemy, who, at the age of 12, became the fourteenth king of that
name to rule Egypt. Within the year, Caesar returned to Rome,
and Cleopatra, by then his mistress and the mother of his son,
Caesarion, followed him, leaving Ptolemy XIV as sole ruler in
Egypt. Their sister, Arsinoe, who had joined in the insurrection
against Caesar, was taken to Rome to be exhibited in his great
triumphal parade. After Caesar's assassination in 44 BC, Cleopatra
returned to Egypt. She is reputed to have poisoned Ptolemy XIV
shortly afterwards, and, in 43 BC, she made her son Caesarion
joint ruler with her, as Ptolemy XV (43–30 BC).

After Caesar's death, his nephew, Octavian, formed a trium-
virate with Lepidus and Mark Antony, but, after the Battle of
Philippi in 42 BC, Octavian assumed rule in the western part of the
Roman Empire, and Antony took control of the east, his eastern

---

[202]   Caesar, *Civil War*, Book III, para. 108.
[203]   Hirtius, *Alexandrian War*, Chapter XXIII.

Plate 6.1   *Cleopatra VII and her son by Julius Caesar, Caesarion: relief from rear wall of the Temple of Hathor, Dendera, showing the queen and her son in Egyptian dress.*

Hellenistic Egypt

portion including Egypt. Summoned to Tarsus to explain her lack of support at Philippi, Cleopatra arrived in state. Her first meeting with Antony took place on the royal barge, a clever move typical of this wily queen because the barge was technically Egyptian soil, which made Antony her guest rather than her master. Antony followed Cleopatra to Egypt and, in 37 BC, they were married under Egyptian, though not Roman, law. By 40 BC, Cleopatra had borne Antony the twins, Alexander Helios and Cleopatra Selene; and five years later, she bore him a second son, Ptolemy Philadelphus.

Cleopatra and Antony were ambitious of uniting east and west into one empire, an aim that inevitably brought them into conflict with Octavian. In August, 31 BC, the rivals met in a great sea battle off the Ionian coast of Greece at Actium. Defeated, the queen set sail for Egypt with Antony not far behind. Antony, in despair, fell on his sword; and Cleopatra, sensing that she would fail to beguile the austere Octavian as she had Julius Caesar and Antony, committed suicide. Her son by Julius Caesar, Caesarion, was murdered on Octavian's orders, but her other children were spared. Ptolemy Philadelphus and Cleopatra Selene were brought up with Octavian's own children, and Cleopatra Selene eventually became the wife of King Juba of Mauretania, in a marriage that, according to ancient Egyptian law, entitled him to claim the throne of Egypt to which she was heiress. Nothing could better illustrate Octavian's supreme confidence in his own power and his contempt for Egyptian custom.

Thus did Dynastic Egypt, after surviving for 3000 years, come to its end. The Ptolemies, who with few exceptions might well be characterized as murderous thugs, could clearly lay no claim to being more civilized than previous rulers of Egypt, nor to being true inheritors of either the Athenian spirit or that of Alexander. Nearly 2000 years later, the Alexandrian poet Cavafy wrote of 'waiting for the barbarians';[204] but it sometimes seems that with the later Ptolemies, and after them the Romans, the barbarians were already there.

---

[204] C. P. Cavafy (1863–1933). For the poem, *see Four Greek Poets* (Penguin Modern European Poets) 1966, pp. 11–12.

Government and Administration

Alexander the Great left the administration of Egypt largely in the hands of Egyptians. Neither he nor his successor, Ptolemy Soter, had any desire to destroy Egyptian traditions, political, religious or otherwise, and both were inclined to leave well alone wherever possible. Ptolemy, however, took control of military, financial and foreign policy himself, and set in train the policy of appointing Greeks, rather than Egyptians, to civil and military posts that was to lead to friction between the two communities.

While satrap of Egypt, Ptolemy was assiduous in carrying out Alexander's plans. Alexander had intended that Alexandria, the city he had founded on the north-west coast of the Delta, should become capital of Egypt. Ptolemy made it so, although Alexandria, always treated differently from the rest of Egypt, was in, but not of, the country. While it had been Alexander's purpose to found a Hellenistic city run on democratic lines, there was never any suggestion that the privileges of democracy might be extended to the rest of Egypt, or even to Egyptians living in Alexandria. Ptolemy granted to every Macedonian and Greek man living in the city the right as a free citizen to bear arms, and to meet in open assembly to discuss grievances. Egyptian and Jewish inhabitants had no such rights; and children of mixed marriages were not granted citizenship. Ptolemy limited the power of the citizens of Alexandria by prohibiting them from the actual use of arms; and the assembly was a mere debating chamber without political clout, government being firmly in the hands of Ptolemy himself. The lack of an Alexandrian senate or city council precluded thoughtful and deliberate discussion so that, when crises occurred, the outcome was often dictated by mob hysteria.

Although the Ptolemies adopted Greek names and titles, the public image of each king was that of a traditional pharaoh. Ptolemaic kings were depicted on the walls of Egyptian temples worshipping Egyptian gods and wearing Egyptian dress. Their names were written in hieroglyphs inside cartouches. They never, however, identified with their Egyptian subjects; and only one of them, the great Cleopatra VII, had any knowledge of the Egyptian language. The collection and distribution of taxes, and the prosecution of war against Alexander's former generals and their descendants in the various parts of Alexander's old empire over which they ruled, seemed to be the concern of a Ptolemaic ruler's Greek subjects, while the payment of taxes and much of the agricultural endeavour that provided them fell to the Egyptians. Few Ptolemies made any effort to dismantle the dichotomy between the two halves of the community, with Greeks despising the Egyptians who in turn detested the Greeks.

On the whole, the Ptolemies treated Egypt as their own private possession, to be exploited for the enrichment of the monarchy. To this end, the administration was rigidly controlled by one of the most efficient bureaucracies ever formed. All aspects of life were regulated by a plethora of officials, who were arranged into a strict hierarchy headed by a minister of finance, known by the Greek term *dioiketes*, second in authority only to the king. Every decree, however unimportant, was not only issued in the name of the king but also, it was claimed, emanated directly from him, the tone of many of them suggesting that several of the Ptolemaic kings did indeed adopt a more than usual hands-on approach to administrative affairs.

As of old, Egypt was divided into administrative districts – in the Ptolemaic period their number reduced to about 30. Each of these districts, or *nomoi*, had its own capital in which the district governor, or *strategos*, was based. The administration was run from the bottom of the bureaucracy, where the village scribes assiduously carried out their paperwork and sent streams of correspondence up to central government: records of local court proceedings, and legal documents concerning wills, land ownership, births and deaths all finding their way to the office of the chief justice, or *archidikastes*, in Alexandria. Inevitably in such a large bureaucracy, there was ample opportunity for corruption. Towards the end of the Ptolemaic era, posts in the administration tended to become hereditary, and throughout the period, they were bought and sold.

Economy

In the Ptolemaic Period, coinage became the official medium of economic transaction in Egypt, though barter and payment in kind was widespread. The use of money in the upper economic levels of society might be expected, but it is clear that lower sections of

Egyptian society were also monetarized to a marked degree. Gold, silver and bronze coins were current, their size, weight and purity carefully monitored and publicly proclaimed. From the beginning of the period until AD 296, the currency of Egypt was 'closed': the export of coins forbidden and the exchange of all foreign currency brought into Egypt mandatory.

A prosperous Egypt being essential to Ptolemy Soter's plans, he made improvements to commerce by establishing state monopolies, in gold mining and linen production, for example, a practice in which he was following earlier kings of Egypt. He also began a process of agricultural reform, in which it became the norm for two crops per year to be grown; and he extended cultivated land through reclamation schemes in the Faiyum. Apart from cereals, the main cash crops were papyrus and olives; and, in 259 BC, Ptolemy II Philadelphus prepared a minutely detailed set of Revenue Laws[205] for the monitoring of these productive industries, which were often run by private individuals under strict supervision, though they are usually termed royal monopolies. He reopened the ancient canal between the Nile and the Red Sea (*see* page 186) to promote Red Sea trade, and was probably the founder of the town of Berenice which Pliny the Elder called 'Panchrysos' (the all-golden),[206] built to exploit the gold mines of the Sudanese Nubian desert between the Wadis el-Allaqi and Gabgaba. Berenice, which had an estimated population of at least 10,000, is now known to have been at Daraheib in the Wadi el-Allaqi.[207]

Philadelphus founded a number of Greek settlements throughout Egypt but especially in the Faiyum which, extensively developed and colonized, was named the Arsinoite *nome* in honour of his wife, Arsinoe II. Their purpose was to exploit the potential of the Faiyum basin and to settle Greeks among the indigenous population, mainly through allocations of land to army veterans. The policy of cleruchy, that is, settling soldiers on Crown land, in return for which they were liable for military service, enabled cleruchs to own large tracts: in 118 BC, for example, a third of the land at Kerkeosiris[208] in the southern Faiyum was owned by cleruchs. Although officially the holding reverted to the Crown on

[205] Austin, 1981, no. 236.
[206] *Naturalis Historia*, Book VI.
[207] See A. and A. Castiglioni, *Egyptian Archaeology*, 4, 1994, pp. 19–22.
[208] Crawford, 1971.

the death of a cleruch, in practice soldiers began to hand their tenancies on to their sons so that, by the first century BC, cleruchial holdings had become fully heritable. At the beginning of the Ptolemaic Period, army service was restricted to Greeks, but, from the reign of Ptolemy IV Philopator, it was opened to native Egyptians so that they, too, benefited from the cleruchial system. Interestingly, a policy of allocating land to army veterans had first been introduced into Egypt over 1000 years before, in the reign of Thutmose III.

The system of canals cut in the Faiyum in the Twelfth Dynasty under Amenemhat III having fallen into disrepair, a new and extensive irrigation system was put into place.[209] During the Ptolemaic Period, half the land of one village, Kerkeosiris, was given over to wheat, between 2 and 16 per cent to barley, and between 13 and 20 per cent to lentils, a distribution which may have been typical. The villagers also cultivated beans, fenugreek, garlic and cumin.

Throughout Egypt, sheep were the most important livestock, with some flocks numbering over 1000 animals. They were shorn twice a year; and for cheese-making, their milk, together with goats' milk, was used in preference to cows' milk. The manufacture and export of glass played a major part in the economy, the most important glass workshops being in Alexandria, where Egyptians were among the leading glass-workers in the world. They invented new techniques, such as cut-glass work, *millefiori*, that is, the process in which many coloured-glass rods are placed together to produce a rainbow-like effect, and gold sandwich glass, in which gold foil is cut into patterns and placed between two layers of glass, still an accomplishment of Egyptian craftsmen. At some time during the first century BC, they may have perfected the art of glass-blowing, although this did not flourish until the late Roman Period.

Religion

Throughout the Ptolemaic Period, Egyptians continued to worship their own gods in much the same manner as before. The Greeks, tolerant as ever of the religion of other nations and inclined to find

209   Diodorus I, 61; and Kees, 1961, pp. 220–3.

aspects of their own gods in foreign deities, were prepared to recognize the Egyptian pantheon. Ptolemy Soter introduced into Egypt a new deity, Serapis, a hybrid with the characteristics of the Egyptian Osiris and Apis (*see* pages 67 and 214) and of the Greek Zeus, Asklepios and Dionysos. A great temple was built for him, the Serapeum in Alexandria, which became a place of pilgrimage until AD 389, when the Emperor Theodosius ordered its destruction. Serapis, however, was designed to appeal to Greek tastes and was never fully accepted by the Egyptians. He did find favour in Greece and in Rome, so that the Ptolemies used him and the even more popular Isis to promulgate Egyptian culture in the classical world.

There is no record from the Ptolemaic Period of Greeks serving as priests in native Egyptian temples. Its kings, however, finding it politic to patronize the Egyptian religion, commissioned the building of temples, five of which are particularly noteworthy: Edfu (begun by Ptolemy III and completed by Ptolemies VIII, IX and XII); Dendera (Ptolemy IX); Philae (Ptolemies IV and V); Esna (Ptolemy VI); and Kom Ombo (Ptolemies V, VIII and XII). Today, they hold an especially important place in any study of ancient Egyptian temples, for three main reasons: they were all built over a comparatively short space of time, and can be seen as entities in themselves rather than as sprawling accumulations, such as the edifices at Karnak which were enlarged and embellished over hundreds of years; the first three are the best preserved of the temples in Egypt; and, in their inscriptions, they offer much information about temple ritual not available elsewhere.

The Egyptian priesthood considered that its duty, as the repository of knowledge, was to protect Egyptian culture and customs from the 'Ionian dogs', as they termed the Greeks. Gradually, however, the Ptolemaic kings developed a *modus vivendi* with the powerful Egyptian priesthood, and, in return for priestly co-operation in handling the native populace, they agreed to be treated like the Egyptian kings of old, by accepting the religious obligations that went with kingship and the rites through which legitimacy was conferred upon a ruler, and by building temples and making offerings to the Egyptian gods. These temples are exercises in Egyptian nationalism, the reliefs on their walls often containing veiled insults to the Greeks in the inscriptions that accompany them, written in such a deliberately elaborate and

confusing hieroglyphic script[210] that they baffled even those few
Greeks who were able to read standard hieroglyphic inscriptions.
They are more extensive and more detailed than those of any other
period, the priesthood of the time realizing that they had to
commit their knowledge to writing rather than to rely on custom
and memory, or even on the records set down on papyrus rolls
which were not indestructible. Ptolemaic temples thus became
source books in stone of Egyptian temple ritual.

In the Late and Ptolemaic Periods there was an extraordinary
revival in animal cults. Although the worship of gods made manifest in animals was one of the oldest forms of religion in Egypt (*see*
page 65), long before the Ptolemaic Period a more intellectual
approach to religion had developed. It seems likely, therefore, that
the popularity of animal cults in the last centuries before Christ
owed much to Egyptian nationalism. Sickened by successive
periods of foreign domination, priests may have encouraged Egyptians to turn to what was perhaps the most characteristic feature
of Egyptian religion, the worship of sacred animals, mummified
after death and buried in tombs. Old animal cults, such as those of
the Apis,[211] Mnevis[212] and Buchis[213] bulls, enjoyed the patronage of
Ptolemaic kings, though the most popular deity was a relative
newcomer, Bastet, the cat goddess, identified with Artemis and
worshipped by Greeks and by Egyptians. Bastet's chief shrine, at
Bubastis in the eastern Delta, consisted of a temple much admired
by Herodotus,[214] and all cats were identified with her. According
to Herodotus,[215] whenever a cat died, the Egyptians shaved their
eyebrows and went into mourning.

[210]   Fairman, 1943, p. 55ff.
[211]   Associated with Ptah and worshipped at Memphis. The introduction of the
new god, Serapis (*see* page 213) brought a new lease of life to the ancient burial
ground of the Apis bulls at Sakkara. In the Ptolemaic Period the burial vaults at
Sakkara, like those at Alexandria, were called the Serapeum. *See* Watterson,
1984, pp. 165–6.
[212]   Associated with Re and worshipped at Heliopolis. Lavish endowments,
recorded on the Rosetta Stone, were provided for him by Ptolemy V Epiphanes.
See Watterson, 1984, p. 68.
[213]   Associated with Montu, the war god, and worshipped at Armant (Greek
Hermonthis) near Luxor. Buried in a catacomb known as the Bucheum, where
the earliest burials so far found date to the reign of Nectanebo II and the latest
to Diocletian, over 600 years later. *See* Watterson, 1984, pp. 190–1.
[214]   Herodotus, II, 138.
[215]   Herodotus, II, 68.

At Sakkara, and Tuna el-Gebel in Middle Egypt, ibises and baboons sacred to Thoth, worshipped in both places, were mummified and buried in subterranean galleries. Eggs found on the site at Sakkara suggest that the birds were bred there – in large numbers if one text is anything to go by. This text, written in demotic on a piece of broken pot, refers to the provision of food for 60,000 ibises.[216] It has been estimated that the average annual rate in the burial of ibises at Sakkara was 10,000, which would suggest that the birds were ritually slaughtered in large numbers. At Elephantine, rams, as representatives of the god Khnum, were mummified, dressed in their regalia, which included a crown, and buried in large sarcophagi. Crocodiles, representing the god Sobek, were buried at Kom Ombo; and in the Faiyum, large numbers of them, in a variety of sizes, have been found, complete with clutches of eggs. Many of the reptiles were prepared for burial simply with black resin poured over the body, which has often been packed into shape with discarded papyrus documents. Large quantities of such papyri were also used to make cartonnage wrappings. The crocodile mummies of the Ptolemaic Period are thus invaluable sources of information for the modern papyrologist.

Domestic Life and Architecture

In the Graeco-Roman Period, native Egyptians tended to live separately from their foreign conquerors, each community with its particular lifestyle. In Alexandria and elsewhere, the Greeks had no wish to grant the Egyptians the privileges of citizenship; and, even in the third century AD, it was said that the Egyptian element of the population could be distinguished not only by its language but also by 'its way of life, the rusticity of which is far removed from the urban style of living'.[217]

New towns and *nome* capitals were built in the Ptolemaic period, the most famous of which is Oxyrhynchus, which lies some 80 kilometres south of the Faiyum. Like the other *nome* capitals, Oxyrhynchus is known, not through its archaeological remains, but because of the mass of papyrus documents found

---

[216] Spencer, 1982, p. 210.
[217] Hunt and Edgar, 1932–34, ii, no. 215.

there.[218] The papyri make it evident that Oxyrhynchus was Greek and not Egyptian, though probably built over an older settlement, which limited the possibility of construction in the form of the regularly planned town that was typical of the Graeco-Roman world. In the third century AD, the town numbered 4000 free men entitled to vote as its citizens, and from this, it may be estimated that the total population was in excess of 10,000.

Oxyrhynchus probably boasted forms of classical architecture such as a colonnaded main street. The public buildings mentioned in the papyri certainly reflected a Greek lifestyle, with at least four public baths, for the use of Greeks and those Egyptians who were Hellenized, the public bath not being a traditional Egyptian institution. There was a hippodrome and a gymnasium, again not Egyptian institutions whereas, to the Greeks, a gymnasium was essential as a place in which to meet not only for exercise but also to discuss politics, activities not traditionally part of the Egyptian way of life. There was a theatre that may have held up to 1000 spectators; the plays performed would be Greek, though religious drama had long been known to the Egyptians.[219] According to the papyri, there were some 20 temples, one of which was dedicated to Serapis and housed a bank.

Cultural Achievements

Alexandria

Alexandria was destined to be the greatest cultural achievement of the Hellenistic period not only in Egypt but elsewhere. Alexander had consided redeveloping Naucratis, founded late in the sixth century BC by Ionian colonists from Miletus, and, in his time, the only major Greek settlement in Egypt, but had discovered that Naucratis, an inland site, was unsuitable for his purposes. From the outset, he intended his city to be a great centre of trade and commerce, a link between east and west, and the intellectual capital of the Hellenistic world. Deciding to found his new city on the coast to the north of Naucratis, Alexander himself outlined its general layout, but it was planned by Deinocrates of Chalcedon,

---

[218]   Grenfell et al., 1900.
[219]   Fairman, 1974.

who had redesigned Ephesus: Alexander did not live to see his foundation completed. The city grew immensely wealthy, not only because of its port but also through the manufacture of glass, papyrus and linen.

Alexandria was 25 kilometres in circumference and laid out on an axial grid system radiating from two main avenues. The city supported a population of some 300,000 free citizens and at least that number of slaves. For the port, the island of Pharos was connected to the mainland by a mole, on either side of which was a harbour. In due course, over a quarter of the city was covered with palaces, temples and other public buildings such as baths, a theatre, a hippodrome and gymnasiums. Many of its greatest institutions, notably the Pharos lighthouse, the Great Library and its adjunct, the Daughter Library, were built in the reign of Ptolemy II Philadelphus; but it was his father, Ptolemy Soter, who established the city as a centre of scholarship. Through his careful management of the economy, he was well able to afford to attract learned men to Alexandria, where they lived at state expense, studying in his Academy of the Muses or Mouseion (Museum).

The Ptolemys had little regard for Egypt's cultural heritage. Alexandria remained throughout the dynasty a great Hellenistic city, and from the wealth that accrued through the endeavours of native Egyptians, nurtured great men of learning who contributed significantly to scientific advance, especially during the early part of the dynasty. In the third century BC, Archimedes spent some time in the city, where he is said to have invented the Archimedean screw.[220] Ptolemy II Philadelphus' guest, Ctesibius, invented the *clepsydra* (water clock) and the pressure pump. The mathematician, Euclid (*c.*300 BC), the third-century BC physician, Erasistratus, and the geographers, Claudius Ptolemy (*c.*150 BC) and Eratosthenes, all worked in Alexandria.

At the invitation of Ptolemy III Euergetes I, Eratosthenes, born in Cyrene in 276 BC, followed Callimachus (*see* page 196) to Alexandria, and at state expense, pursued his studies in philosophy, astronomy, history, geography, mathematics and literary criticism. Such versatility brought from his detractors the soubriquet 'Beta', or second; in other words, jack of all trades and master of none. His admirers conferred on him the title *philologus*, the first

---

[220] Diodorus 5, 37, 3.

Alexandrian so honoured, although he did not claim to be omniscient. Eratosthenes' map of the ancient world was the first to show lines of latitude and longitude. His greatest achievement was his estimation of the Earth's circumference, correct to within less than 200 kilometres, and arrived at by geometrical calculation based on his observations of the length of the Sun's shadow cast at noon on the day of the summer solstice at Alexandria and Syene (Aswan). It was Eratosthenes who inspired the reform of the calendar. In use for millenniums, the Egyptian calendar (*see* page 5) was known to be deficient in that it made no allowance for the fact that the Earth took slightly longer than 365 days to pass round the Sun. To the great majority of Egyptians, who were peasant farmers, such niceties were of no concern because it was the agricultural seasons that composed their year. The bureaucrats viewed things differently, especially as documents of the Ptolemaic Period were dated in a random mixture of the regnal year of the king, the financial year, the Egyptian calendar and the Macedonian calendar.

In 238 BC, Euergetes I convened a meeting of the Egyptian priesthood at Canopus. The results of their deliberations were published as the Decree of Canopus,[221] copies of which were inscribed on stone and set up in the major temples, and of which two copies are extant in the Louvre and Cairo Museums. The Decree was written in hieroglyphs, in demotic and in Greek; and, among other matters, it acknowledged the divinity of Ptolemy III and conferred the title *Euergetai* or 'Benefactor Gods' upon him and his wife, henceforward to be served by a newly established class of priests who would be known as the 'priests of the Benefactor Gods'. The Decree commanded that one day be added to the calendar every four years, the day to be called the Festival of the Benefactor Gods; and that the new calendar should take as its starting point the year 311 BC, the official date of the death of Alexander IV. Eratosthenes' new calendar would be the basis for a calendar, revised by Julius Caesar in 45 BC, and amended by Pope Gregory in AD 1582, which is the calendar in use today. The Egyptians were not impressed by it: Alexandrians continued to use the Macedonian lunar year, the rest of Egypt the old solar calendar.

---

[221] OGIS, no. 56. A translation of the Decree is in J. C. Mahaffy, *History of Egypt under the Ptolemaic Dynasty* (London, 1899).

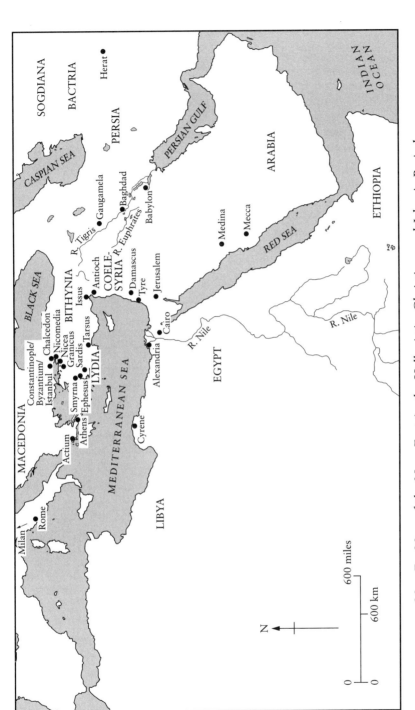

Map 7   Map of the Near East in the Hellenistic, Christian, and Islamic Periods.

Architecture

Tombs

The rich of the Ptolemaic era were buried in stone sarcophagi in
decorated tombs; those unable to afford such luxury in pottery
coffins; and the poor, perhaps wrapped in bandages coated with
bitumen, in communal graves. The tombs were often of the traditional rock-cut type, and tombs of various designs built in stone or
brick were not uncommon. A tomb chapel, designed to resemble a
contemporary house, was popular, with the purpose of sheltering
the families of the deceased on their visits during feasts; there are
good examples at Tuna el-Gebel, a necropolis used from the late
Ramesside period to Roman times. At Tuna el-Gebel, the house
tombs of the later period are arranged in streets and form a
veritable city of the dead.

Perhaps the most unusual of the tombs at Tuna el-Gebel is the
family tomb of Pedusiri, better known by the Greek form of his
name, Petosiris, who was buried with his father and grandfather,
his wife, his children and other family members, in burial chambers below ground, under a single tomb chapel resembling a small
temple, complete with pillared portico and an altar in the courtyard, in the Greek style. All the men of Petosiris' family held high
office in connection with the cult of Thoth at Hermopolis (*see* page
136), Petosiris himself being high priest in the time of Philip
Arrhidaeus. The reliefs on the interior walls of his tomb chapel
mix Egyptian themes, some not in use since the Old Kingdom,
with a style influenced by Greek art, a proof that some Egyptians
at least were susceptible to Greek influence. By contrast, Egyptian
deities and motifs are sometimes found in the decoration of tombs
owned by Greeks.

Temples

The standard layout of a Ptolemaic temple clearly demonstrates
the domestic nature of the building as the house of the god. The
pylon is its entrance gate, beyond which the columns of a colonnaded court represent plants in a garden. Beyond this court is a
hypostyle hall, the reception room, which leads into another hall,
a dining room, with a menu of the meals served to the god listed

Plate 6.2   Temple of Hathor, Dendera (Graeco-Roman period); interior of hypostyle hall. Note column capitals in the shape of a woman's head with cow's ears – a reminder that one of Hathor's manifestations was as a cow goddess.

on its walls. The inner sanctuary is the master bedroom; and the side chapels surrounding it are guest bedrooms and storage cupboards, where the god's regalia and clothing were kept.

Temples of the New Kingdom and Late Period were constructed in stone, their decoration recalling the reeds and mud with which temples were originally built. Columns copy the supports formerly made from tree trunks or bundles of plant stems, often displaying five bands carved at the top as if holding together a bunch of stems. Column bases are carved in imitation of the calyx of a lily, and capitals are varied: lotiform, palmiform, or papyriform, reflecting the vegetable origin of columns. In the Graeco-Roman period, a campaniform capital was particularly popular, a composite capital derived from many varieties of flower, real and imaginary.

The walls of a stone temple are cut as copies of the materials used in the building of reed shrines, as if made of interwoven palm sticks or mats, covered with a thick coating of mud, the corners seemingly strengthened with pseudo-bundles of reeds or palm sticks, bound together and lashed to each corner. The tops of walls were originally left unbound, the palm fronds free to bend, but, in the stone temples, the curve of palm fronds is imitated by a *cavetto* cornice, and the reinforcements by the purely decorative *torus* roll. The stone temple pylons derive from the towers of mud and reed that stood outside primitive reed shrines, the decoration of *cavetto* cornice and *torus* roll reproducing in stone the features of reed architecture. Pylons also played a role in the interpretation of the temple as a reflection of the physical world, the two wings of each pylon representing the hills on the horizon behind which the sun rose and set. At Medinet Habu, the walls of the passageway between the wings of the pylon are decorated with reliefs showing the adoration of the sun: on the eastern wall, the sun is rising, on the western wall it is setting.[222]

Ptolemaic temples display all these features and, in addition, their basic decoration reflects the mythological origins of the temple and of the world. Each major deity had his or her own version of a creation legend, that of the falcon god, Horus, claiming that he was instrumental in the creation of the world. In Horus' temple at Edfu, for example, an inscription[223] tells of how, in the beginning, Chaos reigned until an island appeared in the Nun, the primeval sea that covered the earth. Only when a falcon emerged out of the darkness and alighted upon the island did light break over Chaos and the world begin. A simple reed shelter was built for the falcon, to which rooms were added, gradually giving rise to the first temple. In many temples of the New Kingdom (at Medinet Habu, for instance) and the Ptolemaic Period, a slight but distinct rise in floor level from outer hall to sanctuary, is an architectural feature resonant of the siting of the sanctuary of the original shrine on the highest point of the Island of Creation.

A high mud-brick wall surrounded each temple, and, where it is

[222] Derchain, 1966, p. 18.
[223] Reymond, 1969, Chapter 2.

Plate 6.3   Temple of Horus, Edfu (built between 237 and 71 BC): courtyard.

well-enough preserved, as at Karnak, Medinet Habu and Dendera, it can clearly be seen to have been built in sections alternating concave with convex, giving the impression of wavy lines. This method of building a mud-brick wall apparently serves no architectural function,[224] and may be an attempt to represent the waves of the Nun.[225] Within the temple, the base of a wall is often cut with a dado of lily or lotus plants seeming to spring from the ground of the stone floor, a further reminiscence of the Island of Creation.

By the Ptolemaic Period, a more complex, cosmological interpretation of the temple had been developed. As the home of a god, it represented the sky, the rooms on its eastern side equated with the eastern half of the heavens, and those on its western side with the western sky. It was regarded as a cosmic theatre in which were enacted the great events pertaining to Egypt and its safety.[226] The temple was also regarded as a representation of the physical world, symbolizing Egypt. The rites carried out therein by the

[224]   Spencer, 1979, pp. 232–7.
[225]   Barguet, 1962, p. 32.
[226]   Rochmonteix, 1894, p. 20.

king[227] were designed to maintain the balance between Egypt and the forces of Chaos, an ever-present threat. In the Late and Graeco-Roman Periods, the king was identified with the child of the deity of the temple. Special structures, developed from the sanctuaries which were in earlier periods devoted to the theogamy ritual, were built within the temple precinct. The Ptolemaic structures were known as *mammisi*, and in them the birth of the divine child was celebrated annually.

The exterior of a temple was concerned with its protection and, by extension, the protection of Egypt, its pylons decorated with reliefs that showed the king smiting Egypt's enemies. Exterior walls were carved with reliefs of battles – usually purposefully orientated in that southern walls contain reliefs depicting Nubian enemies, western walls Libyan enemies and northern walls Asiatic foes. On the exterior walls of many temples are lion-headed gargoyles round water spouts intended to remove water, either rain or the water used in rituals, from the roof. They are inscribed with magic formulas which state that, in spitting out this water, the lions are symbolically spitting out evil away from Egypt – a good example of the Egyptian talent for imbuing something that has practical purpose with magical significance.

Literature

Many of the literary works written for Egyptians of the Hellenistic Period display a marked antiquarian tendency. They were works of propaganda – stories set in previous centuries but written by contemporary scribes – so-called pseudepigrapha. The *Bentresh Stele*, purporting to have been written in the time of Ramesses II, carries the story of Ramesses' sister-in-law, Bentresh, who is cured of an illness by the statue of the god, Khonsu. The work is a piece of propaganda on behalf of Khonsu, probably composed in the Ptolemaic Period. Another work of the same period is the *Famine Stele*, supposedly written in the time of King Djoser of the Third Dynasty, but probably composed by the priests of the Temple of

---

[227] In theory the king was high priest of every temple. Reliefs, therefore, show the king carrying out every ritual, although in practice, of course, he must have had a deputy.

Khnum in Elephantine, in an attempt to reinforce their claim to the local tax revenues.

The demotic literature of the time is best represented by narrative tales, and instructions in wisdom such as those of Ankhsheshonq and the Papyrus Insinger, for example.[228] The hero of several vivid demotic stories is Prince Khamwese, a son of Ramesses II and High Priest of Ptah at Memphis. The *Story of Setne Khamwas (Khamwese) and Naneferkaptah* tells in lively detail of how Khamwese, a man much interested in magic, steals a magical papyrus from the tomb of the magician, Naneferkaptah, who, in the end, makes the prince give back the payrus – but not before he has been seduced, made to murder his children and robbed of his clothes by a certain Tabubu! Another hero of a demotic tale is Pedikhons, a prince of the Twenty-third Dynasty, who invades the land of Khor (Syria) and challenges its ruler, the Amazon queen, Serpot, to battle. Serpot's army inflicts heavy casualties on the Egyptians, and Pedikhons challenges the Amazon to single combat. They fight all day until, when night falls, they call a truce and begin to talk to each other – and at last they fall in love. This *Story of Prince Pedikhons and Queen Serpot* is one of several clearly inspired by Greek literature, as it echoes that of Achilles and the Amazon, Penthesilea.

This looking back to the past, a common feature of pseudepigrapha and demotic literature, is often taken as a sign of weakness. In this case, however, it is likely that it allowed native Egyptian literature to play an important part in the Egyptians' struggle to maintain their own culture in the face of the tide of Hellenism. This would more than justify demotic literature's importance; but it is also to be valued on its merits as literature alone.

---

[228] For these and other works of literature of the period *see* Lichtheim, 1980.

7

Roman and Christian Egypt

On the deaths of Cleopatra VII and Caesarion, Egypt passed into the hands of Octavian, who promptly took possession of the royal treasury, which became the foundation of his personal fortune, and levied extra taxes. Egypt also became Rome's granary, the source of the immense wealth that enabled Octavian to reward the loyalty of his legionaries. The Roman Empire was in dire need of reorganization, and, as his first priority, Octavian created a strong, authoritarian government headed by a key figure, himself. Aware of Rome's traditional dislike of tyrants and kings, he played down the fact that he was regarded as a pharaoh in Egypt, and was careful not to style himself 'Emperor'. Instead, he served as head of state under the title *princeps senatus*, Leader of the Senate, despite the conferment on him, in 27 BC, of the title Augustus, (the revered one), which he joined to his family name, and was thenceforward known as Caesar Augustus. Augustus regarded Egypt as his personal property, and it became a land exploited on behalf of a ruler who lived elsewhere.

History

Under Augustus Egypt's prosperity grew for a time. The improvements in administration which brought this about, however, were made not for the benefit of the Greek population, and still less of the Egyptian, but to create wealth for Rome. It was an appreciation of its importance as a source of wealth that persuaded the Roman emperors to take care not to imbroil the country directly in the political crises that plagued the Empire from time to time.

The Romans generally valued Egypt for its productivity, but it was the land itself that held a fascination for many of them, who saw it as a place full of exotic wonders and had a penchant for bringing some of its antiquities back to Rome. On occasion, the emperor took a special interest: Hadrian, for instance, paid a visit to Egypt in AD 130, and founded a new city, Antinoopolis, at the spot where his favourite, Antinous, had drowned in the Nile.

For several centuries after Augustus, religion gave rise to political crises in Egypt. Alexandria played an important part in the development of the new religion, Christianity, which began to spread throughout the Roman Empire in the first century AD. Under Roman rule, the city did not enjoy so many privileges as under the Ptolemies, but it remained one of the most prosperous ports of the Empire; and above all was still a centre of learning. According to Egyptian Christian tradition, St Mark the Evangelist first brought Christianity to Egypt in the early 40s AD, and it was in the Jewish quarter of Alexandria that he made his first convert, a shoemaker named Anianus or Hananiah. St Mark is said to have founded the diocese, or See, of Alexandria, and to have become the first Patriarch of its Church.

In its early years, Christianity was officially classified by Rome as a sect of Judaism: accordingly, Christians suffered in the persecutions carried out against Alexandrian Jews in the first century. Christianity was slow to take hold in Alexandria, many of its newly converted Christians unable to distinguish between Christ and Serapis but worshipping both. The Emperor Hadrian noted that even those Alexandrians who professed to be bishops of Christ prostrated themselves before the pagan god.

For two years from AD 249, Christians throughout the Roman Empire, including Egypt, endured intermittent persecutions, beginning with the Edict of Decius, which was promulgated in that year, and resuming seven years later on the orders of the Emperor Valerian, whose explicit target was the eradication of the Church leaders to weaken the Church. In AD 262, the Edict of Gallienus decreed that Christianity should be tolerated, a respite that lasted until AD 284, when the Emperor Diocletian began what was to be the last great persecution of Christians in the history of the Roman Empire. In Egypt, the Diocletian persecutions, which lasted for four years, were particularly severe, and a great many Christians, including Egyptian-speaking members of the populace, were put to death. Although the number of martyrs was probably not as great as was later claimed, nevertheless, so many Egyptians died that the era marked the beginning of a native, or Coptic (*see* page 252) Church, that was distinct from the Church of Alexandria, which was basically Greek. The period is known in the Coptic Church as 'The Era of Martyrs'; and commemorated in the Coptic Calendar, in which the dating of years begins with the start of Diocletian's reign – 29 August AD 284 – in the Coptic Calendar becoming 1 AM (1 Annus Martyrius or First Year of the Martyrs).

In AD 313, the Emperor Constantine issued his Edict of Milan in which the right to freedom of worship was granted to everyone. In Egypt, native Egyptians had been slow to adopt Christianity: in the Decian persecutions, only four non-Greek Egyptian martyrs were identified by the Patriarch of Alexandria, Dionysius (AD 247–64), who became the first holder of that office to advocate the active conversion of native Egyptians; and Christianity began to spread so rapidly in the non-Greek communities that, within a few years, it was flourishing throughout Egypt.

With the persecutions ended and freedom of worship granted, the Church was riven by great theological disputes, most of them concerning the nature of Christ. Egyptian Christians played no small part in these disputes which would, in time, separate the Egyptian Church from the rest of Christendom for, thanks to the efforts of Patriarch Dionysius, it had become extremely influential throughout the Christian world, its prelates accepted as great international figures. The first dispute was begun in about AD 318 by an Alexandrian priest named Arius. He challenged the doctrine of the Trinity of Father, Son and Holy Ghost, maintaining that God the Father was superior to God the Son, who in turn was superior to the Holy Ghost. In AD 321, a synod of bishops from Egypt and Syria met at Alexandria and excommunicated Arius.

The problems caused by teachers like Arius, who challenged orthodox beliefs, led to a series of ecumenical councils called by the Emperor, the first of which, at Nicaea[229] in AD 325, was attended by Constantine himself. The Council produced the Nicene Creed, which excluded Arianism with the crucial statement that Christ is of one substance with the Father (*homoousion to patri*). Nonetheless, when Constantine was baptized

[229] Iznik in Turkey.

in AD 337, he chose to be baptized according to Arian rites; and by AD 350, Arianism had become the dominant religion of the court.

The Patriarch of Alexandria, Athanasius (*c.* AD 296–373), an influential figure at the Council of Nicaea, became the chief protagonist in the struggles of orthodox Christianity against Arianism. Almost as soon as he became Patriarch, the Arians began to attack him. In AD 330, he was accused of imposing a local tax on linen garments, and, among other claims, of murdering Arsenius, a bishop. Summoned to a council at Tyre to answer the charge of murder, Athanasius was able to refute it by producing Arsenius alive and well. He was then accused of threatening to prevent the grain fleet from sailing, at which he protested, asking how he, a private citizen, could do so. The Emperor Constantine, taking no chances, banished him from Egypt.

Athanasius remained in exile until Constantine's death. The new Emperor, Constantinus, allowed him to return to Alexandria, where again he had to endure the attacks of the Arians, and the Emperor ordered the expulsion of his supporters from the churches. Athanasius himself went into exile in Rome and did not return to his See until AD 346. He then enjoyed a period of relative peace in which he was able to extend the influence of the Egyptian Church when the Christians of Ethiopia asked him to send them a bishop; Athanasius appointed Frumentius, a Syrian, as the Abba Salama (Father of Peace) or Abuna. For the next 1600 years, until the middle of the twentieth century, the bishops and the Abunas of the Ethiopian Church were Egyptians.

During the 46 years of his Patriarchy (AD 328–74), 20 of them spent in exile, Athanasius managed to hold together the disparate elements of his flock: the orthodox Christians of Egypt – the rich, the poor, the peasants, the educated; Greeks and non-Greeks; Alexandrians; and those who lived in Egypt proper. He was the first Patriarch to make a point of visiting his flock in all parts of Egypt. During his third period of exile (AD 356–62) he sought refuge in the deserts of Egypt and Libya, often with the monks (*see* page 243) who lived there, although he took care that they should not come into conflict with the authorities on his account. Athanasius was not only a leading churchman, he was also one of the greatest theologians of his day. Although he had an understanding of the Egyptian language, he wrote in Greek, his finest work his great *Life* of St Antony (*see* page 243).

After the death of the Emperor Theodosius I in AD 395, the Roman Empire was divided into two: Egypt became part of the Eastern (Byzantine) Empire. Three years before his death, Theodosius I issued an imperial edict outlawing paganism, whereupon the Alexandrian mob, as turbulent as ever, came out on to the streets again. The Patriarch, Theophilus, took the opportunity of harrying heretics within the Church and pagans alike, with a zeal that incited the mob to perpetrate a great act of vandalism, the destruction of the Serapeum in which were housed 40,000 books from the Great Library.

In AD 412, Theophilus was succeeded as Patriarch by his nephew, Cyril, even more fanatical than himself. He had spent some time with the monks in the monasteries of Nitria (*see* page 243) and could therefore count upon their support so that, when in AD 415, the Prefect Orestes complained of Cyril's behaviour, a mob of several hundred monks set upon Orestes, and one of them wounded him. When this monk was executed, Cyril proclaimed him a saint and a martyr. Bands of monks milled round the streets of Alexandria looking for an act of piety to perform before they returned to their monasteries: and found it in the unlucky Hypatia. Hypatia, a noted philosopher, taught mathematics at the Mouseion. To the monks, she was the embodiment of heretical Greek thought and, one suspects, a woman who did not know her proper place. They cut her to pieces with tiles. The death of Hypatia symbolized the death of Alexandria as a city imbued with the spirit of Greece, with its passion to discover truth and create beauty.

In AD 431, the Emperor Theodosius II convened a Council at Ephesus to settle yet another theological dispute. Nestorius, the Patriarch of Constantinople, had begun to teach that Christ had two natures, one human, the other divine: in other words, that His nature was diphysite, a tenet that came to be called the Nestorian heresy, and to which Patriarch Cyril was vehemently opposed. He attended the Council of Ephesus accompanied by monks and bishops from Egypt in such large numbers that they made their presence felt, and, intimidated, the Council condemned Nestorius.

Cyril was succeeded as Patriarch by Dioscorus (AD 444–54), who inherited a strong Church, and a See so rich that, able to exert great temporal power, he became a veritable 'pharaoh of the Church'. He was unable, however, to persuade the Council that met at Chalcedon in AD 451 that Christ had one, monophysite, nature. This Council decreed that Nestorius was no heretic and that henceforward a diphysite doctrine would be followed by the Orthodox Church. Refusing to ratify the Council's decision, Dioscurus was excommunicated, stripped of office and exiled to Gangra in Paphlagonia, where he died three years later. The Churches of Egypt and Syria remained attached to a monophysite doctrine.

There were many in Egypt who supported the Orthodox Church. They were called 'Melkites', from the Semitic word for 'king' (*melk*) because they followed the imperial doctrine, and most of them were Greek. Relations between them and their Monophysite compatriots, who were largely Egyptian, grew very bitter at times, and brought bloodshed. When Justinian became Byzantine Emperor in AD 527, he tried to persuade the Monophysites of Egypt and Syria to accept the diphysite doctrine, and offered the Patriarch of Alexandria, Theodosius, increased power in Egypt and Africa if he would accept Chalcedon. Theodosius refused and was forced into exile. He was replaced as Patriarch by a Chalcedonian from the Tabenessi Monastery, Paul, but he could not win over the Monophysites. Abusing his extensive temporal powers, he treated the Monophysites so harshly that in AD 539 Justinian was forced to depose him. There followed a period in which the Monophysite Church in Alexandria became hopelessly disorganized.

In the sixth century, Egypt as a whole was disorganized, subject not only to religious but also to political strife. The Roman legions had been withdrawn in the fifth century and replaced with local troops garrisoned only in the larger towns. They were not adequate to the task of controlling struggles for power between local governors, nor to drive back Nubian tribes, such as the Blemmyes, who constantly mounted raids unchecked on the south of the country. Nor were they capable of preventing the Persians, under Chosroes, from invading Egypt in AD 616, during the reign of Heraclius (AD 610–41), who was the last of the Byzantines to rule the country. For 13 years the Persians occupied Egypt. They inflicted great damage on Coptic institutions, especially those around Alexandria, but for most Egyptians, the Persians were yet another band of foreign invaders whose presence had to be endured.

Under the protection of the Persians, the Monophysite Andronicus became Patriarch in AD 616, and, for his first six years, his successor, Benjamin (AD 623–62), also enjoyed Persian patronage. By AD 629, however, Heraclius had reclaimed Egypt, and two years later, he appointed Cyrus the Colchian, a Chalcedonian, as Patriarch in place of Benjamin. Cyrus set about converting the Monophysites with whatever force was needed. Monks were expelled from their monasteries, and bishops from their sees, and many died. The bickering over religious dogma, however, was about to be brought to an end. In AD 632, the Prophet Muhammad died, and, within a year, Arab forces had erupted from Arabia on a great *jihad*, carrying the newly developed religion of Islam with them. In AD 636, the Emperor Heraclius was defeated in battle at Yarmuk in Syria, and three years later, the Arabs invaded Egypt. Relations between the Monophysites and the Chalcedonians had become so fraught that many native Egyptian Christians hailed the Arabs as liberators.

Government and Administration

In Egypt, Augustus and his successors, the Roman emperors, were officially regarded as heirs to the pharaohs. Although no Roman emperor was ever crowned King of Upper and Lower Egypt, he was accorded the full royal titulary. Transliterated into hieroglyphs, his name was carved on official monuments inside a cartouche and accompanied by epithets such as 'Son of Re'. For the three centuries of Roman rule, reliefs carved on the walls of Egyptian temples depict the emperors making offerings to Egyptian gods, dressed in the Egyptian style, wearing Egyptian crowns, carrying the pharaonic symbols of office. As far as the Egyptians were concerned, Roman emperors, like the Ptolemaic kings before them, were performing the role that a king of Egypt had throughout the centuries been expected to play: maintaining equilibrium between Egypt, as represented by the temple, and the forces of Chaos that were a constant threat (*see* page 224).

Augustus made some changes in the administration. He retained the 30 administrative districts (*nomoi*) into which the country had been divided by the Ptolemies, but he reduced the powers of chief officers, the *strategoi* (commanders), who had exercised civil and military authority, and decreed that they should exercise only administrative and judicial powers. He appointed a prefect to govern the country as his personal representative. A century or so later, the historian Tacitus (*c.* AD 55–115) noted with approval that Egypt,

> together with the forces designed to keep it in order, has been governed ever since Augustus's day by Romans of equestrian rank acting as successors to the Ptolemies. It seemed politic that a province of this sort – difficult of access, exporting a valuable corn crop yet divided and unsettled by strange cults and irresponsible excesses, indifferent to law and ignorant of civil government – should be kept under the immediate control of the imperial house.[230]

It did indeed seem politic to Augustus to keep control of Egypt; and to this end he took care not to make it a province of the Empire. As a province, Egypt would have been administered by a governor of senatorial rank, who may have turned the wealth of the country to his advantage by using it as a power-base from which to challenge Augustus. Such an ambition would be beyond the reach of a mere prefect chosen from the lower, equestrian, order. So jealously did Augustus guard his property that no senator of Rome was allowed to enter Egypt without his express permission.

The Prefect of Egypt was based in Alexandria, and normally served for between one and three years. He spent about two months a year in Upper Egypt and another two at various towns in the Delta, holding assizes, inspecting accounts, settling disputes and reviewing the local administration. Local administration lay largely in the hands of Greeks and Hellenized Egyptians; and official business was conducted in Greek. From the time of the Emperor Vespasian (AD 69–79), the country was divided into Upper, Middle, and Lower Egypt, each part governed by an *epistrategis* (subcommander) responsible to the Prefect. Alexandria, as usual, was treated differently and was administered by *archontes* (magistrates).

Tactitus characterized Egypt as a nation 'indifferent to law' (*see* above), a mistaken view, as the principles of justice and law, and a system for administering them, had been applied for centuries,[231] with every Egyptian, at least in theory, having the right to appeal to the pharaoh in person. In the Ptolemaic Period, separate civil courts had been established for Greeks and non-Greeks. Greek law

---

[230] *The Histories*, Book 1, Chapter II, p. 27.
[231] Pirenne, 1932–5.

was practised in Alexandria and judges travelled to Greek settlements to administer it. Native Egyptians had recourse to Egyptian law which was conducted in their own language by native judges. Neither Greeks nor Egyptians were restricted to their own courts, but could opt to have civil disputes settled in the court of their choice, with the help of interpreters if necessary. In the Roman Period, justice in Egypt, as in other parts of the Empire, was administered locally, with governors having supreme authority in their provinces.[232] By the middle of the first century, the system of separate Greek and Egyptian courts had been phased out. Greeks continued to have recourse to their own courts, but Egyptian law was gradually modified to conform to that of Rome. The supreme judicial authority of the Empire was the emperor, to whom Roman citizens had the right of appeal. This right was absolute in capital cases, and could sometimes be exercised in civil matters; and meant nothing to those Egyptians who were not Roman citizens.

Military affairs were in the hands of the Roman army. Two legions, each with about 10,000 men, were stationed in Egypt, one in Babylon-in-Egypt, about 21 kilometres south of the apex of the Delta, the other in Alexandria. There were fortified camps at the strategically important towns of Pelusium, Coptos, Thebes and Syene (Aswan), to guard frontiers, mines, trade routes and grain depots throughout Egypt. Until the time of Diocletian (AD 284–305), all troops were under the command of the Prefect. Legionaries, always Roman citizens, were supported by a naval squadron based at Alexandria, and by auxiliary units of infantry and cavalry that were largely made up of recruits from provinces throughout the Empire, but commanded by Roman officers. Until the late second century AD, the only Egyptians allowed to serve in the auxiliary units of the Roman army were those of Greek descent, a disadvantage for indigenous Egyptians insofar as an auxiliary who served honourably for 26 years was granted Roman citizenship.

In the year AD 200, the Emperor Septimus Severus decreed that Alexandria and several Egyptian provincial cities should be governed by city councils. The Alexandrians who, in their opinion, had managed very well for centuries without a city council, resented the removal of their special status. They also resented a decline in agricultural activity in the rest of Egypt, which they

[232]　Coles, 1966.

attributed to administrative incompetence, and which adversely affected their prosperity. When Severus' son, Caracalla, arrived in Alexandria in AD 215, he found the city in such a state of unrest that he ordered executions and removed its special privileges, including the endowments supporting its famous Mouseion. For good measure, he gave instructions for a massacre of Alexandrian Christians. Some 70 years later, Diocletian succeeded in placing responsiblity, not only for cities, but also for large areas outwith the city boundaries, in the hands of municipal authorities.

In the reign of Diocletian, Egypt was assimilated into the Eastern Empire, coming under the aegis of the Prefect of the East. Its administration had been somewhat different from that of the rest of the Roman Empire, the traditional method of dating continuing in use, with the regnal year of the king substituted by that of the emperor, and Egypt issuing its own coinage. Under Diocletian, these local customs gave way to the system in use throughout the rest of the Empire. Egypt continued to be divided into three parts, henceforward called provinces: Aegyptus Jovia (western Delta), ruled by the Prefect; Aegyptus Herculia (eastern Delta and Middle Egypt) and the Thebaid (Upper Egypt), ruled by *praesides* (chiefs). Diocletian's policy of separating civil from military authority resulted in a diminution in the power of the Prefect. Military command in Egypt became the responsibility of a newly created post, that of *Dux* (Commander) of Egypt.

About AD 341, a fourth province, Augustus, was added to the other three Egyptian provinces; and some time later Aegyptus Herculia was renamed Arcadia. Each of these provinces was subdivided into two, considerably weakening the power and influence of the *praesides*; and this remained the pattern of provincial administration until the Arab Conquest. In AD 395, the Emperor Theodosius I divided the Empire between his two sons: as part of the eastern Empire, Egypt was thereafter ruled from Constantinople. Life for the Egyptians did not improve: taxation remained onerous; and Egyptian farmers still strove to maintain the grain shipments, the only difference being their destination, to Constantinople instead of to Rome.

Economy

Alexandria, a cosmopolitan city trading in every kind of luxury item conceivable and producing goods of her own, was still the capital of Egypt. In the first century AD, the philosopher, Dio of Prusa, known as 'Chrysostom', delivered a public address in the city in which he stated that it

> ranked second [to Rome] among all cities beneath the sun . . . The trade, not merely of islands, ports, a few straits and isthmuses, but of practically the whole world is yours. For Alexandria is situated, as it were, at the crossroads of the whole world, of even the most remote nations thereof, as if it were a market serving a single city, a market which brings together into one place all manner of men, displaying them to one another, and, as far as possible, making them a kindred people.[233]

During the Roman period, temples continued to own large areas of farmland, though the greatest landowner was the Emperor, an absentee landlord who distributed parcels of land to his favourites, and to army veterans. A few Egyptians owned land, but most of them chose not to work it themselves, preferring to live in the cities, where some were employed as state officials. Most of the native Egyptian population lived under a feudal system similar to that of medieval England. For them, life went on as it always had done – they worked the land as labourers or tenant farmers, sometimes subjected to forced labour; and the efficiency of Roman government was largely felt in the ruthlessness with which taxes were gathered. Farmers were obliged to pay a fixed portion of their produce as taxation, and those who leased land from the state paid rent for it.[234]

Farmers who worked state-owned land were required to swear on oath that they would cultivate crops specified by the government, which provided seed, though its cultivation and harvesting were entirely the responsibility of individual farmers. Preparation of the ground began in November and, by the end of January, sowing had been completed. In April the wheat harvest began – and so did the collection of taxes.[235] As the grain was harvested, it was brought to the threshing-floor, where it was measured, recorded and assessed for taxation. At Karanis (see page 238), and presumably elsewhere, tax payers were allowed to pay what they

---

[233] *Oration*, Section 31 foll.
[234] Wallace, 1938, pp. 1–3; Geremek, 1969, pp. 53–70.
[235] Packman, 1968, p. 59; Youtie and Pearl, 1944, p. 41.

owed by instalments.[236] Grain owed in tax was taken to a central granary, where the superintendent (the *sitologus*) issued a receipt, the formal document acknowledging the settlement.

Grain so paid was taken to Alexandria for shipment to Rome, a journey of nearly 3000 kilometres which could take up to two months.[237] For the first three centuries of Roman rule, the farmers of Egypt provided one-third of the annual amount of grain required to feed the city of Rome. It was sent each spring as tribute, the *annona*, and it amounted to 150,000 tons of grain annually. In addition, the Egyptians were subjected to a land tax levied on agrarian property, such as farm buildings and animals, and on the products of workshops. They also paid a poll tax at full rate, Greeks paying at half-rate, Roman citizens not at all.

Second only to agriculture in the economy were textiles, which were heavily taxed. The weaving trade was highly specialized, and seems to have had at least 19 subdivisions: weaver, dyer, weaver of fine linen, web beater, fuller, wool dealer, wool shearer, wool seller, wool/web beater, weaver of striped patterns, master of looms, weaver of heavy garments, vendor of fleece, flax spinner, flax seller, linen weaver, washer and treater of cloth, and weaver of tapestries.[238] Cloth was also produced domestically, the combing, spinning and weaving undertaken by women for use in their own households. In addition, many would also contribute to the supply of military clothing, by the second century a compulsory charge on even the smallest towns. A document from Karanis (*see* below) records that for the years AD 310–11 the village supplied 24 tunics and eight cloaks,[239] the production of which seems to have taken three years to complete.[240]

For the first two centuries or so of Roman rule, Egypt enjoyed a period of peace and security, and this combined with improvements in agricultural techniques, such as a more widespread use of the waterwheel (*saqiah*), brought prosperity. In the reign of Commodus (AD 190–2), however, Egypt, unable to maintain its grain quota to Rome, was forced to supplement it with supplies purchased from North Africa. Worse still, the coinage was

[236] Gazda, 1983, p. 18, note 11.
[237] Wallace, 1938, pp. 45–46; Rickman, 1980, p. 231.
[238] ibid., pp. 193–202; Johnson, 1936, pp. 538–44.
[239] Boak, 1947, pp. 30–3.
[240] The receipt for these garments is dated AD 314: Jones, 1960, pp. 186–7.

debased. Diocletian's reorganizations made tax collection easier, and an extra tax, the *embollé* or shipment, paid in grain, was imposed as provision for the main cities. From AD 297, new tax assessments, known as 'indictions', were made every 15 years. By the third century, taxation had become an intolerable burden, the struggle to pay the *annona* inflicting growing hardship.

Karanis

Karanis is a town of the Graeco-Roman period which, from its extensive excavations, has yielded a detailed picture of the rural economy of Egypt in Roman times. It is situated in the Faiyum, in the *Nome* which Strabo reckoned was

> the most noteworthy of all in respect to its appearance, its fertility, and its material development, for it alone is planted with olive trees that are large and full-grown and bear fine fruit . . . and it produces wine in no small quantity, as well as grain, pulses, and the other seed-plants in very great varieties.[241]

By the end of the Ptolemaic period, the irrigation system of the Faiyum had been allowed to silt up, affecting local agriculture badly. Augustus recognized the importance of the area and sent in units of the Roman army to restore the dykes and re-excavate the canals.[242] In late Roman times, the irrigation system seems to have broken down again, and the real potential of the Faiyum lay undeveloped for centuries.

The local economy of Karanis, and presumably that of other towns, was enriched by pigeon keeping. Pigeons had long been a favourite food with the Egyptians; it has been assumed that large estates in ancient Egypt had their own dovecotes, now disappeared. Remains of mud-brick dovecotes found at Karanis[243] are similar to those of the Delta region today: some free-standing structures, others built on house roofs and consisting of horizontal layers of pots, each pot a nesting box for a single bird. Columella, a noted first-century writer on agriculture, listed the advantages of keeping pigeons: 'Farmers . . . use the dung of fowls to

[241] 17.1.35.
[242] Wallace, 1938, p. 2.
[243] Gazda, 1983, p. 13.

doctor . . . every kind of soil, and with the fowls themselves they enrich the family kitchen and table by providing rich fare; and lastly, with the price which they obtain by selling . . . they increase the revenue of the farm.'[244] The size of two dovecotes excavated at Karanis, with spaces for at least 1250 birds, suggests that pigeon keeping was not only an activity of individual farmers but sometimes undertaken as a commercial venture. Tax was levied on pigeons throughout the Fayum,[245] and records from Karanis for the period AD 173–5 show that 12 farmers paid a dovecote tax.[246]

Camels did not figure in daily life until Graeco-Roman times. Records from Karanis show that camels (that is, dromedaries) played an important part in the economy. Camel owners were obliged to lend their animals to the state for work on excavating canals and for transport,[247] and thus records were kept of the number owned. They were also declared for tax-levy purposes: the following declaration, made in AD 134 by a camel-keeper at Karanis, is probably an indication of the size of a typical herd:

> I, Dioskoros . . . from the village of Karanis, camel-herd of the same, swear . . . that I declare 55 fully-grown camels in the village, that is 55 plus 16 colts, totalling 72 [*sic*] camels.[248]

Religion

In the Roman period, Greeks in Alexandria as elsewhere in Egypt continued to honour many of the old Egyptian deities, notably Horus the Elder (Haroeris), represented as a falcon-headed man dressed as a Roman legionary; Isis, identified with Demeter or Aphrodite; and Thoth, the ibis-headed god of writing identified with Hermes. Serapis, the hybrid god introduced by Ptolemy I Soter, was never popular with Egyptians, but, in the Roman period, he was associated with Isis and Horus and worshipped

[244] VIII.1.2.
[245] Husselman, 1953, pp. 84, 86, 90; and Youtie and Pearl, 1939, pp. 136–7.
[246] Wallace, 1938, p. 69.
[247] ibid., p. 92.
[248] P. Mich. Inv. 5895: Husselman, 1971, pp. 55–7.

widely in the eastern Empire. The greatest popularity was enjoyed by Osiris, revered by Egyptians and non-Egyptians alike.

Funerary practices

Many Greeks outwith Alexandria adopted Egyptian burial practices. They mummified their dead; and the decoration on funerary shrouds often indicates that they had the same hope as their Egyptian compatriots that Osiris would grant them life after death. During the Roman period, the standard of mummification was not high, and had in any case been in decline since the end of the New Kingdom. Although, during the Graeco-Roman period, mummification became available to a wider range of social classes, it was often incompetently carried out. Damaged bodies were 'completed' under the mummy bandages by the addition of animal bones, stones and other materials. As if to make up for the poor quality of the mummification, greater attention was paid to the external appearance of the mummy, with bandages arranged in an elaborate, coffered design, complete with gilded studs. The head was covered by a cartonnage headpiece, a custom that led to the practice of placing over the face panels painted with a portrait of the deceased.

These panels, of which there are over 1000 extant, are known as 'mummy portraits',[249] and were in use from the first half of the first century AD to the fourth. They were made of canvas or wood, which was sometimes coated with a thin layer of plaster, and painted in hot wax in a technique (wax encaustic) that was new to Egypt. Their style is realistic and life-like, showing Roman rather than ancient Egyptian influence. By the end of the fourth century, mummy portraits and mummification had given way to the practice of burying the dead by simply dressing them in everyday clothes, and laying them out on boards.

Christianity in Egypt

In its early days, the Church in Alexandria was a mixture of Christianity, Judaism, pagan beliefs, Greek philosophy, and even

[249]   Parlasca, 1966 and 1969–80; Montserrat, 1993.

Plate 7.1 Painted plaster mask, Roman Egypt. (Courtesy of the Trustees of the British Museum, London.)

magic. The most influential of the cults was Gnosticism, whose followers combined oriental mysticism with Greek philosophy and Christian doctrines: Basilides and Valentinus, two of the most influential teachers in Alexandria, were Gnostics.

By the beginning of the reign of the Emperor Commodus (AD 180), Christianity was firmly established in Alexandria, principally among the Greek population, although a few Greek-speaking Jews and Egyptians had also adopted the new religion. Converts had been made of Greeks in the provincial towns but, as yet, there was no serious attempt to convert the native Egyptian populace. The Church of Alexandria, whose bishop was the first to be called 'Pope', was well organized. In AD 180, Pantaenus founded a Catechetical School, the only one of its kind, in which aspiring converts, male and female, received instruction and were prepared for baptism by *catechetes* (teachers), some of whom were ordained priests, others not. The first head of the School after Pantaenus was his pupil, Clement, who was in his turn succeeded by his pupil, Origen, two of the greatest Christian scholars (*see* page 253).

The disputes over the nature of Christ (*see* page 228) led to a permanent rift between the Church of Egypt and most of the rest of Christendom. The Church of Egypt remained firmly Monophysite, its reluctance to conform fuelled by resentment that Constantinople had replaced Alexandria as leader of the Christian Church. National pride was wounded, thus adding to the xenophobia always characteristic of the Egyptians; and Monophysitism became an expression of Egyptian nationalism. Egypt was still part of the eastern Empire; the state religion, therefore, was Orthodox and Diphysite. The popular religion of the majority of Egyptians, however, was Monophysite, and remained so even after the sixth century, when the leadership of the Monophysite movement passed to Syria.

Monasticism

Diocletian's persecutions, in particular, exacerbated the despair that many Egyptians felt during the third century, a period of high taxation in a debilitated economy. A significant number sought relief by withdrawing into the desert, where they lived in caves and in the abandoned tombs of the pharaonic period. They were the precursors of the hermits who practised the *anachoresis* that was to become so notable a feature of Christian Egypt. In pre-Christian times, the term meant 'withdrawal of labour' in pursuance of redress for a grievance: the Christian anchorite was a man who withdrew into the desert for a solitary existence of prayer and fasting. This he did, not to escape from the pressures of life, but to struggle with the Devil, who was thought to be incarnated in demons and monstrous animals. The anchorite, in struggling with them as an 'athlete of God', believed that he was protecting his fellow Christians against the wiles of Satan.

An anchorite was much admired, and many villagers considered it an honour to provide him with regular supplies of food. In spite of this, his life was intentionally one of such great hardship that the majority of would-be anchorites could not endure it and were forced to give up. One who did not was St Antony. Antony was born, about AD 251, of an Egyptian Christian family in Coma, the modern Qiman al-Arus, some 75 kilometres south of Cairo. Before he was 20 years old, his parents died, whereupon he gave away his inherited property and began a life of Christian asceticism which lasted until his death, reputedly at the age of 105.

In AD 285, Antony shut himself up in an abandoned fortress at Pispir in Upper Egypt, where he remained for 20 years, sustained by local inhabitants who twice a year supplied him with bread through a hole in the roof. Eventually, his fame spread, and a group of would-be disciples came to Pispir, where they broke down the door of Antony's cell and persuaded him to emerge into the world. Over the next few years, many were encouraged to follow Antony's example and take up the ascetic life; and men who shared his ideals began to form a community around Pispir. To begin with, each man lived by himself in one of the caves or old tombs in the area around Antony's cell, as a true *monachos* or 'one who lives alone'. Gradually, there grew a different type of community in which monks lived a semi-coenobitic (communal) existence, meeting together at intervals for prayers, though continuing to live in isolation at other times. Those who were unable to sustain life on a diet of bread and water, as Antony did, were permitted to grow vegetables, and even to make baskets and mats from palm fibre, which they sold to raise money for food.

Over the years, the Antonian system proliferated throughout Egypt. In AD 315, the first monastic community in Lower Egypt was founded at Nitria, some 60 kilometres south of Alexandria, by the hermit, Amoun. By AD 356, a large community had grown up in Shiet (Greek: Scetis) in the Wadi Natrun in the Western Desert, inspired by the example of Makarius the Egyptian, later known as Makarius the Great. Especially revered anchorites such as Makarius were often focal points for new communities. When such an anchorite died, his followers named their community after him, so that it became known as the *Topos* (Place) of X (the deceased anchorite). Gradually, each *topos* developed a nucleus of buildings known as a *laura*, which consisted of a church and a refectory in which monks could gather together once a week for divine service and a communal meal. Each *laura* appointed a monk to be its 'Father', whose duty it was to advise newcomers.

Antony, the father of monasticism, died in AD 356. Over 40 years before his death, tired of the attentions of admiring followers, he had withdrawn to a cave on Mount Clysma, the modern Kolzoum, or Qulzum, in the Eastern Desert 350 kilometres south of Cairo. For several years after his death, his followers maintained a semi-coenobitic *laura* at the foot of Antony's mountain until, some time between AD 361 and 363, they built a monastery. In the years that followed, 12 of the monks of this monastery became Patriarchs of the Egyptian Church; and today it still supports an active monastic community.

The development of the Egyptian monastery from the eremetical Antonian community into one that was enclosed and governed by strict rules was the work of Pachom, born c. AD 292 into a pagan family in Esna in Upper Egypt. He served in the army for several years, and first became attracted to Christianity when his unit was based in Thebes, where the kindness of local Christians impressed him so much that he applied for military discharge and, still in his twenties, received baptism. Pachom then practised asceticism for seven years until, about AD 323, he set up his first monastic community at Tabennesi in Upper Egypt.

Pachom's army experience stood him in good stead when it came to organizing his monasteries. He rejected the semi-coenobitic monastery of the Antonian system in favour of one in which the monks led a wholly communal life, introducing coenobitic monasticism, perhaps the most significant contribution made by Egypt to Christianity. Christian monasticism spread from Egypt to the west after the Patriarch of Alexandria, Athanasius, travelled to Rome in AD 340 taking two young monks, Isidore and

Ammonius, with him. Seventeen years later, Basil the Great, inspired by his visit to the monasteries of Egypt, began to organize foundations for the Eastern Church in Asia Minor that were similar but observed his code.

In the Pachomian system, a monastery comprised cells for monks, a church, a refectory, a kitchen, a library, workshops, an assembly hall and a guest-house, all surrounded by an enclosure wall in which there was a gatehouse for porters. The monks were allocated to 'houses', each ruled by its own head, who had a deputy, and as far as possible containing monks of one trade (*see* below), or one nationality. By the time of Pachom's death in AD 346, there were 11 Pachomian monasteries, including two for women. Men and women seeking to take up the monastic life simply presented themselves at the gate to be taught a few simple prayers which they were required to commit to memory. The ability to memorize was important because most were illiterate; and anyone failing the initial test of memory was denied admission. Those whose previous life was known to be unsatisfactory were also rejected.

Pachom placed great emphasis on the spiritual benefits of hard work rather than idle contemplation, so that his monasteries were self-supporting, and often produced surpluses that were sold for the benefit of the monastery. The monks were encouraged to work in an organized way, some making baskets and other goods for sale in local markets, others tending cattle, working the land, doing carpentry, cooking, or looking after the sick. All work was performed in silence, except for the singing of psalms. The monks' diet was much the same as that of Egyptian peasants – bread, onions, salt, oil, lentil soup, with very little cheese or fruit. Wine and meat were forbidden, though the extra rations issued to the sick, the old and the infirm included wine. Pachom disapproved of excessive fasting because it impaired the ability to work. During Lent, however, many chose to eat every other day, and some only every five days; and only uncooked food was eaten.

The monks in Pachomian monasteries lived according to strict rules, written in Egyptian, not Greek, for these monasteries were very much native Egyptian institutions. Pachom himself learned Greek only late in life. Nearly 40 years after his death, his rules were elaborated and made more taxing by Shenute, the head of the White Monastery of Sohag. Shenute, born in AD 334 in an Upper Egyptian village near Sohag, was a monk in the White Monastery, which was founded by his uncle, Bgoul, until, at the age of 51, he became its head. He was not only an efficient organizer, considered to be the greatest religious reformer of the Coptic Church, but also an outstanding preacher and theologian (*see* page 251). Like Antony and Pachom before him, he was Egyptian and very little influenced by Greek Alexandria.

Domestic Life

Housing

In many parts of the Roman Empire, but not in Egypt, any large estate would boast a conventional Roman villa. Most Egyptians of the period lived in settlements of densely packed houses, in apartment blocks at least two storeys high, constricted as ever by the nature of the land. The inhabitants of many of the Faiyum settlements seem not to have struggled very fiercely against the encroachment of the desert sand, often abandoning the ground floor of a house to it, and adding a new storey on the roof. Over a wide area of housing at Karanis, for example, there are at least seven discernible changes in level.

In the second century, Karanis covered an area of 125,000 square metres, and had a population of about 5000. By the end of the third century, its population had fallen to less than 500, and a century later the village contained only a handful of inhabitants. Other villages show a similar decline. In the late third century, 40 per cent of the houses were abandoned in one part of Oxyrhynchus, a *nome* capital.[250] The reasons for this decline are not understood, but may have something to do with government neglect of the Faiyum (*see* page 238).

House walls at Karanis were normally of mud-brick, strengthened with wood, and were often 2 metres thick at ground level, although only about a quarter of that width at the top. Under the house there was usually a cellar with a ceiling of barrel-vaulted mud-brick although, in the rest of the house, the ceilings were made from straw mats and mud over wooden rafters. Steps, door thresholds and house corners were made of stone or fired brick; doors were of wooden planks, and were fastened in individual

[250]   P. Osl. 111.

ways, some requiring keys. Window frames, never more than 1
metre high and 50 centimetres wide, were of wood. Some had
bars, others shutters; but there was no window glass.
The interior walls were covered in a black wash, the courses of
mud-brick picked out in white. The only other form of interior
decoration lay within the niches in some of the larger rooms, either
stucco reliefs in geometric designs, or reliefs of minor gods. These
niches may have been household shrines. Whatever its purpose,
the size of a room was usually 3.5 by 2.5 metres although, in a few
houses, there was a larger chamber used, presumably, as a reception room. At the centre of each house stood a pillar and
a square staircase to which all rooms opened. Bedrooms were
never on the ground floor, nor were dining rooms which occasionally were on the roof.[251] The kitchen was outside, and baking was
often done in a communal oven situated, together with a quern-
stone for grinding flour, in an open courtyard shared by the whole
apartment block or by a group of houses.

Furniture

During the Roman era, carpenters began to work on boards of
longer length by preparing timber over a sawpit, using planes.
Furniture for the poorer Egyptians was much the same as it had
been but, for the rich, a variety of high-quality Roman-style pieces
became available, notably the Roman couch. Upholstered and
with turned legs, couches were of wood, often inlaid with ivory,
designed for the dining room, as Romans and Greeks reclined on
one elbow when eating, but often used as beds. Table tops were of
marble; vase stands were cast from bronze; lighting was by a single
oil lamp, or several grouped together to give more light. In the
Greek and early Roman periods, lamps were made of pottery; later
they were of bronze but they conformed to a standard shape – a
covered bowl with a protruding lip to support a wick.
Everyday utensils were made from the cheapest of materials,
such as pottery or wood. Baskets were extensively used, as was
stone for mixing and grinding bowls (*mortarium*). Metal items
were the most costly, and therefore highly valued. A papyrus[252]

[251] P. Lond. V, 1722.
[252] P. St Pal. XX, 67.

dating to AD 200 lists the furniture in one house: downstairs, a bronze lamp and stand, various cups and saucers, a bath and a basin, a cloak and a spare blanket; upstairs, two mattresses, two pillows, three blankets, a couch, a chest, and three cloaks. The kitchen equipment was also upstairs and consisted of a colander, mixing bowls, measures and knives.

Cultural Achievements

Medicine

Surprisingly, perhaps, given that Alexandrian intellectuals were never much interested in studying the ancient culture of Egypt, however impressive, it is from that little regarded source that a great gift to western civilization came. The art of medicine had been practised in Egypt from early dynastic times. It was the Egyptians who produced the first medical books (*see* page 43), made the first observations on anatomy, first used splints, bandages, compresses and antiseptics. Egyptian medical schools attracted students from all over the ancient world, the Greeks later passing on to other countries the medical knowledge that they had learned in Egypt. There are clear traces of Egyptian influence in Greek, Latin, Arabic, Syriac and Persian medical books; and in those of western Europe in the Middle Ages. In addition, mummification familiarized the Egyptians with the dissecting of the human body, a practice largely forbidden elsewhere, so that only in Egypt was it possible for Greek physicians to study practical anatomy, thus enabling the science of medicine to develop.

Architecture

Although it is generally accepted that individual architects must have designed many Coptic buildings, not a single architect's name is known. Coptic architecture, which is best seen in churches and monastic buildings, was perhaps a communal effort. Early Christian Egyptians made use of pharaonic structures, converting temples or parts of temples into churches (Medinet Habu or the Temple of Isis at Philae, for example). At some time before the middle of the third century, Christians in the Faiyum and in

Alexandria congregated in buildings owned by the whole Christian community but whether these were churches is not clear. The earliest churches, now lost, were built in what is now called Old Cairo.

A typical Coptic, non-monastic church is in the shape of a Roman basilica with a *narthex* (porch), a nave and two side aisles with vaulted roofs supported by columns. The *narthex* sometimes contains an Epiphany tank, the water of which can be used for baptism, but its main purpose is to provide a place where penitents are admonished and where catechumens stand during services. The nave is spacious enough to contain seating for the congregation. Originally, some churches had upper galleries over the side aisles, in which women members of the congregation sat. After the tenth century, women were accommodated in the north end of the nave, screened from view. Today, side aisles are usually reserved for women, though men and women may sit together in the northern part of the nave.

Churches are aligned east-west, each with the main entrance at the western end, and one or more sanctuaries at the east. The sanctuaries are covered by domes, each one surmounted by a cross. Almost all churches have three altars, screened from view by a wooden screen [the *haikal* (sanctuary) screen or *higab*]. There are no bell towers or campaniles in surviving Coptic churches, because bells were forbidden under Muslim law. The exteriors of old Coptic churches are plain and unimposing: because of the mob attacks made on Christians from the end of the seventh century to the beginning of the nineteenth, it was felt prudent not to be too distinctive among surrounding houses.

Monastic architecture is perhaps best seen in the four surviving monasteries of the Wadi Natrun which, like those elsewhere in Egypt, are equipped not only with living quarters for the monks in rows of cells, kitchens, mills, refectories, and guest-houses, but also with churches. These churches are similar to non-monastic buildings, but without provision for women; and there is little seating, the monks being expected to stand during services. The earliest monasteries were not surrounded by defensive walls but were equipped with towers (*kasrs* or keeps) in which monks could take refuge if necessary, and where valuables such as books and church regalia were kept for safety. In the ninth century, monasteries were enclosed by high walls as protection against Bedouin attacks. The walls which like the monastic buildings, are of mud-brick, were up to 12 metres high and, apart from where they are buttressed, some 2 metres thick.

Art

Coptic art consists in the main of painting; sculpture, much of it in stone with some small objects in bone, bronze and, occasionally, ivory; and textiles. There are two styles in painting. The Hellenized Alexandrians were influenced by the late Roman style that prevailed throughout the eastern Empire; the provincial Egyptians, in a nationalistic reaction to their Graeco-Roman conquerors, developed a native school of their own, which is at first sight reminiscent of Byzantine style. Unlike their forebears, Coptic painters depicted the human head full face. They used the same limited palette of colours as the ancient Egyptians and, like them, rendered the human figure in outline only with no attempt to indicate movement or differences in light and shade. They abhorred a vacuum, and filled up their paintings with ornamentation in the form of trees, other plants and animals.

The earliest Coptic sculpture extant dates from the fourth century, and seems to have been used to embellish non-Christian

Plate 7.2   Fresco of the Twelve Apostles: from the Coptic cemetery at El-Bagawat. Fifth century AD.

buildings. Its general style is Hellenistic and consists of apses, friezes and column capitals decorated with vine-leaf and acanthus scrolls, sometimes intermingled with birds and other animals. Favourite themes were subjects drawn from classical mythology, such as Leda and the swan; Aphrodite, sometimes rising from the sea, sometimes backed by a scallop shell; and pairs of Eros figures. Most of the surviving sculpture dates from the fifth to the ninth centuries, and consists of architectural fragments of carved stone from monasteries and churches. Apses and niches are decorated with bands of stone carved with vine and acanthus patterns, interspersed with crosses. Column capitals are sculpted, often with motifs inspired by New Testament stories: some, for example, are carved in the shape of baskets filled with stone loaves and fishes. There are also extant large numbers of decorative tombstones and grave stelae.

The art is perhaps best illustrated by the textiles. From the fourth century, the Copts buried their dead in everyday clothes; and it is thanks to this custom that so many of their textiles have survived. Tapestry was used for wall hangings, curtains and altar cloths, and as decorative insertions in clothing. It was made from undyed thread woven on linen, and wool coloured with vegetable dyes. The earliest tapestries were monochrome, purple being a favourite colour, and the decorative themes, like those of the sculpture, show Hellenistic influence. From the sixth century, the use of polychrome became widespread, and themes demonstrate an individual Coptic style, with leaf patterns, vines, dancing figures, hares, lions and fish being most common. Adam and Eve sometimes make an appearance, but Christian subjects were rarely used before the seventh century.

Language and writing

Shenute (*see* page 246) wrote in Egyptian, the language spoken by his ancestors, the ancient Egyptians, although it had, of course, changed over the years, as all languages do. Ancient Egyptian was written in several scripts: hieroglyphic ('sacred sculptures'), largely used for monumental inscriptions; hieratic ('priestly writing'), a cursive form of hieroglyphs used on papyrus documents; and demotic (*see* page 191).

Most Egyptians were illiterate, and depended on the services of scribes. By the first century AD, if not before, it had become clear that the understanding of hieroglyphs and hieratic was rapidly being lost. In any case, the old scripts were unsatisfactory, for they did not indicate vowel sounds, only consonants. When the need arose for providing Egyptian-speaking converts to Christianity with translations of the scriptures, an attempt was made to convey the exact pronunciation of words through a script that employed both vowels and consonants.

Greek letters were chosen as the basis of the new script, to which were added a number of signs taken from the demotic to express sounds present in Egyptian but not in Greek. The new Egyptian alphabet finally decided upon consisted of 31 letters. It is clear from the earliest texts extant, which date to the late first century AD, that the new script originated with non-Christians. It was not long, however, before the Egyptian of the day was standardized into a literary language, with a grammar and a regular orthography of its own; and that above all it had become the language of Christian Egyptians.

This language, and the script in which it is written, is now called Coptic, a term by which the whole culture of Christian Egypt is known. The noun Copt is a foreshortened form of the ancient Greek noun *Aiguptios*, meaning an indigenous inhabitant of Egypt. After their conquest of Egypt, the Arabs corrupted *Aiguptios* to *qibt*, pronounced 'Copt'. Although the term originally had no religious connotation, meaning simply 'Egyptian', since the sixteenth century it has been used specifically to mean Christian Egyptian.

The Coptic language is no longer spoken, though knowledge of it has not been lost; and it is employed in the Coptic Church much as Latin was until recently in the Roman Catholic liturgy. There are several dialects, the most widespread being Bohairic, the dialect of Lower Egypt, and Sahidic once spoken in the district of Thebes (Luxor). Shenute wrote in Sahidic which, because of his extensive literary output of sermons, homilies, ordinances and letters, and because it was also the medium chosen by Pachom, became the classic form of the language.

Literature

Shenute was the earliest and, in his own country, the most famous, Egyptian Christian writer. His impact, however, was largely confined to Upper Egypt. It was left to two natives of Alexandria, Origen and Athanasius (*see* page 229), to achieve worldwide recognition, and, together with Clement, contribute to Christian learning as a whole.

Titus Flavius Clemens (*c.* AD 160–215), better known as Clement of Alexandria, was probably born in Athens. He already enjoyed a reputation as a philosopher before arriving in Alexandria and converting to Christianity. Three of his treatises, the *Paidagogos* (Tutor), a manual of instruction in Christian manners and morals; the *Protreptikos* or Exhortation to the heathen Greeks to embrace Christianity; and the *Stromateis* (Miscellanies); and his various writings on historical, theological and philosophical topics, formed the basis of Clement's instruction in the Catechical School. His reputation, and the erudition shown in his works, were of great importance in the growth of Christianity in Alexandria. In the *Paidagogos*, for example, he refrained from a direct challenge to the upper-class Greeks of Alexandria to give away their wealth, in accordance with Christ's teachings, and instead encouraged them to turn away from riches to the contemplation of higher things. The *Protreptikos* contained a brilliant attack on paganism expressly designed to appeal to intellectuals.

Origen, born into an Alexandrian Christian family about AD 185, was appointed as a *catechetes* in Clement's School when only 18 years old. In search of greater erudition, he later spent some time in Rome, where he gained many admirers, and widened his experience of different schools of philosophy by studying with Ammonius Saccas, a Neoplatonist. He is reputed to have written 6000 works, most of which are lost, and specialized in the textual criticism of the Bible, in comparing the Greek versions with the original Hebrew. Ptolemy II Philadelphus (285–246 BC) ordered a Greek version of the Old Testament to be produced for the Jews of Alexandria. This, the Septuagint, so-called because it was said to have been produced by 70 scholars in 70 days, was a controversial work because of disagreements over Greek interpretations of Hebrew words. Accordingly, Origen prepared a new edition of the Old Testament – the Hexapla – in which he set out the six different versions of the text in parallel columns. But his greatest work was perhaps *Contra Celsum*, a refutation of the attack on Christianity made by the Epicurean philosopher, Celsus, considered by many to be the most convincing defence of Christianity ever made.

8

Islamic Egypt

On the death of the Prophet Muhammad in AD 632, his father-in-law, Abu Bakr, became the first Khalif (Successor), and, in accordance with the Prophet's wish, prepared to carry the word of God to the 'peoples of the north'. The spread of Islam was remarkably successful, in part to compensate for the harsh living conditions in the Arabian peninsula which, for centuries, had forced Arabs to migrate into the Fertile Crescent and the Syria-Palestine area where, eventually, they came to serve as a buffer between the Persian and Byzantine empires, alternately paid to fight in their armies, then taxed to pay for the fighting. The Zoroastrians of Persia and the Byzantine Christians had been in a state of enmity for over two centuries, and when, in AD 634, the forces of Islam emerged from Arabia, King Yezdegerd in Ctesiphon and Emperor Heraclius in Constantinople were so preoccupied with each other that they failed to recognize the Islamic threat, much less to counter it. The Arabs in the north welcomed the Arabs of Arabia as liberators from their Persian and Byzantine oppressors, and joined in the fight against the infidels.

Abu Bakr died in AD 634, naming 'Umar his successor. 'Umar is regarded as one of the greatest Khalifs, and, at his death in AD 644, the Islamic Empire stretched from North Africa to the borders of India. Eleven years later, a new Khalif was elected: Ali, the son of Muhammad's uncle, Abu Talib, and husband of the Prophet's daughter, Fatima. In AD 661, Ali was assassinated, and Mu'awiya, the governor of Syria and a powerful member of the 'Umayyad family, became Khalif. The custom of electing Khalifs was abandoned when Mu'awiya became the founder of the 'Umayyad Dynasty (AD 661–749), choosing Damascus as his capital city in preference to Medina, which had been the capital of the first four Khalifs. The ʿUmayyads gathered rivals; among them a group of dissidents known as Shiʿites, so-called because they were the party, or *shiʿa*, of Ali. Believing that the Khalifate rightfully belonged only to the descendants of Ali and Fatima, they looked on the ʿUmayyads as usurpers. Thus, though the majority of Muslims were Sunni and followed the traditional practices of Islam (Sunnah) as laid down by the Prophet, the Shiʿites became their antithesis.

History

In December AD 639, an Arab force of 3500 Yemeni cavalrymen rode across the Sinai Desert and advanced through the Wadi el-Arish to Bilbeis. They were led by an Emir, ʿAmr ibn al-ʿAs; and, in July AD 640, they defeated the Byzantine army at the Battle of Heliopolis. The Byzantines fled, leaving Egypt to the Arabs. Twelve thousand troops were sent to Egypt to reinforce ʿAmr's army, and, on 6 April AD 641, after a seven-month siege, Egypt's second city, Babylon-in-Egypt (*see* page 274), was taken. Alexandria held out for a year but, in September AD 642, the capital city of Egypt and one of the cultural centres of the Christian world finally fell to the Arabs. ʿAmr became governor; and Egypt became part of the Arab empire.

The ʿUmmayed Dynasty came to an end in AD 749, when the last ʿUmmayed Khalif, Marwan II, was overthrown. The next Khalif was Abbas, founder of the Abbasid Dynasty, the most long lasting (AD 750–1258) and celebrated of them all. He was succeeded in AD 754 by his brother, Mansur, who ordered a new capital to be built between the Tigris and the Euphrates: much of its architecture inspired by Ctesiphon, the ancient Persian capital, Baghdad was to become the intellectual centre of the Islamic world. The romance attached to the names of two of its rulers, Haroun al-Rashid (AD 786–809) and his son, Maʿmun (AD 813–33), lent it glamour, the glory of Haroun matched only by that of his western contemporary, Charlemagne. Nevertheless, just four decades or so after Maʿmun's death, the authority of the Khalif in Baghdad was challenged by Ahmad ibn Tulun, son of a Turkish slave.

In AD 868, Ibn Tulun, who had been brought up in the Abbasid court, was appointed governor of Egypt. An enterprising man, he was not content to be a mere governor, not least because his governorate supplied the whole of the Arabian peninsula with grain. He made Egypt virtually independent of the Khalifate in Baghdad, so effectively that, in AD 877, he was allowed to annex a large part of Syria. Ibn Tulun's dynastic achievements, however, were short lived, for a punitive expedition was sent from Baghdad to crush Egyptian independence just over a decade after his death in AD 844. For the next 30 years, Egypt was once more ruled by governors appointed by, and loyal to, the Khalif until, in AD 935, another Turk, Muhammad ibn Tughj, achieved independence, to become the founder of the Ikhshid Dynasty, called after the Persian term meaning 'governor', undistinguished and, like its predecessor, short lived. The Ikhshids gave way in AD 969 to the Fatimids, and, for the first time in nearly 1000 years, Egypt became a fully independent state, with a ruler who owed no allegiance, religious or otherwise, to the Khalif in Baghdad, but exercised the office himself (*see* below). Egypt became one of the leading countries of the Islamic world.

The Fatimid Dynasty had been founded 60 years earlier by Abu-Muhammad Obaidallah, who claimed to be the grandson of Fatima, daughter of the Prophet Muhammad, and was therefore a Shi'ite (*see* page 255). Obaidallah, who traced his descent through Isma'il (died AD 760), was the *imam* or spiritual leader of the Isma'ilis, also called the Seveners, Isma'il being the seventh *imam*, a sect in which *imams* were valued more highly than military or political leaders. Obaidallah and his followers rapidly conquered North Africa, from the Straits of Gibraltar to the borders of Egypt, and, establishing their headquarters in Tunis, made preparations to realize the Fatimid dream of controlling a universal Islamic empire. Egypt at that time was Islam's richest province, and the Tulunid and Ikhshid Dynasties had added to their areas of influence the Hejaz, part of Syria, and Palestine, including Jerusalem, sacred not only to Jews and Christians, but also to Muslims, for it was there that the Prophet was said to have rested on his journey to heaven, making Jerusalem third only to Mecca and Medina as a holy city. Believing that Jerusalem will be the meeting place on the Day of Judgement, Muslims chose it as the first *qiblah* (direction) towards which to turn when praying. Conquest of Egypt would bring to the Fatimids the control of great wealth; Syria, being contiguous with Iraq, would provide a stepping-stone to the Khalifate in Baghdad; and Mecca and Medina, the holy cities of the Hejaz, would add enormous prestige.

The Fatimids made several unsuccessful attempts to invade Egypt,[253] until a series of low Niles led to a famine, and the Ikhshid Dynasty gave way to Moez, Obaidallah's successor as *imam*. In AD 969, a Fatimid army of 100,000 men entered Egypt, led by the greatest general of the day, Gohar al-Siqilli al-Rumi, who, as his name makes clear, was of Christian slave origin, al-Siqilli meaning 'the Sicilian' and al-Rumi 'the Greek'. His army met with no resistance, and Gohar reassured the Egyptians that their lives and property were safe, and promised them freedom of religion,[254] a keystone of Moez's policy. Moez's son and successor, Aziz (AD 975–96), continued his father's enlightened religious policy, even marrying a Christian; and the reign of Aziz's son, Hakem (AD 996–1021), started promisingly for Christians when, four years after it began, he promoted his maternal uncle Arsenius (*see* page 272) Patriarch of Alexandria. Hakem, however, became a controversial figure, accused of cruelty, melancholia, schizophrenia and even madness.

One act in particular earned him opprobrium throughout Christendom. On 4 October AD 1009, he ordered the destruction of the Church of the Holy Sepulchre in Jerusalem. While the Abbasids controlled Jerusalem, access to the holy shrines was guaranteed to all Christians, including those of western Europe. Hakem's action rendered the guarantee less reliable, and gave the first impulse towards the Crusades. To increase his popularity among the non-Ismaʿilis, Hakem relaxed the strict observance of certain religious practices,[255] and alienated his fellow Ismaʿilis. In AD 1012, he declared that he was no longer to be considered their *imam*;[256] and soon after broke with the strict Ismaʿili tradition of primogeniture by naming his cousin as his heir.[257] Five years later, he declared himself an incarnation of God. On 13 February AD 1021, Hakem disappeared, killed, it was rumoured, by his sister. After his death, some Ismaʿilis believed that his actions must have been divinely inspired, and, in AD 1017, the Druze movement was founded. It

253 Shaban, 1976, pp. 193–4.
254 al-Maqrizi, *Ittiʿaz*, vol. 1, pp. 151–2.
255 al-Maqrizi, *Khitat*, vol. 2, pp. 340, 343.
256 ibid., pp. 285, 288.
257 ibid., pp. 288, 289.

still exists in the Lebanon, where Druzes expect Hakem's reappearance as the Messiah.

Hakem's successors adopted a policy of protecting and supporting Christian pilgrims bound for Jerusalem. In the early Middle Ages, European pilgrims were few in number because of the difficulties of travel to Palestine, but, by the late eleventh century, Hungary and Bulgaria had been incorporated into the Byzantine Empire, so that it became possible to travel overland to the Holy Land through Christian countries. Unfortunately, the importance of Jerusalem to western Christians increased just as the Fatimids came into conflict with the Seljuk Turks, who had occupied Palestine. The Seljuks originated in the steppes of central Asia, and started to migrate south-westwards in the middle of the eleventh century, conquering Persia in the 1040s and capturing Baghdad from the weakened Abbasids in AD 1055. Like the Abbasids whom they replaced, they were Sunnites; and they proved an effective counterbalance to the Shi'ite Fatimids of Egypt. Palestine became the buffer zone between the two powers, threatening the safe passage of pilgrims. The Turkish occupation of the Holy Land was claimed as the cause of the First Crusade of AD 1095–9, by the end of which Jerusalem had been captured by the Crusaders and a series of Latin kingdoms established on the coast of Syria.

In AD 1168, the Crusaders attacked Egypt. The Khalif of Baghdad, Nur-ad-Din, put aside his rivalry with the Fatimids and sent one of his army commanders, Shirkuh, a member of a Kurdish military family from Takrit (Iraq), to Egypt to advise the Khalif, al-Adid, on methods of combating the foreign Christians. Shirkuh became *wazir* or chief minister to al-Adid but died soon afterwards. He was succeeded by his nephew, Salah-ad-Din, who had accompanied him to Egypt; and, when al-Adid died in AD 1171, Salah-ad-Din was appointed to govern Egypt on behalf of the Khalif of Baghdad, bringing the Fatimid dynasty to an end. Four years later, Salah-ad-Din (Saladin, AD 1137–93) made himself Sultan of Egypt. Though he was an independent ruler, he acknowledged the suzerainty of the Khalif of Baghdad and, once again, Egypt became part of the Sunnite Islamic Empire. Within a year, Saladin had also made himself Sultan of Syria, so establishing the Ayoubite (after his family name, Ibn Ayub) dynasty. In AD 1187, he recaptured Jerusalem from the Crusaders and precipitated the Third Crusade of 1189–92 which, in spite of the capture of Acre in 1191, ended in failure for the Crusaders.

For a decade or so after 1175, when he became Sultan, Saladin maintained peaceful relations between Egypt and the Crusaders, using the respite to reinforce the Egyptian army and fleet. At the same time, he promoted the concept of *jihad* or holy war to unite all Muslims. Renowned for his knightly courtesy, the Crusaders praised his magnanimity, despite their bitter defeat at Jerusalem. Many Muslims, however, criticized him for losing Acre, and accused him of nepotism and extravagance. He had appointed both his brothers to commands in the army, but the charge of extravagance does not accord with the disposition he made of the contents of al-Adid's treasury. A contemporary Arab historian, ibn-al-Athir, described the treasures Saladin found in the khalifal palace, which included a 2400 carat ruby, and peerless pearls and emeralds, one four fingers in length.[258] He sent a share of the treasure to Nur-ad-Din and distributed some of it among his officers, as was expected, but the rest was sold and the proceeds paid into the Egyptian treasury. Saladin kept nothing for himself.

Saladin died in Damascus in March 1193 and was buried, not in Cairo, but in his Syrian capital, in the great mosque that was built in his name. Six months before his death, he had concluded a peace with Richard I of England. The Crusaders, however, had begun to realize that, if they were to be successful in the Near East, they needed to capture Egypt, and Saladin's successors were forced to fight in defence of their territory against western Christian invaders. The Fourth Crusade of 1202–4 was intended to be directed against Egypt but, fortunately for the Egyptians, the Venetians diverted it to Constantinople which was sacked. In the Fifth Crusade of 1218–21, however, the Crusaders laid siege to the strategically important port of Damietta in the eastern Delta. The sufferings of its inhabitants during the long siege, which lasted from August 1218 to November 1219, from wounds, starvation and disease, were described by the German secretary to the Spanish Cardinal Pelagius, Oliver of Paderborn:[259]

> Famine was great and there was a lack of wholesome food, although there was an abundance of mouldy bread . . . The people's sufferings from hunger made them susceptible to various diseases . . . Sultan al-Kamil deceived the poor wretches from day to day with empty promises and persuaded them not to surrender.

[258]   Tornberg, 1851, p. 242.
[259]   Hoogeweg, 1894.

A low Nile flood forced al-Kamil, fearful of famine but intent on defending Damietta at all costs, to try to make terms with the Crusaders. He offered to return the Holy Cross, which had been captured in one of Saladin's victories, together with Jerusalem and all the captives who could be found alive in the kingdoms of Cairo and Damascus. He also offered to pay for the repair of the walls of Jerusalem and, moreover, to restore the whole kingdom of Jerusalem except for Kerak in Transjordan and Montreal in the Idumaean hills. Incredibly, the Crusaders refused al-Kamil's offer. The final decision had to be taken by Pelagius, and he refused ever to countenance negotiations with Saracens.

Damietta fell in November 1219, and, 18 months later, the Crusader army set out on a disastrous advance up the Nile, in full and dangerous flood, towards Cairo. According to Oliver of Paderborn, the troops had been allowed to guzzle the wine left behind by the Saracens because there was too much of it to carry away. Many of the Crusaders lay in a drunken stupor and were captured; others struggled helplessly in deep mud; yet others clambered into boats in such numbers that they capsized. They also lost many of the camels and mules that carried their clothes and tents, and even the arrows needed for defence. The Templars[260] led a disciplined rearguard, but 'the men in front headed off in different directions and wandered through the dark night like stray sheep.' On 30 August 1221, the Crusaders were forced to make 'a lamentable peace', insisting, with some justification, that they had been defeated not by the bow or the sword, but by flood and famine – and, one must add, by drunkenness and indiscipline. On 8 September 1221, Damietta was handed back to the Muslims, who were pleased to note that its fortifications had been greatly strengthened during the Christian occupation.

In the Sixth Crusade of 1228–9, the Christians negotiated the recovery of Jerusalem with the Sultan of Egypt, but finally lost the city in 1244. The Seventh Crusade of 1249–54 was led by Louis IX of France (St Louis). Once again, Egypt was attacked; and, once again, conditions in the Delta were to prove the Crusaders' undoing. In May 1249, the Crusader army sailed from Cyprus to Egypt with the intention of taking Damietta. The old, sick, Sultan,

---

[260] The Knights of the Temple, an order founded in AD 1118 in the Temple of Solomon, whose purpose was to protect pilgrims making for the Holy Land.

as-Salih Ayub, was in Cairo, and the defenders of Damietta communicated with him by means of carrier pigeons, a method which they, like the Crusaders, had learned from the Turks. Messages were sent on three occasions, but no answer was received, and it was assumed that the Sultan was dead. The city was surrendered.

In November 1249, the Crusaders marched on Mansourah, a town built by al-Kamil to celebrate his victory over the Fifth Crusade. Like his predecessors in that Crusade, Louis underestimated the difficulties of the terrain, but this time the army maintained discipline until a deputy commander in the Egyptian army, Rukn ad-Din Baybars, engineered its defeat. On 7 April 1250, the Frankish forces fled Mansourah, and Louis of France was captured. A month later, on payment by the French of a large ransom, Louis was set free, eventually to die in Carthage 20 years later leading yet another Crusade, the Eighth, which began in 1270 and ended two years later. During his captivity, Louis had arranged for the surrender of Damietta, and the Crusaders left Egypt never to return.

Eleven years after the Crusaders had been driven out from Mansourah, Baybars became Sultan of Egypt. Baybars, whose name means 'panther', was born in about 1228 on the Russian steppes, the son of a nomadic Turk. He was captured in the Crimea by slavers and taken to Syria, where he was sold for training as a slave soldier or *memalik* (Mameluke). Mamelukes were captured as young men from non-Islamic peoples, usually hardy nomadic tribes with a tradition of horse riding and archery. They were converted to Islam, received a rudimentary education, and given military training, then freed to serve the state as mounted archers in a Mameluke regiment. At the beginning of the thirteenth century, 12,000 Caucasians, mostly Circassians and Turks, were taken to Egypt, where they formed an elite corps in the army. A year or so before the Battle of Mansourah, Baybars came into the service of the Egyptian Sultan, as-Salih Ayub, and was appointed deputy commander of a Mameluke regiment.

The decade following the death of Sultan as-Salih was turbulent. Baybars belonged to the most powerful corps in the Mameluke army, the Bahriyya, a unit of about 1000 men named after its barracks on an island in the Nile (*bahr al-nil*). The Bahriyya murdered as-Salih's son and successor, Turanshah, who

they thought was discriminating against them, and, in 1254, installed Ibegh, one of their own men, as Sultan of Egypt. Five years
later, Ibegh was in turn murdered and replaced by Qutuz, another
Mameluke. He was faced with the challenge of Mongols, led by
Hulagu Khan, who had invaded Iraq and, in 1258, captured
Baghdad. On 3 September 1260, Qutuz's army defeated them in a
great battle at Ain Jalut near Hama in Syria; a month later, he was
assassinated and Baybars, who had been the outstanding commander at Ain Jalut, became Sultan in 1261.

Like all Mamelukes, Baybars was a Sunni Muslim, and owed
allegiance to the Khalif of Baghdad. Gaining control of the
Khalifate himself by installing one of the last of the Abbasid
princes as titulary Khalif of Baghdad and forcing him to live in
Cairo, he turned his attention to expanding his area of influence
into Syria. He had to defend his Syrian territory on two fronts: the
Mongols continued their attacks in the north, and Crusaders still
controlled fortresses that extended from Antioch to Jaffa. Baybars'
greatest military achievement was the storming of Antioch in
1268, in which 16,000 of its garrison and inhabitants were killed
and 100,000 captured.

Baybars died in Damascus in July 1277, possibly after drinking
fermented mare's milk, for which he had a great fondness, and
which had become polluted; or, as it was rumoured, from inad-
vertently drinking poison which he had intended for someone else.
An austere man, ruthless and secretive, he was a great soldier and
administrator, energetic, but to the last a Turk and never fully at
ease in Arab or Egyptian society. He despised the Christians of his
time as weaklings who in no way compared with their illustrious
forebears; and he intimidated his fellow Mamelukes with political purges. His military victories impressed his subjects. The
Egyptians thought him an enlightened ruler, strict but just. He is
still a folk hero in Egypt, and tales are told of his prowess, of his
legendary speed of travel between one area of battle and the next,
and of the time when he swam across the Nile wearing full
armour.

Another veteran of the Bahriyya corps, Qalawan, became Sultan after Baybars. He was nicknamed *al-Alfi* (a thousand) because
it was said that he had been bought in the slave market for 1000
dinars. He chipped away at the Crusaders' positions until their
only possession in Syria was Acre and its surrounding area.
Qalawan was succeeded by his son, Al-Nasir Muhammad, who

ruled until 1340, in a reign that marked a most prosperous time for Egypt; but he was followed by a series of incompetent Bahriyya Mameluke Sultans, 11 of them in 40 years. Hassan is the only one worthy of note. In 1347, the Black Death (bubonic plague) struck Egypt, killing off, it is estimated, a third of the population. Nevertheless, in 1356, Hassan ordered the construction of a huge mosque (*see* page 281), just below the Citadel in Cairo, which he funded by cutting the pay and pensions of his army officers, thus alienating them. One of the mosque's minarets collapsed in 1361, killing several hundred people in the street below; and 33 days after this unlucky event, Hassan was overthrown. His body disappeared without trace, and his mausoleum within the great mosque remains empty.

The Sultanate was taken from the Bahriyya Mamelukes in 1382 by others from the Burgi barracks in the Citadel. The Burgis, who were Circassians, ruled Egypt until 1516. During that time, the country prospered and trade increased, enabling the Burgi Mamelukes to construct a plethora of fine mosques, *madrasas*, mausoleums, public buildings and fountains. An eye-witness account of the Mamelukes, written in about 1421, was given by Sir Gilbert de Lannoy[261] (*c.*1386–1462), the soldier from Burgundy commissioned by Henry V of England to carry out a survey of Egypt and Syria with a view to mounting a crusade. He noted that a Mameluke sultan was chosen by his fellows not only for his intelligence, courage and self-control but also because, during the reign of his predecessor, he had contrived to surround himself with loyal and powerful supporters. Though power and vested interests kept him in authority, he was ever fearful of rivals. Even if he reached an agreement with his emirs that one of his sons should succeed him, this seldom happened: the unfortunate heir was either thrown into prison or strangled or poisoned on the orders of a rival emir.

Mamelukes, fighting from horseback, were protected by simple, silk-covered breastplates and small round helmets, and used bows and arrows, swords and clubs; drums were beaten to terrify the enemy's horses. Their reward was women, castles and clothing; according to merit, one was placed in command of 10, or 20, or 50, or 100 lances. In this way, a Mameluke could rise to become emir of Jerusalem or Damascus or Cairo. According to de Lannoy,

[261] Potvin, 1878.

the indigenous Egyptians had little enough concern in governing the country; and, when a sultan waged war, neither the townspeople nor the farmers went to fight but continued with their own businesses, leaving those who wanted to become lords to get on with it.

De Lannoy observed that Alexandria was very large and well fortified, with two ports. The old port, forbidden to Christians, was about 1.6 kilometres wide, shallow, and liable to be affected by west-south-west winds; the new port was 9.5 kilometres in circumference. There were no wells or cisterns in the city: its excavated subterranean conduits were filled from the end of August to the beginning of October by Inundation water from the Nile. He saw Egypt with a soldier's eye, noting that the ground under Alexandria was firm and suitable for the digging of mine tunnels by invasion forces. A military view is also evident in his appraisal of the Egyptians, whom he thought wretched, being clad only in shirts with no leggings or breeches, bands round their heads, and carrying few weapons of any sort. However large the number of Christians in Egypt, they could, he was certain, be of very limited help to invading western Christians.

Less than a century after de Lannoy's visit to Egypt, the country had fallen to the Ottoman Turks. In 1392, the Ottomans wrested control of the old Byzantine empire from the Mongols, capturing Constantinople in 1453 and renaming it Istanbul. They then turned their attention to Egypt and the weakened Mamelukes. In August 1516, the army of the Ottoman Sultan, Selim the Grim, using artillery for the first time, defeated the Mameluke army at Aleppo in Syria, in a battle in the course of which the aged Mameluke Sultan, al-Ghuri, died of apoplexy. Three years later, the Ottomans took easy possession of Cairo, and Egypt, removing to Istanbul the last survivor of the Abassid dynasty, the puppet through whom the Mamelukes had controlled the Khalifate. Later Ottoman Sultans claimed that the wretched Khalif had transferred his rights to the Khalifate to Selim, but, although Istanbul became the capital of the Islamic empire, its rulers were not true Khalifs, because they were unable to claim descent from the Prophet or his family. In spite of this, the Ottoman Empire flourished, while Egypt was reduced to the status of a province, rapidly declining into a decadent and backward country.

In 1798, Egypt was drawn into the conflict between revolutionary France and Britain. Napoleon Bonaparte, realizing he was as yet in no position to attack Britain directly, mounted an expeditionary force with the aim of securing control over the Red Sea route to India, where Britain had an important trading empire. The first step in this campaign was the invasion of Egypt, and, on 1 July 1798, a French army of 36,000 men arrived in Alexandria. Two weeks later, after an arduous march across the desert, the French reached Giza where the Turkish-Egyptian army was drawn up in the shadow of the pyramids. The Egyptian army consisted of 16,000 native infantry spearheaded by an elite cavalry of 8000 Mamelukes; the French had little cavalry but superior weaponry. The Battle of the Pyramids lasted for only two hours. The Egyptian infantry, which had never seen heavy guns, panicked and scattered; and the Mamelukes, though they fought bravely, could not withstand French fire-power.

The French took possession of Cairo and Egypt with relative ease, but, while they were doing so, a British fleet under the command of Admiral Nelson destroyed their fleet lying at anchor in the Bay of Abukir at Alexandria. His expeditionary force now stranded in Egypt, Napoleon was nonetheless able to view the situation with optimism, because it allowed him to concentrate on the second purpose of his mission, which was to bring to Egypt the ideals of the French Revolution, to the benefit of all native Egyptians. He appointed a body of 189 prominent Egyptians who, he considered, would in the course of advising him become accustomed to ideas of assembly and government; and in each of the provinces of Egypt, at that time 14, he set up an assembly of up to nine Egyptians, with responsibility for food distribution, sanitation and policing, as advised by a French official.

Napoleon issued a series of decrees, in which the first postal service in Egypt was to be organized, and a stage-coach line between Cairo and Alexandria inaugurated. In Cairo, he founded a 300-bed hospital for the poor and ordered street-lamps to be erected on the main streets at 30-foot intervals. He set up four quarantine stations in an attempt to check bubonic plague, at that time a scourge in Egypt. Using a type-fount of Arabic letters which Napoleon had brought to Egypt with him, the first printed books in Egypt were produced: manuals on the treatment of smallpox and bubonic plague, and a treatise on ophthalmia, another of Egypt's scourges. Newspapers were published for the first time, a mint was set up to re-stamp Mameluke coins as French; windmills were built for grinding corn and raising water; and the mapping of Egypt began.

Napoleon had brought with him to Egypt a large body of French scholars, artists, engineers, writers and scientists, to study the natural history of Egypt and the diseases prevalent in the country, and, above all, to record its antiquities. To facilitate the work of these scholars, he founded the Institut d'Égypte in Cairo, a branch of the Institut de France. In 1802, one of the scholars, Dominique Vivant Denon, published an account of his Egyptian travels in *Voyage dans la Basse et la Haute Égypte*. His drawings formed the basis for the great *Description de l'Égypte* published by François Jomard between 1809 and 1822. These works had a profound effect on European scholarship, and were in large part the means through which the western world would learn of Egypt's great cultural heritage.

In August 1799, after 14 months in Egypt, Napoleon returned to France, leaving General Kléber in command of an army much reduced by disease and battle which, nevertheless, repulsed a Turkish invasion force in March 1800. Three months later, Kléber was assassinated by a Muslim fanatic. His replacement, General Baron de Menou, declared Egypt a French colony but finally, in September 1801, a combination of British and Turkish forces compelled the French to relinquish their hold on Egypt and to withdraw.

The impact of French culture and technology upon a land that had, until Napoleon's arrival, been living in the Middle Ages, was extremely unsettling, and, when the French departed from Egypt, they left it in chaos. When the British withdrew in 1803, seemingly content to leave Egypt in the hands of the Turks, there was every prospect of Egypt becoming a desolate backwater.

Government and Administration

For over a century after the Arab Conquest, Egypt was administered on behalf of the Khalifs by governors responsible for finance, police and the supervision of Friday prayers. The Khalifs imposed Koranic law, but were content to leave the traditional forms of government in each conquered territory more or less untouched, so that the existing Byzantine system of finance and administration of Egypt was left in place, except that the four duchies into which the country had, in the Byzantine era, been divided, were reduced to two, Upper and Lower Egypt, subdivided into *kura* or districts. The Fatimids (969–1171) established the most hierarchical and centralized administrative system known to the Islamic world. Moez realized the need for administrative reform, and entrusted the task to Yaqub ibn-Killis, a converted Jew, whose efficiency was recognized in the reign of Moez's son, Aziz, when he became the first man in the Fatimid era to have the title of *wazir* conferred upon him. In an attempt to deter bribery, the new *wazir* decreed that palace and government officials and the army should be paid fixed salaries; and he set his own annual salary at 100,000 dinars.

The system was headed by the *imam* himself, who was also commander-in-chief of the army. The affairs of Egypt were divided into three branches: administrative, judicial and missionary. The administration was divided into departments, each with its own head responsible to an official called the *wasita*, who functioned as intermediary between the *imam* and the departments. The Chief Justice administered justice, and also supervised the mint.[262] The Chief Missionary, who had representatives throughout the Fatimid and the Islamic empires, was in charge of foreign missions, both diplomatic and trade. He was also in charge of education in Egypt, and responsible for the collection of certain taxes. It was not illegal for one man to hold the positions of Chief Justice and Chief Missionary at the same time.

Saladin was acknowledged to be a great general and a competent administrator. After his death, his Egypto-Syrian empire fragmented, split between his sons and brothers. The Mamelukes, who took control of Egypt in 1249, were not generally gifted with administrative abilities. Baybars and al-Nasir undertook a programme of public works but administrative incompetence, compounded by corruption and negligence, resulted in Egyptians paying for them through forced labour and greater taxation. As a *vilayet* or province of the Ottoman Empire, Egypt was administered by a Turkish *vali* but governed from Istanbul. The 24 Mamelukes the Ottomans left in position as *beys*, or local governors, had no real political power, although they were still a potent military force, in continual conflict with their Turkish overlords, and replenished their numbers by recruiting new slaves.

[262] al-Maqrizi, *Khitat*, vol. 1, p. 404.

Economy

As soon as their conquest was completed, the Arabs imposed land
and poll taxes on the Egyptians, to be collected in two forms: in
grain, which was sent to Arabia, and in money, which was sent to
the governor. At the beginning of the eighth century, Khalif 'Umar
II decreed that Muslims should be exempt from all taxes except
the *zakat*, the mandatory 'loan to God'. The annual revenue from
monetary taxes, which was between 10 and 15 million dinars,
had, by the end of the eighth century, disastrously fallen to about
three million annually, thanks to 'Umar's decree.

From the beginning of the eighth century, the tax burden on the
reducing numbers of Christian Egyptians became heavier. Even
monks, previously exempt, had to pay a tax of 1 dinar a head.
Discontent led to sporadic revolts against the Arabs,[263] the greatest
of them taking place between AD 829 and 831, when Christians
were joined by disaffected Muslims, When, in 832, Ma'mun became the first Khalif to visit Egypt, he instituted a reform of the
land tax that had been in operation for nearly two centuries. The
Church, which had played an important part in the assessment
and collection of taxes, had fewer members and had become less
effective. Khalif Ma'mun decreed, therefore, that some Copts
should be put in charge of tax districts, with Muslims as their
deputies.

As so often in the past, Egypt's natural resources, allied with the
endeavours of the native Egyptians, brought the wealth that enabled the Fatimid Khalifs to feed their vast army of slave soldiers
from many countries; and to make the khalifate into a Shi'ite rival
to the Sunnite Abbasids in Baghdad. At the beginning of Moez's
khalifate, however, the economic organization of the country was
badly in need of reform. Ibn-Killis (*see* page 267) ordered that land
illegally sequestered in the past be returned to its rightful owners,
and took action against profiteers and grain monopolists. In
Cairo, a public depot was set up under state control for the
collection and distribution of wheat. The fleet was enlarged and
new docks built so that Egypt might play a fuller role in the
commerce of the eastern Mediterranean. The country's economic
prosperity was enhanced through the arrival in Alexandria of

---

[263] Ya'qubi, vol. 2, p. 466.

Venetian merchants with all kinds of western European goods, the most valuable of which was amber from the Baltic, silk from Italy and cloth from Flanders.

Goods from Europe were traded for precious spices and essences – cloves, aloes, cardamom, aromatics – that arrived in Egypt from Ethiopia, India and China through the Red Sea and overland on the ancient Silk Route. The main pack animal, the camel, was often likened to a 'ship of the desert', indicating that the domestication of camels first took place in southern Arabia on the coast of the Arabian Gulf, the only area in which Arabs of ancient times had direct acquaintance with the sea and ships.[264] Whatever their history, because camels are uniquely adapted to travel in the desert, they were crucial to the desert economy of Arabia. In the Fatimid era, great camel trains became a common sight in Egypt, wending their ways between Cairo and the oases, Nubia, and the east.

With their usual thoroughness, the Fatimids taxed trade. Nothing and nobody escaped. Every item entering a town, whether by land or by sea, passed a tax-collection point where tax was duly exacted. Fishes were taxed when brought ashore, and at the place where they were preserved. Cattle were taxed on farms, when transported and at the slaughterhouses.[265] Everybody, from leather tanners to pottery makers, from oil pressers to winemakers, from bakers and spinners to prostitutes, paid tax; and in addition, Muslims paid the *zakat* (*see* page 268) and Christians and Jews a poll tax. There was even a value-added tax on all stages of textile production,[266] a flourishing part of the economy. Fustat (*see* page 274) produced a great deal of fustian, the cloth made famous by Chaucer and Shakespeare; and Tinnis in the Delta was noted for its *tinnisi* cloth, with which tennis balls are now covered.

In the Fatimid period, a new system of taxation was introduced. As God's representative on earth, the *imam*, like the Pharaohs before him, owned all land in Egypt, and made gifts of it to his followers. Those who had originally been in possession of the land lost their title to it, although they were allowed to stay on to cultivate it, and even to pass it down from father to son. These

[264] Bulliet, 1990, p. 47.
[265] al-Maqrizi, *Khitat*, vol. 1, pp. 104–5.
[266] al-Maqdisi, p. 213.

'landowners', however, were no better than serfs: they paid a land tax called *kira* (rent),[267] at a not excessive rate.[268] The Fatimids replaced the *kira* with a new system of land-tax collection, however, whereby a contract to pay a fixed sum for a district was auctioned to the highest bidder,[269] not necessarily a member of the local community, a system that led to misery for the peasants, with government officials and army commanders buying up the contracts simply to make money.[270]

Such contractors undertook responsibility for the maintenance and repair of canals, vitally necessary if the irrigation system were to remain in place; and they were given allowances for the work,[271] but, within a short time, the Fatimid administration had short-sightedly let this arrangement slip, having no interest in the maintenance of the irrigation system. For the first time in millenniums, peasants were left without state support in the task of building and mending dykes and digging canals. The irrigation system fell into disrepair with the inevitable result that agriculture deteriorated and there was famine year after year. Taxes also fell.[272] Al-Maqrizi, the fifteenth-century Egyptian scholar, noted that, since time immemorial, a quarter and perhaps a third of Egyptian revenues had been spent on the upkeep of the irrigation system,[273] and lamented that the northern half of the Delta had become a wasteland since the arrival of the Fatimids.[274]

In 1011, the level of the Nile fell disastrously low. According to al-Maqrizi, Hakem abolished several taxes in an attempt to alleviate hardship, but prices rose and bread was so scarce that it became prohibitively expensive. Sickness and death were widespread but medicines were as scarce as the bread. The sale of intoxicating drinks was prohibited, and people were forbidden to indulge in pleasure cruises on the river or to hold public musical performances – an interesting sidelight on the lifestyle of at least some of Hakem's subjects. In an attempt to promote the cultivation only of essential foods such as grain, Hakem ordered the

267 al-Maqdisi, pp. 64–5.
268 al-Maqrizi, *Khitat*, vol. 1, p. 82.
269 al-Maqrizi, *Khitat*, vol. 2, pp. 5–6.
270 al-Maqrizi, *Khitat*, vol. 1, p. 85.
271 al-Maqrizi, *Khitat*, vol. 1, p. 82.
272 al-Maqrizi, *Khitat*, vol. 1, pp. 249–50.
273 al-Maqrizi, *Khitat*, vol. 1, pp. 61, 76, 100.
274 al-Maqrizi, *Khitat*, vol. 1, p. 171.

destruction of vines and forbade the growing of watercress and *mulukhiyya*.[275] He also forbade the eating of fish without scales[276] and ordered the killing of all dogs except hounds for hunting.[277]

The economy recovered so that, in 1048, the Persian traveller, Nasir-i-Khusrau, was able to describe the splendours of the Cairo of Sultan al-Mustansir and how, on one December day, he saw in the market not only plentiful supplies of the usual vegetables and pulses but also roses, lilies, oranges, lemons, apples, grapes, dates and sugar canes. Prices were fixed: a shopkeeper found cheating was paraded through the streets on a camel, preceded by a proclamation that he had cheated and been punished. Nasir observed that:

> Cairo is a great city to which few cities can compare. I estimated no fewer than 20,000 shops in Cairo owned by the sultan... Caravanseries, baths and other public structures are so numerous as to be difficult to count – all the property of the sultan... as many as 20,000 houses belong to the sultan.[278]

According to Nasir, the Sultan's palace housed 30,000 people, including 12,000 servants and 1000 guards; but, some 22 years later, al-Mustansir was destitute.

During the Mameluke era, Alexandria remained important to Egypt's trade. Sultan Qayt Bey strengthened its defences in 1480 by ordering a great fort, called Qayt Bey, to be built on the site of what had been the famous Pharos or Lighthouse, a fort still used

---

[275] *Corchorus olitorius* or Jew's Mallow: a vegetable with deep-green leaves which are used to make a soup that is thought to have been eaten since pharaonic times. *Mulukhiyya* is widely cultivated in summer time and its leaves can be eaten fresh, or dried for use in the winter. The soup is made simply and cheaply by boiling *mulukhiyya* leaves in water to which a few vegetables have been added. It can also be made with meat or chicken stock; and in medieval times pieces of chicken or fried diced meat seem to have been added to make a richer version of what is one of Egypt's national dishes.

[276] Presumably the barbel, a mud-fish which cleans the bottoms of canals and wells.

[277] al-Maqrizi, *Khitat*, vol. 2, pp. 286, 87, 88, 342. Even today, Egypt has many seemingly stray dogs (often, in fact, guard dogs) which live largely on scraps of bread. Hakem was presumably trying to save bread.

[278] Schefer, 1881, p. 127.

by the Egyptian military today. In 1488, however, Bartholomew Diaz became the first European to sail round the tip of Africa, thus opening up a sea route round the Cape, and enabling Europe to trade with the Orient without recourse to routes through Egypt and Alexandria. Much Mameluke wealth, once based on a monopoly of trade with Venice, had been lost by the beginning of the sixteenth century.

To the Ottoman Turks, the welfare of Egyptians, whether Muslims, Jews or Christians, was of so little account that they laid upon them all the burden of heavy taxation.

Religion

After the Conquest, the Arabs made no attempt to persuade Egyptians to convert to Islam. Some Christians, however, found conversion expedient, not wholly as a matter of conviction or because they were under direct pressure, but largely to avoid the taxes imposed on non-Muslims; many believed that, after conversion, they could revert to their former religion, not realizing that the penalty for apostasy was death. Even by the beginning of the Fatimid era (AD 969), proselytizing was not encouraged, Moez perhaps coming to understand that the great majority of Egyptians were still firmly Christian, having resisted conversion to Islam, and perhaps seeing them as counterweight to Egyptian Muslims, most of whom, unlike himself, were Sunni.

Moez's son Aziz (975–96) demonstrated his tolerance of Christianity by marrying a Christian and appointing one of her brothers, Orestes, as Melkite Patriarch of Jerusalem, and another, Arsenius, as Metropolitan of Cairo. Although the majority of Aziz's subjects in Egypt were Egyptian Christians, the country was largely run by, and for, Muslim Arabs. Relations between Muslims and Christians remained good for most of the Fatimid dynasty, however, and many Christians became valued counsellors to the Muslim authorities who saw that they had much to contribute to the well-being of the country, as did Jews. In addition, Christian artists and craftsmen influenced Fatimid art through the legacy of Hellenistic and Coptic styles that they brought to their work.

In contrast to Aziz, his son and successor, Hakem (996–1021), was not kindly disposed towards Christians, nor, for that matter, towards Jews and orthodox Sunni Muslims. He ordered that notices be posted on the doors of mosques, shops, army barracks and cemeteries cursing the early Muslims; and his persecution of Christians and Jews began with the razing of churches and synagogues. From 1009, Christians were forced to wear black – the colour associated with Hakem's hated enemies, the Sunni Abbasids in Baghdad – and also made to wear round their necks large wooden crosses, each weighing about 12 kilograms. Jews were compelled to wear wooden discs in similar fashion. Hakem's orders were so strictly enforced that, according to al-Maqrizi, many Christians converted to Islam to escape his strictures. In 1011, relenting towards Sunni Muslims, he ordered the notices cursing them to be removed.

In the years that followed the Fatimid dynasty, Christians lost their influence at court, and the Coptic community in Egypt dwindled in number. From the fourteenth to the nineteenth centuries, they sank into a long period of obscurity; and it was not until the twentieth century that Copts again achieved a significant position in Egyptian political and religious life.

Burial customs

The last vestiges of pharaonic practice in burying the dead were lost in the Islamic period. The ritual period of 70 days between the day of death and the day of burial was abandoned, and Muslims and Christians observed Islamic law, which decrees that the dead must be buried within 24 hours, wrapped simply in shrouds and without coffins. There was no mummification.

One of the *hadiths* (traditions), the sayings and actions attributed to the Prophet, forbade such vanities as elaborate superstructures over burial places; and none of the early Muslim graves was marked in this way. When Khalif al-Mustansir died in AD 862, however, his Greek mother had a canopy erected over his grave. She observed the letter of the *hadith*, if not its spirit, as the canopy lacked walls and was therefore not a building; and the fashion of erecting a dome over the grave was adopted by the Fatimids. At first, domes were supported by four brick piers, with a *mihrab*, a prayer niche, set into one of them. Because this meant that the *mihrab* was placed asymmetrically, however, it soon became the custom for the space between the piers of the *qiblah* (prayer direction) side to be filled in so that the *mihrab* could be positioned in the centre of the wall, from where it was a short step to filling in the spaces between all four piers, thus producing a tomb building.

Cultural Achievements

Cairo

Under the Arabs, Alexandria lost its position as capital city of Egypt. Khalif ʿUmar ordered a new Arab capital to be built near the apex of the Delta, where it would have command of the place where the two halves of Egypt converge; and, in AD 641, ʿAmr ibn al-ʿAs established an administrative centre for Egypt near the ruins of Babylon-in-Egypt, today called Old Cairo, some 5 kilometres south of the centre of the modern city. According to an inaccurate tradition, Babylon-in-Egypt was constructed in the thirteenth century BC by Babylonian prisoners of Ramesses II. The site had, however, been named after a fort built by the Romans, who considered it strategically important enough to station a whole legion there. To Christians, it was the place in which the Holy Family had taken refuge on their flight into Egypt; and Egyptian Christians believed that St Mark had written most of his gospel there. For strategic and for religious reasons, therefore, Babylon-in-Egypt was a canny choice for the site of a new capital; and ʿAmr, who was wise and humane, left its Christian and Jewish inhabitants undisturbed as construction began on the first Muslim city to be built in Egypt. The city was named al-Fustat or 'The Tent' because, it was said, as he was about to set out from Babylon-in-Egypt for his attack on Alexandria, ʿAmr found two doves nesting on the roof of his tent. Accordingly, he left the tent standing until he returned victorious from Alexandria; and, in due course, his new city grew up round the site. ʿAmr ordered his mosque, the first to be built in Egypt (*see* page 279), to be erected on the spot where his tent had stood.

In AD 868, Ahmad ibn Tulun founded a new Egyptian capital on raised ground to the north-east of Fustat, and named it al-Qataʿiyeh (the Quarters). Al-Qataʿiyeh was designed not only as the site for Ibn Tulun's residence but also to meet the needs of the varieties of people and nationalities serving him. The walls of his palace were covered in gold, and the city boasted the first hospital in Egypt; today all that remains of this once splendid capital is the mosque built for its founder (*see* page 279).

When, in AD 969, Egypt became the centre of the Fatimid empire, Moez ordered General Gohar to build him a new capital to outdo Baghdad in its splendour. Choosing a site to the north of Fustat, Gohar founded a city named *al-Qahirah,* so called because the planet Mars (in Arabic *Qahir al-Aflak* or Subduer of the Skies) was in the ascendant as the walls of the new city were being built. The full name of the city was Misr al-Qahirah, 'Misr' being the Semitic term for Egypt. Even today, many Egyptians speak of going to Misr when they mean Qahirah or Cairo. The Fatimid Khalif moved his residence to Cairo four years after its founding, by which time the city wall, complete with its four gates, was completed, as was the mosque, al-Azhar (*see* below) and the palace, which occupied an area of nearly 100,000 square metres in the centre of the city. The palace was designed to accommodate the khalifal family, their servants and bodyguards, and army officers and government offices were located within it. Over the years, it was enlarged so that eventually it boasted over 4000 rooms.

Gohar's *al-Qahirah* was a city of magnificent buildings, chief among which was the great mosque, al-Azhar or 'The Flowering', founded in AD 970. In the thirteenth century, the mosque became the Islamic University, and, to this day, is dedicated to the study of Islamic laws and Arabic. Cairo rapidly became a brilliant cultural centre, famous for the study of three disciplines for which the Arabs were noted: astronomy, mathematics and medicine; and graced by the work of the many highly skilled craftsmen who had been brought in to build the new city but who remained to make it a centre of artistic excellence.

Saladin undertook the remodelling of the capital. In 1176, he ordered a great citadel to be built to the south of *al-Qahirah,* on a rise in the Moqattam hills which dominated the city. It was laid out in the form of a Crusader castle in Syria, and parts of it were constructed from stone taken from the small pyramids at Giza. The residence in the Citadel built for him continued to be used by his successors until the middle of the nineteenth century. Saladin set up many *madrasas* (theological schools) and mosques in Cairo, and men of learning enjoyed his patronage so that Cairo once again became a cultural centre. He also founded hospitals, notably an asylum (*maristan*) for the insane. According to the Spanish

Plate 8.1 The Al-Azhar Mosque, Cairo (founded in AD *970): interior. (Photograph David Couling.)*

Plate 8.2   Gate to the Citadel, Cairo (begun by Saladin in AD *1176).
(Photograph David Couling.)*

Muslim traveller, ibn-Jubayr, who visited Cairo in 1183, the
maristan was supervised by a highly qualified director. It was a
palatial building, provided with 'cupboards full of drugs and a
variety of medicinal drinks'; and the Sultan in person oversaw the
institution 'making sure that proper care is constantly given.'[279]
Saladin's court physician, ibn-Maimun, enjoyed his fullest support. A Spanish Jew, better known as Maimonides, he wrote on
theology, philosophy and astronomy as well as on medicine. His
medical works include commentaries on Galen and Hippocrates,
and his observations on diet and hygiene are still read with interest
today, as is his most famous book, *A guide for the perplexed*,[280] a
philosophical study combining Aristotle's scientific teachings with
religion.

During the Sultanate of the ninth Mameluke, al-Nasir (between
1293 and 1340), Cairo was visited by the Moroccan traveller, ibn-
Battutah, who was impressed by its 'boundless number of buildings, peerless in beauty and splendour', surging with 'inhabitants
whom it can hardly contain despite its spaciousness and capacity'
– a description that still applies today. Ibn-Battutah noted that
36,000 ships owned by the Sultan and his subjects plied the Nile,
and that drinking water was carried into the city by 30,000
muleteers and 12,000 cameleers.[281] Less than 200 years later, in
September 1519, the Ottomans had captured the city. They built
very few public buildings and reduced the great capital, which had
for centuries been at the heart of Islam, to a provincial city.

Architecture

Houses

After the Arab Conquest, the rural inhabitants of Egypt continued
to live in traditional mud-brick houses. The Arabs, who had little
in the way of architectural traditions of their own, at first built
houses in Egypt that, judging by what little remains, were based on
Mesopotamian models. In the twelfth century, they introduced a
type derived from western Asiatic houses, a new style that con-

---

279   Broadhurst, 1952, pp. 43–4.
280   S. Munk, (ed.), (Paris, 1856–66). Also H. Atay (Ankara, 1974).
281   Gibb, 1958, vol. 1, p. 41.

sisted of a high, central, covered courtyard, with two large open-ended halls (*liwans*) opening off two opposing sides. Interior apartments led off the central court and were divided into two sections, one for men, the other for women. The building material was largely stone, marble inlays set into the walls being the chief form of decoration.

Until the nineteenth century, when European architecture was introduced, large private houses in Egypt conformed to this basic plan. The houses of the rich often had several storeys; and all had bedrooms, bathrooms, kitchens and servants' quarters, and a sitting-room overlooking the courtyard. The windows throughout were filled with *mashrabiyyah*, wooden screens made of decorative open-work; and on the roof was a *mulqaf* (ventilator) which caught the cool breeze. The exterior of an Egyptian Arab house is austere, but its courtyard is an oasis of shade, cooled by a pool or a fountain, its marble walls often covered with flowering plants.

Mosques

The mosque as a place of worship is not strictly necessary to the practice of Islam: the Prophet himself prayed in the courtyard of his house. The earliest mosque in Egypt was built at Fustat for ʿAmr ibn al-ʿAs a decade or so after the Prophet's death, and lacking certain later features of mosque architecture. A distinctive feature of a modern mosque is its minaret, the origin of which is unclear. The earliest mosques had none; instead, the muezzin simply climbed on to the roof to call the faithful to prayer. It is possible that the building of minarets was inspired by the Pharos of Alexandria, which was still standing when the Arabs invaded Egypt, a speculation reinforced by the meaning of the Arabic word for minaret, *manara*, the 'place of flames'. A minaret was added to ʿAmr's mosque in AD 672, nearly 30 years after its foundation. In early mosques, the *mihrab*, the indication of the direction of Mecca towards which the faithful pray, was probably shown as a mark on the wall. Decorated *mihrabs* seem to date from the ʿUmayyad period; and the *mihrab* in ʿAmr's mosque was not installed until AD 712.

The architectural centrepiece of al-Qataʿiyeh was the great mosque, covering an area of some 2.6 hectares, that was built for Ibn Tulun between AD 876 and 879, and designed, it is said, by a Christian architect. Today, it stands preserved almost intact,

Plate 8.3   Ibn Tulun Mosque, Cairo (built between AD *876 and 879):
courtyard. (Photograph David Couling.)*

although the other mosques and the splendid palaces and gardens of al-Qataʿiyeh have long since disappeared. The mosque's square plan is of the classical Iraqi type, inspired by Christian basilicas, but its decoration and the materials used in its construction show Persian influence. There were no fixed rules for the architecture of mosques beyond the emphasis to be placed on achieving an appearance of lightness and elegance. Ibn Tulun's mosque, therefore, has a great open courtyard, 92 metres square and Cairo's largest, surrounded on three sides by arcades. On the fourth (southern) side is the sanctuary, made up of five aisles that run parallel with the courtyard, its *mihrab* (prayer niche), ornamented with glass mosaic, being in the outermost wall. The arcades are formed from wide arches resting on great brick piers; arches which, unlike the standard curved Arab arch, are pointed. The walls between the arches have windows, each filled in with open-work stucco carved while still wet, their window frames beautifully decorated with plaster sculpted in a typically Persian vine-leaf motif.

Several of the Mameluke Sultans, though particularly known for foreign conquest and short, violent reigns, also commissioned the building of great mosques, in which artistic innovation was encouraged. The most important architectural achievement of Baybars' reign was the mosque built for him in Cairo, on the site of the eastern palace of the Fatimids. With its adjoining *madrasa* (theological school), the mosque was constructed between 1262 and 1263 and named al-Bunduqdari. It consists of a vast colonnaded courtyard, with square towers at its corners, entered through monumental gateways. By the time of the Napoleonic invasion of 1798, it had fallen into disuse. The French turned it into a fort, Fort Sulkowski, and later it was converted into stables, a bakery and finally a soap factory. Its minaret collapsed in 1882.

The mosque of the Mameluke Sultan Hassan, which was built with astonishing speed and on an unprecedented scale between 1356 and 1362, is regarded by many as the finest in Cairo. Almost twice the size of other mosques, its exterior walls are over 36 metres high, and its entrance portal, which curves outwards so that it can be seen from the Citadel, is built on the same scale. In contrast to its austere exterior walls, its portal is lavishly decorated, and leads to a domed vestibule as large as the prayer hall in many mosques; and the central court beyond is on an equally large scale, measuring 35 metres by 32 metres. The whole edifice is dominated by a minaret some 86 metres high, originally one of a pair of the same size. After one collapsed in the seventeenth century, it was rebuilt on a much smaller scale. A second pair of minarets, intended to stand above the entrance, was part of an original design that was not completed

The internal plan of Sultan Hassan's mosque differs from that of a classic mosque, in that it has a central court or *sahn*, surrounded by four halls (*liwans*), each of them large, rectangular and barrel vaulted. Mameluke mosques always have *madrasas* within them; and each of Sultan Hassan's *liwans* contains a college devoted to the study of one of the four orthodox branches of Islam. The largest *liwan*, which is on the south-east side of the *sahn*, is used as the prayer hall; and, in this great hall, an Islamic dream was finally realized, in that it is larger than the Taq-i Kisra, the throne room of the ancient Shahs of Persia. The hall is decorated with a fine, white marble frieze inscribed with texts from the Koran in Kufic script; its walls, and especially the *mihrab*, are lavishly inlaid with coloured marbles and porphyry. Behind the hall is Hassan's cenotaph. The chief interior ornaments of a mosque are its lamps, for the myriad of which the mosque of Sultan Hassan was once famous. Most of these lamps are now in the Museum of Islamic Art in Cairo.

In its heyday, the Sultan Hassan mosque would have employed hundreds of people ranging from mosque officials and teachers to accountants, cooks and cleaners. To meet their needs, it had its own well, kitchens, stables, housing and lavatories, and a market. It was, in essence, a self-sufficient community, probably larger than many contemporary villages in Egypt. Its huge scale and the quality of the materials used in its construction meant that the cost of building it was enormous. Al-Maqrizi stated that 1000 dinars, the equivalent of 4 kilograms of gold, were spent each day, a sum also equivalent to the annual income of 30 skilled fourteenth-century archers. Part of the cost was financed by those who died during the Black Death (*see* page 263): the State collected the property of the many who died without surviving heirs, and spent much of it on the mosque. At Hassan's death, it was still unfinished. His nephew completed the vital structures of the building, including Hassan's cenotaph, but abandoned the decoration.

The mosque of the first Burgi Sultan, Barquq, is one of the finest. Built to the east of the Citadel between 1399 and 1411, it heralds the beginning of a distinctive style of Mameluke

*Plate 8.4   The Mosque of Sultan Barquq, Cairo (built between AD 1399
and 1411): exterior showing dome decorations.
(Photograph David Couling.)*

Plate 8.5   The Mosque of Sultan Qayt Bey, Cairo (built AD *1472): interior. (Photograph David Couling.)*

architecture, with a square ground plan, and two minarets on its western front; but its glories are the domes, two large and several small, the first stone domes to be built in Cairo. One covers the tomb of Sultan Barquq, another those of his female relatives. The large domes are decorated on the outside with zigzag patterns, the small with a ribbed design. Seen together from within the mosque, they give the impression of soaring light.

In 1472, Sultan Qayt Bey caused his mosque, which is considered to be the outstanding achievement of Mameluke art, to be erected near that of Barquq. It was the first mosque laid out in the cruciform shape that was to become the standard design; but its chief claims to fame are the fine, elaborately carved stonework decorating its dome and the borders round the windows and doors, and the beauty of its stained-glass windows. Other khalifs and *imams* chose to be buried in the vicinity of the mosque tombs of the Sultans Barquq and Qayt Bey; and later many private individuals added their tombs, so that the area became known as the City of the Dead.

The private tombs were large enough to allow the relatives of the dead owner to stay with him during important Muslim festivals, a custom owing nothing to Islamic tradition but still a practice of Egyptian Muslims, and probably derived from the funerary practices of the ancient Egyptians, who were not usually afraid of the dead, and who often paid visits to a tomb to share a meal in the presence of the deceased.

Language

During the two centuries of ʿUmayyad rule (AD 685–750), Greek, the official language of Hellenistic and Roman Egypt, died out; and Coptic, the surviving language of pharaonic Egypt, spoken by native Egyptians, dwindled. In the eighth century, Arabic became the official language of the Arab empire, of which Egypt was a part. The Copts or native Egyptians gradually abandoned their own language and customs in favour of those of the Arabs, retaining only their Christianity, although even this did not flourish for long, cut off as it was from the churches of East and West.

By the eleventh century, liturgical manuscripts, grammars and vocabularies were being written in Coptic and in Arabic. Two centuries later, Coptic had been almost entirely superseded by

Arabic as the literary language, although in the fifteenth century, al-Maqrisi reported that Coptic was still spoken in villages in Upper Egypt. A century later, it was dead, preserved only in Church liturgy, and 'spoken' rather as Latin was 'spoken' until recently in the Roman Catholic Church.

9

Modern Egypt

Poverty and obscurity engulfed the country in the Ottoman era. It was Mehmet Ali (*c*.1769–1849), a native of Kavalla in Macedonia and the son of a Turkish Aga, who delivered it from oblivion. He arrived in Egypt in 1801 as second-in-command of 6000 troops from Kavalla, part of the Ottoman army sent to drive out the French. Two years later, he secured command of what was the most powerful force in Egypt; and, in 1805, with the support of the people of Cairo and their religious leaders, he overthrew Koshrew, then Ottoman Pasha (Governor). The departure of the British had left Egypt in a state of civil disorder, with the Mamelukes engaged in a bitter struggle for power with the Ottoman authorities. Mehmet Ali successfully played them off against each other and, within two years, had gained control of the whole of Egypt.

In 1807, Mehmet Ali was recognized as Pasha by the Sublime Porte in Istanbul, to all intents and purposes independent of Ottoman authority, and thenceforward known by the Egyptian form of his name, Muhammad Ali. A man of vision, but not an impractical idealist, he was a despot who invested Egyptians with a sense of nationhood, ruthlessly carrying out plans which brought large benefits to the country, and justly seen as the founder of modern Egypt.

History

Muhammad Ali's hold on Egypt could not be secure until Mameluke power was broken. Accordingly, on 1 March 1811, he invited nearly 500 Mameluke beys to a feast in Cairo's Citadel, where they were beheaded one by one as they passed through its entrance gate. Muhammad Ali followed up the 'Massacre of the Mamelukes' by having some 1200 more slaughtered throughout Egypt. Thus, Mameluke power, which had lasted for over 500 years, was brought to an end forever.

Muhammad Ali was technically still a vassal of the Ottoman Sultan, and, from time to time, he was called upon to give military assistance to the Turks. In 1813, he was asked to send a force to Arabia to suppress the Wahhabi revolt in the Hejaz, a task that took five years to accomplish. In 1824, he became Governor of the Morea in southern Greece during the Sultan's attempt to quash Greek independence, and appointed his eldest son, Ibrahim, to be commander of the Egyptian forces. Ibrahim defeated the Greeks on land, but, on 20 November 1827, his fleet was destroyed by the allied European Powers during the Battle of Navarino.

For his co-operation, the Turks rewarded Muhammad Ali with the island of Candia (Crete). Having greater territorial ambitions, he had already brought first Kordofan and then the rest of the Sudan under Egyptian control; he now decided to expand his dominion northwards into Ottoman territory, and in 1831 sent Ibrahim to attack Syria. Ibrahim occupied Damascus and defeated the Turks at Homs. Eight years later, Egypt declared war on Turkey a second time, and Ibrahim threatened to capture Istanbul. The Sultan appointed Muhammad Ali as Pasha of the conquered territories; and, in 1841, with the help of the European Powers, he persuaded Muhammad Ali to sign a treaty, in which he agreed to give up Syria, Candia and the Hejaz. In return, the office of Pasha of Egypt was proclaimed hereditary to the family of Muhammad Ali; and, in 1866, the title 'Khedive' or Viceroy was conferred upon his grandson, Ismail.

In September 1848, the state of Muhammad Ali's health led to his son, Ibrahim, assuming control in his father's name. The son died two months later, the father outliving him by nine months, to die on 2 August 1849. He was buried in a tomb carved from Carrara marble, in the great mosque that crowns the Citadel of Cairo and bears his name. The Muhammad Ali mosque was built in conscious imitation of the Santa Sophia mosque in Istanbul, with a central dome surrounded by four small and four semicircular domes, and, in classic Byzantine style, four corner towers. Its two minarets are tall, slender and elegant. The interior is faced

Plate 9.1   Muhammad Ali Mosque, the Citadel, Cairo (nineteenth century). (Photograph David Couling.)

completely in alabaster, hence the building is sometimes called the 'Alabaster Mosque'. It was to be the last great achievement of Islamic art in Egypt; and, with its shining domes and dagger-shaped minarets, it is like no other building in Cairo.

Muhammad Ali was succeeded by his grandson, Abbas I (1849–54), who, unlike his grandfather, was anti-reform and anti-European. In any case, he proved to be such an unpopular ruler that, less than five years after becoming Pasha, he was murdered. The succeeding two rulers, Said (1854–63) and Ismail (1863–79), the son of Ibrahim, had been educated in Europe, were French speaking and wore European dress. They were both bent on modernizing Egypt along European lines and in co-operation with Europe: Ismail, in particular, was determined to make Egypt independent of Turkey. Having expansionist aims, he greatly enlarged the army, annexed extensive areas of Ottoman territory on the Red Sea coastline, and, in the best imperialist traditions of the day, even sent an English explorer, Samuel Baker, to lay claim on his behalf to parts of Equatorial Africa.

Ismail's grandiose ideas and lack of financial acumen led him into debt (*see* page 304) and thus into the hands of foreign bankers. In reaction against his policies, Egyptian nationalism began to grow, instigated largely by al-Sayyid Jamal al-Din al Afgani, who, as his name implies, came from Afghanistan. He addressed large public meetings in Cairo calling for Egyptians to reject the West and become part of a pan-Islamic world. Expelled from Egypt, he left many sympathizers. Army officers, especially Arabic-speaking Turks, were among those who resented the foreign control of Egyptian financial affairs. Many were convinced that the country was being unfairly punished by European bankers for Ismail's mistakes.

When, under pressure from France and Britain, the Sultan forced Ismail to give up his office, in 1879, to his son, Muhammad Tewfik, resentment reached a peak. An army colonel, Arabi, became a symbol of Egyptian resentment of foreign control, whether British, French or Turkish; and, in 1882, he attempted a military coup. In July of that year, Alexandria was bombarded by British and French ships. That was as much as the French felt inclined to do, and the expeditionary force sent to Egypt, ostensibly in the interests of protecting European lives and property, was entirely British. Troops under the command of Sir Garnet Wolseley defeated Arabi's forces at Tel-el-Kebir in September, 1882, and the leaders of the revolt, including Arabi, called Pasha by his followers, were banished. The British occupation of Egypt began.

Sir Evelyn Baring[282] had from 1879 been British controller in Egypt, co-operating harmoniously with Khedive Tewfik. Disbanding the Egyptian army, he set up a new force under the command of Sir Evelyn Wood, and accorded him the title of Sirdar. The new army, with 4000 men considerably smaller than the old, was, nevertheless, more efficient. Conditions of pay and service were improved, and the army was led by a combination of Egyptian and British officers. It failed, however, to prevent the loss of Egyptian control in the Sudan. The rebellion started by the Mahdi in 1883, and compounded by the vacillation of Gladstone and the British Government, caused the death of General Gordon at Khartoum two years later, after which Egyptian forces were withdrawn. The Sudan south of Wadi Halfa was abandoned to the Mahdist forces, which remained in control until their defeat by Kitchener in the Battle of Omdurman in September 1898. Nubia, as a buffer between Egypt and the Sudan, was made a military zone. The British Government maintained an army of occupation in Egypt that at no time exceeded more than 14,000 men, and were anxious to withdraw it.

In January, 1892, Abbas Hilmi (1892–1914) succeeded his father, Muhammad Tewfik, as Khedive. Although the new Khedive resented British control of Egypt, he was wary of encouraging the re-emergent nationalist movement. Arabi Pasha returned from exile in Ceylon (now Sri Lanka) in 1899, to find himself a forgotten man. Mustafa Kemal, a young lawyer, was leader of a new nationalist party. He had been educated in France, and rejected violence in favour of gaining independence by legal means, his views publicized in the newspaper published by his party. He was supported not only by Muslims but also by Copts, though the Copts simply wanted an Egypt that was independent rather than pan-Arabic. Lord Cromer, totally out of sympathy with moves for independence, resigned in April 1907. His replacement, Sir Eldon Gorst, was rather more liberal but died in July 1911, and two months later, Field Marshal Kitchener took over as Consul General and British Agent in Egypt.

Kitchener's time in Egypt was short: on Britain's entry into World War I in August 1914, he was elevated to War Minister

[282] Created Baron Cromer in 1892.

and, incidentally, granted an earldom. He never returned to Egypt. Khedive Abbas Hilmi was resentful of the British Occupation; and, at the beginning of World War I, was in Istanbul, making it known that he would fully support the Turks should they decide to enter the war on the side of Germany. He was forbidden to return to Egypt, and, by December 1914, he had been deposed. His uncle, Hussain Kamil, was appointed head of state in his place, with the title of Sultan. The British Government considered that the alliance Turkey had made with Germany posed a threat to the strategically important Suez Canal, and, to safeguard the waterway, suspended the Egyptian National Assembly and, on 2 November 1914, introduced martial law. On 18 December of that year, Egypt became a British Protectorate.

Egypt was vital to the British campaign in the Near East. Cairo was used as the staging post for an Allied offensive to free Arabia, Palestine and Syria from Ottoman control. The war thus brought a certain amount of prosperity to Egypt,[283] but most Egyptians remained anti-British, feeling that their country had been drawn into a war which was not its concern. In October 1917, Sultan Hussain Kamil died, and Ahmed Fuad (1917–35), the youngest son of Ismail (*see* page 290), succeeded him. The war ended and Egypt tried to win independence, but it was not until 1922 that it was able to secure a treaty in which its independence was recognized, though responsibility for the country's defence and for the Suez Canal remained with Britain. In March 1922, Ahmed Fuad became King, the first for nearly 2000 years.

The Treaty of 1922 was negotiated by the Wafd (Nationalist) Party, which took over as governing party in a new assembly, though the King retained considerable privileges, a situation that did not advance democratic aspirations. The Wafd, led by Saad Zaghloul Pasha, became the focus for the nationalism that dominated Egyptian politics in the years before World War II. The numbers of Britons occupying posts in the administration, thus denying opportunities to Egyptians, fuelled resentment that promises of self-determination made before the Great War had been forgotten. Relations between King Fuad and the Wafd under

---

[283] An evocative account of the attempts of poor Egyptians to improve their financial circumstances by obtaining work with the British Army is found in *Midaq Alley*, one of the novels of the Egyptian writer, Naguib Mahfouz, winner of the Nobel prize for literature in 1988.

Zaghloul Pasha were as poor as they were between the Wafd and the British, and did not improve when, in 1935, Fuad was succeeded by his son, Farouk (1935–52), and Saad Zaghloul Pasha by Nahas Pasha.

The international situation increased domestic political tension. Mussolini controlled Libya, and, fearing his intentions towards neighbouring Egypt, the Egyptian government sought to strengthen links with Britain, signing an Anglo-Egyptian treaty in 1936. One of its clauses committed Egypt to give aid to Britain in case of war. When war broke out in 1939, Egypt fulfilled its obligations. Britain was permitted to mount the North African Campaign from Egypt and, in 1942, halted the Axis forces at el-Alamein, some 90 kilometres west of Alexandria. After the war, Egypt began to seek support for its attempts to win full independence from Britain. In March 1945, it was a chief signatory to a pact drawn up by the Arab countries of the Middle East, meeting in Cairo to form a league of Arab states dedicated to resisting western imperialism, and presenting a united front when putting forward their claims.

Farouk, the last King of Egypt, was noted for the corruption and the extravagance of his regime, which did nothing to reduce the country's high unemployment and rampant inflation. Opposition to him and to the British was led by an extreme right-wing movement, the Muslim Brotherhood, which advocated Islamic principles as the solution to Egypt's problems. The creation of the State of Israel in 1948 brought further deterioration. The Arab League, of which Egypt was a part, attacked the newly formed state but to no avail; and Israel was granted recognition by the major powers. With Nahas Pasha dismissed as leader of the National Assembly, a 'committee of free officers' led by General Muhammad Neguib staged a *coup d'état* on 23 July 1952, forcing Farouk to abdicate; and, on 18 June 1953, Egypt was declared a Republic.

In due course, General Neguib was replaced as head of the revolutionary council by another general, Gamal Abdel Nasser, whose immediate concern was to free Egypt from what he considered to be the economic and military imperialism of the West. In 1954, Nasser began negotiation with the British, which led to a partial withdrawal of troops from the Canal Zone; and, in 1955, he took part in the Bandung Conference of Afro-Asian nations, which proclaimed their opposition to colonialism and formulated a policy of neutrality between East and West. Egypt became a leader of what were called the third-world nations; and Nasser became chief spokesman for the policy of non-alignment. In June 1956, after a referendum, he was elected President of Egypt, a position he retained until his death in 1970.

The industrialization of Egypt was a key element in Nasser's economic policy. For this, electricity was needed; and the building of a great hydro-electric dam was proposed. Nasser tried to raise finance for his projected dam in the United States and from the World Bank. The United States, however, was less than pleased with Nasser's policy of non-alignment, and his requests for monetary aid were refused. Nasser, therefore, decided to nationalize the Suez Canal Company (*see* page 303), so that its revenues could be used to pay for the dam; this action precipitated the Suez Crisis of 1956. Egypt was attacked by the combined forces of Britain, France and Israel, but the rest of the international community, led by the United States, compelled them to withdraw. This episode earned Nasser great kudos in the Arab world, but the Canal, blocked during the war, remained closed until April 1957, and the much-needed revenues were lost. Nasser turned to the Soviet Union, which agreed to provide finance and technical assistance for the building of the Aswan High Dam (*see* page 307); for the next few years, Egypt was a client of the Soviet Union.

In 1967, Nasser made an attack on Israel that proved so disastrous that he offered his resignation. The Cairo crowds, on occasion just as vociferous as the Alexandrian crowds of old, refused to accept it. Gamal Abdel Nasser died in September 1970 at the age of only 52: in the years of his presidency, Egypt had, for the first time since 343 BC, been ruled not by a Macedonian Greek, nor a Roman, nor an Arab, nor a Turk, but by an Egyptian. Nasser was a man of great charisma, and through him, Egypt regained its sense of national pride. At his funeral, the ordinary people of Egypt demonstrated their grief in an unprecedented manner.

His successor was Anwar Sadat (1970–81), another true Egyptian, a former journalist, once at military college with Nasser, and a member of the revolutionary council that deposed King Farouk. Breaking off relations with the Soviet Union, Sadat turned to the West for aid. Egypt faced intractable problems of underdevelopment and a population that had reached over 40 millions by 1970. A carefully planned attack across the Suez Canal and into

Sinai on 6 October 1972 opened another war between Egypt and Israel, and gave a great boost to Egyptian morale. The time chosen for the onslaught was the day of Yom Kippur, one of the holiest days in the Jewish calendar, and it caught the Israelis by surprise. His success enabled Sadat to open negotiations with Israel from a position of strength.

But a programme of social and economic reform was desperately needed, and Sadat realized that, if such a programme were to succeed, Egypt could not afford to waste its slim resources in forever maintaining a state of war with Israel. In 1978, he signed the Camp David Agreement that led to a peace treaty between Egypt and Israel in March the next year. Sadat was the first Egyptian to receive the Nobel prize for peace, which he shared in 1978 with Menahem Begin, then Prime Minister of Israel.

The peace treaty lost Egypt the support of the Arab League, which moved its headquarters from Cairo; and only Jordan and Saudi Arabia did not break off diplomatic relations. Sadat had grown more popular abroad than at home, many Egyptians believing the price paid for his policy of peace with Israel too high. At an anniversary parade held in Cairo in 1981 to mark the 6 October victory, a group of young army officers and religious dissidents assassinated him.

His successor as President was his vice-president, Hosni Mubarak, who had been in command of the air force from 1972 to 1975, and was responsible for its victories in the 6 October War. He continued many of Sadat's foreign policies, with some success. In 1989, Egypt was restored as a member of the Arab League while still maintaining friendly relations with the West, as evidenced during the Gulf War of 1990–1. Egypt played a full part in the struggle to free Kuwait from occupation by Saddam Hussain's Iraqi army, allowing airfields in Egypt to be used as bases for United Nations operations, and sending Egyptian troops to join the international forces.

It seems appropriate that a country which can claim to be the bridge between Africa and the rest of the world and between the Arab world and the West, provided the United Nations in 1991 with its fifth Secretary-General, Boutros Boutros-Ghali, a member of a distinguished Coptic family, whose grandfather, Boutros Pasha, had signed the Anglo-Egyptian Treaty, and whose uncle, Wassif Pasha, had in 1937 taken Egypt into the League of Nations.

Egyptology

As a result of Muhammad Ali's modernization of Egypt, the country opened up to foreigners, most significantly to those whose curiosity had been aroused by the publications of Napoleon's scholars. Muhammad Ali knew little about ancient Egypt, and cared less, but he seems to have been of the opinion that, if it amused foreigners to come to Egypt to study its ancient monuments, he was willing to allow it for the sake of good relations with European governments. Unfortunately, his open policy was disastrous for the preservation of Egypt's antiquities, which were torn up and shipped wholesale to museums and private collectors all over the world. In 1865, the French philosopher, Ernest Renan, noted despairingly:

> For more than half a century Egyptian antiquities have been pillaged. Purveyors to museums have gone through the country like vandals. To secure a fragment of head precious antiquities have been smashed to smithereens.

Renan was unable to resist a special dig at English and American travellers, who he claimed were the worst enemies of Egyptian antiquities, tartly prophesying that:

> The names of these idiots will go down to posterity since they were careful to inscribe themselves on famous monuments, across the most delicate drawings![284]

In the half-century or so that Renan spoke of, there had also been visitors to Egypt who had journeyed there in the spirit of curiosity rather than for the pillaging of antiquities. Chief among them was John Lewis Burckhardt, the Anglo-Swiss explorer who, disguised as a Muslim sheikh, visited Petra in Jordan in 1812, the first European to do so. A year later, he journeyed to Nubia and became the first modern European to set eyes on Ramesses II's great temple at Abu Simbel, despite it being almost engulfed in sand. Benjamin Disraeli landed in 'the ancient land of Priestcraft and of Pyramids' and, in 1831, spent four months visiting the sights, and, incidentally, collecting material for his novel,

---

[284] J. E. Renan, *Correspondance de Renan* (Paris, 1926–8).

Contarini Fleming. Seven years later, the Scottish artist, David Roberts, arrived to spend some time in Egypt and Nubia, eventually publishing the lithographs that brought further fame to Egypt's antiquities.

Perhaps the most infamous of the early visitors was Giovanni Belzoni, an engineer who unwisely became involved in politics and fled his native Italy to seek refuge in England, where, for a time, he became a music-hall strongman act known as the 'Italian Giant'. Belzoni then decided to make his fortune by looting antiquities from Egypt. Among other things, he discovered the tomb of Sety I in the Valley of the Kings in 1818, and removed the beautiful alabaster mummiform sarcophagus to London, where it reposes today in Sir John Soanes's house in Lincoln's Inn Fields. He also cleared away the sand from Ramesses' temple at Abu Simbel. For Belzoni and all other early travellers and scholars alike, the greatest puzzle of ancient Egypt was its language as expressed in hieroglyphs, that strange, beautiful, pictorial script. To them, it was completely unreadable; and it was not until 1822 that the work of several eminent European scholars finally enabled the French philologist, Jean-François Champollion, to decipher it.[285] This he did thanks largely to the Rosetta Stone (*see* page 198), which had been rediscovered in 1799 by French sappers working at Fort Rashid, near Alexandria.

Said Pasha saw the advantages of preserving the antiquities of ancient Egypt, a task which he entrusted to a young Frenchman, Auguste Mariette, an archaeological assistant in the Louvre sent to Egypt in 1850 to collect Coptic manuscripts. In 1858, Mariette was appointed the first director of the Office of Antiquities and chief supervisor of excavations. In that same year, he founded a museum of Egyptian antiquities at Boulaq, near Cairo, which in 1900 was transferred to Cairo, becoming the great Egyptian Museum. Once director, Mariette set about putting a stop to the wholesale plunder and unrestrained sale of Egyptian antiquities; and thanks to him, Egypt began to take care of its past glories. He made possible the great scientific excavations of the last century or so.

It was not only Europeans who were interested in the ancient history of Egypt. In 1838, Rifaʿa at-Tahtawi published the first book in Arabic on the antiquity of Egypt, and for the first time,

[285]   Watterson, 1993, p. 11ff.

Egyptians could see that their country had a past to be proud of. His views were shared by his contemporary, Ali Mubarak, the founder of the modern school system in Egypt; and great nationalist leaders of the early twentieth century, such as Mustafa Kemal and Abd al-Aziz Fahmi, inspired by Ali Mubarak's enthusiasm, made pride in Egypt's pharaonic past a cornerstone of their nationalism. Other Egyptians took a more mercenary view. Tomb robbery was an ancient art; and in the 1870s at Luxor, it reached new heights, with objects appearing on the antiquities market that had obviously come from a royal tomb still unknown to Egyptologists. In 1881, Gaston Maspero, the new Director of Antiquities, managed to persuade members of the Abd er-Rassul[286] family to disclose the location of the cache of royal mummies that they had found at Deir el-Bahri.[287] When the mummies were taken to Cairo on board a Nile steamer, *fellahin* lined the banks wailing in a show of solidarity with their pharaonic past: the authorities were more prosaic – they taxed the mummies, and at the rate set for dried fish.

Government and Administration

The essential preliminaries to Muhammad Ali's modernization of Egypt were the reorganization of the administration and the rebuilding of the army. Having been impressed by what he had seen of French and British armed forces, he reformed army and navy along European lines: in its new structure, the navy was to become one of the most powerful fleets in the Mediterranean. No longer able to recruit to the army from the old sources in Ottoman territory, he experimented with slaves from the Sudan, of whom 20,000 were brought to Egypt between 1820 and 1824, only 3000 of them surviving. Muhammad Ali then did the unthinkable – he conscripted local, Muslim, peasants into his modern Egyptian army to serve under officers who were Turkish or came from the Caucasus (Turko-Circassians). Though these Egyptian conscripts were reluctant to serve, and spoke Arabic while their officers spoke Turkish, the army worked well.

[286]   The Abd er-Rassul family still lives at Gurna, Luxor.
[287]   The story of the discovery was the theme of a film made in 1969 by the Egyptian director Shady Abd es-Salaam, *The Night of Counting the Years* (*Il Mummiya*), the first Egyptian film to win a prize at the Cannes Film Festival.

By 1824, it comprised six regiments, all highly trained by European (mostly French) instructors. By 1840, there were 115,000 men in 38 regiments, in addition to a European artillery corps, an engineering corps, and 10,000 cavalry, the largest forces in the Near East. The army and navy together accounted for about 4 per cent of the population, much larger numbers than were under arms in European countries, and certainly the cost of maintaining them was enormous. After Muhammad Ali's defeat by the European powers in 1840–1, he was forced to reduce the size of his army to 18,000 men. In the reign of Ismail Pasha, it was increased once more to 80,000.

In reforming the administrative system, Muhammad Ali set up six new departments: of commerce, industry, education, foreign affairs, navy and war. His successors established four more: of the interior (1857), of public works (1864), of justice (1872) and of agriculture (1875). Egyptians were sent abroad, usually to France, to learn governmental skills, but the language of the administration remained Turkish rather than French or, as might have been expected, Egyptian Arabic. Each department had its own minister, advised by a council. Muhammad Ali also had advisers, but he himself made all the important decisions, paying particular attention to bringing the finances under strict control.

Muhammad Ali laid foundations for a provincial administration that lasted for generations. From 1824, Egypt was divided into provinces and districts, rather as it had been in the past, but there were also subdivisions consisting of towns and villages. All were under the control of a central office, but the responsibilities of the provincial officials were considerable, ranging from taxation, public works, security, and conscription to the army, to the organization of labour, the distribution of seed, and the management of industry. Only in the lowest divisions of this administration did Arabic-speakers serve, and then in small numbers; and between 1849 and 1879, there were only eight Egyptian ministers.[288] Otherwise, the administration, civil and military, was dominated by Turko-Circassians, Armenians and Europeans, a situation that obtained until the British Occupation; and its ethos, a legacy of Ottoman rule, was one in which traditional Ottoman concepts of patronage prevailed. Because the State was not concerned with the welfare of individual citizens, each had to protect

---

[288] Yapp, 1987, p. 148.

his own interests and get on in the world through the patronage of other, more powerful, men.

In March, 1883, Sir Evelyn Baring was appointed Consul General and British Agent, with a remit to implement reforms that the British Government considered essential. A legislative council was set up, with 30 members, some appointed, some elected. In each province, consultative councils were inaugurated, in the larger provinces with eight members, in the smaller with three. The 30 members of the legislative council were augmented by departmental ministers and by 46 elected members to form a National Legislative Assembly. Real government, however, was in the hands of British civilian agents who directed most of their efforts to improving Egypt's economy. Baring improved the efficacy of local government in Cairo with a municipal council composed of 28 members, half appointed, half elected, headed by the city governor. The National Assembly was re-constituted in July 1913, to consist of 66 elected members, plus 17 appointed to represent minorities.

Egypt today is a democratic, socialist, Arab republic, in which the President is also Prime Minister. In addition, he holds the offices of Supreme Commander of the Armed Forces, Commander-in-Chief of the Police and of the Judiciary, and Head of the National Democratic Party; and is commissioner on all military and economic matters, and on those touching national security. To these, Sadat added his own favourite title, 'Elder of the Egyptian Family'. The President, who is nominated by the People's Assembly (*Majlis Ash-Sha'ab*), is elected for a six-year term by popular referendum, and is eligible for re-election. He decides on the general policies of the State; and is advised by a 210-member assembly, the Shura Council.

Legislative power lies with the People's Assembly, a single chamber elected by universal suffrage, which, under the Constitution of 1971, has 454 members, nearly half of whom must be chosen from among working people and peasants. Ten are nominated by the President and 444 are elected for a five-year term from 222 constituencies. There are four main political parties, but the National Democratic Party traditionally has the majority. The country is divided into 26 administrative districts, each with a governor and a council, and towns and villages have councils, each headed by a mayor. Some council members are elected, others co-opted. The official religion of Egypt is Islam and the law is based on the Koran; but it is administered with the tolerance that has been a characteristic of Egyptians since pharaonic times.

Economy

To pay for his huge army, for education and for the bureaucracy, Muhammad Ali needed to maximize Egypt's resources. As ever, the main source of wealth was agriculture. The State owned the land, but most of it was held under the *iltizam* or tax farm system, which meant that the revenues from it accrued not to the State but to Mamelukes. Villages were convenient instruments of tax collection. Many tenants, however, avoided taxation by claiming that large tracts of land were *waqfs* (charitable donations). Muhammad Ali, leaving the genuine *waqfs* in place, abolished bogus donations, and sequestered all agricultural land, giving life pensions to the former beneficiaries of the tax farm system. With the help of foreign experts, he began to reform agriculture.

The development of perennial irrigation in Muhammad Ali's reign was introduced to accompany a new system of land tenure and registration. Large amounts of land were distributed among villages, inducements were offered in the form of tax-free tenancies to encourage peasants to reclaim waste land, and many new canals were built and old canals and dykes repaired. By the end of his reign, cultivated areas had been increased by about a third. The Delta received special attention, with the deployment of large gangs of labourers to construct irrigation works, permitting a more intensive cultivation of the area. There followed a growth in the production of summer crops such as rice, sugar cane – an Upper Egyptian crop introduced by the Arabs in the eighth century – and indigo; and above all, cotton.

Cotton seems to have reached Egypt from India during the Saite Period, and was quite common by Roman times when, according to Pliny the Elder, it was grown in Upper Egypt and Nubia. It is now a Lower Egyptian crop because growing conditions in Upper Egypt are not suitable. Cotton became important during the Ottoman Period but, because it was of the short-fibre type, it was not acceptable for the European markets. In 1822, Muhammad Ali introduced long-staple cotton from America, thus laying the foundation of what was to become so important a commodity in the economy that, less than 30 years later, it accounted for over 30 per cent of the export trade. The American Civil War of 1861–5 prevented the production of American cotton and led to a boom in the production of Egyptian cotton which, between 1861 and 1864, increased to 90 per cent of Egypt's total exports. Only during war years, when food crops were given preference, did cotton growing decline thereafter.

Alarmed at the possibility of Muhammad Ali overthrowing the Ottoman sultanate, the European Powers imposed commercial agreements which effectively destroyed the state monopolies of cotton, gum-arabic and indigo he had established. From 1841, despite all the encouragement he gave to trade, cotton and cheap European goods flooded the Egyptian market, and for a time affected the rate of its recovery. His reforms brought great wealth, but most of it remained in the hands of his own family which, by the 1870s, owned one-fifth of all the land under cultivation in Egypt. The Egyptian peasants remained for the most part desperately poor and bore the main tax burden. Foreign communities in Egypt paid little tax, the nobility paid at a 33 per cent rate, the ruling family none at all. The peasants, who often forfeited what little land they had to meet tax demands, were reduced to desperate poverty and, in search of a livelihood, were forced to labour for others.

Increase in productivity led to a growth in exports, and Alexandria flourished once again as a great commercial port, its population expanding tenfold between 1805 and 1847, from 15,000 to 150,000. A shipping service between Marseilles and Alexandria was started by the French in 1835, and, two years later, the British Peninsular and Oriental Line began a steamer service to take travellers on from Suez to Bombay. From 1848, the journey from Alexandria to the Nile was facilitated by the Mansouriah Canal, which had been constructed, using forced labour, to link the city with the river. Within a few years, the building of an even greater canal to link the Mediterranean with the Red Sea would be accomplished.

The Suez Canal

The ancient canal that had once linked the Red Sea with the Bubastite arm of the Nile continued in use until AD 98, when the Emperor Trajan had its western course altered so that it might meet the Nile in the area of Babylon-in-Egypt. The River of Trajan, as the canal was called, had fallen into disrepair by the time of the Arab Conquest, and ʿAmr ibn al-ʿAs reopened it as 'The Canal of the Prince of the Faithful' to facilitate the transportation of Egyptian grain to Arabia. This canal was deliberately destroyed 100 years later when Medina revolted against the Khalif and he decreed that no more Egyptian corn should reach the city.

The Venetians, the Ottomans, and the French of Louis XIV's time, all contemplated schemes for reviving the canal, but all came to nothing. Napoleon was eager to build a canal through the Isthmus of Suez as a means of expediting passage to India; but his chief engineer, calculating that the level of the Red Sea was 10 metres higher than that of the Mediterranean, declared the project unfeasible. At last, in 1854, Ferdinand de Lesseps, the French Consul in Cairo, having proved that the difference in levels between the two seas was not as great as had been estimated, applied to Said Pasha (1854–63) for a *firman* (an exclusive permit) for the construction of a ship canal to run from Suez on the Red Sea to Tineh on the Mediterranean. It was two years before he managed to persuade Said Pasha to grant the *firman*, and two more to raise the capital for the project, but, on 25 April 1859, the construction of the Suez Canal began.

Just over half the finance for the project came from private sources, largely French, and the balance from Said Pasha. Because of doubts expressed by Robert Stephenson about the engineering feasibility of the project, and because of Lord Palmerston's dismissal of the whole thing as a pretext for French interference in the East, few if any of the shares in the Suez Canal Company were purchased by British investors. It was estimated that the work would take five years to complete at a cost of six million pounds sterling. In the event, it took 10 years and cost over 19 million pounds sterling. An Egyptian work-force of 25,000 men dug the canal out of the sand, many dying from cholera, dysentry and the accidents which seem to have been commonplace. Before the building of the canal, the Isthmus of Suez was a waterless area – even Lake Timsah and the Bitter Lakes were dry – and it was necessary to provide a supply of fresh water for the canal workmen. To begin with, 1600 camels per day carried water to the work-force, but, in 1863, a waterway was constructed, using ancient canals, from Boulaq in Cairo across the Isthmus to Ismailia and thence to Suez. This, the Freshwater or Ismailia

Canal, provided a plentiful supply of water not only to the canal workers but also to the local population: and does so to this day.

Said Pasha did not live to see the completion of the Canal. It was his successor, Ismail (1863–79), who presided over the official opening which took place on 17 November 1869. The principal attraction at the splendid ceremony, apart from the Canal itself, was the Empress Eugénie of France, who attended with the Emperor of Austria, Franz-Josef. Ismail had ordered palaces and rest houses to be built for the comfort of his eminent guests, and a wide, paved boulevard to be laid between Cairo and Giza, so that they could be taken to view the Pyramids riding comfortably in their landaus and other European-style horse-drawn carriages. An opera house had been constructed in Cairo to mark the occasion, and, in the summer of 1869, its director invited Giuseppe Verdi to compose a hymn for its inauguration. Verdi declined, and the audience was instead entertained by a performance of his *Rigoletto*. Nearly two years later, on 24 December 1871, another of Verdi's operas, *Aida*, had its first performance in the new Opera House, but Verdi refused to attend the première of this story of ancient Egypt, claiming that he was afraid lest the Egyptians mummify him.

Khedive Ismail's ambitious schemes for the modernization of Egypt were financed with loans from international bankers, at usurious rates of interest. Revenues from the Suez Canal, which had reached over a million pounds sterling by 1874, were not nearly enough to save Egypt from bankruptcy. Ismail was unable to raise more loans and so, in 1875, he was forced to put his shares in the Suez Canal Company up for sale, and, in addition, was compelled by his creditors to accept British and French supervision of Egypt's finances. The Khedive owned 44 per cent of the shares in the Company, French investors the rest. Disraeli, on learning of Ismail's imminent bankruptcy, outfoxed the French in acquiring his shares with the help of a four million pounds sterling loan from Baron Rothschild, and, on 24 November 1875, he was able to write to Queen Victoria: 'It is just settled; you have it, Madam. The French Government has been out-generaled . . . The entire interest of the Khedive is now yours, Madam!'[289]

In the 1870s, Egyptian cotton exports, which had fallen initially on the restoration of American cotton supplies, began to recover

[289] Monypenny and Buckle, 1910–20, v, 448–9.

and, by 1880, had risen to 50 per cent above their 1865 peak of 14 million pounds sterling annually. Sugar cane exports had also risen. The foreign exchange earned from exports eased the acquisition of foreign loans for development in Egypt, a large part of the finance going into improvements in communications. The Suez Canal had been an outstanding achievement; but almost as important was the development of a railway system. The first railway in Africa, a line from Cairo to Alexandria, had been opened in 1856. It was followed by a link between Cairo and Suez; and, in the reign of Ismail, a network of railways was constructed in the Delta and Upper Egypt which facilitated the movement of the cotton and sugar cane crops. Roads and bridges were built, and over 13,000 kilometres of canals cut. Ismail, however, overreached himself and, by 1880, his Government was bankrupt.

The Mahdist revolt of 1883–98 (*see* page 291) did nothing to improve Egypt's financial situation, weakened by British and French insistence that the repayment of creditors should be the highest priority. Under the terms of the London Convention, drawn up in 1885, the interest on Egypt's national debt was rescheduled, and this permitted the Government to raise a fresh loan with international bankers. Baring, as Consul General, was then able to concentrate on making reforms. Under his guidance, the system of forced labour was abolished, modernization of the larger towns undertaken, and advances made in public health, education and the law. In Cairo, roads were improved and a system of public sewers begun. Kitchener's great interest, while he was responsible for Egyptian affairs, was the welfare of the peasants. Gorst had set up the first peasant co-operatives in 1907, and Kitchener continued the policy. The year 1912 saw the introduction of the Five Feddans Law, with the aim of giving each landless peasant five or six *feddans*[290] of land, a water-buffalo and a water-wheel; and exempting peasants from the possibility of having their land seized in repayment of debts.

The next important period of economic and social reform came in the 1950s, when President Nasser ordered the reallocation of land. Before 1952, half of the cultivable land was owned by 2 per cent of the population, and there were nearly two million landless peasants. Nasser ordered big estates to be subdivided, and a law was passed stating that no-one should hold more than 100 *feddans*

[290]   One *feddan* equals approximately 1 acre (0.4 hectare).

of land. The ultimate aim was for all peasants to own their own land, a truly difficult task. The population of Egypt was about 13 million people when the Five Feddans Law was passed (*see* above); by 1956, it had almost doubled. Changes in agricultural practice and an enlargement in the amount of agricultural land available were key to the fulfilment of Nasser's plans.

To increase perennial irrigation so that farmers in particular might enjoy a constant supply of water, unaffected by the droughts to which the region was susceptible, Nasser directed that a dam at Aswan be built (*see* page 307). It was to have a huge reservoir; and, as an added bonus, it was decided that it should be a hydro-electric dam designed to generate cheap electricity in the quantities that were needed for the industrialization of Egypt. Despite initial difficulties with finance (*see* page 294), the construction of the Aswan High Dam, one of the most impressive in the world, was inaugurated in 1960. Nasser did not live to see its completion, but the great reservoir behind the dam was named Lake Nasser in his honour. The official name of the dam is al-Sadd al-Aali, but appropriately enough, because Nasser was often said to be a latter-day pharaoh, it is often called 'Nasser's Pyramid'.

The Aswan dams

The American Civil War of 1861–5, which freed the slaves who had worked the cotton plantations, rendered American cotton in short supply, making the Egyptian cotton crop even more valuable. The American long-staple cotton, introduced into Egypt by Muhammad Ali, was grown in the Delta, but the vagaries of the Nile Inundation caused difficulties. The Nile was in full flood between July and October, but the cotton plants were at a critical stage in growth, demanding the maximum amount of water, between March and July when the Nile was at its lowest ebb. Khedive Abbas Hilmi (1892–1914) was advised that, during the Inundation, over 40 per cent of Nile water debouched into the Mediterranean and was wasted. If, however, some method could be devised of retaining this surplus water, and storing it until the spring, when it could be released to irrigate the cotton plants, then the cotton crop would be greatly increased.

A proposal for the 2000 million tonnes of water involved to be stored in natural depressions in the desert was considered, but eventually rejected in favour of a dam across the Nile itself. Aswan, 1000 kilometres south of Cairo, was chosen as the site because of its granite: granite was the ideal rock on which to build, and from which to build, the structure. William Willcocks, a British engineer, was commissioned to design a dam, and work began on it in 1898. There were to be three elements: the dam itself; navigation locks at its western end; and a barrage or subsidiary dam for further water-control at Assiut, half-way between Aswan and Cairo. Willcocks designed a dam some 1625 metres long, 30 metres thick at the base, and 28 metres high. It was built by John Aird and Company, who undertook to complete the job in five years at a cost of two million Egyptian pounds.

The masonry of the Aswan Dam was completed in June 1902, a year in advance of the time stipulated in the contract, although, during the dam's construction, the Nile was ceaselessly flowing by at a rate of between 500 and 12,000 tonnes a second, carrying with it 100 to 150 million tonnes of silt, 10 per cent of which would be distributed over the flood plain, in layers of about 1 millimetre thick, the rest being washed out into the Mediterranean. Perhaps the most ingenious feature of the construction was the method devised to allow the Nile silt to pass through the dam: it was provided with 180 sluice gates at its base. The problem of raising the sluice gates, when the pressure of water against them was up to 200 tonnes per gate, was solved by inserting rollers between moveable gates and fixed frames – Stoney Rollers, a simple but effective invention of the English engineer, R. G. H. Stoney – a method already used for the Manchester Ship Canal and elsewhere in England. The Aswan Dam was inaugurated on 10 December 1902.

The construction of the Aswan High Dam, which was designed by Soviet engineers, was begun on 9 January 1960, and was to cost about one billion US dollars to build.[291] It opened on 15 January 1971. It is 111 metres high, and 980 metres wide at the base, narrowing to 40 metres at the top, on which there is a two-lane highway. The High Dam which, unlike the old dam, is rock filled, measures 3600 metres in length, 530 metres of which actually span the Nile. Its six giant turbines are capable of generating over two million kilowatts of electricity. To its south lie the damned waters of the Nile, forming the Lake Nasser reservoir, which

[291] $10 billion at 1994 prices.

measures 500 kilometres long and averages 10 kilometres wide (up to 60 kilometres in some places). These impressive statistics make the Aswan High Dam one of the engineering wonders of the modern world: but it has not been an unalloyed success.

Within five years, farm output increased by between 10 and 20 per cent; and the new dam provided half of Egypt's electricity. Several years of drought in East Africa followed in the 1980s, leading to famine; but Lake Nasser enabled the Egyptians to store what water there was and safeguard agriculture from collapse. The Dam now provides only about 10 per cent of Egypt's electricity requirements, however, though still worth about 500 million US dollars a year; and environmental damage has been considerable. The snails that carry the debilitating disease bilharzia (schistosomiasis) proliferate in the waters of canals and irrigation ditches that were once cleaned out by the Inundation but are now stagnant. The river is clogged in places by water hyacinth and clouded with algae. Even the disappearance from the Mediterranean of the sardines that once bred in the sea off the Nile estuary has been blamed on the effects of the Dam, because the Inundation no longer debouches the silt on which the sardines flourished.

The loss of the silt that the Inundation used to deposit on the flood plain in Egypt has been the most serious damage. It is estimated that the Nile brings down from the Ethiopian highlands about 130 million tonnes of silt in a good year. Much of it is now accumulating in Lake Nasser, although it is expected that it will take a century or more before it seriously reduces the capacity of the reservoir. Because the soil of Egypt is no longer replenished naturally, the fertility of the Nile Valley and the Delta has been reduced. Despite the loss of silt, the pressure to grow more crops increases with the growth of population, and farmers have had to turn to the heavy use of chemical fertilizers: ironically, fertilizer factories are among the biggest users of the electricity produced by the High Dam.

The loss of silt brought other problems. The ever-increasing demands for mud-brick for housing depleted Egypt's agricultural land, and in 1985, the Government was forced to pass a law forbidding brick-making with soil that was no longer being replenished annually. Shale was to be used instead: but even this damaged the environment – the demand for brick with which to build houses for a burgeoning population led to a proliferation of kilns along the Nile near Cairo, polluting the atmosphere with their smoke. Another law was passed, and today many of the brick factories lie abandoned. Salination of the soil is another problem for which the High Dam is blamed, although modern irrigation methods are culpable. Water used to be lifted on to fields manually (through the use of shadufs, for example) and was therefore used sparingly. Today, pumps constantly flood the fields, from which water evaporates, leaving salts behind. About two billion US dollars have been spent on a drainage network to remove excess water from some two million hectares, but about a tenth of the Delta has already been lost to salt.

The old Aswan Dam itself caused environmental damage: the controlled 'inundation' led to a progressive silting up of the marshes in which Egyptian papyrus had once proliferated, causing it to die out. Changes in their environment finally brought an end to crocodiles and hippopotamuses in the Egyptian part of the Nile. The old dam, of course, was built in a less environmentally conscious era: even when its reservoir flooded the Temple of Isis at Philae, partially submerging this famous 'Pearl of the Nile', the benefits of the dam were the paramount concern. The High Dam's reservoir also threatened to flood the great archaeological monuments which lay in Nubia, such as Abu Simbel. Although some were abandoned, the most important were rescued, largely under the auspices of UNESCO; and Abu Simbel, Philae and several lesser temples have been relocated.

The operations to rescue drowning temples received worldwide publicity, but the world does not seem to have been overly concerned with the human inhabitants of the area flooded by Lake Nasser. These are the 100,000 or so Nubians, some of whom were moved to the Sudan, though most were rehoused in new villages in the area between Aswan and Kom Ombo. Fittingly, this area, once jealously guarded by the Egyptians against incursions from the south, has become the New Nubia.

Before the High Dam was built, Nasser consulted the Sudanese Government on the proposal to flood part of its territory: the Nile Agreement of 1959 gave Egypt two-thirds of the Nile's average flow, estimated to be 84 cubic kilometres, the balance going to the Sudan. Nasser made no agreements with other Nile nations further upstream,[292] notably Ethiopia, where the headwaters of the

---

[292] Ethiopia, Uganda, Zaire, Tanzania, Kenya, Rwanda and Burundi. Today, an eighth nation must be added – Eritrea.

Blue Nile[293] are located, and Burundi, where the White Nile rises, warning them that he would go to war with any that took 'Egypt's water'. The 1959 estimate of the Nile's average flow has proved incorrect: during the 1980s, it was 76 cubic kilometres, and in 1984, it fell to 42 cubic kilometres. Dire predictions have been made that global warming will reduce the flow still further. So far, Egypt has been able to take advantage of Sudan's failure to use its full entitlement to the water; but the day may come when all eight upstream nations will want their share.

Meanwhile, Egypt tries to save water and to irrigate the desert. The original plan for the High Dam envisaged using some water to link up the oases in the Western Desert by canals, and extend the irrigation network eastwards towards the Nile Valley. In the 1960s, a great deal of money and effort was put into 'greening' a large area of desert west of the Delta; but Liberation Province, as that area became known, was not a great success. More schemes are contemplated.[294] If the Egyptians are to gain more water, they must solve the problem of evaporation from Lake Nasser, which occurs on an enormous scale: the hot Sahara sun draws an estimated 14 cubic kilometres of water from the surface of the lake each year. The problem of evaporation from the Sudd[295] was first recognized by Garstin[296] who proposed, as a solution, to build reservoirs in the cold upland areas far south of Egypt through which the Nile flows. This may have to be the radical policy adopted by the Egyptians, even though it would result in the loss of the hydro-electric power generated by the High Dam. In any case, co-operation with the upstream countries, possibly including the purchase of 'their' water, will certainly be necessary if 'water wars', which threaten to be a scourge of the twenty-first century in several areas of the world, are to be avoided.

---

[293] The Blue Nile, together with the tributaries Atbara and Sobat, make up 85 per cent of the main river's flow.

[294] Pearce, 1994, p. 31.

[295] *Report on the basin of the upper Nile* (Cairo Government Press, 1904).

[296] Sir William Garstin (1849–1925): engineer, undersecretary of state in Egyptian Ministry of Public Works 1892.

The modern economy

An important part of modern Egyptian economy is the oil that is found in the Eastern Desert and the Gulf of Suez. The petroleum industry accounts for almost 50 per cent of total foreign currency earnings, with Egypt exporting nearly a million barrels of oil a day. Suez Canal dues net over 1000 million US dollars a year; and tourists, attracted to Egypt by its pharaonic monuments and, in increasing numbers, by the Red Sea resorts, are capable of bringing in a similar amount, although the activities of Islamic fundamentalists since 1993 (see page 314) have caused a fall in tourist numbers. Nevertheless, the country is still an economy largely dependent on agriculture and animal husbandry, with over 50 per cent of the work-force engaged on the farms where the principal crops are wheat, maize, rice and sugar cane. In spite of the loss by 1992 of appreciable areas of agricultural land to urban and other forms of encroachment, what is left still supports over four million sheep and the same number of goats, over three million cattle, three million buffaloes, over one-and-a-half million asses, 170,000 camels and 26,000 pigs, over eight million ducks and 36 million chickens.[297]

The human population is expanding rapidly despite government encouragement of family planning programmes.[298] In 1990, it was over 52 million and growing at an annual rate of some 2 per cent. To put it more dramatically, in 1994 there were a million Egyptians born every 10 months. Land reclamation, therefore, has for some time been seen as vital: between 1965 and 1980, over 60 per cent of the agricultural investment budget was allocated to it, and over 0.44 million hectares were brought into production. In the 1980s, expenditure could be reduced to a quarter of the budget, in part because greater emphasis was placed on more intensive farming methods.

Over the last decade or so, modern machinery has increasingly been employed to work the land. Some *fellahin*, however, still use the traditional methods: ploughing with simple wooden ploughs

---

[297] 1993 estimates: statistics here and below culled from the *Europa World Year Book, 1995.*

[298] In 1969 the birthrate was 7.1 children a mother; in 1994 it was 3.9.

drawn by animals such as water-buffalo, cows, sometimes even camels, and raising water by means of a shaduf, despite the availability of modern pumps. The mechanizing of agriculture has not been without its problems: a machine suitable for picking the Egyptian long- and extra-long-staple cotton remains to be developed; and the small, Japanese-made combines imported for the transplanting and harvesting of rice have not proved successful.

In the early 1970s, Egypt adopted an 'open-door policy' or *Infitah*, by which was meant the removal of restrictions on national investors, the gradual withdrawal of the State from an active role in the economy, and the permitting of unrestricted importation of foreign goods and capital. Had the Government regulated private investment and itself invested more in agriculture and industry, the policy of *Infitah* would have had a greater chance of success. Instead, there was a balance of payments deficit; and the Egyptians blamed the *Infitah* for all their troubles. In the 1990s, at the behest of Western monetarists, subsidies on essential foods such as flour, rice and meat were reduced, causing hardship to an already poor populace.[299]

Religion

Most Egyptians are Sunni Muslims, but there is a sizeable minority of Christians and a small Jewish community. There are officially two million Coptic Christians and about a million Christians of other denominations. The figure for Coptic Christians is disputed, with the Copts themselves claiming to be over six million in number, though the Coptic authorities maintain a diplomatic vagueness over the exact figure. For some years past, the Copts have felt discriminated against because of their religion: they are underrepresented in parliament, government, the armed forces and the universities. They also resent the fact that mosques receive free water and electricity supplies from the Government; and that a licence, which is difficult to obtain, is needed before a Coptic church can be built.

---

[299]   In 1994 an army conscript earned E£4 per month; a government employee, typically, E£80 (rate of exchange: E£5 to £1 Sterling). The cost of an egg was 10 piastres (about 2p), a litre of cow's milk E£2.50; *eish baladi* (pitta bread) 5 piastres, beef E£6 a kilo.

The Koran recognizes Jews and Christians as 'the People of the Book', and accords them protection; and religious freedom is guaranteed by the Egyptian Constitution. There have been, however, clashes between Muslims and Copts. At present, Coptic personal and matrimonial law is administered by bodies such as the Patriarch's Court or the *maglis milli* (the Coptic lay council); but Copts are concerned at moves to bring them under the jurisdiction of the same State courts as Muslims. They resent the fact that Muslim laws on marriage and divorce encourage Copts to convert to Islam: if a Christian man wishes to marry a Muslim woman he must convert, but, although a Christian woman may marry a Muslim without converting, she is not eligible to inherit his estate, neither is she entitled to custody of the children if she loses her husband through divorce or death. Divorce is difficult to obtain for Copts, but is tolerated under Islamic law, so a Copt wishing to divorce his wife sometimes converts to Islam.

A few weeks before his assassination, in September 1981, President Sadat ordered that Shenouda III, the 117th Patriarch of the Coptic Church, be stripped of his temporal power and exiled to his monastery, Anba Bishoi, in the Wadi Natrun, for 'inciting strife'. As Patriarch, Shenouda, elected to his post in 1971 at the age of 49, was considered by Copts to be in direct line of descent from St Mark, and his exile caused great offence. After 40 months of house arrest, he was released by President Mubarak, as a New Year's gesture; and, a few day's later, in his Christmas Eve sermon (5 January in the Coptic calendar), Shenouda called for Copts and Muslims to embrace, vowing that he would stay out of secular politics. But both Patriarch and President know that the rise of Islamic fundamentalism (*see* below) may force him to renege on his promise.

Egypt Today

Like Sadat before him, Mubarak is faced with formidable cultural and economic problems, made all the more serious by the enormous changes that Egypt has undergone since the mid-1980s. Economic pressures have forced men, young men especially, to leave their home towns and villages in search of work. Many Egyptians have moved to Cairo, swelling its population. Before the

Gulf War of 1990–1, large numbers worked in Kuwait and the Gulf States, earned good livings, and were able to send money and luxury goods back to their families in Egypt. Greater social mobility has led to an inevitable breakdown in the traditional structures of society.

Since 1992, Muslim extremists have posed a growing threat. The Egyptians are a pious people, but, over the last decade, there has been a more ostentatious display of religiosity, especially among the young: the number of bearded men has increased, as has the number of women wearing 'religious dress', covering the head, at least, with a *hijab* (scarf).[300] In the past, Egyptians attracted by extreme groups of Islamists, such as the Muslim Brotherhood (*see* page 293), have tended to be either from the officer class or idealistic university students. Today, Islamists are also found among the growing numbers of unemployed labourers. Most simply become more observant Muslims, finding comfort in the slogan 'Islam is the solution'; others are attracted by the social welfare programmes of the Islamists, through which medical and monetary aid is given to the needy. The source of funds for such aid is a matter of dispute, with several foreign governments put forward as candidates. The ability of Islamists to provide aid that the State should give but does not was demonstrated after the earthquake of October 1992, when government tardiness allowed Islamists to provide emergency supplies of food and blankets.

A small number of Islamists are militant activists, belonging not to the Muslim Brotherhood which is banned but tolerated, but to the more extreme and violent secret society, *al-Gamaat al-Islamiya* (the Islamic Group). The aim of *al-Gamaat*, under the leadership of Mohamed Shawki al-Islambouly, a brother of President Sadat's assassin, is to bring down the Mubarak government and replace it with a fundamentalist Islamic state. Their chosen means of bringing this about is to deprive Egypt of much-needed income from foreign investment and tourism, exacerbating its economic problems to such an extent that the army stages a coup. By 1994, attacks on foreign tourists had cost Egypt much of its tourist trade, losing the economy an estimated 700 million pounds, although, by 1995, the tourist trade had begun to revive.

[300] Married women traditionally have covered their hair with a scarf, not for religious reasons, however, but as a sign that they are married.

Domestic Life

In recent years, social welfare services have greatly improved, with the introduction of sickness benefit, health insurance schemes, and pensions. There is a national health service; and the general health of most Egyptians has improved through better nutrition and hygiene. The average life-expectancy has risen to well over 50 years for men and for women.

The family is as closely knit in Egypt today as it was in pharaonic times. The husband is head of the household, and considers himself to be responsible for his siblings, especially widowed or unmarried sisters, and elderly relatives. Above all, he loves and respects his mother, sometimes even more than his wife. It is common among Egyptian men to believe that, although a wife's feelings towards her husband may change, a mother's love for her son is constant. Marriage between cousins is often preferred in traditional families, and the birth of children welcomed. The Government has encouraged family planning but, in country districts, where the infant mortality rate is high and farms are labour intensive, children can be valued as economic units.

Because of their innate conservatism, the Egyptians have managed to retain an identity over the centuries in the face of many invaders, and to maintain:

> to a remarkable extent very many of their ancient customs, beliefs and industries, adapting the older beliefs and rites to the Christian and Islamic faiths, and preserving many of their social customs practically unchanged from ancient times.[301]

This statement is as true today as it was when it was made nearly 70 years ago.

The desire of Egyptian women to bear children leads some of them to turn to superstition and folk medicine, practices frowned on by all religious authorities. Almost every village in Egypt possesses the tomb of a local spiritual leader or sheikh. Childless women often visit a sheikh's tomb and walk round it three, five or seven times, reciting passages from the Koran and praying to the sheikh to intercede for them. The so-called Osireon, a flooded temple at Abydos, is believed to have magic properties, and

[301] Blackman, 1927, p. 48.

bathing in its waters a help in conceiving children. In the Temple of Sety at Abydos, there is a relief of Osiris lying upon a bier: the god's penis shines with a patina created by the fingers of the many barren women who have touched it. Sometimes, women with difficulty in conceiving make a pilgrimage to one of the crypts in the Temple of Hathor at Dendera, to touch a relief depicting the goddess with her son upon her knee – a gesture that would be understood by Roman Catholic women the world over who find comfort in a statue of the Virgin with the Christ Child on her knee.

Unmarried young people in Egypt are not permitted to meet alone and unchaperoned. The morality code is strict, especially in rural districts where the pregnancy of an unmarried girl, a disgrace to her family, may bring her death at the hands of male relatives. One reason cited for performing female circumcision, which unfortunately is practised in many traditional families, is to stifle female sexuality and prevent unwanted pregnancies. Arranged marriages are usual: the mothers and aunts of the bride and groom often play a major part in introducing a couple one to the other. There is normally an engagement party, attended by large numbers of family and friends, and a second celebration which, in the case of the more affluent, can be lavish, marks the marriage. There is no marriage ceremony for Muslims: the groom and male members of his family simply record the contract. Coptic weddings comprise church and civil ceremonies. At both forms of wedding, it is the custom for the groom to buy the wedding-dress, often in the style of the latest European wedding-gown. It has also become the custom for the groom to provide the house or apartment in which he and his wife will live, and for the bride and her family to furnish it. The cost of accommodation, which is scarce, is so great that many Egyptians have to delay marrying.

For the first time in history, nearly half the population of Egypt is urbanized, and half that number live in and around Cairo, where the population in 1994 was an estimated 15 million and expected to rise to 20 million by the end of the century. Cairo has become a twentieth-century city with high-rise apartments, luxury hotels, ultra-modern office buildings, even a Metro and a fine new Opera House, all cheek-by-jowl with medieval mosques and nineteenth-century palaces and apartment buildings that are mostly dilapidated but are still fine examples of the French-style architecture then the vogue. In the last few years, a lack of housing

*Plate 9.2   Mameluke tombs, City of the Dead, Cairo.
(Photograph David Couling.)*

together with poverty have forced Egyptians to go to extraordinary lengths in the search for accommodation in the city, which is gaining 1000 new inhabitants daily. Nearly half-a-million of these highly adaptable people have taken up residence on roof-tops, where they breed rabbits and keep chickens, in effect creating a village life-style at roof-top level. An estimated three million have found accommodation in the great Mameluke cemetery which stretches for nearly 7 kilometres at the foot of the Citadel. The City of the Dead has become the abode of the living.

Many squatters in the City of the Dead live in shacks built between tombs, but others live in the tombs themselves. Their occupation of the site is illegal, but the authorities have bowed to the inevitable and laid on drains, electricity and piped-in water, so that living conditions in the cemetery are better than in many other places. Nearly 20,000 of the inhabitants are Copts, belonging to a sect called the Zaballeen. For over a century, they have been rubbish-collectors, and, in the 1980s, they were awarded the contract for collecting Cairo's refuse. Their approach is 'green': they cannot afford to employ refuse lorries with engines that would contribute fumes to Cairo's already heavily polluted atmosphere.

Instead, they use donkeys and deep-sided carts. Each family specializes in the recycling of different materials: of plastic, paper, glass, rags. Discarded clothes are shredded and made into fluff, which is sold for use as filling for car seats. So successful are the Zaballeen that, at the Rio Earth Summit of 1993, they won an environment award.

Throughout the millenniums, the wealth of Egypt, largely created by the ordinary people of the country, has been used for the benefit of the ruling class, from the Pharaohs to Persian and Greek kings, from Roman Emperors to Arab Khalifs, Turkish Sultans, Khedives and Kings. Sadly, wealth is still not evenly distributed, and many Egyptians are desperately poor. But it is they, with their patience, endurance and good humour, and above all, their resourcefulness, who are the hope for the future.

Bibliography

Abbreviations

ANET J. B. Pritchard (ed.), *Ancient Near Eastern Texts relating to the Old Testament*, 3rd ed., (Princeton, 1969).

ARE J. H. Breasted, *Ancient Records of Egypt*, (Chicago, 1906).

BIFAO *Bulletin de l'Institut Français d'Archéologie Orientale.*

CAH Cambridge Ancient History.

JEA *Journal of Egyptian Archaeology.*

JNES *Journal of Near Eastern Studies.*

KMT [A Modern Journal of Ancient Egypt], (San Francisco).

MDAIK *Mitteilungen des Deutschen Archäologischen Instituts Abteilung Kairo.*

OGIS W. Dittenberger, *Orientis Graeci Inscriptiones Selectae*, 2 vols, (Leipzig, 1903–5).

Onom. A. H. Gardiner, *Ancient Egyptian Onomastica*, 3 vols, (Oxford, 1947).

P. Lond. *Greek Papyri in the British Museum*, 5 vols, (London, 1893–1917).

PM B. Porter and R. L. B. Moss, *Topographical bibliography of ancient Egyptian hieroglyphic texts, reliefs and paintings*, 7 vols, (Oxford, 1927–51).

P. Osl. *Papyrus Osloensis*, 3 vols, (Oslo, 1925–36).

P. St Pal. *Studien zûr Paläographie und Papyruskunde*, 23 vols, (Leipzig, 1904–22).

The works of the Classical Greek and Roman writers are published by the Loeb Library of Classics; or by Penguin Classics.

References and Further Reading

Introduction

Gardiner, A. H., 'Regnal years and civil calendar in pharaonic Egypt', JEA, XXXI, pp. 11–28, (1945).

Kitchen, K. A., *The Third Intermediate Period in Egypt (1100–650 BC)*, 2nd ed., with Supplement, (Warminster, 1986).

Kitchen, K. A., 'The basics of Egyptian chronology in relation to the Bronze Age,' in Åström, P. (ed.) *High, Middle or Low?* Acts of an International Colloquium on Absolute Chronology Held at the University of Gothenburg 20–22 August 1987. Part 1, pp. 37–55, (1987).

Kitchen, K. A., 'Supplementary notes on the basics of Egyptian chronology', in Åström, P. (ed.) *High, Middle or Low?* Acts of an International Colloquium on Absolute Chronology Held at the University of Gothenburg 20–22 August 1987. Part 3. pp. 152–9, (1989).

Petrie, W. M. F., *Diospolis Parva. Egypt Exploration Fund Memoir*, 20, pp. 4–8, (1901).

Chapter 1

Brewer, D. J. and Friedman, R. F., *Fish and fishing in ancient Egypt*, (Warminster, 1989).

Butzer, K. W., *Environment and archaeology: an ecological approach to prehistory*, 2nd ed. (Chicago, 1971).

Butzer, K. W., *Early hydraulic civilization in Egypt: a study in cultural ecology*, (Chicago, 1978).

Butzer, K. W. and Hansen, C. L., *Desert and river in Nubia*, (Madison, N.Y., 1968).

Cockburn, A. and Cockburn, E., *Mummies, disease and ancient cultures*, (Cambridge, 1980).

Giddy, L., *Egyptian oases*, (Warminster, 1987).

Houlihan, P. F., *Birds of ancient Egypt*, (Warminster, 1986).

Lhote, H., *The search for the Tassili frescoes: the story of the prehistoric rock-paintings of the Sahara*, (London, 1958).

Lichtheim. M., *Ancient Egyptian Literature*, vol. I, (Berkeley, 1975).

Lichtheim, M., *Ancient Egyptian Literature*, vol. II, (Berkeley, 1976).

Majno, G., *The healing hand: man and wound in the ancient world*, (Harvard, 1975).

Pestman, P. W., *Marriage and matrimonial property in ancient Egypt*, (Leiden, 1961).

Reeves, C., *Egyptian medicine*, (Princes Risborough, 1992).

Strouhal, E., *Life in ancient Egypt*, (Cambridge, 1992).

Trigger, B. G. et al., *Ancient Egypt: a social history*, (Cambridge, 1983).

Tyldesley, J., *Daughters of Isis*, (Harmondsworth, 1994).

Vercoutter, J., *The peopling of ancient Egypt*, Proceedings of the symposium held in Cairo 1974, pp. 15–36, (UNESCO, 1978).

Watterson, B., *Women in ancient Egypt*, (Stroud, 1991).

Chapter 2

Ayrton, E. R. and Loat, W. L. S., *The predynastic cemetery at el-Mahasna*, (London, 1911).

Ball, J., *Contributions to the geography of Egypt*, (Cairo, 1939).

Benedite, G., *Le couteau de Gebel el-Arak*, in Monuments Piot, 22, pp. 1–34, (1916).

Brink, E. C. M. (ed.), *The archaeology of the Nile Delta Egypt: problems and priorities*, (Amsterdam, 1988).

Brink, E. C. M. (ed.), *The Nile Delta in Transition, 4th–3rd Millennium B.C.*, (Tel Aviv, 1992).

Brunton, G. and Caton-Thompson, G., *The Badarian Civilisation*, (London, 1928).

Butzer, K. W., 'Archaeology and geology in ancient Egypt', in Caldwell, J. R. (ed.), *New roads to yesterday*, (New York, 1966).

Case, H. and Crowfoot Payne, J., 'Tomb 100: the decorated tomb at Hierakonpolis', in JEA, 48, pp. 5–18, (1962).

Caton-Thompson, G. and Gardner, E. W., *The desert Fayum*, 2 vols, (London, 1934).

Debono, F. and Mortensen, B., 'El Omari', *Archäologische Veroffentlichungen 82*, (Mainz, 1990).

Emery, W., *Archaic Egypt*, (Penguin Books, 1961).

Flannery, K. V., 'The origins of the village as a settlement type in Mesoamerica and the Near East: a comparative study', in Ucko, P. J. Trimingham, R. and Dimbleby, G. W. (eds), *Man, settlement and urbanism*, (London, 1972).

Ginter, B., et al., 'El-Tarif and Qasr el-Sagha', in MDAIK, 41, pp. 15–42, (1982).

Hassan, F. A., 'Radiocarbon chronology of Neolithic and Predynastic sites in Upper Egypt and the Delta', in *African Archaeological Review*, 3, pp. 95–116, (1985).

Hoffman, M. A., *Egypt before the Pharaohs*, (London, 1980).

Kantor, H., Further evidence for early Mesopotamian relations with Egypt, in JNES, 11, pp. 239–50, (1959).

Kemp, B. J., 'The decorated tomb at Hierakonpolis', in JEA, 59, pp. 36–43, (1973).

Klees, F. and Kuper, R., *New light on the northeast African past: current prehistoric research*, (Cologne, 1992).

Kroeper, K. and Wildung, D., *Minshat Abu Omar*, (Munich, 1985).

Krzyzaniak, L., *The Nile Delta in transition: 4th–3rd millennium BC*, ed. van den Brink, (Tel Aviv, 1992).

Krzyzaniak, L. and Kobusiewicz, M. (eds.), *Late prehistory of the Nile basin and the Sahara*, (Poznan, 1989).

Lucas, A., *Ancient Egyptian Materials and Industries*, 4th ed. revised by J. R. Harris, (London, 1962).

Rice, M., *Egypt's Making*, (London, 1991).

Said, R., et al., 'A preliminary report on the Holocene geology and archaeology of the northern Fayum desert', in *Playa Lake Symposium 1972*, ed. C. C. Reeves, pp. 41–61, (Lubbock, Texas, 1972).

Spencer, A. J., *Early Egypt: the rise of civilisation in the Nile valley*, (London, 1993).

Stanley, D. J. and Warne, A. G., 'Sea level and initiation of predynastic culture in the Nile delta', in *Nature*, vol. 363, June, pp. 435–8, (1993).

Trigger, B. G., 'History and settlement in Lower Nubia', *Yale University Publications in Anthropology*, 69, (1965).

Trigger, B. G., et al., *Ancient Egypt: a social history*, (Cambridge, 1983).

Vandier, J., *Manuel d'archéologie égyptienne*, vol. 1, (Paris, 1952).

Wendorf, F. and Schild, R., *Prehistory of the Nile Valley*, (New York, 1976).

Watterson, B., *Introducing Egyptian hieroglyphs*, 2nd ed., (Edinburgh, 1993).

Chapter 3

David, A. R., *The pyramid builders of ancient Egypt*, (London, 1986).

Davies, W. V. (ed.), *Egypt and Africa*, (London, 1991).

Edwards, I. E. S., *The pyramids of Egypt*, (Harmondsworth, 1970).

Emery, W., *Archaic Egypt*, (Harmondsworth, 1961).

Faulkner, R. O., *The Ancient Egyptian Pyramid Texts*, (Oxford, 1969).

Gardiner, A. H., *Egyptian Grammar*, 3rd ed., (Oxford, 1966).

Habachi, L., *The Second Stela of Kamose, and his struggle against the Hyksos ruler and his capital*, (Gluckstadt, 1972).

Hart, G., *Pharaohs and pyramids*, (London, 1991).

James, T. G. H., *The Hekanakhte papers and other early Middle Kingdom documents*, (New York, 1962).

Jenkins, N., *The boat beneath the pyramids*, (London, 1980).

Johnson, G. B., 'The mysterious cache tomb of Fourth Dynasty queen, Hetepheres', in *KMT* 6 (1), pp. 34–50, (1995).

Killen, G. P., *Ancient Egyptian furniture*, vol. 1 c.4000–1300 BC, (Warminster, 1980).

Kitchen, K. A., 'Byblos, Egypt and Mari in the early second millennium B.C', in *Orientalia*, 36, pp. 39–54, (1967).

Lauer, J. P., *Saqqara, royal cemetery of Memphis*, (London, 1976).

Lichtheim, M., *Ancient Egyptian Literature*, vol. 1: *The Old and Middle Kingdoms*, (Berkeley, 1975).

Petrie, W. M. F., *Gizeh and Rifeh*, British School of Archaeology in Egypt, No. 13, (1907).

Reisner, G. A., 'The tomb of Hepzefa, nomarch of Siût', in JEA, 5, pp. 79–98, (1918).

Reisner, G. A. and Smith, W. S., *A history of the Giza Necropolis*, vol. II: *The tomb of Hetepheres*, (Cambridge, Mass., 1955).

Chapter 4

Aldred, C., *Akhenaten, pharaoh of Egypt: a new study*, (London, 1968).

Bietak, M., *Tell el-Dab'a II*, Untersuchungen der Zweigstelle Cairo des oesterreichischen Archäologischen Institues, Band 1, (Vienna, 1975).

Carter, H., *The tomb of Tutankhamen*, (London, 1972).

Carter, H. and Gardiner, A. H., 'The tomb of Ramesses IV and the Turin plan', in JEA, IV, 1918, (1967).

Černy, J., 'Prices and wages in Egypt in the Ramesside period', J. World Hist., I., (Paris, 1954).

Černy, J., 'Egyptian oracles', in Parker, R. A., *A Saite Oracle papyrus from Thebes*, Chap. 4, (Providence, N.J., 1962).

Černy, J., 'The workmen of the king's tomb', in 'Egypt from the death of Ramesses III to the end of the Twenty-first Dynasty', CAH, vol. II: 2, Chapter XXXV, pp. 606–75, (1975).

Connan, J. and Deschesne, O., *La Recherche*, 22, pp. 152–9, (1991).

Connan, J. and Dessort, D., Comptes rendues hebd. Seanc. Acad. Sci. Paris, 309, pp. 1665–72, (1989).

Connan, J. and Dessort, D., ibid., 312, pp. 1445–52, (1991).

Cook, J. M., *The Persian Empire*, (London, 1983).

Daressy, G., *Ostraca*, (Cairo, 1901).

David, A. R., *The pyramid builders of ancient Egypt*, (London, 1986).

David, A. R. and Tapp, E., (eds), *Evidence embalmed: modern medicine and the mummies of ancient Egypt*, (Manchester, 1984).

Davies, N. de G., *The tomb of Rekh-mi-Re at Thebes*, (New York, 1943).

Dodson, A. M., Letter in KMT, 4 (2), p. 4, (1993).

Dorman, P. F., *The monuments of Senenmut*, (London, 1988).

Drioton, E., 'Notes diverses, 15 – Deux scarabées commemoratif du roi athlete', in Ann. Serv., 45, pp. 85–92, (1947).

Edgerton, W. F., 'The strikes in Ramses III's twenty-ninth year', in JNES, 10, pp. 137ff., (1951).

Engelbach, R., 'A "Kirgipa" commemorative scarab of Amenophis III presented by His Majesty King Farouk I to the Cairo Museum', in *Ann. Serv.*, 40, pp. 659–61, (1941).

Erman, A., *The ancient Egyptians: a sourcebook of their writings*, (New York, 1966).

Fairman, H. W., *The Triumph of Horus: an ancient Egyptian sacred drama*, (London, 1974).

Faulkner, R. O., *The Book of the Dead*, (London, 1985).

Bibliography

Forbes, D. C., 'The tomb of the fanbearer Mahirpre in the Valley of the Kings', in *KMT*, 4 (3), pp. 70–83, (1993).

Gardiner, A. H., *The Kadesh Inscriptions of Ramesses II*, (Oxford, 1960).

Gelb., I. J., *Hurrians and Subarians*, (Chicago, 1944).

Habachi, L., *Features of the deification of Ramesses II*, (Gluckstadt, 1969).

Hansen, K., 'The chariot in Egypt's age of chivalry', in *KMT*, 5 (1), pp. 50–61, (1994).

Harris, J. E. and Weeks, K. R., *X-raying the pharaohs*, (New York, 1973).

Hayes, W. C., *Glazed tiles from a palace of Ramesses II at Kantir*, (The Metropolitan Museum of Art, New York, 1937).

Hayes, W. C., *A papyrus of the late Middle Kingdom*, (The Brooklyn Museum, 1955).

Helck, W., 'Bemerkungen zum Ritual des dramatischen Ramesseumspapyrus', in *Orientalia*, 23, pp. 383–411, (1954).

Janssen, J. J., *Commodity prices in the Ramesside Period*, (Leiden, 1975).

Kitchen, K. A., 'Punt and how to get there', in *Orientalia*, 40, pp. 184–207, (1971).

Kitchen, K. A., *Pharaoh Triumphant: the Life and Times of Ramesses II, King of Egypt*, (Warminster, 1982).

Kitchen, K. A., *Ramesside Inscriptions, Translated and Annotated – Translations, I.* Also *Notes and Comments, I*, p. 12ff. (Oxford, 1993).

Knudtzon, J. A., *Die el-Amarna-Tafeln*, (Vorderasiatische Bibliothek), 2 vols., (Leipzig, 1908, 1915).

Krieger, P., 'Le scarabée du mariage d'Amenophis III avec la reine Tij trouve dans le palais royal d'Ugarit', in Schaeffer, C. F.-A., *Ugaritica*, 3 (Mission de Ras Shamra, 8), pp. 221–6. (Paris, 1956).

Lansing, A., 'A commemorative scarab of Amen-hotpe III', in *Bull. M. M. A.*, 31, pp. 12–14, (1936).

Lichtheim, M., *Ancient Egyptian Literature*, vol. II: *The New Kingdom*, (Berkeley, 1976).

Martin, G. T., *The hidden tombs of Memphis*, (London, 1991).

Meyer, C., *Senenmut: eine prosopographische Untersuchung*, (Hamburg, 1982).

Mond, R. and Myers, O. H., *Temples of Armant: A Preliminary Survey*, (London, 1940).

Moran, W. L., *The Amarna Letters*, (Baltimore/London, 1992).

Murnane, W. J., *United with Eternity: a concise guide to the monuments of Medinet Habu*, (Chicago, 1980).

Newberry, P. E., *Egyptian antiquities: Scarabs*, University of Liverpool Institute of Archaeology, (London, 1906).

Peet, T. E., *The great tomb-robberies of the Twentieth Egyptian Dynasty*, 2 vols, (Oxford, 1930).

Petrie, W. M. F., *Six Temples at Thebes, 1896*, (London, 1897).

Posener, G., *Ostraca hieratiques*, vol. II, fasc. 3., pp. 43–4, (Cairo, 1972).

Quibell, J. E., *Tomb of Yuaa and Thuiu*, (Cairo, 1908).

Romer, J., *Valley of the Kings*, (London, 1981).

Sadek, A. I., *Popular Religion in Egypt during the New Kingdom*, (Hildesheim, 1988).
Schiaparelli, E., *Relazione sui lavori della Missione Archeologica Italiana in Egitto*, 2 vols, (Turin, 1927).
Shorter, A. W., 'Historical scarabs of Tuthmosis IV and Amenophis III', in *J.E.A.*, 17, pp. 23–5, (1931).
Spencer, A. J., *Death in ancient Egypt*, (Harmondsworth, 1988).
Teeter, E., 'Popular worship in ancient Egypt', in *KMT*, 4 (2), p. 28ff., (1933).
Uphill, E. P., *Egyptian towns and cities*, (Aylesbury, 1988).
Van den Boorn, G. P. F., *The Duties of the Vizier*, (London, 1988).
Vercoutter, J., 'The Gold of Kush. Two Gold-Washing Stations at Faras East', in *Kush*, 7, pp. 120–53, (1959).

Chapter 5

Kitchen, K. A., *The Third Intermediate Period in Egypt (1100–650 BC)*, 2nd ed. with Supplement. (Warminster, 1986).
Leahy, A., *Libya and Egypt c.1300–750 BC*, (London, 1990).
Lichtheim, M., *Ancient Egyptian Literature*, vol. I: *The Old and Middle Kingdoms*, (Berkeley, 1975).
Lichtheim, M., *Ancient Egyptian Literature*, vol. III: *The Late Period*, (Berkeley, 1980).
Montet, P., *Tanis: douze années de fouilles dans une capitale oublie du delta Égyptien*, (Paris, 1942).
Trigger, B. G., et al., *Ancient Egypt: a social history*, (Cambridge, 1983).
Watterson, B., *Women in ancient Egypt*, (Stroud, 1991).

Chapter 6

Arrian, *The Campaigns of Alexander*, (Penguin Classics).
Austin, M. M., *The Hellenistic world from Alexander to the Roman conquest*, (Oxford, 1981).
Barguet, P., *Le temple d'Amon-Re à Karnak*, (Cairo, 1962).
Bell, H. I., *Egypt from Alexander the Great to the Arab Conquest*, (Oxford, 1948).
Bevan, E., *A History of Egypt under the Ptolemaic Dynasty*, (London, 1927).
Bowman, A. K., *Egypt after the Pharaohs: 332 BC–AD 642*, (London, 1986).
Crawford, D., *Kerkeosiris: an Egyptian village in the Ptolemaic period*, (Cambridge, 1971).
Derchain, P., 'Reflexions sur la decoration des pylons', in *Bull. Soc. Francç d'Ég.*, Nr 46, pp. 17–24, (1966).
Diodorus, *History* (Book XVII for Alexander), (Loeb Classics).
Elgood, P. G., *The Ptolemies of Egypt*, (London, 1938).

Elgood, P. G., *The Later Dynasties of Egypt*, (London, 1951).

Fairman, H. W., 'Introduction to the study of Ptolemaic signs', in BIFAO, XLIII, pp. 51–138, (1943).

Fairman, H. W., *The Triumph of Horus: an ancient Egyptian sacred drama*, (London, 1974).

Forster, E. M., *Alexandria: a history and a guide*, (Alexandria, 1922).

Fraser, P. M., *Ptolemaic Alexandria*, (Oxford, 1972).

Grant, M., *From Alexander to Cleopatra*, (London, 1982).

Grenfell, B. P., Hunt, A. S., and Hogarth, D. G., *Fayum towns and their papyri*, (London, 1900).

Hunt, A. S. and Edgar, C. C., *Select papyri*, 4 volumes, (Harvard, 1932–4).

Kees, H., *Ancient Egypt: a geographical history of the Nile*, ed. T. G. H. James, trans. L. F. D. Morrow, (Chicago, 1961).

Lewis, N., *Greeks in Ptolemaic Egypt*, (Oxford, 1986).

Lichtheim, M., *Ancient Egyptian Literature*, vol. III: *The Late Period*, (Berkeley, 1980).

Mahaffy, J. C., *A History of Egypt under the Ptolemaic Dynasty*, (London, 1899).

Packman, Z., 'The taxes in grain in Ptolemaic Egypt', in *American Studies in Papyrology IV*, (New Haven, 1968).

Préaux, C., *L'économie royale des Lagides*, (Brussels, 1939).

Reymond, E. A. E., *The mythological origin of the Egyptian temple*, (Manchester, 1969).

Rochmonteix, M., 'Le temple Égyptien', in *Oeuvres diverses*, pp. 1–38, (Paris, 1894).

Rostovtzeff, M., *The social and economic history of the Hellenistic world*, 3 vols, (Oxford, 1941).

Sauneron, S., *The priests of ancient Egypt*, (London, 1960).

Spencer, A. J., *Brick architecture in ancient Egypt*, (Warminster, 1979).

Spencer, A. J., *Death in ancient Egypt*, (Harmondsworth, 1982).

Tarn, W. W., *Hellenistic civilisation*. 3rd ed., (London, 1952).

Watterson, B., *The gods of ancient Egypt*, (London, 1984).

Chapter 7

Badawy, A., *Coptic art and archaeology*, (Cambridge, Mass, 1978).

Bell, H., 'Popular religion in Graeco-Roman Egypt', in JEA, 34, pp. 82–97, (1948).

Boak, A. E. R., 'Tax collecting in Byzantine Egypt', in JRS, 37, pp. 24–33, (1947).

Bourget, P. M. du, *Coptic art*, (London, 1971).

Brady, T. A., *The reception of the Egyptian cults by the Greeks (330–30 BC)*, The University of Missouri Studies X, 1, (Columbia, 1935).

Coles, R. A., 'Reports of proceedings in papyri', in *Papyrologica Bruxellensia*, 4, (1966).

Columella, *De Re Rustica*, (Loeb Library).

Du Bourget, P., *L'art Copte*, (Paris, 1968).

Gazda, E. K., (ed.), *Karanis: an Egyptian town in Roman times*, (Kelsey Museum of Archaeology, University of Michigan, Ann Arbor, 1983).

Geremek, H., 'Karanis: communauté rurale de l'Égypte romaine au IIe-IIIe siècle de notre ere', in *Archiwum Filogiczne*, 17, (Warsaw, 1969).

Grenfell, B. P., Hunt, A. S. and Hogarth, D. G., *Fayum towns and their papyri*, (Egypt Exploration Fund, Graeco-Roman branch, London, 1900).

Griffiths, J. G., (ed.), *Plutarch's de Iside et Osiride*, (University of Wales Press, 1970).

Hardy, E. R., *Christian Egypt*, (New York, 1952).

Husselman, E. M., 'The granaries of Karanis', in TAPA, 83, pp. 56–73, (1952).

Husselman, E. M., 'The dovecotes of Karanis', in TAPA, 84, pp. 81–91, (1953).

Husselman, E. M., *Papyri from Karanis*, [American Philological Association, Philological Monographs 29 (Mich Pap IX). Case Western Reserve University Press, 1971].

Johnson, A. C., 'Roman Egypt', *An economic survey of ancient Rome*, II, ed. T. Frank, (Baltimore, 1936).

Jones, A. H. M., 'The cloth industry under the Roman Empire', in *Economic History Review*, ser. 2, vol. 12, pp. 183–92, (1960).

Kees, H., *Ancient Egypt: A geographical history of the Nile*, ed. T. G. H. James, trans. L. F. D. Morrow, (Chicago, 1961).

Khs-Burmester, O. H. E., *A guide to the monasteries of the Wadi 'n-Natrun*, (Cairo, 1955).

Kybalova, L., *Coptic textiles*, (London, 1968).

Lewis, N., *Life in Egypt under Roman rule*, (Oxford, 1983).

Lindsay, J., *Daily life in Roman Egypt*, (London, 1963).

Meinardus, O. F. A., *Monks and monasteries of the Egyptian deserts*, (Cairo, 1961).

Milne, J. G., *A history of Egypt under Roman rule*, 3rd ed., (London, 1924).

Montserrat, D., 'The representation of young males in "Fayum portraits"', in JEA, 79, pp. 215–25, (1993).

Packman, Z., 'The taxes in grain in Ptolemaic Egypt', in *American Studies in Papyrology*, IV, (New Haven, 1968).

Parlasca, K., *Mumienportrats und verwandte denkmaler*, (Wiesbaden, 1966).

Parlasca, K., *Repertorio d'arte dell'Egitto greco-romano*, Ser. B, 1: *Ritratti di mummie*, (Palermo, 1969–80).

Pirenne, J., *Histoire des institutions et du droit privé de l'ancienne Égypte*, 3 vols, (Brussels, 1932–5).

Richter, G. M. A., *The furniture of the Greeks, Etruscans and Romans*, (London, 1966).

Rickman, G., *The corn supply of ancient Rome*, (Oxford, 1980).

Rostovzeff, M., *The social and economic history of the Roman Empire*, (Oxford, 1926).

Tacitus, *Annals*, Penguin Classics.
Tacitus, *The Histories*, Penguin Classics.
Thompson, D., *Coptic textiles*, (New York, 1969).
Waddell, H., *The desert fathers*, (London, 1936).
Wallace, S. L., *Taxation in Egypt from Augustus to Diocletian*, (Princeton, 1938).
Walters, C. C., *Monastic archaeology in Egypt*, (Warminster, 1974).
Watterson, B., *Coptic Egypt*, (Edinburgh, 1988).
Youtie, C. and Pearl, O. M., *Tax rolls from Karanis*, (University of Michigan Studies, Humanistic Series XLIII: Michigan Papyri IV, Ann Arbor, 1939).
Youtie, C. and Pearl, O. M., *Papyri and ostraka from Karanis*, (University of Michigan Studies, Humanistic Series XLVII: Michigan Papyri VI, Ann Arbor, 1944).

Chapter 8

Broadhurst, R. J. C., *The travels of Ibn Jubayr*, (London, 1952).
Bulliet, R. W., *The camel and the wheel*, (Cambridge, Mass., 1990).
Ceram, C. W., *Gods, graves and scholars*, Part II, (London, 1966).
Gibb, H. A. R., *The travels of Ibn Battuta*, (Cambridge, 1958).
Hoogeweg (ed.), 'Oliver of Paderborn, Chronicle,' from *Die Schriften . . . Oliverus*, (Stuttgart, 1894).
Lewis, B. (ed.), *Islam from the Prophet Muhammed to the capture of Constantinople*, (Oxford, 1987).
Maalouf, A., *The crusades through Arab eyes*, Trans. J. Rothschild, (London, 1984).
al-Maqdisi, S. al-D., *Ahsan al-Taqasim.*, ed. M. J. de Goeje, (Leiden, 1877).
al-Maqrizi, A., *Al-Khitat*, (Oxford, 1987).
al-Maqrizi, A., *Itti'az al-Hunafa'*, vol. 1, ed. J. Shayyal, (Cairo, 1948).
Poliak, A. N., *Feudalism in Egypt, Syria, Palestine and the Lebanon, 1250–1900*, (Philadelphia, 1977).
Potvin, C. (ed.), *Oeuvres de Ghillibert de Lannoy*, (Louvain, 1878).
Runciman, S., *A history of the Crusades*, 3 vols, (Cambridge, 1951–4).
Saunders, J. J., *A history of medieval Islam*, (London, 1965).
Shaban, M. A., *Islamic history: a new interpretation*, (Cambridge, 1976).
Schefer, C., (ed.), *Nasir-i-Khosrau, 'Sefar Nameh'*, (Paris, 1881).
Tornberg, C. J., (ed.), *Ibn-al-Athir, 'Kamil al-Tawarikh'*, vol. XI, (Uppsala, 1851).
al-Ya'qubi, A. bin a.Y., *Tarikh*, (Beirut, 1970).

Chapter 9

Adams, C. C., *Islam and Modernism in Egypt*, (Oxford, 1933).
Ahmed, J. M., *The intellectual origins of Egyptian nationalism*, (Oxford, 1960).

Blackman, W. S., *The* fellahin *of Upper Egypt*, (London, 1927).

Bowie, L., 'The Copts, the Wafd and religious issues in Egyptian politics', in *Muslim World*, 67, April, pp. 106–26, (1977).

Bratton, F. G., *A History of Egyptian Archaeology*, (London, 1967).

Commander, S., *The state and agricultural development in Egypt since 1987*, (London, 1987).

Cooper, M., *The transformation of Egypt*, (London, 1982).

Cromer, Earl of (Evelyn Baring), *Modern Egypt*, 2 vols, (London, 1908).

Cromer, Earl of, *Abbas II*, (London, 1915).

Dawn, C. E., *From Ottomanism to Arabism: Essays on the origins of Arab nationalism*, (Urbane, Illinois, 1973).

Edwards, A. B., *A Thousand Miles up the Nile*, (London, 1877, reprinted 1982).

Fagan, B. M., *The Rape of the Nile: Tomb robbers, tourists and archaeologists in Egypt*, (London, 1977).

Gershoni, I. and Jankowski, J. P., *Egypt, Islam and the Arabs: the search for Egyptian nationhood, 1900–1930*, (Oxford, 1986).

Goldschmidt, A., 'The Egyptian Nationalist Party, 1892–1919', in P. M. Holt, (ed.), *Political and social change in modern Egypt*, pp. 308–33, (London, 1965).

Greener, L., *High Dam over Nubia*, (New York, 1962).

Greener, L., *The Discovery of Egypt*, (London, 1966).

Hinnebusch, R., *Egyptian politics under Sadat*, (Cambridge, 1985).

Hirst, D., 'Legacy that Mubarak must grasp', in *The Guardian*, (7, 8, 9 April, 1986).

Holt, P. M. (ed.), *Political and social change in modern Egypt: Historical studies from the Ottoman conquest to the United Arab Republic*, (London, 1968).

Hussaini, I. M., *The Moslem Brethren*, (Beirut, 1956).

Kilpatrick, H., *The modern Egyptian novel: a study in social criticism*, (London, 1974).

Kramer, G., 'L'Égypte du President Mubarak', in *Politique Étrangère*, (Autumn, 1983).

Mahfouz, N., *Midaq Alley*, (American University Press, Cairo, 1947, reprinted 1989).

Marsot, A. L. as-S., *Egypt in the reign of Muhammad Ali*, (Cambridge, 1984).

Monypenny, W. F. and Buckle, G. E., *The life of Benjamin Disraeli, Earl of Beaconsfield*, 6 vols, (1910–20).

Pearce, F., 'High and dry in Aswan', in *New Scientist*, No. 1924, pp. 28–32, (1994).

Raymond, A., *Artisans et commerçants au Caire au XVIIIe siècle*, (Damascus, 1973–4).

Reid, D. M., 'The return of the Egyptian Wafd, 1978', in *International Journal of African Historical Studies*, 12 (3), pp. 389–415, (1979).

Richards, A. R., *Egypt's agricultural development 1800–1980: technical and social change*, (Boulder, 1982).

Rivlin, H., *The agricultural policy of Muhammad 'Ali in Egypt*, (Cambridge, Mass., 1961).

Scholch, A., *Egypt for the Egyptians*, (London, 1981).

Shamir, S., 'Basic dilemmas of the Mubarak regime', in *Orbis*, 30 (1), (1986).

Somekh, S., *The changing rhythm: a study of Nagib Mahfouz's novels*, (Leiden, 1973).

Sullivan, E. L., *Women in Egyptian public life*, (Syracuse, 1986).

Tignor, R., *Modernization and British colonial rule in Egypt, 1882–1914*, (Princeton, 1966).

Tripp, C. and Owen, R., (eds), *Egypt under Mubarak*, (London, 1989).

Vatikiotis, P. J., *The modern history of Egypt*, (New York, 1969).

Vatikiotis, P. J., *Nasser and his generation*, (New York, 1978).

Waterbury, J., *The Egypt of Nasser and Sadat: the political economy of the two regimes*, (Princeton, 1983).

Watterson, B., *Introducing Egyptian hieroglyphs*, 2nd ed., (Edinburgh, 1993).

Wilson, J. A., *Signs and Wonders upon Pharaoh*, (Chicago, 1964).

Yapp, M. E., *The making of the modern Near East 1792–1923*, (London, 1987).

General Index

Index of Ancient Egyptian Terms